Basements and Attics, Closets and Cyberspace

LIFE WRITING SERIES

In the **Life Writing** Series, Wilfrid Laurier University Press publishes life writing and new life-writing criticism and theory in order to promote autobiographical accounts, diaries, letters, and testimonials written and/or told by women and men whose political, literary, or philosophical purposes are central to their lives. The Series features accounts written in English, or translated into English from French or the languages of the First Nations, or any of the languages of immigration to Canada.

From its inception, **Life Writing** has aimed to foreground the stories of those who may never have imagined themselves as writers or as people with lives worthy of being (re)told. Its readership has expanded to include scholars, youth, and avid general readers both in Canada and abroad. The Series hopes to continue its work as a leading publisher of life writing of all kinds, as an imprint that aims for both broad representation and scholarly excellence, and as a tool for both historical and autobiographical research.

As its mandate stipulates, the Series privileges those individuals and communities whose stories may not, under normal circumstances, find a welcoming home with a publisher. **Life Writing** also publishes original theoretical investigations about life writing, as long as they are not limited to one author or text.

Series Editor
Marlene Kadar
Humanities Division, York University

Manuscripts to be sent to
Lisa Quinn, Acquisitions Editor
Wilfrid Laurier University Press
75 University Avenue West
Waterloo, Ontario N2L 3C5, Canada

Basements and Attics, Closets and Cyberspace

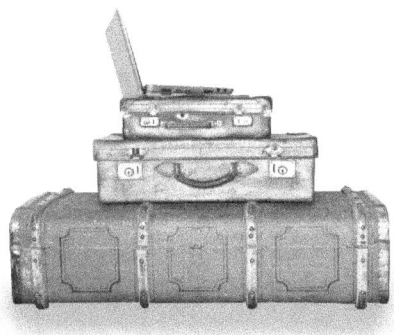

Explorations in Canadian Women's Archives

LINDA M. MORRA and JESSICA SCHAGERL, *editors*

WILFRID LAURIER UNIVERSITY PRESS

This book has been published with the help of a grant from the Canadian Federation for the Humanities and Social Sciences, through the Aid to Scholarly Publications Programme, using funds provided by the Social Sciences and Humanities Research Council of Canada. Wilfrid Laurier University Press acknowledges the financial support of the Government of Canada through the Canada Book Fund for our publishing activities.

Library and Archives Canada Cataloguing in Publication

    Basements and attics, closets and cyberspace : explorations in Canadian women's archives / Linda M. Morra and Jessica Schagerl, editors.

(Life writing series)
Includes bibliographical references and index.
Issued also in electronic formats.
ISBN 978-1-55458-632-5

    1. Women—Canada—Archives. 2. Women—Canada—Archival resources. 3. Archives—Moral and ethical aspects. 4. Archivists—Canada. I. Morra, Linda M. II. Schagerl, Jessica, 1975– III. Series: Life writing series

HQ1453.B374 2012   305.40971   C2012-900194-5

Electronic monograph in PDF format.
Issued also in print format.
ISBN 978-1-55458-650-9 (PDF).—ISBN 978-1-55458-887-9 (EPUB)

    1. Women—Canada—Archives. 2. Women—Canada—Archival resources. 3. Archives—Moral and ethical aspects. 4. Archivists—Canada. I. Morra, Linda M. II. Schagerl, Jessica, 1975– III. Series: Life writing series (Online)

HQ1453.B374 2012   305.40971   C2012-900195-3

© 2012 Wilfrid Laurier University Press
Waterloo, Ontario, Canada
www.wlupress.wlu.ca

Cover design by David Drummond using an image from Shutterstock. Text design by Daiva Villa, Chris Rowat Design.

The poem "Stuff," on page v, is reprinted from *Paper Affair: Poems Selected and New* (Black Moss Press, 2010), by Susan McMaster. Reproduced with permission of the poet.

Every reasonable effort has been made to acquire permission for copyright material used in this text, and to acknowledge all such indebtedness accurately. Any errors and omissions called to the publisher's attention will be corrected in future printings.

No part of this publication may be reproduced, stored in a retrieval system, or transmitted, in any form or by any means, without the prior written consent of the publisher or a licence from the Canadian Copyright Licensing Agency (Access Copyright). For an Access Copyright licence, visit http://www.accesscopyright.ca or call toll free to 1-800-893-5777.

Stuff

When I was young I gave all my secrets to you, spilling over in great armfuls,
messy slops of unmanageable entrails, rags and boxes, piles and tail-ends of rolling
milling bits that kept tumbling from my fingers worse than handfuls and handfuls of
marbles—here, I said, here, I can't contain these any more, my bags are stuffed
and splitting, the zippers completely shot, I have no cupboards with doors that close,
they're stuck in their guides, gummed up with leftovers, my drawers jam open,
scatter underwear torn and stained—help me, I said, I can't hold on, please take
me in hand, clean and sweep and dump or at least pile away all my messy
leavings on your own ordered shelves—

And you rolled up your sleeves—

So why this residue? Twenty years later,
the secrets you swept up, dumped into the trash,
like bleach and old paint keep seeping back,
the anger you burned still hangs in the air,
opens blisters inside if we breathe too deep.

Now it's you who sits slumped, hands spread wide—
Your turn, you say, your job this time—

Time for finer siftings
to separate simple rot
from what will always cut,
time to grind up, melt down, discard
the useless at last.

Time to make room—my turn
to make room for you.

— *Susan McMaster*

Contents

Introduction: No Archive Is Neutral
Linda M. Morra and Jessica Schagerl   1

I. Reorientations

Of Mini-Ships and Archives
Daphne Marlatt   23

Finding Indian Maidens on eBay: Tales of the Alternative Archive (and More Tales of White Commodity Culture)
Cecily Devereux   29

"Faster Than a Speeding Thought": Lemon Hound's Archive Unleashed
Karis Shearer and Jessica Schagerl   47

"I remember...I was wearing leather pants": Archiving the Repertoire of Feminist Cabaret in Canada
T. L. Cowan   65

"In the hope of making a connection": Rereading Archival Bodies, Responses, and Love in Marian Engel's *Bear* and Alice Munro's "Meneseteung"
Catherine Bates   87

An Archive of Complicity: Ethically (Re)Reading the Documentaries of Nelofer Pazira
Hannah McGregor   107

Psyche and Her Helpers, under Cloud Cover
Penn Kemp   125

II. Restrictions

Archival Matters
Sally Clark   133

Keeping the Archive Door Open: Writing about Florence Carlyle
Susan Butlin   141

The Oral, the Archive, and Ethics: Canadian Women Writers Telling It
Andrea Beverley   155

Halted by the Archive: The Impact of Excessive Archival Restrictions on Scholars
Ruth Panofsky and Michael Moir   169

Personal Ethics: Being an Archivist of Writers
Catherine Hobbs   181

Invisibility Exhibit: The Limits of Library and Archives Canada's "Multicultural Mandate"
Karina Vernon   193

III. Responsibilities

Rat in the Box: Thoughts on Archiving My Stuff
Susan McMaster   207

Letters to the Woman's Page Editor: Reading Francis Marion Beynon's "The Country Homemakers" and a Public Culture for Women
Katja Thieme   215

Archival Adventures with L. M. Montgomery; or, "As Long as the Leaves Hold Together"
Vanessa Brown and Benjamin Lefebvre   233

The Quality of the Carpet: A Consideration of Anecdotes in Researching Women's Lives
Linda M. Morra   249

"I want my story told": The Sheila Watson Archive, the Reader, and the Search for Voice
Paul Tiessen   263

"You can do with all this rambling whatever you want": Scrutinizing Ethics in the Alzheimer's Archives
Kathleen Venema   281

Locking Up Letters
Julia Creet   303

Afterword
Janice Fiamengo   319

Contributors   325

Index   331

Introduction: No Archive Is Neutral
Linda M. Morra and Jessica Schagerl

Basements and Attics, Closets and Cyberspace is, first and foremost, about researching the archives created by, about, and for Canadian women. This book asks questions about the theories, methodologies, and assumptions at work when we, as researchers, gather information about Canadian women's lives, whether this research takes place in an institution such as Libraries and Archives Canada, or at a kitchen table with a stack of dated letters. The contributors to this collection examine the negotiations and contradictions involved in ethically dealing with the records of Canadian women's public and private lives and with the material conditions of women as cultural workers. The essays, therefore, are as much about the *processes* involved in creating, locating, accessing, using, and interpreting archival materials—even in deciding what constitutes an archive—as they are about the ethical questions generated by such processes.

The collection addresses the real and sometimes peculiar challenges that affect archival work today; the essays therein reflect upon the dilemmas, ethical and otherwise, that arise partly out of shifting understandings of the archival researcher's role, and partly as a function of the extension of what archives have come to mean to those same researchers. From questions of acquisition, deposition, and preservation, to challenges concerning the interpretation of material, the contributors track how fonds are created (or sidestepped) at various stages in response to political imperatives and feminist commitments; how archival material is organized, restricted, accessed, and interpreted; how alternative and immediate archives might be conceived and approached; and how exchanges might be read when there are peculiar lacunae—missing or fragmented documents, or gaps in communication—that require imaginative leaps on the part of the researcher.

This book has a fairly direct genealogy. The critical reach of the essays included in *Basements and Attics, Closets and Cyberspace* is a logical response to and a fruitful extension of Helen M. Buss and Marlene Kadar's path-making book, *Working in Women's Archives: Researching Women's Private Literature and Archival Documents* (2001), and Jennifer Blair, Daniel Coleman, Kate Higginson, and Lorraine York's *ReCalling Early Canada: Reading the Political in Literary and Cultural Production* (2005). Buss and Kadar collected essays that explored the "challenges and opportunities that arise from encounters with female subjects" (1). Given the increasing use of archives and archival material to "rescue a female tradition in writing," the essays provide the indispensable groundwork for formulating theories and approaches to women's archives "as a complex and incomplete site of feminist knowledge" (1). The editors note that the difficulty of researching women in Canada was complicated by the paucity of materials: the lack thereof was a function of both women's marginal importance and a country whose nationhood remained quite young. Since archival papers that were considered worth keeping usually related directly to the official process of nation-building, with which women could only have had a limited part, the material retained tended to perpetuate women's marginalization.

As Buss notes in an earlier publication, *Mapping Our Selves: Canadian Women's Autobiography in English*, these difficulties are further compounded when working with women's autobiographical or biographical texts because of the "assumption of a history and cultural experience that is male and, by implication, a subjectivity that is gendered male" (5). The interrelation of women's subjectivity and its archival traces, as some of our contributors show, is an important consideration when researching women in Canada. From the problems encountered in conducting such research and how these come to dictate the methods subsequently employed (Carole Gerson), to the need to justify one's research on women's journals (Mary Rubio), to the ethical question of exploring the private life of more prominent literary women (Christl Verduyn), *Working in Women's Archives* raises a series of ethical questions and establishes the foundation for researching women's lives and literature in Canada (Buss and Kadar 2).

Ten years later, *Basements and Attics, Closets and Cyberspace* enlivens some of the challenges posed by *Working in Women's Archives* with its focus on the archives of Canadian women.

ReCalling Early Canada, for its part, seeks to refine the methodologies used in the literary and cultural deployment of archives, while simultaneously refreshing the terms, explanatory models, and tendencies that have gained prominence in discussions of the historical past. Attentive to the nuances of critical historical thought, the editors of *ReCalling Early Canada* argue that "the politics of recollection inhabits a tension between what we might call the 'directions' of history," an "intuition of our responsibility to imagine accurately, as far as possible, the otherness or difference of the past," and "our capacity for imagination itself" (Blair et al. xviii). Taking a diverse range of historical investigations about pre-First World War cultural production in Canada as their focus, the contributors to *ReCalling Early Canada* suggest that productive re-visionings of the past can indeed take shape, for instance, through new understandings of Indigenous kinship networks and family photographic archives (Julia Emberley) or through an expanded awareness of what counts as the sanctioned view of Canadian art history (Paul Hjartarson), as Susan Butlin also observes in this collection. In both *ReCalling Early Canada* and *Working in Women's Archives*, the contributors argue that researchers must acknowledge the subject-position of the archivist or researcher involved in the archive's formation and comprehension; in the words of the editors of *ReCalling Early Canada*, there is an increasing "awareness of the institutionalization of the objects of study and its ideological negotiations" (xliii). The contributors to that volume, several of whom are also, happily, in our collection, challenge the archival document as a medium of "truth," and explore various archival methods of research. The essays in their totality seem to buttress the argument implicit in this book—that no archive is neutral.

There are several intersections between the contributions to this volume, however, that bear further explanation and elaboration. In the rest of this introduction, we offer one way to read across the chapters. Three axes of understanding—reorientations, responsibilities, and restrictions—serve as a provisional frame for reading these essays. Responsibilities and restrictions are discussed simultaneously because they are so closely related. The goal of this reading of the essays in *Basements and Attics, Closets and Cyberspace* is to consider some of the issues that we, as editors, see brought to light in the collection. Our strategy in this introduction is not to offer a prescriptive reading; rather, it is to underscore some of the insights afforded by the collection as a whole.

Reorientation: What Are Archives?

One specific preoccupation of *Basements and Attics, Closets and Cyberspace* relates to the current range of what "archival deposits" and "archival materials" may embrace: which criteria are used to determine what is worthy of being preserved and used for (feminist) scholarship, how archives are formed, how to approach and read extant archives, and what kind of challenges are presented by the advent of new forms of technology. As Michael O'Driscoll and Edward Bishop explore in "Archiving 'Archiving,'" archives are not merely "institutional sites, but also spatio-temporal processes" that "expand our understanding of 'the archive' beyond its physical instantiations and towards a richer appreciation of archiving as an historical, material, and ideological set of practices" (3). For the purposes of this collection, the working definition of *archive* includes the fond—that is, the material that forms a deposit at an institution; it also includes the institution authorized by the state. Various contributors also examine archival deposition in relation to Derrida's notion of "consignation," not only the act of consigning or depositing in a place but also the "act of *con*signing through *gathering together signs*" (3; emphasis in original). For the most part, however, the contributors discuss traditional (print) archives as a research resource, one that invokes multiple and sometimes conflicting responses as a result of this consignation.

The authors of the essays in this volume also make a conscious effort to consider the scope of what "archives" mean and could mean and to imagine how extant archives might be approached and read. It is this diversity of archives and of approaches to reading the archives that might point the way—or a way—in our research. Enriching and expanding the definition of archive and archive preservation are the oral narratives of the Indigenous or working class, who were less likely to leave written traces of their lives. Western forms of epistemology are inadequately equipped to approach, interpret, and preserve them (see Margaret Kovach's helpful study *Indigenous Methodologies*). Some contributors, such as Cecily Devereux, define what is meant by "alternative archives" and "alternative archival material" in relation to official institutional archives and materials, and explain why and how these archives are forged. Alternative archival material might also refer to those non-institutional records conceived of as sufficiently unconventional in subject or genre such that it would not be represented in officially sanctioned, public archives; it may also refer to materials excluded when they are written by those whose national citizenship was not regarded as mainstream. Since women's letters and memoirs—especially those by racialized subjects—were considered of little historical significance until recently, many of these materials disappeared, remained unarchived, were dismissed as "ephemera," or were relegated to attics, basements, closets, and increasingly, cyberspace, rather than public institutions. Yet, as Richard Cox elsewhere notes, personal recordkeeping "raises a remarkable array of issues and concerns about records and their preservation," since the records eventually acquired by an institution were usually first kept by an individual citizen or were "the product of personal and family efforts to gather, organize, and maintain their documents" (*Personal* i, ix). At least one of the contributors herein makes the same argument: Kathleen Venema retains personal documentation about Alzheimer's disease and showcases its significance by contextualizing those papers in larger issues related to ethics and feminist scholarship.

Archives secondarily encompass, "the ways and means of state power; power itself, perhaps, rather than those quietly folded and filed documents that we think provide the mere and incomplete records of some of its inaugural moments" (Steedman 6). Derrida argues that the *arkhe* is the place "where authority, social order [is] exercised, *in this place* from which *order* is given" (1; emphasis in original); it is this place from which power originates and emanates, and which appears "to represent the *now* of whatever kind of power is being exercised, anywhere, in any place or time" (Steedman 1). The fever to which Derrida refers is therefore bound up in the "establishment of state power and authority" (1). In these engagements, we recognize what Ann Laura Stoler has referred to as the shift from "archive-as-source to archive-as-subject" (86).[1] Indeed, *arkhe* in this sense has expanded in the modern period, so much so that it

> appear[s] to lose much of its connection to the idea of a place where official documents are stored for administrative reference, and be[comes] a metaphor capacious enough to encompass the whole of modern information technology, its storage, retrieval and communication. (Steedman 4)

Opening up the definition of archive may suggest the dispersal of state power, an undermining of the centralization and interests of the state. There are implications for such a shift in the definition of *arkheion*, which was initially "a house, domicile, an address, the residence of the superior magistrates" (Derrida 2). The practical and conflicted responses to the deposition of papers, even the outright refusal to deposit such papers in state institutions, may signal a shift in approach to what is regarded as "archives" or archival material. Given the increasing lack of financial support for public archives, such a shift in approach may become a necessity.

Newer technological media and the preservation of material online, like personal recordkeeping, gesture toward writers who work independently and make their own decisions about what is worth preserving even if state institutions may approach that material differently or deem it as lacking in value. As Devereux, Karis Shearer, and Jessica Schagerl show, the archive thus can encompass what we may refer to as "renegade" electronic caches: those in which material is sometimes haphazardly gathered by individuals using an approach that is less methodological than what an archivist might employ, and therefore certainly unauthorized and ungoverned by the state. Louise Craven notes in *What Are Archives?* that technological changes "have led to a new way of thinking about archives.... The individual and the community, not the organization or the government, are the significant units now" (8). As academic conversations about digital archives show, the process sometimes isolates the material from librarians and archivists who are equipped with practical or theoretical approaches that extend beyond those accessing the digitized form. To be sure, the so-called triumph of the digital archive has its drawbacks, but it opens up possibilities both for those who create archives and those who access them.[2] Paul Tiessen reveals in his essay that writers like Sheila and Wilfred Watson had anticipated—even hoped for—a medium like the blog before it was invented, although they did not anticipate the inherent challenges. Wilfred, for example, believed that writers "should circulate their work only in unpublished form, thus speaking without the interference of any number of hands.... I cd. [sic] envision a day when serious writers everywhere... will only circulate their writings in MS." With the advent of the blog, as Shearer and Schagerl show, writers can indeed "circulate" their writing without concerning themselves with the interventions of publishers, editors, and the like. The instant self-publication offered by the medium of the blog allows women to provide important critical responses—and provides researchers with another archive upon which to draw. These forms resist what Derrida refers to as *domiciliation,* or house arrest, this "uncommon place, this place of election where law and singularity intersect in *privilege*" (2–3; emphasis in original). Archives, habitually seen as the purview of the state, may increasingly be set up independently in this manner. One might say that the shift in the ownership of knowledge and the individual agency being exercised through new technological forms moves against the state-instituted and privileged archival grain.

In *Ethics, Accountability and Recordkeeping in a Dangerous World*, Richard Cox assumes the sanctity of the archive, even arguing that the danger of allowing the concept of the archive "to dissipate into a thousand different views" is that its "real power and importance... may be lost and beyond repair" (256); yet the contributors to this book argue collectively that broadening the definition has its uses and applications. Certainly, one result of this expansion of the meaning of "archive" is that the positivistic elements of archival research are questioned further, with productive results. Ann Laura Stoler argues that, when researching in "official" or state-sanctioned archives, researchers must learn to read "[a]gainst the sober formulaics of officialese...on the ragged edges of protocol produced [by] administrative apparatus," and in the face of those limits imposed by the absence of evidence or uncertain knowledge (2). Researchers are obliged to adopt alternative approaches to reading extant archives, since the latter can no longer be viewed solely as repositories of documentary evidence used by an objective researcher in search of the truth.

Still, Carolyn Steedman notes that social and cultural historians who work with primary materials are sometimes depicted as "those sad creatures who fetishize" archives: "they are warned about the seductions of the archive, the 'entrancing stories' that they contain, which do the work of the seducer" (x). Steedman, of course, is referring to how researchers might be, at certain stages, infected by "archive fever" as Derrida has famously defined it—that is, the passionate desire to have, access, or be in the archive and to locate or recover a point of inception, "where things *commence*" (1; emphasis in original). To some extent, the seduction and appeal is indeed present for most researchers: in his dialogue with Vanessa Brown, Benjamin Lefebvre discusses, for example, how the Lucy Maud Montgomery archives are "highly addictive" because they provide the "opportunity to *keep on reading*—to postpone indefinitely the end to Montgomery's work." When researchers undertake such work, they often do so with the desire to generate a sense of coherence, or with the understanding that the archive is a way of seeing and knowing. In *The Intimate Archive*, Maryanne Dever, Sally Newman, and Ann Vickery write that the passion for archives "is concerned with the desire to record—and implicitly to control—memory, history and canonicity, and thus aid the production of selective views of national cultures" (1). "Archive desire," which maybe expressed individually or collectively, is thus also marked by an anxiety about and the recognition of the "possibility of forgetfulness" and "finiteness" (Derrida 19).

The possibility of forgetfulness is heightened when researchers only have fragments with which to work. As T. L. Cowan argues, a problem we face is how to conduct research about a woman's life, or an event to which she may have contributed, for which we only have a "trace"—the memory of a person present, a bystander's snapshot, a scrap of paper with an allusion to said event. To many researchers, these traces might be considered irrelevant or "'trivial,' that is, imagined to be without explanatory significance" (Enloe 220), but Cowan argues differently. Making reference to Lorraine Code, Cowan notes that even gossip might be seen as a "valuable and...subversive form of knowing/knowledge." The ethical questions generated by the use of such sources are related to legitimacy and authority: how do we know the difference between respectable scholarship and vulgar, sensationalist pursuits? How do we—and should we—avoid posing as spokespersons for the women about whom we write? When is gossip integral to what needs to be articulated? As the editors of *The Intimate Archive* suggest, scholars are often compelled to distinguish between "what separates legitimate scholarly intent from plain old voyeurism" (23). This issue is often particularly fraught, and the boundaries are unclear for feminist and queer scholars (see, for instance, the work of Julie Rak and Wendy Pearson). Ethical questions must be generated, however provisionally, to determine what indeed separates legitimate from illegitimate scholarship.

When confronted with archives that are limited in scope or by intent, feminist researchers are compelled to think laterally or seek out unconventional sources—eBay, blogs, anecdotes, and other ephemera. Shearer and Schagerl, for instance, put into practice Cowan's smart observation that "sometimes research is about who your Facebook friends are." Yet, if practices related to deposition and collection create gaps, so do these newer forms of technology. Email is an unreliable form; for some it is only erratically preserved, as Cowan discusses, but others, like Penn Kemp, are more systematic. Some interactions, as Tiessen notes in his archival research on Sheila Watson, are simply not documented. Others, as Linda M. Morra reveals in her contribution, are worth documenting even if anecdotal in nature, in order to make a larger point about laying bare one's ethical commitments, even as these are contextually derived.

Archival sources that are addressed in this collection therefore extend from paper to electronic media and to oral and ephemeral forms. In *Dust*, Steedman argues thus for such an extension of the archive:

> By insisting that "writing" includes all signs, traces, mnemonic devices, inscriptions and marks—by thus interrogating the word "writing" in order to release it from the empirical understanding that is held in place by the usual opposition between "speech" and "writing," we are—perhaps—led to understand that it *includes* its opposite, "speech." (6)

Indeed, as Cowan, Morra, Andrea Beverley, and Catherine Bates show in their respective essays, conceptions of "writing" must challenge that opposition in order to accommodate the oral medium, which sometimes becomes a crucial source of research material. In her literary reading of archival representation in Alice Munro's "Meneseteung" and Marian Engel's *Bear*, Bates argues that part of the problem is the privileging of written documents and the consequent denial of lived voices and bodily experiences. These "experiences raise the place of 'empathy and affect' in recuperative and historical practices" (Dever 21). That such a practice is needed for archival research is confirmed by Beverley's essay on the conflicts surrounding the *Telling It* conference, which took place in the late 1980s. Understanding *Telling It* as an *oral* research site with particular complicated silences that should be respected by the researcher prompts Beverley to conclude these silences enable "both the possibilities and vulnerabilities of cross-cultural feminist dialogue." Even so, she is able to glean a "more complete" picture through the contents of various archival collections, but is careful about making disclosures or violating the privacy that such silences are intended to protect. In a similar vein, Cowan's essay shows the merit of a flexible methodology that is attentive to the affective dimensions of research. In colloquial terms, she connects the dots of the stories that remain in what's left of one's immediate archive. Her re-theorizing of the problem of information-gathering begins with an extended argument for the merit of the "anecdote in writing a rhizomatic historiography" of what she terms "repertoire knowledges" of performances. To put it bluntly, as Cowan does to great effect in her chapter, "the fact that we haven't kept our shit might enable, out of necessity, the creation of an archive that straddles the specific and the non-specific."

This expansion of what constitutes an archive has definite implications for archival research, its uses, and the value that we accord to it in the academy. We must consider several factors when reorienting ourselves in relation to what we define as archive, chief among these being the responsibilities of the researcher, and the restrictions, both implicit and explicit, that may limit the research.

Responsibilities and Restrictions: What Imperatives Inform Archival Research? What Are the Limits and Impasses in Archival Research?

Of course, archives are not necessarily fixed historical records, but the mediations of the archivist, academic, historian, and independent scholar or writer. Craven notes that an individual finds meaning in archival documents

> because the document means something to him and, at the same time, because of that individual's cultural or community identity the individual finds other meaning, other things to identify with. Over time then, identity as meaning making is perpetually constructed and reconstructed through the experience of archival documents. (17)

The researcher becomes an active participant in the forging of meaning when engaging with archival material. Meaning, then, is not "inherent in the archival artefact": "it is actively produced through engaged reading, which is always provisional inasmuch as it remains open to challenge and contestation" (Dever, Newman, and Vickery 20). In her discussion of Pazira's documentaries, Hannah McGregor warns of the potential for merely repeating a narrative that has assumed the status of truth. A researcher must be mindful of how she uses the materiality of the archives so that the production of another type of archive is not restaged. Researchers, however, may find ways to "'speak back' to the archives, to resist the imperialist discourse they encountered, and to connect to communities and cultural memory that reside outside of the traditional archives" (Kirsch and Rohan 6).

As this collection developed, certain broad questions that problematized the role of the researcher drawn to archival research began to reappear: How do archivists and researchers characterize their engagement with women's archives? How do researchers proceed in relation to constructing and evaluating the lives and aesthetic contributions of Canadian women? How do researchers read and make sense of the changing nature of the materials that are available to them? What are the implications for such engagement and for such readings? What are the limits of such availability? How does one even recognize them? By what principles do feminist researchers decide to use certain materials and omit others? We see these questions as an important recognition of the researcher's positionality and agency in interpretation. As a result, many of the chapters in this volume self-consciously recall the time and place of research, the dead ends and successes on the research path. For Susan Butlin, for instance, the pursuit of a fuller understanding of Florence Carlyle's cultural production was at times quite literally a search across Southwestern Ontario, in small galleries and houses.

The questions about the changing role of the researcher complemented those about the legitimacy and acquisition of Canadian women's archives. How does one recognize and then read omissions in institutional archives? What would archivists and scholars sanction as legitimate archives and archival materials, and why? What principles inform the decisions not only to research the lives of women but also to create archival deposits? How does one approach the shifting, unstable forms of new technologies? How does one determine what is worthy of being included within a specific archival deposit? What are the implications for such decisions?

From the point of view of the archivist, there are certain commitments—ethical, socio-political, familial, and institutional—to which one must pay heed. Catherine Hobbs looks at the decisions that archivists make, how they must be made responsibly, and considers their effects. As Cox notes in *Ethics, Accountability, and Recordkeeping in a Dangerous World*, archivists are "transformed into the gatekeepers of the stored materials" and archives are "a kind of sanctuary or purgatory where older materials are sent for keeping but not always use[d]" (235). Elsewhere, Lucille M. Schultz notes that archivists' criteria include an institution's mission in addition to other factors that "might affect an institution's holdings at a given moment; something as simple as 'available space,' for example, could be a factor in decision-making" (viii). Knowing the rationale behind such decisions about acquisition can impact the course of research (Creet) as much as assuage the anxieties of the writer's ego (McMaster).

The institutions in which papers are retained thus contribute both to the context that gives rise to the papers but also to the meaning and shape of the papers themselves; to how the writer or artist envisioned his or her own creative life; and to the national or local imaginary of which the writer or artist may (or may not) wish to be a part. In other words, alternative archives must be matched by alternative forms of reading archives: how to read archival material, even reading imaginatively against the "intention" of an archive, is an integral part of the research process. An archive may have been instituted with a different set of objectives from those of the researcher approaching the archive, creating a disjunction that needs to be queried. As a result, questions will arise about what place serves the best interests of the various parties involved, including the archivist who represents the institution, the writer, the general public, and even the nation at large. The place of deposition thus becomes an articulation of meaning. So, for example, Wilfred Watson's papers were deposited in Edmonton, separately from those of Sheila Watson. She decided not to "respond to overtures from Library and Archives Canada made as early as 1992, nor to encouragement from Flahiff that she consider Ottawa—where lay the literary remains of McLuhan—as a home for her work" (Tiessen), nor did she leave them with those of her husband in Edmonton. Even a decision *not* to deposit papers with a particular institution or an institution's refusal of papers becomes a comment in itself: these refusals are revealing, as is the decision eventually made by her executor, Fred Flahiff, to deposit her papers with St. Michael's College at the University of Toronto, where she acquired her doctorate under the supervision of Marshall McLuhan.

The flipside of deposition is, of course, acquisition. The archivist represents an institution's mandate and collecting practices. After being approached by a potential donor (or actively seeking one out), the archivist must consider if the material corresponds to the socio-cultural and historical imperatives set out by the institution. The archivist is also involved in the interpretation of that material when he or she acquires, catalogues, and describes it for the purposes of formally conferring the status of a collection: "It is only after a fond has been created through these processes that the researcher enters the reading room and begins to read: sifting, transcribing, interpreting and analysing" (Dever, Newman, and Vickery 16–17). At times, a writer's sense of agency is curtailed or prevented by the prospective institution approached as a possible host for the deposition of materials: institutions may refuse such desires, and so the artist or writer must renegotiate the terms or attempt to find another place that may not have been what he or she first intended. These negotiations demonstrate that there is no consensus about what the author may have achieved or that the understanding of the artists' or writers' place in socio-political and cultural history must be shared. In such instances, institutions exercise some control over shaping the cultural and political landscape to which researchers will gain access, and to what will eventually become part of public knowledge.

Another factor in the process of conducting such research is related to permissions. Ruth Panofsky and Michael Moir identify the complex issues that arise when working on a project that has been limited by either the owner of the papers or the archivist proper. The *private* nature of papers appears as a contradiction to their storage in a *public* institution. Access to papers seems to belie the intimate aspect of materials housed in fonds and gives rise to questions about what might be disclosed further through a researcher's subsequent publications. On the one hand, restrictions may be imposed by the owner of the papers or the archivist responsible for their care; on the other hand, they may be the result of the researcher's limited time and resources. Outside of this collection, one of the more renowned cases is outlined in *Reading In: Alice Munro's Archives*; therein, JoAnn McCaig shows that questions about "fair use" can be hotly debated and contested, and may result in the foreshortening of research about a literary figure.

The individual who seeks to deposit material, or refuses to do so, must consider a range of ethical and legal issues. Karina Vernon's chapter, for example, demonstrates tellingly how refusals to deposit papers with a national institution might be regarded as "empowered self-exemption," a refusal to participate in the national imaginary that excluded—and continues to exclude—racial minorities. Vernon's essay, while not always explicitly focusing on the lives of women, interrogates the problems of casting records of lives in national terms. In so doing, she puts into sharp focus ideas of legitimacy, access, and national feeling. The papers of black Prairie settlers have been preserved, but outside of the national archives, and this tendency suggests that where material is stored or not stored is politically inflected. From the point of view of Julia Creet, who is considering where to leave her mother's letters about experiences of the Holocaust, these ethical commitments must be "painstakingly deciphered." Is the "preservation of her papers" in the best interests of the public, or "a further intrusion on her private life"? Should she place these papers in a public institution in Canada, or abroad? Creet's chapter reminds us that Canadian women's archives extend well beyond national borders, for political, cultural, financial, or personal reasons. Researchers are obliged to consider the impediments to and implications for cross-border research and the globalizing trends that invite reconsideration about archives in national terms. Creet also invites us to consider a "basic tenant of archival theory" that the fonds "should reflect a complete life, or as complete as possible," rather than dividing the papers between two countries. As she poignantly explores, when the creator has not made such a decision, the literary executor must intuit what he or she would have chosen to do. This task is far from easy in the absence of explicit instructions. Even so, sometimes the instructions left behind are best left unheeded, since the artist or writer may not have anticipated complications related to deposition. Researchers, certainly, are not under the same obligations as literary executors, but they do mull over these questions when interpreting why and where papers are retained.

Creet grapples with ethical questions that may not be precisely the same when an artist or writer initiates the process of deposition. Typically, the archives of creative writers offer a view of the literary landscape, be it through personal correspondence, private journals, or other archival material. As Hobbs puts it, "the fonds of an individual is where personality and the events of a life interact in documentary form" (127). In this volume, however, the four contributions from creative writers Daphne Marlatt, Penn Kemp, Sally Clark, and Susan McMaster only incidentally offer perspectives on writing. Instead, they offer various perspectives on the woman whose professional creative life is archived and whose everyday life is deemed archivable (although perhaps with some restrictions imposed). It is a different kind of "archive fever" that Clark reveals, for instance, when she recounts learning how writer friends began to "sell" their archives. The decision to leave material with an archive implicitly reflects associations, values, priorities, and exchanges of importance to understanding the writer or artist, and to the national imaginary. The choice becomes an expression of what place the author believes his or her work has, or will eventually serve, in a political or cultural landscape—when it is the author, of course, who renders that decision, rather than someone on his or her behalf.

The "worth" of papers sometimes thus begins with the author or artist who decides that some material is not meant to be included as part of the career being constructed. First, of course, the artist or author must consider her work worthy of inclusion in an archive. This dilemma seems to be one with which women wrestle. Clark and McMaster both remind us that even when women writers are accomplished, the question of depositing papers stirs up feelings of inadequacy. So Clark asks, what "convinces people like me to deposit papers? Worth. Historical value—who doesn't want to be part of the historical record, preserved indefinitely in humidity and temperature controlled vaults?" She cheekily adds that a secondary reason is "tax receipts." For McMaster, it took a gentle conversation with an archivist to overcome her feelings of being an imposter, unworthy of the apparently selfish act of archiving. McMaster's decision to leave her papers where she did signals how much women writers grapple with the decision in the face of an invisible feminine tradition of validating their own work by association with male counterparts.

Questions of deposition are, as Creet, Vernon, and Venema take pains to elucidate, critical to collective memory. Venema locates herself in scholarship that raises questions related to privacy, confidentiality, and both individual and family memory. She refers to her mother's Alzheimer's disease to consider "a quintessential, extended, and unrepeatable engagement with historical indeterminacy, the partial and constructed nature of subjectivity, and the extraordinarily partial nature of both partial and provisional truths." Charting how the lacunae of correspondence tragically mimics the lacunae of memory as her mother is increasingly affected by the degenerative disease, her contribution movingly nuances how memory functions in relation to building and researching an archive.[3]

Gaps in what becomes public knowledge are in part created in terms of who and what is seen as "archivable"—that is, the writer or artist whose papers are considered worthy of being retained. As Susan Butlin's essay reminds us, gaps in the record are also formed by institutions themselves because of their sometimes limited collecting practices. Such biases are the very reason women's papers were often omitted from the national record, as *Working in Women's Archives* so thoroughly addressed. These biases are restaged in detectable omissions in the archival record. Indeed, it can be argued that a process of *archival canonization* emerges in institutions which not only privileges gender but also genre—certain documents are considered worth preserving over others. So it is that newspaper articles about Florence Carlyle's popular or commercial production were almost completely omitted from the record at the Archives of the National Gallery; conversely, those articles that addressed her career as a genre painter were retained. The former articles were retained, however, in a local institution that privileged local and regional matters. The institution and its corresponding mandate may work against a researcher's own objectives; to this end, a researcher is obliged to work imaginatively around or against preserved materials. Katja Thieme's essay shows that, sometimes, newspapers preserved for different purposes other than formulating women's history still showcase the kind of work in which women were involved: Beynon was a woman's page editor for *The Grain Growers' Guide*, and as such she was "in a privileged position for fostering a sense of collectivity among Anglo-Canadian women."

This collection showcases the range of critical debates that animate thinking about women's archives in Canada. It is not necessarily about historical figures or case studies themselves, although it includes essays that look at specific figures such as Lucy Maud Montgomery, Emily Carr, Sheila Watson, Francis Marion Beynon, and Florence Carlyle. On the one hand, this book answers the call Hobbs makes to grapple with "the flotsam of the individual life" (127). On the other hand, it strikes out into new territory and expands its scope beyond women's private literature and traditional approaches to consider what is understood as an archive and archival material, that is, to question the nature of archival research itself. It is a collection that suggests new and creative approaches for pursuing an archival path, the result of the contributors' focus on how a supple research process might allow for greater engagement with unique archival forms or critical absences in the narratives of the past and present.

The Essays

The book is divided into three sections, along the axes of reading we proposed earlier in this introduction, "Reorientations," "Restrictions," and "Responsibilities." We have arranged the essays so that the larger concerns and research interests of our contributors are in dialogue. Every section includes at least one submission by a creative writer to showcase the archival interactions between creator, researcher, and archivist. In the first section, "Reorientations," the seven contributors consider variant forms of archival material. This section opens with an essay by Daphne Marlatt titled "Of Mini-Ships and Archives." Marlatt considers the ethical issues involved in archiving her own material when the privacy of others is also at stake. In "Finding Indian Maidens on eBay: Tales of the Alternative Archive (and More Tales of White Commodity Culture)," Cecily Devereux focuses on images of the Indian maiden in relation to questions of race, gender, and commodity culture. The source of such images is not the institution proper but, much more unconventionally, the Internet auction site eBay. In "'Faster Than a Speeding Thought': Lemon Hound's Archive Unleashed," Karis Shearer and Jessica Schagerl also consider the value of digital technologies for a revised understanding of the archive. T. L. Cowan's "'I remember...I was wearing leather pants': Archiving the Repertoire of Feminist Cabaret in Canada," begins with a discussion of how best to document an event when one's immediate archives are ephemeral and anecdotal. In so doing, she commits to writing a "rhizomatic historiography of the feminist cabaret specifically, but more generally, about feminist community-based, or grass-roots, performance."

In the same section, Catherine Bates provides strategies of reading the archive that are revealed in the work of Marian Engel and Alice Munro. In her chapter, "'In the hope of making a connection': Rereading Archival Bodies, Responses, and Love in Marian Engel's *Bear* and Alice Munro's 'Meneseteung,'" she suggests that these writers develop alternative, embodied strategies of reading within an archive. Hannah McGregor shares a similar focus on the discursive components of archives. In "An Archive of Complicity: Ethically (Re)Reading the Documentaries of Nelofer Pazira," she specifically questions conflicting readings of Pazira's work and emphasizes that her' artistic archive (films and memoir, chiefly) needs to be read against what she calls "the official Canadian archive of publicly disseminated information about Afghanistan into which Pazira as a public figure has been absorbed." Penn Kemp's autobiographical piece, "Psyche and Her Helpers, under Cloud Cover," closes the section with a reflection on the challenges of archiving sound, email, and digital files.

The second section, "Restrictions," is opened by Sally Clark's essay, "Archival Matters." She wittily tracks those "matters"—both the archival material proper and the concerns authors may have—which arise and may impede the process of archiving one's own papers, and sometimes those of others. Susan Butlin reminds us in her essay, "Keeping the Archive Door Open: Writing about Florence Carlyle," that exclusions from the archival record "result in a distorted view of women artists' and writers' professional careers and production." For instance, a range of difficult-to-unearth resources exists for Carlyle that suggests an institutional lack of attention to popular commercial culture, and these allow Butlin to question the traditional narrative surrounding the creative production and remunerative activity of female artists. In "The Oral, the Archive, and Ethics: Canadian Women Writers Telling It," Andrea Beverley considers the limits to both what might be preserved in the archives and what a researcher may disclose after his or her discoveries therein. These kinds of limits are what temporarily prevented Ruth Panofsky from completing her research on Adele Wiseman, as she discusses with Michael Moir in "Halted by the Archive: The Impact of Excessive Archival Restrictions on Scholars." Moir explains the process by which archivists make decisions to preserve material and allow or prevent access. Similarly, in "Personal Ethics: Being an Archivist of Writers," Catherine Hobbs elucidates what the responsibilities and ethical commitments of the archivist are when dealing with the papers of literary authors. In spite of such responsibilities and commitments, the archival institution is not consistently regarded as an ideal repository. As Karina Vernon explores in "Invisibility Exhibit: The Limits of Library and Archives Canada's 'Multicultural Mandate,'" black Prairie community members have avoided depositing their materials with Libraries and Archives Canada because they feel that their exclusion from the national imaginary would be restaged in the institution itself, even if LAC has been reoriented to reflect an institutionally conceived "Multicultural Archives."

In the third section, "Responsibilities," the contributors turn to archival material to consider the involvements of the researcher and how, at times, there is a personal, familial, or communal investment at stake. In "Rat in the Box," Susan McMaster reflects upon the deposition of her own papers, but also notes that these cannot be viewed in isolation; they must be regarded as a part of the work of a larger cultural community. In "Letters to the Woman's Page Editor: Reading Francis Marion Beynon's 'The Country Homemakers' and a Public Culture for Women," Katja Thieme likewise suggests the need for turning to underused archives for investigation. She charts the rhetoric of Canadian suffrage debates through the archive of *The Grain Growers' Guide* under the women's page editorship of Francis Marion Beynon. Through the archival traces of her editorship, Thieme suggests how we might consider Beynon significant to a larger and burgeoning feminist community in the pre–First World War period. In "Archival Adventures with L. M. Montgomery; or, 'As Long as the Leaves Hold Together,'" Vanessa Brown and Benjamin Lefebvre approach Montgomery archives from two different professional backgrounds in order to consider how their archival discoveries might be characterized, and how such discoveries have an impact on currents in Montgomery scholarship. In "The Quality of the Carpet: A Consideration of Anecdotes in Researching Women's Lives," Linda M. Morra traces the use of anecdotes in researching women's lives and contemplates the ethical implications for their inclusion or exclusion from feminist research.

In the same section, Paul Tiessen considers the complicated and sometimes troubling means by which a researcher must approach his or her archival subject. As his title, "'I want my story told': The Sheila Watson Archive, the Reader, and the Search for Voice," suggests, the researcher is implicated in how the story is told and the subject's voice is rendered. So the researcher must also consider the responsibilities involved in "voyeuristically occupying a corner of a triangular position" when reading correspondence between two literary figures. Kathleen Venema's moving essay, "'You can do with all this rambling whatever you want': Scrutinizing Ethics in the Alzheimer's Archives" theorizes the absences of and gaps in archives in resonant ways. She notes that "Alzheimer's disease means that my mother's life and mine are defined these days by discontinuities, disconnections, and absences like the ones that the archive simultaneously performs and seeks to redress." Julia Creet's poignant rumination, "Locking Up Letters," considers the ethical implications of depositing her mother's Holocaust letters in archives. The place to which these papers are consigned, she notes, is important in order to honour and respect her mother's complicated national histories. Janice Fiamengo's "Afterword" assesses, by turns, what archives are; where and how they may be located; how they may be approached, characterized, and interpreted; and what processes ought to be adopted for the material under scrutiny.

This book is not a final word on the subject of Canadian women and archives, but offers a response to questions being raised by currents in scholarship, research methods, and shifting definitions of what constitutes archival material.

Notes

1 Scholars such as MacNeil and Cook have elsewhere examined the implications of postmodernism upon archival research. See also Banting.
2 See, for example, conversations regarding digitization of materials that appeared on the listserv for the Society of the History of Authors, Readers and Publishers. Between July 17 and 18, 2011, several emails were exchanged by participants such as Terrance G. Shults, who considered how digitization separated "material from the librarians, archivists"(July 18, 2011, 9:22 a.m.) and Jerry Blaz, who noted,

> [just as the] creation of written texts was called a harbinger of the destruction of the human memory, and to a large degree it was a correctly diagnosed harbinger, the digitalization will result in other "destructions," which, in the course of not too many generations, will be overlooked and a new unremarkable, taken-for-granted and unnoticed version of reading and investigation will evolve. It happened in the creation of writing, and again with the invention of printing, and it is happening again in our lifetime. Luckily, it will not mean the disappearance of preservationists and conservationists; they will still be ready to jump into the breach as they are today. (July 18, 2011, 7:17 p.m.)

3 See also Millar's "Touchstones: Considering the Relationship between Memory and Archives."

Works Cited

Banting, Pamela. "The Archive as Literary Genre: Some Theoretical Speculations." *Archivaria* 23 (1986–7): 119–22. Print.

Blair, Jennifer, Daniel Coleman, Kate Higginson, and Lorraine York, eds. *ReCalling Early Canada: Reading the Political in Literary and Cultural Production*. Edmonton: U of Alberta P, 2005. Print.

Buss, Helen M. *Mapping Our Selves: Canadian Women's Autobiography in English*. Montreal: McGill-Queen's UP, 1993. Print.

Buss, Helen M., and Marlene Kadar, eds. *Working in Women's Archives: Researching Women's Private Literature* and *Archival Documents*. Waterloo: Wilfrid Laurier UP, 2001. Print.

Cook, Terry. "Fashionable Nonsense or Professional Rebirth: Postmodernism and the Practice of Archives. " *Archivaria* 51 (Spring 2001): 14–35. Print.

Cox, Richard J. *Personal Archives and a New Archival Calling: Reading Reflections and Ruminations*. Los Angeles: Litwin, 2009. Print.

———. *Ethics, Accountability, and Recordkeeping in a Dangerous World*. London: Facet, 2006. Print.

Craven, Louise. *What Are Archives? Cultural and Theoretical Perspectives: A Reader*. Aldershot: Ashgate, 2008. Print.

Derrida, Jacques. *Archive Fever: A Freudian Impression*. Trans. Eric Prenowitz. Chicago: U of Chicago P, 1996. Print.

Dever, Maryanne, Sally Newman, and Ann Vickery, eds. *The Intimate Archive: Journeys Through Private Papers*. Canberra: National Library of Australia, 2009. Print.

Enloe, Cynthia. *The Curious Feminist: Searching for Women in a New Age of Empire*. Berkeley: U of California P, 2004. Print.

Hobbs, Catherine. "The Character of Personal Archives: Reflections on the Value of Records of Individuals." *Archivaria* 52 (Fall 2001): 126–35. Print.

Kirsch, Gesa E., and Liz Rohan, eds. *Beyond the Archives: Research as a Lived Process*. Foreword by Lucille M. Schultz. Carbondale: Southern Illinois UP, 2008. Print.

Kovach, Margaret. *Indigenous Methodologies: Characteristics, Conversations, and Contexts*. Toronto: U of Toronto P, 2009. Print.

MacNeil, Heather. "Trusting Records in a Postmodern World." *Archivaria* 51 (Spring 2001): 36–43. Print.

McCaig, JoAnn. *Reading In: Alice Munro's Archives*. Waterloo: Wilfrid Laurier UP, 2002. Print.

Millar, Laura. "Touchstones: Considering the Relationship between Memory and Archives." *Archivaria* 61 (Spring 2006): 105–26. Print.

O'Driscoll, Michael, and Edward Bishop. "Archiving 'Archiving.'" *ESC* 30.1 (2004): 1–16. Print.

Pearson, Wendy Gay. "Queer Matters: A Response to Robert Fulford." *Studies in Canada*. 32.4 (2006): 13–17. Print.

Rak, Julie. "Introduction." *English Studies in Canada*. 32.4 (2006): 1–3. Print.

Shults, Terrance G., and Jerry Blaz. "Re: digitization of materials." *Society of the History of Authors, Readers and Publishers Listserv*. July 18, 2011, 9:22 a.m; 7:17 p.m. Web. Oct. 10, 2011.

Steedman, Carolyn. *Dust: The Archive and Cultural History*. New Brunswick: Rutgers UP, 2002. Print.

Stoler, Ann Laura. *Along the Archival Grain: Epistemic Anxieties and Colonial Common Sense*. Princeton: Princeton UP, 2009. Print.

I. Reorientations

Of Mini-Ships and Archives
Daphne Marlatt

To think about women's archives is to think about how recently (say, in the last century and a half) women's lives in the Western world have moved from the private and domestic sphere to the public cultural-political one, becoming "collectable." This transit from private to public is embedded in the origin (or at least as far back as written records will reveal) of the word archive in Greek: *arkhë*, or first place where government records were kept. Despite its ark-like association, *arkhë* is the word for a process, the process not only of recording and keeping what has been said in the moment but also eventually making it public for posterity (for long-after-the-fact eyes) in a waterless and dust-free atmosphere.

Does writing itself, even the writing of women's "private" journals, inherently contain the possibility of going public? After all, writing is an act of externalizing, of potentially making ideas and thoughts available for other eyes to peruse, even one's own eyes at a later date. Printing and distributing are steps beyond that. Preserving in amenable conditions is also a step further. It is the reverse of instantly, on an impulse, pressing the "delete" button before pressing "send."

But then, from a broader perspective, language itself is a living archive. More specifically, the history of a language is an archive of the cultural changes and linguistic borrowings of its speakers through centuries of usage. As a poet, I recognize this fact from hours at my desk behind a closed door (the gift of not just solitary but uninterrupted time) where I trace glimmers of half-erased, half-perceived connections between words and their historic trade routes through time. Nouns, little ships freighted with meaning, fossilized verbs that once sailed their way through seas of speech, language to language. My tracing of these routes will find their way (or not) into sentences composing a larger verbal structure that may (or may not) eventually find its way into print. Often these mini-ships, hand jottings on draft pages of print or nearly illegible scribbles on scraps of paper, get lost in file folders in drawers or boxes, eventually to land, years later, on a library shelf under bright lights in what is termed an archive. Docked, documented. Archivally (re)constructed.

Reconstruction: putting together scattered fragments, putting together what once occurred or was experienced as a *gestalt*, a whole, but is now available only in shards, odd notes on variously sourced, undated pages or bits of paper. To some degree, the drive behind collecting a writer's archive is rather like what drives archaeology. It is similar to resurrecting the dead, if such a thing were possible. But then there is also what is lost in the living, layers and layers of memory that are now simply recalled by outline, by the repeated telling of an event that the body's complex sensoria once experienced fully in all the emotional and mental reverberations of a moment's impact. Perhaps this desire is the drive behind oral history and its effort to uncover and make public what people have experienced as personal. It is the memories of individual lives that together make up the particular history of a community—another kind of archive—recorded and made public as the unofficial history of the legislated-upon, rather than the official history of the legislators. These memories, often considered too personal to be of public value, when collected and published compose alternative or alternate views of official history, views that deepen our understanding of the impact of past events. So I discovered in 1972, when I first began working on a team collecting the Japanese Canadian oral history of Steveston, which at that point was largely untold outside of the community.

In the early 1970s, Maya Koizumi began interviewing members of the community about their experiences fishing and boat-building on this coast. The oldest, Asamatsu Murakami, then in his late eighties, recalled arriving in Victoria by ship in 1899, and then, once in Vancouver, travelling by stage coach down a still partially forested Granville Street to Steveston, where he began fishing for one of the canneries—in one man's lifetime, the forest terrain was transformed into something completely urban. He and others had clear memories of the living conditions in Steveston's cannery camps, the strikes, the bringing over of picture brides, and the early formation of their *Dantai* (benevolent society). They recalled the complexities caused by labour disputes with white unions, and feeling the pressure of constant racism, which led up to a series of fishing-licence cutbacks and the eventual internment of the entire community during the Second World War. As writer for and editor of the oral history we gathered, *Steveston Recollected*, I would go with Maya to meet her interviewees. Not understanding Japanese, I relied on her for both on-the-spot interpreting and translation of the taped interviews and several historical accounts written in Japanese that were lent to us by a community member. But I listened for tonal gestures, watched various emotions shadow faces and disappear. For factual background, I explored the Richmond City Archives and the Historic Photos Archive of the Vancouver Public Library to gain a sense of what was going on in the larger community at various points in time. Gazing at black and white photos by Philip Timms and Dundas F. Todd gave me a remarkable sense of the materiality of Steveston's booming cannery row and waterfront in its early days. Contemporary photographs by Rex Weyler and Robert Minden, sometimes of the same buildings and streets, gave us all a visual measure of the intervening years.

Certain phrases people used to express their remembering, as well as the visual detail of historic photographs, prompted my own imagining of what it must have felt like, say, to fish by hand at night on a freshet-swollen river, or to find yourself newly arrived in a sea of hip-high marsh grass. Thus began a cycle of poems I wrote in a sustained act of research-fuelled imagination and critique about the history of this multiracial, multicultural boom town at the mouth of what had once been an incredibly fertile salmon river. With Robert Minden's portraits of people on its contemporary streets, it became our collaborative book, *Steveston* (1974).

A few years earlier, while writing *Vancouver Poems* (1972), I had started exploring the Vancouver City Archives, which houses, among other documents, Major Matthews's collection of accounts by early residents of the settlement known as Granville before the disastrous fire of 1886 wiped out most of its frontier buildings. This curiosity about the origins of my adopted city and what was here before the so-called white civilization arrived to log the coast's luxuriant forests was sparked by Pauline Johnson's *Legends of Vancouver*, a book of stories Chief Joe Capilano told her before his death in 1910. My great-uncle gave me a copy of the eighth edition (1913), bound in deer hide with a hand-painted profile of an Indian head in feathered headdress on its cover, soon after my family had immigrated to Vancouver in 1951—it was the first Canadian book I received, and my first encounter with oral history. Pauline's listening ears in a dugout canoe transformed into a verbal ship of print carrying traditional Squamish stories about one version of pre-contact history, ghosting its way through the written records of white settlers.

And there were always settlers who spoke languages other than English. Those settlers of diverse ethnicities who brought their cultures with them, made up the poly-linguistic fabric of Strathcona, the earliest residential area of Vancouver, a hilly piece of terrain lying north of the original shore of False Creek, south of the harbour, and east of Main Street. When I first moved into the area in 1976, I wanted to find out more about its history, as did the artist Carole Itter, who lived a couple of blocks away. Together we began another oral history project, and for this purpose we interviewed people from various communities that, in successive waves of immigration, had established themselves in these few blocks: Chinese, Italian, Jewish, Irish, Japanese, black, Ukrainian, and Yugoslav, with the neighbourhood elementary school described as a sort of mini United Nations in the thirties. Photographs in interviewees' albums or from the city archives would prompt memories. In turn, the stories that arose prompted archival research to try to establish period context and the unrecalled names of people involved in particular events. Newspaper clipping files in the Vancouver Public Library, books about the city's history by various authors, photographs of East End streets through the years, city directories (who lived where in what years), maps with earlier names for streets that had been subsequently renamed—all these sources proved useful.

By the time I began writing *Ana Historic*, I was used to archival research and enjoyed doing it so much that hours went by devoted to my study of the city's early history. The Major Matthews collection, with its eyewitness accounts and anecdotal details, its hand-drawn maps and early photographs, gave me a time-telescope sense of the small frontier settlement and mill surrounded first by woods and then stumps in the early 1870s, before the fire. No one appointed Major Matthews to undertake this task, he apparently decided to do this on his own initiative, recognizing that the lived experiences of people vividly recreate the feel of an event that most official versions reduce to facts. Thus, the tradition of an alternative and somewhat renegade history for this city began. Consequently, Vancouver has one of the best-documented histories of any city in the world (of course, despite its short life thus far, it also has managed to erase much of the architectural evidence from its earlier phases—wood frame buildings in what was once a rain forest don't last long, especially when the boom town mentality constantly seeks to reinvent itself).

The Major Matthews collection gave me a sense of the friendships and community stratifications already beginning in Granville in the 1870s. But the "squibs," basically satirical male gossip and in-jokes of a column protectively titled "Falsehoods of the Hour" that appeared in *The Moodyville Tickler* (1878), delighted me because they imparted the humour and irritations of daily life in the water-based communities on the edge of Burrard Inlet. The *Tickler* was the Inlet's first newspaper, based in the sawmill at Moodyville in what is now North Vancouver. Its editor, lumber clerk William Colbeck, had a gift for sending up his fellow workers and airing his political views in delightfully sarcastic terms while also reporting on events of the day like the fourth of July boat race. His was a distinctly individual voice, educated and literary, yet steeped in his community and locale. Reading his columns opened a further window into the meshwork of memories and anecdotes that Major Matthews had collected, along with his considerable array of carefully notated historic photographs. Then there was Ralph Andrews's chattily descriptive voice in his *Glory Days of Logging* (1956), which opened another window. Whether in Vancouver's city archives or its public library, these voices were available in print. Women's voices, like the women themselves, were much harder to find from that period. So I decided to invent the voice of Mrs. Richards, writing her diary entries and thoughts to herself about that frontier settlement. I did so using Keats's letters as a model, particularly their dash-heavy punctuation and the immediacy of syntax, freighted with nineteenth-century diction and phrasing. I wasn't sure this method had succeeded until someone asked me where to find Mrs. Richards's diaries in the city archives.

This sense of the life of an event or community, the feel of it, the intermeshed relationships that build community, perhaps that is what certain kinds of archives best offer. I wanted more than the often-repeated outlines of a series of events that make up most historical accounts. I wanted the daily feel of a lifetime in a now-vanished period that underlies, as the underwater hull of a boat frames its deck, what we now inhabit. Without that awareness, it seems to me, we don't understand the full shape of our own present.

As a writer whose archive is slowly accumulating in Library and Archives Canada, I struggle with a sense of invaded privacy around more personal documents. I have not delivered any of my journals to LAC, partly because I still have to access them from time to time, but mainly because the working out of certain ideas and notes on reading have as much to do with the working out of my psyche through various relationships and periods of disquiet as it has to do with my writing. In this sense, they feel "private." But is this a failure to recognize my own disquiet as a reflection of the larger feminist issues of the decades in which I've lived thus far? Is it a hanging onto what seems personal, despite the recognition that "the personal is political," or the further awareness that each one of us who so prizes individuality is actually a knot in a vast mesh of interdependent circumstances and events, constantly shifting our collective culture in and out of focus?

Perhaps the distinction between a writer's private life and her writing life is a false one, particularly for a poet and novelist who works at crossing the limits of what can be designated as fiction and what can be designated as memoir. And yet I find that, to write at all, I need to maintain a sense of silence and invisibility. That seems to be the source out of which arises the improvisational act of composition, its little ships darting through a wordless sea of pure possibility.

Finding Indian Maidens on eBay: Tales of the Alternative Archive (and More Tales of White Commodity Culture)
Cecily Devereux

At the beginning of the twentieth century, the image of the "Indian maiden" was a well-established and familiar motif in popular cultural representations in North America. Used in advertising and in easily accessible and affordable art (such as prints, lithographs, photographs, postcards, calendars, and three-dimensional objects), the primary purpose of the image was to sell things to non-Indigenous consumers. Its function and ideological work should thus be understood in relation to the exchange of particular commodities. These commodities fall into a range of categories: first, the product that the image represents or stands in for (such as butter or vegetables); second, the thing itself that uses the image at a formal or representational level (such as salt and pepper shakers, or pictures to hang on a wall); third, and most important for the purposes of this paper, the complicated ideology of femininity constructed in the image itself. This ideology is complicated by femininity's constitution as an object of exchange, a familiar problem in patriarchal cultures that depend precisely on the exchange of women. It is also complicated by a foundational clash between the image's purported representation of Indigenous femininity and its simultaneous construction of white femininity in the Indigenous woman's image. This clash is evident in the extent to which the Indian maiden, in many early-twentieth-century representations, not only is devised for marketing goods to non-Indigenous consumers but also becomes, by the second decade of the century, a figure who suggests a white woman in costume or masquerade rather than an Indigenous woman in "real life."

In the production and circulation of this image, it is possible to discern the work of a white colonial economy that has historically depended both on the overwriting of Indigenousness through the appropriation and consumption of its representation and the exchange of women across racial and cultural categories as commodities with a specifically sexual value. The image's racial and cultural ambiguity is central to this economy and exchange. On the one hand, the Caucasian Indian maiden renders ambiguous her own racial and cultural location and mystifies the space of contact and colonization: the space she marks and inhabits in representation is *either* Indigenous land occupied by white people, or a white people's territory that still contains nostalgic vestiges of Indigenous people. On the other hand, the image serves to affirm a commerce in women, without making clear the object of exchange along the lines of racial and cultural identity. Both Indigenous and white women have been central to the construction and occupation of white colonial space as objects of exchange and as sexual and reproductive commodities. Although this aspect of the real experience of Indigenous and white women is only one part of their histories, it is a crucial part of colonial history. The image of the Indian maiden in late-nineteenth- and early-twentieth-century advertising is a crucial location for the representation of a specifically colonial desire to identify and maintain femininity as a commodity.

Although the broad circulation of the image of the Indian maiden in advertising and commercial representation at the end of the nineteenth century has been observed by critics such as Gail Guthrie Valaskakis, Rayna Green, and Daniel Francis, tracking the image through early advertising and product branding is not necessarily an easy thing to do. Commercial media is ephemeral: people throw away their butter wrappers and calendars. Advertisements in periodical and print publications are not always catalogued with textual materials. Libraries and archives do not necessarily have a mandate to acquire ephemera, and when they do, they may not catalogue it using search terms that identify it with reference to an image in an advertisement or product wrapper; such ephemera might be instead categorized by product, company, or genre, rather than with reference to what is represented. In light of these conditions and the commercial function of the Indian maiden's image, it is perhaps not surprising that, while many libraries and archives have materials related to this image and its circulation at the end of the nineteenth century and the beginning of the twentieth, the Internet auction site eBay may currently be the largest searchable and digital repository of commodity objects related to the Indian maiden.

A search of an institutional repository such as the digital "American Memory" record of the Library of Congress turns up many textual items and images under the term "Indian maiden" (70 hits on Nov. 11, 2009) and slightly more in both categories under the term "Indian princess" (120 hits on Nov. 11, 2009).[1] Other relevant digital and non-digital items are listed in the Library of Congress catalogue, which is also the case for Library and Archives Canada and a number of institutional special collections. These collections include, among others, the John W. Hartman Center for Sales, Advertising and Marketing History at Duke University Library, the Early Advertising Collection at Bryn Mawr College, the Early Advertising of the West Collection at the University of Washington, and in the UK the Evanion Collection of Victorian Printed Ephemera at the British Library. Although some of the items in institutional repositories, and particularly in those focused on advertising history, represent the commodity culture record of the image, a search using the term "Indian maiden" on eBay will generally yield hundreds of objects.

Certainly, that was my experience when I started looking. On November 6, 2009, for instance, 666 items appeared in a search using this term. Some of the items for sale are contemporary, including paintings and prints (Indian Maiden Daughter of Setting Sun R. Atkinson Fox! for $5.95), plates, dolls, and figurines (Native American Indian Maiden 16" Porcelain Lloyd 1990 for $9.99), the occasional Barbie, and various costumes. Some of these costumes are based on Disney's later twentieth-century representations of Pocahontas or, from *Peter Pan*, Tiger Lily. eBay also offers a range of more explicitly eroticized Indian maiden costumes (Indian Maiden—Sexy Indian Women's Adult Costume for $39.99). Some of the items listed on eBay are not contemporary. These include images in print and a variety of practical and decorative objects, such as mugs and ashtrays, bas-relief wall plaques, old souvenirs from just about anywhere in North America, postcards, the occasional wood carving, and the classic Pez candy dispenser (Vintage Pez Indian Maiden or Squaw for $19.99). Many of the items are advertising and commodity culture ephemera that use the image of the Indian maiden to market particular products. The November 6, 2009, search turned up, among many other items, an Ink Blotter, Indian Maiden Princess, Wausau, WI, 1921 for $9.99; a package or advertising card for a 1933 Goudey Indian Gum R73 Hopi Maiden #84/216 for $1.25;

a Leinenkugel Indian Maiden Character Beer Stein for $69.95, and two Vintage Land O'Lakes Indian Maiden Decal Cheese Boxes for $14.99.

Any search for Indian maiden objects on eBay makes clear that there is considerable material, old and new, using this image, and that there is a demand for it and a range of values related to both the image and the item. (The Pez dispenser, for instance, might be collected for itself rather than for its iconography; the Leinenkugel beer stein might be collected in relation to beer advertising, rather than for the Indian maiden image on the product.) As is the case for many electronic records, older items and newer ones are mashed together indiscriminately. eBay is searchable with a range of categories, but these have mostly to do with price, date of listing, date of closing, or the nature of the object, rather than with varying degrees of antiquity or the nuances of cultural location or signification. The randomness and disorder of eBay is sometimes challenging for a searcher and, as I suggest, for a researcher. But it is also compelling in the way it erases discontinuities between old and new commodities and thus highlights significant continuities in the circulation and valuation of the Indian maiden in the early twentieth and the twenty-first centuries. This is a matter both of the new products' suggestion that the image continues to have a particular currency and the older products' new value, since they have become what Jean Baudrillard describes as a "mythological object," working to establish in the present a continuous relation to a founding moment (for the buyer) (75). The image of the Indian maiden, like the antiques Baudrillard describes, "presents itself as a myth of origins" (76) and, moreover, when attached to antique objects, links the buyer "authentically" to that point of origin.

At the same time as eBay serves as a cultural marketplace—or, indeed, as a kind of museum store or antique shop, in which the current value of the Indian maiden is foregrounded and maintained in old and new products—it also functions as a useful, if always shifting and provisional, archive of the Indian maiden's image. It is not only a primary resource for anyone wanting to buy Indian maiden objects but also for anyone engaging in research related to the image of the Indian maiden and the ways in which this image operates in colonial culture from the early twentieth century to the early twenty-first. Indeed, it is possible to find popular cultural objects on eBay that represent the Indian maiden in ways not currently possible in institutional repositories or even online institutional databases, not necessarily to buy them but to track, compare, organize, and analyze them. In other words, it is possible to do the kind of work academic researchers normally do in the archive, and to use this contemporary online shopping catalogue to investigate the materials of cultural history. That research on the image of the Indian maiden, and thus on the ways in which white colonial culture has used the representation of Indigenous and white women to reference a practice of gendered commodity exchange, may well be best done outside of the institutional repository; it is an index not only of the commercial function of the image but also of a pervasive problem of "the archive" for research in women and women's history and Indigenous women's history. Although many libraries and archives such as Library and Archives Canada have undertaken significant initiatives in acquisition, the relative paucity in many institutional repositories of material related to Indigenous culture and to women across cultural categories is well documented.[2] eBay is an important example of the kind of alternative archive to which anyone undertaking research in non-institutional categories of knowledge or in areas of study that are not always substantially represented in institutional archives must inevitably turn.

Founded in 1995 by computer programmer Pierre Omidyar, eBay is an e-commerce website based on the principle of the auction. It is not an archive in the conventional sense. This unconventionality is not a bad thing, but it does mean that, as an archive, the site presents problems for academic research. Its random and shifting inventory is not stable enough to work like the holdings of an institutional repository: once sold, items disappear. Sometimes items are removed before they are sold, and a search, even if it is saved, will not bring you back to an item that was once there. Indeed, there is no real guarantee that the items exist at all: although eBay undertakes to ensure its reliability as a marketplace and established a dispute process for sellers and buyers, it houses independent vendors. Despite Omidyar's founding principle that "[p]eople are basically good" (eBay, "What We Believe"), not all vendors actually are, of course. The connection between the object represented and its existence or availability cannot always be ensured for each of the millions of items exchanged every day on eBay. Further complicating the academic use of eBay as an archive, moreover, are its own practices, which (unsurprisingly) for a shopping resource include none of the careful work of acquisition, cataloguing, description, and controlled access that characterizes the collection practices of institutional archives. Although it is a catalogue in a sense, eBay does not "catalogue" its inventory for ordinary users; items can be found only by searching the descriptions sellers provide. The site does not apply a centralized system of identification, but rather lets sellers use labels that they hope will be captured in the web searches of potential purchasers. The search term is ultimately the organizing principle that activates a collection or, in this case, an archive of materials on eBay.

Since researchers might use eBay—and in some cases, as I am suggesting here, should use it—like an archive to find repositories of material not always present in institutional archives, it is necessary to consider the site's impediments to scholarly research and the implications of using it in this way. As I have suggested, however, it is not surprising that an e-commerce site is not like an institutional archive, something it did not set out to be. eBay, a private, money-making enterprise, operates with a different mandate from those of the publicly funded major North American national archives, such as Library and Archives Canada (LAC) (formerly the National Archives), and the U.S. Library of Congress. The stated mission of the Library of Congress is "to makes its resources available and useful to the Congress and the American people and to sustain and preserve a universal collection of knowledge and creativity for future generations" (Library of Congress, "About the Library"). LAC's mandate is similar, although it undertakes to serve the people first, "[t]o preserve the documentary heritage of Canada for the benefit of future generations... [t]o be a source of enduring knowledge accessible to all, contributing to the cultural, social, and economic advancement of Canada," and "[t]o facilitate in Canada cooperation among communities involved in the acquisition, preservation and diffusion of knowledge," and the government last ("[t]o serve as the continuing memory of the government of Canada and its institutions") (Library and Archives Canada, "Mandate").

eBay does not have a mission statement. The history section of the site describes eBay as "a remarkably efficient market created by connecting individuals who wouldn't otherwise be connected" (eBay, "Who We Are: History"). "With more than 88 million active users globally, eBay is the world's largest online marketplace, where practically anyone can buy and sell practically anything. With a diverse and passionate community of individuals and small businesses, eBay offers an online platform where millions of items are traded each day" (eBay, "Who We Are: Overview"). While its function as a commercial resource is emphasized, eBay is also presented in its own descriptions as a service that does very different work from that of national archives; yet it shares some of the same objectives of enabling access for individuals to systems of exchange that are putatively intended to build community through networking and exchange. Although it is objects that are being exchanged in a process of transaction, the principles of community formation, and of (advancement through) access and change are not fundamentally dissimilar to that of national archives. eBay's work, if not necessarily national, might well be framed in terminology like that used by Library and Archives Canada: to preserve people's stuff for the benefit of future generations; to be a source of stuff accessible to all, contributing to the cultural, social, and economic advancement of individuals and communities; to facilitate cooperation among communities involved in the acquisition, preservation, and diffusion of stuff.

What eBay does not propose explicitly to do is to serve as a repository for cultural memory in particular communities. That it actually does do so is an indication less of its objectives than of significant gaps in the institutional record. Broadly understood, eBay is a big archive of the stuff a community does *not* typically keep as a part of the official cultural historical record, but unofficially preserves elsewhere, at home, in private collections, in shoeboxes. It thus works, albeit inadvertently, to fill in the gaps in institutional archives and to function as a popular cultural repository that may, in some cases, connect researchers with materials that remain otherwise hidden in people's personal collections or obscured by masses of objects in antique and thrift stores. This material and the information it provides is enormously valuable to scholars and researchers. My own first encounter with the image of the Indian maiden in late-nineteenth- and early-twentieth-century commercial media occurred in an exhibition at the Confederation Centre for the Arts in Charlottetown, Prince Edward Island. This exhibition, first presented at OBORO in Montréal in May 1992, was based on materials collected by Marilyn Burgess and Gail Guthrie Valaskakis. Burgess and Valaskakis describe the exhibition's images of Indian princesses as "part of a collection which has grown over the years through the contributions of family and friends," a private archive of "dusty and dated prints of Indian princesses" (7). These private collections, a motivating principle for eBay, organize materials and draw attention to particular problems and questions that may not be highlighted in institutional repositories, but are nonetheless significant.

In "Traces of the Familiar: Family Archives as Primary Source Material," Wendy B. Sharer described the ways in which her grandmother's closet yielded materials that "dovetailed" with her own research and fundamentally changed how she perceived the relationship of the scholar to what she calls the "family archive" (47). Her essay appeared in *Beyond the Archives: Research as a Lived Process* (2008), the title indicating its attention to a range of non-institutional records and the ways "less frequently consulted resources can enrich our understanding of history, culture, and rhetoric" (2). Barry Rohan, another contributor, outlined how the discovery of his grandfather's trunk not only enabled him to better understand his own family but also engaged him in the research of a figure whose work is significant to early performance history in the U.S. In an important sense, eBay is grandmother's closet or grandfather's trunk opened up and distributed—for sale, it is true, but with the effect of making broadly available the contents of those family archives in ways that have important implications for cultural memory. I think this renders eBay an alternative archive, a repository in which materials can be found that are otherwise not held institutionally; it has its pitfalls, but it is a record of the material not always in the official cultural memory of a community that persists nonetheless. This material continues to circulate between (as the title of this volume suggests) people's basements, attics, and public space, and thus continues to be present in the ways in which a community remembers. Although researching in eBay may be an unconventional practice for academic work, it makes sense in relation to the record of commercial images, objects, and ephemera that constitute the archive of the Indian maiden. By forming a category of objects for sale under the search terms "Indian maiden" or "Indian princess," eBay *makes* an archive, or to think about it another way, makes it clear that there *is* an archive. The lists of objects, the search terms that find representation on eBay, make it possible to see that the system of representation informing the production and circulation of these images existed.

* * *

The history of representation of the Indian maiden's image is much longer than the early-twentieth-century starting point for this discussion might suggest in art and in literature, and even in terms of commodification and marketing. It begins, as Rayna Green has observed, with the European invasion and settlement of Indigenous territory in the late sixteenth century (701), a point to which many of these representations often romantically return, and a part of the origin myth that continues to function as an object of colonial desire in the image of the Indian maiden. Disney's 1995 animated feature *Pocahontas*, with its narrative of colonization facilitated by an eroticized Indigenous woman, is a case in point. David Stymiest has drawn attention to the circulation of Pocahontas images (c. 1595–1617) in early modern colonial advertisement for the purposes of promoting settlement in Virginia to demonstrate the ways "symbolic capital [was created in travel and emigrationist pamphlets] out of the sexualized image of Pocahontas that could then be turned into actual capital, in the form of investments in the Virginia Company" (116). As Stymiest notes, the marriage of Pocahontas and John Rolfe, the first "legal" marriage of an Indigenous woman and an English settler in the American colony (111), provided a symbolic narrative of the white occupation of Indigenous territory, which the Disney film suggests is welcomed. In the process of constructing this narrative for the purposes of colonial occupation and expansion, Pocahontas comes to be understood in the early seventeenth century as a figure of Indigenous femininity who serves to connect the settler-invader culture to the land, and to authorize, in her portrayed sexual availability and desire for the white colonial man, the occupation of that land.

Pocahontas, Stymiest suggests, "was the pre-eminent symbol of Virginia and forms an iconic representation of how the virgin territory of America welcomes the colonizer to make his mark on her" (122). She is also the first example of the ways in which Indigenous femininity was "subsumed, commercialized, and converted into an image of exchange in a symbolic economy, which continues, albeit in a highly transformed aspect, up to the present day" (124). This image of Indigenous femininity becomes, in representation, a brand for the colonial nation itself, and a gesture of colonial appropriation. Images of Pocahontas on these terms proliferate from the seventeenth century to the nineteenth, and reappear, as I have already indicated, recently in the popular Disney film. Disney's reactivation and reaffirmation of the Pocahontas image's value can be traced in the number of items that appear on eBay under the search term "Pocahontas" that are products associated with the film. A significant portion of the 1,806 items identified in a search on November 10, 2009, are related to Disney's animated feature (Mint Disney Princess Barbie Doll Pocahontas Barbie for $7.00; Wilton Disney Pocahontas Cake Pan w/Instructions 1995 for $3.25). And even if eBay offers none of the very early materials associated with Pocahontas, such as paintings and prints now held by museums and galleries by virtue of their antiquity, it nonetheless offers many significant pre-Disney materials. One example is a Vintage Poster Sign from Pocahontas Fuel Co. Coal Metal for $173.73. The seller's description of the poster indicates that the "Top of the sign states 'Pocahontas Fuel Co Miners, Shippers and Bunker Supplies of Original Pocahontas Coal'" (eBay Nov. 10, 2009).

As this poster suggests, in the context of nineteenth-century imperial expansionism in North America, the value of the image of the Indian maiden as an iconic representation of the colony welcoming the colonizer persists. By the end of the nineteenth century, the image begins to undergo significant transformations. First, it shifts from marketing the land and the economy of patriarchal colonization (a symbolic marriage between the colonizer and the territory) to a fungible icon of the land that could be and often was used to market the commodities produced from the land (coal, for instance, or vegetables). Daniel Francis suggests that this shift is evident across gender categories; in addition, he notes that the shift in the representation dates to a time earlier in the history of imperial commerce, "going back at least to the travelling medicine shows of the late eighteenth century, in which potions and elixirs were peddled on the strength of their connection with Indian healing practices" (174). But the first decades of the twentieth century, as he also notes, saw a radical increase in the ways the image functioned. He draws attention to "the appearance of dozens and dozens of products which tried to find favour with consumers by identifying with the Indian: Pocahontas perfume, Red Indian motor oil, Iroquois beer, Squaw Brand canned vegetables—the list goes on and on" (174). Francis suggests that early twentieth-century advertising "used the Indian as a symbol to appeal to modern consumers who admired values they associated with pre-industrial society" (176). It is also possible to argue that advertising "used" images of First Nations and Native American people, and in particular, of First Nations and Native American women for two reasons: first, to represent industrial society as if it were a natural "product" of the old imagined exchange between settlers and Indigenous people, and second, to affirm over and over again the idea of the occupation of Indigenous land as a marriage by choice and ultimately what should be regarded a "fair trade."

The Indigenous woman who had, according to two hundred years of advertising propaganda and white fantasy, welcomed colonists, is a foundational image for this colonial conception of the "fair trade." Francis, as I have suggested, notes that this image appeared, with particular frequency and resonance, on many products. By the end of the nineteenth century, the image of the Indian maiden was well established as an icon of colonial commodity culture in North America. As Burgess and Valaskakis point out, by the early twentieth century "[t]here are gold-leaf princesses on cigar boxes and bare-breasted, primitive princesses—and sometimes squaws—advertising Swamp-Root herbal cures and a range of food products, including corn, peas, beans, apples and Mazola Oil, Land O' Lakes butter and Kraft foods" (27). Attaching this image to something always identified it for white consumers as a commodity in circulation for and within the colonial community. As Rayna Green demonstrates, the Indian maiden had functioned since the early days as a "controlling metaphor in the American experience" (703), and had been embedded in the semiotics of commercial exchange and national representation as an image that stands in for other commodities. The containers and advertising for turn-of-the-century objects continue to circulate on eBay; they comprise a substantial part of the catalogue of Indian maiden objects still in circulation in 2010, and thus indicate the pervasiveness of the image's use.

Attached to and indicative of particular products, the image was arguably stripped of any referentiality to actual Indigenous women it may have had. It became more and more a matter of fantasy, imagination, and projection than anything even vaguely mimetic. The image developed into the kind of imprisoning stereotype Greek/Cherokee writer Thomas King depicts in the story "How Corporal Colin Sterling Saved Blossom, Alberta, and Most of the Rest of the World as Well"; therein, Indigenous people turn into "cigar store Indians," literally immobilized by the stereotype circulated in white commodity culture. As King's story suggests, the image of the "cigar store Indian" does symbolic work in the marketing of colonial culture's commodities, and by doing so has serious consequences for those who are simultaneously represented and stripped of intrinsic meaning.

These consequences are evident for Indigenous women compelled to signify the iconic Indian maiden in white culture according to the practice of tropic representation. Kuna/Rappahannock writer Monique Mojica takes up the question of some of these consequences in her 1991 play, *Princess Pocahontas and the Blue Spots*, which parodies the stereotype of the Indian maiden and works to undermine its continued function. Cree/Métis poet Marilyn Dumont's 1996 "Squaw Poems" also draw attention to the ways Indigenous women in colonial culture are called upon to perform as the "squaw" or the "Indian maiden," identities invented by white culture. In her 1996 collection *A Really Good Brown Girl*, it is significant that Dumont chose to follow "Squaw Poems" with "Helen Betty Osborne," a work that commemorates a young Cree woman sexually assaulted and killed in The Pas, Manitoba, in 1971. She makes the point that the poem could be about herself or "any one of/[her] female relatives" (3–5), all equally subject to what she describes as "'open season' on native women" (25). Dumont's and Mojica's responses strongly suggest that these longstanding images of Indian maidens—now so readily found on eBay—have contributed to the social climate these texts delineate.

This suggestion is also made by other writers. Cree writer Tomson Highway compellingly implicates the commodity symbolism white culture imposes on Indigenous femininity. He represents a cultural practice of sexual exploitation and the discarding of women as though they are excess commodities in his 1998 novel *Kiss of the Fur Queen*. First Nations women in this narrative are left dead with commodity markers—screwdrivers, beer bottles—buried in their own bodies. In M. Elise Marubbio's 2006 study of the repeated violence done to Indigenous women in North American cinema, she draws attention to statistical evidence of the problem Highway foregrounds in *Kiss of the Fur Queen*. She notes the persistence of stereotypes that are "often played out violently on [the real] bodies" of Native American women (231). As Green puts it, images of Indian maidens, like those of "squaws," "offer unendurable metaphors for the lives of Indian women" (714). That is, the non-referentiality of the image of the Indian maiden does not mean its function as a metaphor for colonial experience and as an icon for white culture's commodities does not have significant effects on the ways Indigenous women's bodies are understood to bear a version of that image.

* * *

If the image of the Indian maiden, from early representations of Pocahontas to the late nineteenth century, is symbolic and indicative of a fantasy perception rather than mimesis (or affirms that mimesis is always a fantasy), the image is also, more often than not, recognizably Indigenous.

Images from this period, even if they represent, as Green suggests, the figure of the Indian maiden or princess as "darker than the Europeans, but more Caucasian than her fellow natives" (704), utilize a conventional repertoire of characteristics in skin colour, physiognomy, posture, and dress. Green notes that the most famous image of Pocahontas, "the only one said to be done from life (at John Rolfe's request)," emphasizes her Indigeneity. While undertaking to convey that her Indigenousness is obscured and re-presented by putting her "in Elizabethan dress, complete with ruff and velvet hat—[a] Christian, English lady" (700), the portrait also indicates clearly that she *is*, if in white costume, Indigenous. However, in the second major transformation of the image at the beginning of the twentieth century, this practice of representation is reversed. In commercial media and popular representation, Indian maidens cease to be "Indian" per se, taking on, as Valaskakis has suggested, what are considered to be Caucasian features.

Valaskakis has drawn attention to popular images of the Shoshone woman most frequently known as Sacajawea, Sacagawea, or Bird-Woman (c.1788–1812), famous in white colonial culture because she was the guide of Lewis and Clark in their expedition across the western United States between 1804 and 1806. Like Pocahontas, Sacajawea is a crucial figure in non-Indigenous American cultural memory, primarily because the history of her work is understood to serve white culture, making her, as Green puts it, a "good Indian" (703). Her particular value, in eBay terms, is evident in the fact that a search for "Sacagawea" produces 2,651 results (Nov. 9, 2009). That many of these results relate to the American mint's issue of Sacagawea dollars, moreover, clearly conveys the commercial value of the image: she *is* what is exchanged. Although Sacajawea is unique in her appearance on national currency, she is certainly not alone in being contained within the conventions of representation. Burgess and Valaskakis outline a genre they call the "red tunic lady," an image that they suggest served as the dominant representation of the Indian maiden from about 1915 through the 1940s (27). It is evident in most of these representations that the salient characteristics are their Indigenous costume (that is, sort of Indigenous, or for white culture, like a "sexy Indian maiden costume," Indigenous enough) *and* their "perfect Caucasian features" (11). Valaskakis describes this figure in one image as a "Brooke Shields replica posing in a buckskin dress, circa 1910" (37), or a white woman—indeed, an actor—posing as an Indigenous woman.

It is this image of the white woman in Indigenous costume, rendered increasingly "Caucasian," that circulates in the early twentieth century *as* the Indian maiden, an image in which Indianness has been reduced to decoration and white masquerade. The implications of this reduction are significant. On the one hand, this cultural blanching indicates a familiar process of white culture's overwriting and erasure of Indigenousness, something that began at contact and goes on into this moment not only *in* representation but also in a range of social and cultural practices, including historical accounts, archival representation, and land appropriation. In this process, the whitening of the Indian maiden also indicates an equally familiar process of rendering the "vanishing race." On the other hand, however, the representational space of Indianness, reduced in the image, is filled up with whiteness. This is not to suggest that the white woman is imagined to stand in for Indigenous femininity in the same way the Indian maiden is imagined to stand in for the nation. Rather, what is actually represented is the white body as the product or commodity that is exchanged and has been marked or branded for exchange, like so many other products at the same moment, by imprinting the image of the Indian maiden on that body. An index of displacement and overwriting that creates a crucial signifying gap for Indigenous women in white colonial representation, and a stereotype with demonstrably negative effects for Indigenous women, the Caucasian Indian maiden is also a problem of white femininity.

The problem of the white Indian maiden is not the same problem for white and Indigenous women, who are not necessarily brought together in the image's ambiguous representation. Moreover, while serving to draw attention to problems specific to both Indigenous and white femininity, this image cannot be understood to evince a foundational principle of gendered equality across cultural categories or in relation to forms of oppression. White women and Indigenous women in North America do not notably share histories either of representation within white culture or empowerment within that culture. White women, for instance, were enfranchised in Canada in 1919 under the Act to Confer the Electoral Franchise upon Women, and in the U.S. in 1920 under the Nineteenth Amendment (also called the Susan B. Anthony Amendment). In Canada, First Nations women could not vote without giving up their status until 1960. In this, as in other contexts, the social and political histories of Indigenous and white women remain foundationally discrete. They do not come together in the figure of the Indian maiden, despite the extent to which this image uses a well-established brand, has symbolic value associated with Indigenous femininity to represent and, in effect, to market white women in colonial and imperial North America. At the moment the image of the Indian maiden converges with the representation of white women, the effects of functionalizing Indigenous femininity in white commodity culture were well established. These effects would not be altered—or, at any rate, ameliorated—by the representation of white women *as if* they were Indigenous. What is evident at that moment, however, is an affirmation of functionalizing white femininity as a commodity for exchange within the context of white colonial culture.

That the white woman represented, circulated, and marketed is comprehensible as a specifically sexual commodity is evident in the increasing eroticization of the image through the twentieth century. By the second decade of the twentieth century, as Burgess and Valaskakis have shown, the image of the Indian maiden becomes "more enticing, with low necklines, net stockings, and outfits that are more sexually explicit" (31). She also notes the appearance, in mid- to later-twentieth-century "girlie" magazines, of photographs of white women dressed in beaded buckskin bikinis and headdresses, their costumes only minimally and theatrically Indigenous; white women, in effect, "playing Indian" (Burgess and Valaskakis 30, 31; Green 30). Indeed, she notes Virginia Driving Hawk Sneve's suggestion that, for many of these early-twentieth-century images of the Indian maiden, "the models...were not American Indian women but attractive Caucasian women who frequently begged the artists to be allowed to pose as an Indian Princess" (Burgess and Valaskakis 31; Sneve 72–74). Evidence of white culture's practice of marking appropriation through performing Indigenousness, the early-twentieth-century emergence of the white woman in Indigenous costume, and particularly in erotic display, is also an index of an expansion in the exchange of white women's bodies. Always implicitly sexual, if not always explicitly erotic, the image of the Indian maiden as a white woman shifts the commodity value already established by this marker to white women's bodies, without notably minimizing its already well-established commodification of Indigenous femininity.

Since this imbrication of two systems of representation is not about parity between the representation of Indigenous and white femininity, and since it does not alter or improve the ways Indigenous women occupy white culture in the early twentieth century, two questions arise: First, why does this image circulate with such frequency in the early twentieth century? And second, what is the function of the white woman as commodity? These questions are as complex as those pertaining to the ways in which the image of the Indian maiden represents or does not represent Indigenousness. One answer is that by the end of the nineteenth century, women, a foundational unit of exchange in patriarchal society, come to be identified with greater urgency as racialized reproductive agents crucial to the maintenance of imperial and colonial space. By the late nineteenth century, it became increasingly necessary to remind women in many imperial contexts of their duty to their "race," however it was defined in terms of the dominant category and the particular nation. In the final quarter of the nineteenth century, we thus see in many national contexts the emergence of the woman constituted as one version or another of what is usually called the "mother of the race." The "mother of the race" was an entity valued in imperial and colonial space precisely for her reproductive function, even as her sexuality (what makes her valuable) was repressed or eradicated from her representation in favour of an ennobling concept of destiny and duty and an increasingly sentimentalized ideology of maternalism.

The sexual value of the "mother of the race," repressed in the representation of the apparently non-sexual mother, is revealed in the contemporary eruption of a range of other representations. It is in relation to this ideology of racial maternalism that we see the appearance of the white slave figure. This figure, as I have suggested elsewhere, can be understood as the "mother of the race" captured in the process of circulating through imperial space en route to racial duty. Her reproductive value is thus annihilated by her circulation as a sexual commodity outside of the frame of marriage and the nation. It is also in relation to this ideology of racial maternalism and sexual function that we see the practice of erotic dance emerge in North America during the 1860s, a profession where the repressed function of the "mother of the race"—sexual, genital, reproductive—is rendered as spectacle. In late-nineteenth-century erotic dance, the circulation of women as erotic commodities is performed theatrically as it is also made, perversely, less obscure: it is, clearly and unequivocally, based on the practices of commodity culture. It is in relation to this ideology that the Indian maiden, the icon of white commodity culture, comes to be represented as a white woman.

The Indian maiden is not the only image of femininity circulated as an erotic commodity in the construction and representation of North America, but it is an important one in a history that appropriates and overwrites Indigenousness and undertakes to fill colonial space with white bodies. It is not an image that comes from Indigenous culture, but one that represents the imposition of colonial ideology and commerce on that culture. The archive of representations thus serves as a crucial record of this history, preserved in the commodity objects that history is marked upon and, in effect, expelled—something that eBay importantly highlights in its function as an archive of this "waste" history. In this capacity, eBay significantly contributes to defining the alternative archive as precisely what is expelled, a record not necessarily of what is remembered but what is repressed in a culture. eBay is still a better place to begin to look for images of the Indian maiden than institutional repositories not only because it has more stuff but also because it disarticulates this stuff from the kind of official national narrative archives typically, as Joan Sangster has suggested, undertake to construct. eBay emphasizes the circulation of these images in terms of advertising and commodity culture and draws attention to the value of these images in the present. By emphasizing the commercial and mixing objects related to the image of the present Indian maiden with materials from the historical record of the white commodity culture that image circulated within, the site makes a different point than the official record of cultural memory in an institutional archive. eBay reminds us, crucially, through the democracy of the search term and the openness of the marketplace, that we are the agents of cultural memory and that we *make* archives, not only with what we keep in shoeboxes under our beds or in our basements, attics, and closets but also in what we look for online.

Notes

1 Because eBay changes constantly, as I explain, I have included the search terms and dates that the searches were conducted on the Web auction site to indicate when and how I conducted the research.
2 The National Archives of Canada, as it was then known, "established a long-term project to collect women's archives in the early 1970s" (Dean and Fraser 1).

Works Cited

Baudrillard, Jean. *The System of Objects*. 1968. Trans. James Benedict. London: Verso, 2002. Print.

Burgess, Marilyn, and Gail Guthrie Valaskakis. *Indian Princesses and Cowgirls: Stereotypes from the Frontier*. Montréal: Oboro, 1995. Print.

Dean, Joanna, and David Fraser. *Women's Archives Guide: Manuscript Sources for the History of Women*. Ottawa: National Archives of Canada, 1991. Print.

Dumont, Marilyn. "Squaw Poems." "Helen Betty Osborne." *A Really Good Brown Girl*. 1996. London: Brick, 2000. 18–20. Print.

eBay. "What We Believe." "Who We Are: History." "Who We Are: Overview." *eBay.com*. n.d. Web. Nov. 6, 2009.

Francis, Daniel. *The Imaginary Indian: The Image of the Indian in Canadian Culture*. 1992. Vancouver: Arsenal Pulp P, 1997. Print.

Green, Rayna. "The Pocahontas Perplex: The Image of Indian Women in American Culture." *Massachusetts Review* 16.4 (1975): 698–714. Web. Nov. 11, 2009.

Highway, Tomson. *Kiss of the Fur Queen*. Toronto: Doubleday, 1999. Print.

King, Thomas. "How Corporal Colin Sterling Saved Blossom, Alberta, and Most of the Rest of the World as Well." *one good story, that one*. Toronto: HarperCollins, 1993. 49–66. Print.

Kirsch, Gesa E., and Liz Rohan, eds. *Beyond the Archives: Research as a Lived Process*. Carbondale: Southern Illinois UP, 2008. 47–55. Print.

Library and Archives Canada. "About Us: Mandate." *Library and Archives Canada*. Mar. 30, 2004. Web. Oct. 13, 2009.

Library of Congress. "About the Library: Welcome Message from the Librarian of Congress." *Library of Congress.* n.d. Web. Oct. 27, 2009.

———. "The Mission and Strategic Priorities of the Library of Congress FY 1997–2004." *Library of Congress.* Sept. 20, 1999. Web. Oct. 27, 2009.

Marubbio, M. Elise. *Killing the Indian Maiden: Images of Native American Women in Film.* Lexington: UP of Kentucky, 2006. Print.

Mojica, Monique. *Princess Pocahontas and the Blue Spots.* Toronto: Women's P, 1991. Print.

Rohan, Barry. "My Grandfather's Trunk." Kirsch and Rohan 73–82. Print.

Sangster, Joan. "Archiving Feminist Histories: Women, the 'nation' and Metanarratives in Canadian Historical Writing." *Women's Studies International Forum* 29.3 (2006): 255–64. Print.

Sharer, Wendy B. "Traces of the Familiar: Family Archives as Primary Source Material." Kirsch and Rohan 47–55. Print.

Sneve, Virginia Driving Hawk. "Remembering Minehaha." *Country Living* (1987): 72–74. Print.

Stymiest, David. "'Strange Wives': Pocahontas in Early Modern Colonial Advertisement." *Mosaic* 35.3 (2002): 109–26. Print.

"Faster Than a Speeding Thought": Lemon Hound's Archive Unleashed
Karis Shearer and Jessica Schagerl

Some newer digital forms, such as blogs, now numbering in the millions and growing rapidly, are new versions of older document forms, such as diaries, except that they won't be physically collected by archives as their predecessor documentary sources have been. In many ways, blogs and other new digital documents replace older record forms, but it is not certain whether these documents can be collected in the same way as older sources once used to be. Few archives, of any type, are actually dealing with document forms such as blogs; they are generally left to their creators, and maybe, in the face of a documentary universe far larger than anyone ever anticipated, this may be an acceptable approach.
—*Richard Cox,* Personal Archives, xvii

But I think that in embracing, and working rigorously and critically with these new technologies, we may not only be finding new ways of publishing, but new ways writing and thinking, and ultimately new ways of reading.
—*Sina Queyras,* "The lost poems, or the space of blogging"

A Note to the Reader
Except for some marginalia in several books and on photocopied articles, there is no paper record of this essay's production. Karis and Jessica's collaboration was a digital one. It was not even conducted chiefly over email. We discussed the ideas for the paper over the telephone on occasion, usually when one of us needed some encouragement (or when the anxiety of "the subject of my article may disappear!" got to be too much). The main ideas for the paper—its shape, arguments, digressions, and a good number of phrases that found their way into the final copy—were all written using the chat feature of a major social networking site. Technically, according to the terms of use on this particular site, which are subject to frequent amendment, we do not even maintain ownership of our postings. Our archival activity is limited to what we collected for our own files. To wit, we have notes saved in word processing files that reveal some of the challenges of documenting online collaboration. At one point, for example, Karis noted, "I went to look through the archive of our conversation for something you'd mentioned, but couldn't find it because part of the 'chat history' is now gone—i.e., it doesn't seem to save it all—just the more recent exchange." It is important that readers know about the process and our perhaps unorthodox methodology, since we begin from the premise that digital media is changing the nature of public discourse. In this paper, we argue that a blog is an archive or body of knowledge which allows a researcher to perform potentially risky research about the histories of the contemporary moment in unique and rewarding ways. We suggest that blogs prompt new ways of thinking about what constitutes an archive and, as a result, they invite a rethinking of the research process. To make these claims, we look at "Lemon Hound," the blog authored by the poet Sina Queyras.

Introduction
This chapter[1] is not about Sina Queyras's poetry. It is not about the feminist politics surrounding the "Lemon Hound"[2] blog, contemporary poetry in Canada, or critical discussions of poetry in the blogosphere. It is about digital technology, which has "challenged traditional views of the nature of records and archives and the role of archivists" (Brown 15). This paper is not, by any stretch of the imagination, about demeaning the value of traditional print archives or the role of archivists in the acquisition, preservation, and promotion of literary figures. Their job, which is not well understood even by the researchers who rely on their expertise, has arguably been made more difficult since the language of "archives" has been appropriated by the computer industry for digital storage, chronological

ordering of posts, and data backup (Cox, *Ethics* 237). Our essay might be viewed as continuing this trend; however, as literary critics we note that it is worthwhile to highlight the term's fluidity, since archives are often misunderstood as static entities. Like the authors of many essays in this collection, we are concerned with process, but the archive that we have chosen to work with itself attends to erasures in the (literary) history of the present. The instant self-publication offered by the medium of the blog allows women like Queyras to provide important critical responses to the work of other female poets and artists who might otherwise be ignored by poetry institutions—institutions that, as Lemon Hound points out, still strongly favour male poets.

We are engaged by the often messy and surprising features of the blog as an archive. We explore our own relationships as literary researchers interested in archival research through our engagement with the blog of Lemon Hound, the online persona created by Canadian poet Sina Queyras. The "Lemon Hound" blog charts a process of making public and making publics; at its most basic, it may be read as a blog about claiming a voice (and with it, some authority) and "externalizing the space of our [women's] texts" by bringing them to a wider public (Queyras "Letters"). It is also an archive of the social practices that help shape a (writing) life in the twenty-first century. In this essay, we want to ask broader questions about our own interactions as critics and researchers with the blog as both a research tool and publication venue: what kind of information does the blog archive disclose and what remains inaccessible to the researcher? What are the specific advantages of this interactive archive for women poets, critics, and researchers, and how might it redress some of the current conditions of the academy and literary field? What are the limitations of the blog as archive? Is it worthwhile to attempt to bridge what the editors of *ReCalling Early Canada: Reading the Political in Literary and Cultural Production* call the "methodological and theoretical divide between scholars who identify themselves as archival scholars, often working in earlier periods of study, and those who take up more recent subjects of analysis" (xliv)? Or is this notion of blog as archive just a fantasy, a reference to Derrida's overused "archive fever," a longing for the freedom to call something an archive (thus research, thus "fundable," and thus a good use of our time as scholars working within and without the traditional academy) that we can access through a wireless connection, while sitting on the couch in pajamas, for instance, or with a three-year-old at our feet? To this end, we're also interested in what kind of impulse in critical thought is marked by our desire to understand a blog as an archive and how we can chart that impulse as researchers.

As much as both of us relish most aspects of archival research, there are certain things about archives that have always made us slightly uncomfortable. It's not because of the little white gloves, the slightly chilly room, or the surveillance, since we tolerate those in order to learn the "stories [that] emerge from the particular intimacies that we have associated with entering the physical space of the archive" (Dever, Newman, and Vickery 32). The discomfort has more to do with the fact that we often research Canadian writers who are still alive. We attend their readings, we've met them, and maybe even had a drink with them. The frisson of excitement that attends a bit of literary gossip quickly gives way to the realization that there is someone's very real life under scrutiny. There's something a little too personal about sifting through the confessional correspondence of a writer we may run into at a literary event the next month—although, as Susan McMaster and Catherine Hobbs both note in this collection of essays, these confessional letters are in the publicly accessible archives after plenty of discussion and deliberation between donor and archivist. So when we started to think of the "Lemon Hound" blog as an archive, one aspect that attracted us was the seemingly impersonal nature of this particular archive. There was an explicit distance between the self-conscious writer-persona Lemon Hound (the performative self) and the person who is "Sina Queyras" (the self who writes at a given moment), a gap explicitly signalled by her use of the pseudonymous hound-as-critic persona. We were drawn to "Lemon Hound's" potential not only to provide a view of the contemporary literary landscape but also to tell a particular story of social identity and community that, we argue, has a bearing on how contemporary Canadian poetry is read, theorized, and promoted. "Lemon Hound" is the name of the blog Sina Queyras began in May 2004, when she was living in Brooklyn, New York. The blog—subtitled "Concerning Contemporary Poetry, Visual Art, & Letters"—contains in its archive[3] over 1,597 entries as well as hundreds of comments posted in response to those entries (as of January 17, 2010). A selection of the posts has also appeared in print as Queyras's fifth book, *Unleashed*. Organized in reverse chronological order with the most recent posts appearing first, "Lemon Hound" is hosted by the website blogspot.com. "Lemon Hound" is recognizable as a blog by its appearance: "three columns, the middle one wider than the two on the sides, a logo at top left, some navigation devices in a bar across the top, lots of highlighted text indicating lists of links down the left side, and an image on the right. [In addition, there are] long sections of written language in the middle" (Myers 18). That a generalized description of a blog's appearance can be thus summarized and then used to describe a specific one suggests that blogs belong to a recognizable subset of online publications.

As is typical of blogs, "Lemon Hound" displays the most recent post or entry at the top of the webpage, followed by a month or so of previous posts. Unless the blogger actively chooses to erase old posts systematically, the blog automatically generates an archive. The ease of a blog is what makes it "a simple tool, not a democratized informational utopia," to borrow the words of Robert Sheppard, another poet-blogger (102). "Lemon Hound" features a sidebar of hot links that allow readers to access an archive of the previous years' posts from 2004 to 2009, as well as a search feature which a reader may use to explore the archive. The archive is organized by temporal unit (e.g., year, month, day): options on the left-hand taskbar allow a reader to select a hot-linked year (e.g., 2005), that then produces a drop-down menu offering the option of selecting a specific month (e.g., April). Each month and year shows the total number of posts per temporal unit, so it is also possible to access the material in the archive when the author was most active as well as when she was least active. Searching all fields by date is just one of the many search methods rarely available in conventional institutional archives that may or may not have chronological files, depending on the material archived and the system used by the archivist. (A catalogue that organizes letters and documents chronologically would be an example of an exception.)

In its early stages, the blog was the third-person account of Lemon Hound, the persona Queyras developed as a way of establishing a public voice. The blog eventually became Lemon Hound's cultural commentary in the first person. In an interview with Heather Milne, Queyras explains that in both her blog and the book of the same name, *Lemon Hound*, she "took on that persona because it just felt comfortable to speak publicly that way. I think of the blog as creating a public space because I really feel women are struggling still with the creation of a public persona. I don't know a woman, actually, who doesn't struggle with it" (Interview 317). The project, however, is not without its own ambivalence; Queyras admits in the same interview that she nearly abandoned the blog several times, but ultimately hasn't done so because she feels it serves as an important toehold for women in public discourse (317–18). The digital record of this "toehold in public discourse" provides readers not with the confessional emotive journal entries that one might find in a traditional archive, but instead with critical commentary on contemporary art and poetry that they may not have encountered previously.

What is important about a blog—any blog, not just "Lemon Hound"—is its ordinariness, its potential to reveal aspects of lives that might be overlooked by traditional archives. Even "Lemon Hound," a blog with an informational, critical, and creative bent, has posts generated by the cultural texts encountered during everyday activities like walking and reading. In this paper, we draw on Lemon Hound's blog for several reasons. As literary critics, we are keen to draw on our experiences of using this archive for literary research. Working with the "Lemon Hound" archive, however, proved more complex than we anticipated: Queyras had published over 1,300 posts before we discovered the blog, which meant there was a significant archive of posts and comments to work through. Where would we begin? As readers, both of us prefer to start from the beginning and work through the posts chronologically in order to learn how the blog changed over time; as researchers, however, we find it much more useful to organize our rereading through the blog's search feature. How many times had Queyras included the word "feminism" in a post, for example? How many of those posts generated responses? Almost instinctively, we found ourselves recontextualizing the role of the researcher as one who explicitly collaborates in the production of meaning. The potential for collaborative, non-hierarchical critical work suited our feminist sensibilities, too. Before we reach that discussion, however, we need to elaborate on what a blog archive is, how it operates for a researcher, and how it differs from a paper archive (if it does at all).

No White Cotton Gloves Required Here: Understanding a Blog as an Archive

> A blog archives itself, doesn't it[?]—which is deceptive. I was talking to Los Glazier about the marvelous Electronic Poetry Center at Buffalo, and he said that the university which hosts it could pull the plug at any moment. The same could happen with any blog, but we behave as if it won't. Look at all the links...that are dead-ends.... We've got to save that "now" before it becomes a vanished "then." (Sheppard 103–4)

Let's get one thing straight: a blog is an unstable form of documentation. It is unreliable, shifting, doubtful—in short, it is all the things a good source should not be. Yet, as Linda Morra shows for the anecdote and T. L. Cowan shows for remembered descriptions of the feminist cabaret scene, these uncertain sources that test the limits of the archive have a real value for any reconceptualization of archival research.[4] After all, as Richard Cox notes, "people still continue to create personal documents and to use every means, no matter how insecure, to create, store, and use these records...of lives lived and stories yearning to be heard" (*Personal* xi). In the following section, we address several powerful conventions of thinking about the archive that, to us, have direct bearing on the value of a blog as archive. These conventions concern authorship, transparency, access, and the fixity of the historical record, and they point to the dis/similarities between print and digital archives. The blog operates in tension with these conventions. Indeed, we'll argue in the next section that the blog as an archive necessitates a flexible research process, especially for those researchers who are guided by the assumptions they bring as a result of their engagement with traditional (paper) archives.

On the broadest level, we argue that a blog functions as an archive because it provides a particular socio-historical context to the particular moment; that is, like a traditional archive, a blog provides an account that can be used to articulate a version of a specific historical moment. Its contents offer something for a researcher's understanding and, just like traditional archives, the contents of the blog and its holdings may or may not be important for every research situation. In the blog's case, it mimics the institutional record of holdings, but also has holdings in the same place (i.e., lists of documents and the documents themselves). Granted, a blog is an ongoing cultural production—one that is always in process and whose documents are always in dialogue with one another—but this fact alone does not make it any less an archive. Archival holdings, especially those created by living literary figures, are just as much ongoing cultural productions (see the essays by McMaster, Marlatt, Clark, and Kemp in this collection). One of the explicit ways a blog differs from a traditional archive, however, is in the expressed individual control exerted by the creator over the content, discussion, and preservation of the material. In other words, the blog writer is also the blog's archivist.

The blog's technologically deterministic act of archiving gives it a certain documentary power which mimics the administrative and discursive authority of the institutional archive. Indeed, although it is not the intention of this paper to offer a discussion of the theories surrounding the blog as archive, both the Foucauldian concept about the ordering of a discursive network and the Derridean concept of the technologies associated with memories and archiving seem to offer explanatory models for understanding the blog as archive. As an online blog archive, "Lemon Hound" is accessible to virtually any reader who has an Internet connection, making it far more public than a traditional institutional archive. Particularly interesting is the way in which the "Lemon Hound" blog archive introduces the work of Canadian poets to American and international readers. Due to limited print runs and circulation of poetry volumes in Canada, these readers would not likely encounter this work otherwise (see "Margaret Christakos" and "The positive power"). Moreover, the online archive is accessible not only to a *larger* public but also to *different* or marginalized publics, unlike many institutional archives. On a practical level, "Lemon

Hound" is searchable from a reader's own home or local library computer: researchers do not do not need to incur travel and accommodation costs that might prevent low-income researchers—or those whose research time does not coincide with regular opening hours—from working with traditional archives.

One of the most significant aspects of the blog, then, is the way in which it foregrounds questions of authorship and readership in a way that traditional archives do not. The "Lemon Hound" archive cannot be read as a traditional archive in that the records cannot "reveal the character and intentions of the writer herself" (Douglas and MacNeill 28). Moreover, it openly defies the notion of a knowable, stable identity by self-reflexively theorizing authorship and denying the notion that the text transparently conveys the experience of the individual writer. One particular aspect of the blog archive that sets it apart dramatically from institutional archives is the collaborative properties available. In the latter, for example, one is not only forbidden from penning marginal comments in special collections texts but also institutions go to great security lengths (requisite pencils, white gloves, surveillance) to ensure one does not attempt to "co-author" any rare manuscripts. The massive archive of Sina Queyras's "Lemon Hound" blog posts is online for all the world to read on a computer screen, wherever that might be. The blog does not require special permission to look through it nor to engage with it—although importantly, it does require special permission from the blogger to comment on it, a point to which we will return. As enticing as the unique collaborative potential of this archive appears at first glance, it also brings with it a host of new ethical issues that we explore in the next section. Queyras, too, anticipates many of these issues, however, and self-reflexively discusses them on the blog.

Challenges and Opportunities, as Read through "Lemon Hound"

As a feminist spectator, a feminist *flâneur* if you will, Lemon Hound also scrutinizes indices and archives, such as that of *The Paris Review*,

> look at the archive index of interviews from 2000 to 2005. That's a long time, a "modern" time, a time when feminism was "post," right? I mean, we were being told that there was no need to continue the shrill banter. But here are the recent numbers: in the five-year period between 2000 and 2005 there were 51 interviews, 39 of those with men.... ("More on the Paris Review")

With this post, Lemon Hound announces one of her ongoing preoccupations: the absence of women's voices in public discourse. Whereas Lemon Hound tracks statistics by counting women's names in the archival index, we track Lemon Hound's discussions of these absences by entering the terms "feminism" and "women" into the blog's search engine. Effectively, as researchers, we have reorganized the archive to suit our interests, in this case the literary or rhetorical strategies Lemon Hound deploys to address issues around women and poetry in Canada. Even a very good search tool for a conventional archive cannot rival the digital archive's search option that allows us to read and research in such a highly selective manner.

From the perspective of a researcher, however, one limitation of this blog archive is that the information about the traffic on the blog (aside from the obvious comments) is available to the blogger herself, who is a researcher in her own right. Meanwhile, we are left to speculate that, although they have no comments, the posts on feminism have at least been accessed and read by a substantial number of people; only the author-archivist knows this for certain. Indeed, one of the most interesting and frustrating aspects of the blog from the perspective of a researcher is that features such as the RSS *Site Meter* allows the blogger or author to obtain information about *each of us* every time we visit the blog to conduct research. Traditional archives do this too, of course, but digital technology allows the archivist to track more than names, dates, and folders visited. Lemon Hound's blog uses a *Site Meter*, for example, that—depending on which version she is using—tells her how we found the site, where we are accessing it from, and what interests us on the site (i.e., what blog posts we visit and what search terms we enter) (*Site Meter*). Therefore, just as we are reader-authors whose comments become part of the archive, the archivist-author can also be a researcher collecting information on readers. Although we may feel a comforting sense of anonymity as we access the blog from the privacy of our own living rooms, some of our personal data may nevertheless become part of the archive.

Although the technology is relatively new, the management of an archive as public as "Lemon Hound" must take into account some of the same privacy concerns that institutional archives negotiate. In fact, the degree of public access and the blog's illusion of immediacy make this all the more imperative, if not laborious, as Queyras explains: "the simple, constant fact of being public, of opening oneself up for criticism, for inappropriate intimacies and so on, is fatiguing" (*Unleashed* 8). As a blogger, Queyras can negotiate the boundaries of public and private by managing the public's interaction with her blog. If a reader wishes to leave a comment, for example, Queyras must approve that comment before it is published, a practice that limits inappropriate or harmful statements, and encourages a general tone of respect.

The interactive and public format of the "Lemon Hound" archive opens up space for marginalized voices to enter the public discourse on poetry and for their comments to be archived. Specifically, the blog encourages women readers to become authors in their own right by responding to posts. Occasionally, Queyras uses the content of the post to implicate women readers directly:

> Tired old dialogue that it is, I notice there are not enough women engaged in the discussion of poetry and poetics. Over and over again the voices seem to be male, shouting out about this or that school or lineage...deciding what is important and what not in such confident and reductive tones as to shut out the more cautious, or considered voices.
> Where, one might ask, are the women? ("Women Blogging Women")

Good question: where are the women? Are women directing their critical energies elsewhere? At a time when public commentary in the avant-garde literary scene, of which Queyras is a part, continues to be dominated by men,[5] it seems especially crucial for women to seize the means of production in order to make their voices heard. By doing so and encouraging other women to participate in the project, "Lemon Hound" works to counter the notable absence of criticism concerning the work of younger women poets that Barbara Godard finds rooted in academic labour conditions:

> The lack manifests itself in the increased economic insecurity of young writers faced with a greater challenge in getting published and of critics who, as the casualized labour in the corporatized university, find writing informative criticism that would accord recognition to the poets of their own generation a "luxury" they cannot afford in light of the necessity to produce texts about canonical writers of earlier generations who "count" in the increasingly conservative scale of academic value. (Godard 13)

Taking publishing into her own hands and offering spots to guest bloggers, Queyras's work via "Lemon Hound" provides some of the critical response to which young untenured and non-tenure-track academic writers do not (and, perhaps, cannot) necessarily choose to devote their labour.

Lemon Hound's question—"Where...are the women?"—nevertheless also implicates us as individual readers: why, as women, have we not responded? It's not too late. We could even take a moment to respond right now, and yet we don't. Instead, we're writing a print-based article. Perhaps it is because as women—scholars and writers ourselves—we feel the need to be cautious about how we use our time and to which projects we devote our respective labour. Our worries are not unlike Queyras's, for she too has wondered whether blogging is a fruitful use of her time:

> I've also found that it has become a distraction, a curious leak in my daily focus and practice—whether I post or not, it takes up psychic space. And

furthermore, I'm not sure I'm comfortable with the practice of instant publication. What does one expect when one blogs? Replies? Silence? The creation of a community? ("To blog or not to blog")

From the perspective of a reader, we might also ask, what does one expect when one comments on a blog post? Do these expectations have any bearing on our research role?

Readers' comments make up an important part of the blog archive and provide a unique record of reader response, yet the status of these comments within the archive is perhaps the most contentious issue of all. For example, who owns comments on a blog? Bloggers retain copyright to their posts, as Greg Myers notes in *The Discourse of Blogs and Wikis* (162), but it is far less clear who owns the comments that are posted in response. This question of comment "ownership" is one Queyras asked her readers while she was assembling the manuscript *Unleashed* for print publication. Did she need permission from readers to publish their comments as part of her book? For all that blogs have revolutionized literary culture by offering the benefits of instant publication, the same technology also allows for text to be *un*published with the click of a button. This kind of technology raises a new set of ethical questions: if a reader requests that her comment be erased from the blog archive, does the archivist have an ethical obligation to do so, the way an institutional archivist might impose restrictions on access at the request of an author? Conversely, does the archivist have a responsibility to maintain the record of conversation, including the comment strings that have developed over time? The answers to these questions depend on whether comments are considered "legitimate" publications or pieces of intellectual property. If they are the latter, the erasure of comments or of the blog altogether may pose ethical issues that have emerged for other online publications: see *Joyland Vancouver*, for example, wherein writer Alex Leslie's short story was recently erased from the archive—effectively unpublished—owing to a private and unrelated dispute between the author and editor Kevin Chong ("A Cautionary Tale").

In another case, the public record of reporter Thomas Crampton's entire career as a journalist disappeared when the *New York Times* merged with *The International Herald* and deleted the archives containing his articles ("Reporter"). In both cases, as Cox notes, there are "implications for weakening governance and social order," if the digital record is removed or altered, "since the record is essential for accountability and evidence" (*Ethics* 238). For the researcher, the "delete" button poses a concern because it threatens to unfix the historical record, the narrative she relies upon. It would be disingenuous to suggest that the comments posted by the readers of "Lemon Hound" are parallel to articles by journalists or short stories by professional writers, but the parallel nevertheless raises important questions about the ethical obligation an archivist has to his or her contributors in this age of digital media. The analogy also requires us to think about whether comments ought to be treated as a new form of serious criticism. Since Queyras has considered erasing her blog at least twice (Interview) and has recently published a selection of her blog posts (including a small number of reader comments) in print as the book *Unleashed*, the stakes of such a move are worth considering.

Although, on the one hand, controlling the means of publication can be a powerful tool for shaping the literary field, on the other hand, it does have its own implications for women's labour. As Queyras has pointed out on "Lemon Hound" and elsewhere, blogging is a commitment that takes time, particularly because of the response it generates: "I realized that part of what is making me reluctant to post is not the posts themselves, but the question of how much time I can give to the ensuing discussion. There are several posts in draft, but when I think of posting them, I know that in a way, the post is only the beginning" ("Slow Blogging"). Queyras effectively participates in establishing the cultural capital of her own work and those of her generation. In doing so, Lemon Hound works to counter the notable absence of criticism about the work of younger women poets. Taking publishing into her own hands and offering spots to guest bloggers, Queyras's work via "Lemon Hound" provides the critical response to which young untenured and non-tenure-track academic writers cannot necessarily afford to devote their labour.

If the postmodern writer exhibited a loss of faith in language, the Lemon Hound persona as late modern subject expresses yet another anxiety: what form, if any, should writing take? Should it be print or digital? In an age when the Internet has democratized publishing to the extent that there are now more published authors than ever before, what is one more blog? What, if any, is the value of the blog's content? The "she" of Lemon Hound's first blog entry expresses just such anxiety:

> Now she is blogging. Now she is sitting on the black couch listening to the sirens wail and the rain fall. Now she is thinking of oysters. Now she is wondering why this is worth sharing. Now she is thinking, how decipher what is worth reading? Who is to say? Sifters. She thinks we have become a nation of sifters. We dial up and sift through the wreckage. ("Untitled")

These short paratactic phrases create the sense of—or even parody—the inattentive sifting associated here with Internet readers, and likely remind readers of the frequent updates that characterize social networking sites. Each preposition "now" marks the beginning of a new activity, while the present progressive ("is blogging," "is sitting," "is thinking," "is wondering," etc.) refer to ongoing action, for which no temporal end is indicated. The action "blogging," for example, does not end when Lemon Hound begins "sitting" or begins "thinking"; in fact, in theory, the action of "blogging" begun on May 9, 2004, continues to date and until the reader has evidence that Lemon Hound is no longer blogging. The self-reflexive skepticism about the value of blogging is marked not only by the invocation of the sifting reader but also through the parody of the self-absorbed blogger who records and shares with the world the minutiae of daily life: listening to sirens and rain, and thinking about oysters. Just as this first blog entry moves quickly away from minutiae to larger concerns about writing and reading, so too does the blog as a whole.

Lemon Hound is also a poet of course, and the "Lemon Hound" blog and archive that is open and available to public readers has been assembled by the writer-archivist using unpaid labour and time that might otherwise have been devoted to working on a new poetry manuscript for a print-based publication, since refereed, print-based publications continue to hold more symbolic capital than electronic self-publication at present. They may also be a source of some revenue in the form of royalties, unlike blog publications. Those self-reflexive moments in "Lemon Hound" and in Queyras's writing in general that prompt critical consideration of women's labour (the labour of reading and writing) seem to be crucial to us in any conversation about poetic production, scholarship, and the cultural capital of women's writing today. (Unfortunately, this self-reflexivity does not extend to what it means to include other-authored comments within *Unleashed*.) Although online publication has gained more recent credibility within the academy,[6] blog posts—in part because they are not refereed—do not count toward tenure or academic status, nor does blog maintenance count as academic service. Regardless of how insightful a blog post might be, the reproduction of the post or any reference to it fails to move its author any closer to securing arts grants, promotions, or the like. Clearly, more attention needs to be paid to how the discounting of the blog proper as a genre has a bearing on the blog as archive. "Lemon Hound" has generated important discussion about poetics and, as Queyras foregrounds, it also represents her ethical commitment to provide space for and critical commentary on women's writing. How, then, to negotiate the tension between online and print publication?

Conclusion: What's in Sina's Closet?
In writing this chapter, it struck us that there must be a "paper archive" that exists somewhere, stored in boxes in Sina's closet, perhaps. Recently nominated for a Governor General's Award for her poetry, Sina Queyras is a writer of some renown who is attracting increasing critical attention; there

is every reason to think that her "paper" archives will be sought after by scholars and archivists at some point (if they haven't been already). What would the paper archive surrounding Lemon Hound (the persona as well as the blog) consist of? How does it differ from *Unleashed*? Where does her digital archive fit into this picture? Will it be ignored or rendered useless because technologies change or because certain archivists are hesitant to catalogue digital media?

At this juncture of literary history, with the future of the book in doubt and new technologies becoming obsolete in a matter of months, it is paradoxically all the more imperative to argue for the blog to be accepted as a legitimate archive of the times. These same technologies, however unstable, constitute new ways of writing and interacting with text; to ignore them is to deny the way in digital technology affects how many—and perhaps most—twenty-first-century writers compose, edit, and document their own writing, as well as the way in which readers read, respond, and interact with text. To acknowledge the potential of the blog as an archive is to embrace new modes of *research* generated, in part, by new modes of *writing*. We must, as Lauren Berlant suggests, "welcom[e] the risk of formlessness, the unpredictable consequence of ideas.... Those who turn away from a scene of thought performed in unusual modes of critical intensity, theoretical acumen, or referential familiarity miss an opportunity for surprise learning" (447). The blog as archive is shifting and unpredictable; it puts different demands on researchers. These demands need to be read as opportunities, not restrictions. We grant that our focus on research opportunities is an optimistic view of the blog as archive, one filled with questions and promise because of its changeability.

The dramatic instability of newer technologies like blogs also reminds us that, as the introduction to the collection suggests, the print or digital archival record is never neutral; the very form of the archive mediates the way we think about and interact with textual records. We've argued that "Lemon Hound" foregrounds some of the ways in which new technologies of writing inform the lives of writers and researchers in the contemporary moment; it does so first and foremost by calling attention to the instability of the blog archive (Queyras's threats of erasure), and by addressing the tensions between print and digital culture that impact writers' careers and literary production. Although we've been optimistic about using the blog as a research tool, like Queyras, we're also aware that, to a large extent, our identities are produced by the same technology we use for research. In her poetry collection, *Lemon Hound*, Queyras offers an extended consideration of technology's effect on humans in a poem whose speaker finds herself unable to dissociate her physical body from the technology that has come to facilitate and define it:

> Here she is walking down
> Bleecker thinking, how? How can she describe
> the windmill of her aorta? How tibia is her confu-
> sion? How like the Microsoft song, her frustration
> flits and crescendos. How like the blue of the XP
> screen her mood flickers in the traffic-jam hour.
> ("On the Scent 1" 25)

The symbiosis of body and technology is such that her moods can only be rendered by means of technological similes: her frustration is now best described as "like the Microsoft song" that plays when one turns on one's computer, while her shifts of her mood flicker "like the blue of the XP screen." If technology brings greater order to the archive and expands the possibilities of cultural production, Lemon Hound asks, what is the cost? As blog readers and researchers, surely we must also ask such questions of ourselves.

A Further Note to the Reader

We lied. There is some hard-copy evidence to show that we collaborated on this paper—a series of documents with various parts of "chats" pasted, the back-and-forth of our collaboration there, times and all, complete with chat short forms and digressions. It's actually a pretty accurate reflection of the process of writing this paper. We should probably print that out and save it. Or at least back it up on an external hard drive.

Notes

1. We thank Sina Queyras for talking with Karis about her blog and book, as well as for sharing a draft of *Unleashed*. We also acknowledge the support of the Social Sciences and Humanities Research Council of Canada. Kit Dobson, Mark McDayter, and Linda Morra offered helpful and generous feedback.
2. To avoid confusion, we will use the notation "Lemon Hound" with quotation marks to refer to the blog www.lemonhound.blogspot.com, and Lemon Hound to refer to the persona, in order to distinguish these from *Lemon Hound* (2006), the volume of poetry by Sina Queyras.
3. "Archive" is the accepted term for the collection of entries on a blog. We will be following the now-standard usage, even as we recognize that "archivists bristle at home computer programmers and other techies who appropriated the term archives for data back-ups and storage" (Cox, *Ethics* 237). It is worthwhile highlighting the term's fluidity, since archives are often misunderstood as static entities.
4. In *Against the Archival Grain*, Stoler likewise privileges those "uncensored turns of phrase, loud asides in the imperative tense, hesitant asides in sotto voce. These register confused assessments, parenthetic doubts about what might count as evidence, the records of eyewitnesses with dubious credentials, dismissed rumours laced with pertinent truths, contradictory testimonies called upon and quickly discarded" (23).
5. Currently, the best-known blogs about contemporary poetry are maintained by men—Ron Silliman in the U.S., while in Canada, rob mclennan has perhaps the

most prolific blog about contemporary poetry. The recent and well-publicized "Cage Match of Canadian Poetry" was again dominated by male voices, pitting the avant-garde Christian Bök against the formalist Carmine Starnino. For more on gender representation and the "Cage Match," see Hajnoczky's blog post "Helen Hajnoczky: Report from Calgary," in which she notes that

> [d]espite their belief that poetry needs to narrow its field of vision, the poets and critics that Bök and Starnino offered as examples throughout the match were almost exclusively male, and almost exclusively of Anglo, Christian descent. When I asked why they thought, in a country as ethnically diverse as Canada, that the most prominent writers they could call to mind were white men, neither Bök nor Starnino answered completely.

6 The online publications and hypertext editions of The University of Western Ontario English professor Mark McDayter counted toward his tenure.

Works Cited

Berlant, Lauren. "Critical Inquiry, Affirmative Culture." *Critical Inquiry* 30.2 (2004): 445–51. Print.

Blair, Jennifer, et al. Introduction. *ReCalling Early Canada: Reading the Political in the Literary and Cultural Production*. Edmonton: U of Alberta P, 2005. xiii–xlvi. Print.

Brown, Caroline. "Digitalisation: opportunities or compromises?" *Archives and Archivists*. Ed. Ailsa C. Holland and Kate Manning. Dublin: Four Courts P, 2006. 15–27. Print.

Cox, Richard J. *Personal Archives and a New Archival Calling: Readings, Reflections and Ruminations*. Duluth: Litwin Books, 2008. Print.

———. *Ethics, Accountability, and Recordkeeping in a Dangerous World*. London: Facet, 2006. Print.

Crampton, Thomas. "Reporter to NY Times: You Erased My Career." *thomascrampton.com*. May 12, 2011. Web. May 2, 2010. (http://www.thomascrampton.com/newspapers/reporter-to-ny-times-publisher-you-erased-my-career/).

Dever, Maryanne, Sally Newman, and Ann Vickery. "Introduction." *The Intimate Archive: Journeys Through Private Papers*. Ed. Maryanne Dever, Sally Newman and Ann Vickery. Sydney: National Library of Australia, 2009. 1–32. Print.

Douglas, Jennifer, and Heather MacNeil. "Arranging the Self: Literary and Archival Perspectives on Writers' Archives." *Archivaria* 67 (Spring 2009): 25–39. Print.

Godard, Barbara. "Of Generations and Generativity." *Open Letter* 13.9 (2009): 11–20. Print.

Hajnoczky, Helen. "Helen Hajnoczky: Report from Calgary." *Lemon Hound*. Dec. 9, 2009. Web. Apr. 28, 2010. (http://lemonhound.blogspot.com/2009/12/9helen-hajnoczky-report-from-calgary.html).

Leslie, Alex. "A Cautionary Tale: Story Vanishes from *Joyland Vancouver*." *Alex Leslie*. Apr. 9, 2010. Web. May 2, 2010. (http://alexleslie.wordpress.com/2010/04/09/underwaterpublishing).

———. "Resolution." *Alex Leslie*. Apr. 11, 2010. Web. May 2, 2010. (http://alexleslie.wordpress.com/2010/04/11/swimmingonward).

Myers, Greg. The *Discourse of Blogs and Wikis*. London: Continuum, 2010. Print.

Queyras, Sina. "The lost poems, or the space of blogging." *Poetry Foundation*. Mar. 30, 2010. Web. Apr. 28, 2010. (http://www.poetryfoundation.org/harriet/2010/03/the-lost-poems-or-the-space-of-blogging/#more-8275).

———. Interview with Heather Milne. *Prismatic Publics: Innovative Canadian Women's Poetry and Poetics*. Toronto: Coach House, 2009. 316–28. Print.

———. *Lemon Hound*. Toronto: Coach House, 2006. Print.

———. "'Letters of our generation': An interview with Sina Queyras." By Jillian Harkness. *Book Thug News*. n.d. Web. May 28, 2012. (http://bookthugnews.wordpress.com/interviews/q-a-with-sinaqueyras/).

———. "Margaret Christakos, notes toward an essay on." *Lemon Hound*. Oct. 26, 2008. Web. May 2, 2010. (http://lemonhound.blogspot.com/2008/10/margaret-christakos-notes-toward-essay.html).

———. "More on the Paris Review." *Lemon Hound*. Nov. 12, 2007. Web. May 1, 2010. (http://lemonhound.blogspot.com/2007/11/more-on-paris-review.html).

———. "The positive power of blogging." *Lemon Hound*. May 11, 2006. Web. May 2, 2010. (http://lemonhound.blogspot.com/search?q=rawlings).

———. "To blog or not to blog." *Lemon Hound*. Sep. 3, 2005. Web. Apr. 28, 2010. (http://lemonhound.blogspot.com/2005/09/to-blog-or-not-to-blog_03.html).

———. "Untitled." *Lemon Hound*. May 9, 2004. Web. Apr. 28, 2010. (http://lemonhound.blogspot.com/2004_05_01_archive.html).

———. "Women Blogging Women." *Lemon Hound*. Nov. 27, 2005. Web. Apr. 28, 2010. (http://lemonhound.blogspot.com/2005/11/women-blogging-women.html).

———. "Slow Blogging." *The Poetry Foundation*. Jan. 16, 2010. Web. Apr. 27, 2010. (http://www.poetryfoundation.org/harriet/2010/01/slow-blogging/).

———. *Unleashed*. Toronto: BookThug, 2009. Print.

Sheppard, Robert. "Literary Netscapes: Web Poetry and Blogging." Interview by Graeme Harper. *Authors at Work: The Creative Environment [Essays and Studies 2009]*. Ed. Ceri Sullivan and Graeme Harper. Cambridge: D.S. Brewer, 2009. 101–5. Print.

"Site Meter." *Site Meter*. n.d. Web. Apr. 5, 2010. (http://www.sitemeter.com/).

Stoler, Ann Laura. *Against the Archival Grain: Epistemic Anxieties and Colonial Common Sense*. Princeton: Princeton UP, 2009. Print.

"I remember...I was wearing leather pants": Archiving the Repertoire of Feminist Cabaret in Canada
T. L. Cowan

Emira and I spent last night—about five hours of it, starting at 7:30 and ending well past midnight—at the Vancouver East Cultural Centre soaking in the brilliance of twenty or so freaking amazing artists at the Choice Words Cabaret. This year's Rock For Choice benefit was expanded to include this night of mostly words, some music and a bit of dancing, and Lordisa, was it powerful. So powerful I'm sure I'm going to be full of the sounds for days. So powerful I wanted to kiss every performer. Powerful enough I need to tell you about every single woman who took part. I'll try to be brief...but then, I can't be too quick or you'll lose out on the flavour of sitting still for five freaking hours with your knees and ass aching but not wanting to get up 'cause you can't bear to miss any of it.
—*"choice words: You know what we did last night"*
  Lauren Bacon, Soapbox Girls, *Jan. 12, 2001*

tara said she would interview me about it. maybe she can jog my memory. was ivan coyote there? i am a fun guy to ask for memories as my ADD and 80s drug damage renders me pretty useless. but sometimes you can shake something loose.
—*Lynn Breedlove, Message to the author, Aug. 21, 2009*

> Yes, I do recall the cabaret, now that you have mentioned it.
> What I do recall has to do with feelings and emotions—that we were a part of something powerful and meaningful. My group members and I were there for each other, and we wanted to do our best. We must have read some solo pieces, and one or two shared ones. I remember one of the members from another group giving us a thumbs up and also telling us where the backstage was. It was quite a flow or a wave, so it was not specifics I focused on but it felt like the audience and our group connected. I/we were simply honoured to be invited to share. Seema, Helen and I were part of a group from Monsoon: Asian Lesbians and Bisexual Women of Vancouver, who were interested in getting together to share our voices and our creative work.
> —Sook C. Kong, Message to the author, Aug. 29, 2009

I have told this story before. When I was twenty-six, I organized a spoken word cabaret called Choice Words for the Rock for Choice Festival in Vancouver.[1] The show was at the Cultch (the Vancouver East Cultural Centre). It was 2001. The San Francisco-based all-girl spoken-word circus, Sister Spit, was coming to Vancouver for the show. I was nervous. The rehearsals early in the afternoon were chaotic. There were two pianos that had to be interchanged in the middle of the show. It became clear that none of the performers were going to stick to the fifteen-minute time limit I had allocated. It also became clear that I had invited too many performers, and that the show was going to go on forever. The festival organizers, Meegan Maulstaid and Denise Sheppard, were hanging around, bringing in food for the performers, and checking things out. I was sure they were going to take over the show, since it was clear that I had seriously botched the job. I was an emerging performer on the scene, one with a habit of saying yes when people asked me to do things like organize shows. For my own part in the show, I was planning to do a new performance poem—a piece about my childhood experiences attending pro-life/anti-choice rallies with my very religious parents—accompanied by a friend who was playing bass in public for the first time. I was also hosting the show, something I was not yet comfortable doing. The only thing that wasn't going wrong in that moment was that I was wearing a new pair of motorcycle boots. The shiny success of the boots was mitigated substantially by the fact that, earlier that week, inspired (I imagine) by the punk aesthetic of a number of the other performers in the show, I'd given myself a dye job in stop sign red and a helmet-style haircut. It wasn't a flattering look, as the extant video reveals.

It was in this context that I experienced the following events: in the moments leading up to our 7:30 p.m. scheduled start time, Lynn Breedlove, front man for the dyke punk band Tribe 8, approached me skeptically and asked me to find him "a pretty young fag to suck my dick." It was clear that he doubted my capabilities not only in general but also particularly

Figure 1 The boots, nine years later. "Big John" style, designed by John Fluevog, purchased circa 2000. Author's photo.

with respect to this request. Reliably, I looked panicked and confused. He whipped a big, fleshy dildo out of his 501s by way of explanation. I found my friends in the audience, and they trolled the room for the kind of talent Breedlove was looking for. Several hours later, when it was Breedlove's turn to perform, a "pretty young fag" materialized onstage and dropped to his knees. With his dick in the boy-prop's mouth, Breedlove held him there by the hair while reading a poem/story about sexual violence—or maybe it was about something else. I don't remember what Breedlove said onstage, but the image of him standing and the boy-prop on his knees is still fresh in my memory.[2] Beyond this image, the thing I remember most from this moment in the show was watching Breedlove's performance with fascinated glee from backstage as shocked faces throughout the audience took the bodies they were attached to and left the show, while others laughed in recognition and cheered with the fervour of drunk football fans revelling in a Hail Mary touchdown for the home team. The room was a conflicted scene of disgusted sneers and frightened stares, triumphant grins and celebratory whistles.[3]

It seemed clear to me then that the divergent responses of the audience that night enacted the rifts that were consuming the feminist/dyke/queer scenes in Vancouver at the time. Women-only/trans-inclusive spaces was perhaps *the* primary dividing issue among feminists and queers at the time of the show. Breedlove's in-yer-face, radical, and even violent performance of gender-bending in a space dedicated, at least on the surface, to the issue of reproductive rights—arguably the most galvanizing women's/feminist issue of the 1970s and 1980s—was a sign of how the politics of choice were no longer only tied to the project of securing safe and legal access to abortions. I vowed to become less like me, and more like Breedlove.

At the time of Choice Words, there was a high-profile case going on concerning a transsexual woman who was denied full participation in a woman-only space in Vancouver: Kimberly Nixon v. the Vancouver Rape

Figure 2 "Hard-won Freedoms." Article written by Mel Wales and published in *Xtra West*, Jan. 11, 2001. Reprinted courtesy of the author.

Relief and Women's Shelter. While I have no explicit "evidence" of how the climate in the feminist/queer scene in Vancouver at the time had an impact on the audience's reception of Breedlove's performance and those of the others, I do have another anecdote: a few days after the show, I was interviewed by someone who had attended Choice Words who was preparing a media report about the cabaret. During the course of the interview, I was questioned about the expansiveness of my curatorial theme, which deliberately encompassed a broad notion of choice, extending particularly to the issue of trans-identifications. I remember this person was angry that I had, as she put it, "used a pro-choice event to promote a pro-trans agenda" (this is, of course, a paraphrase). To my knowledge, this exchange was never made public, so I cannot confirm the interaction. However, I think that this is an important piece of missing information about the night: I remember feeling attacked by the intensity of this woman's anger. Then—after speaking with some of the other performers who had also been interviewed by this person, and had similar experiences in their interviews—I connected the dots and realized that the interviewer was dating someone actively involved in defending Rape Relief's "women-born-women" policy at that time. She was perhaps representative of the anger and disappointment expressed that night over Breedlove's performance.[4]

> **What is a woman?**
>
> *Vancouver Rape Relief dodges questions*
>
> **KIMBERLY NIXON CASE**
>
> Tom Yeung
>
> he personal became political, and vice versa, in the resumption of hearings into Vancouver Rape Relief's policy on transgendered women. The opinions of individual Rape Relief members on sex re-assignment surgery was an issue during the cross-examination of Lee Lakeman, the longest-standing member of Rape Relief's governing collective. The BC Human Rights Tribunal hearing resumed Jan 8 after a holiday break.
>
> Repeating a question left hanging when the tribunal adjourned in December, lawyer barbara findlay asked Lakeman why she felt the medical profession had much to answer for.
>
> "I think it advertises itself as being able to do what it can't do: change sex, as a whole sex, being able to transform a human being in ways it cannot do."
>
> Findlay's client is Kimberly Nixon, a transsexual woman who launched a human rights complaint against Rape Relief. In 1995 Rape Relief rejected her as a volunteer counsellor because she was born male. In its defense Rape Relief's lawyers have argued it's a bona fide requirement for its volunteer counsellors to be born female.
>
> The tense cross-examination was rife with objections from Rape Relief lawyer Victoria Gray, who contested the relevancy of some questions. Findlay was trying to draw out the personal views of Lakeman and other members about transsexual women.
>
> Findlay put Lakeman on the spot, asking: "In Rape Relief's view, what is Ms Nixon's gender?"
>
> This prompted an objection and exchange between the lawyers. Eventually Lakeman answered: "Rape Relief has never tried to answer that question."
>
> Later findlay grilled Lakeman on why the latter resisted addressing Nixon by her full name—Kimberly—as opposed to Kim, which Lakeman said was "more accurate."
>
> "I don't think that having a sex change operation totally transforms a male into a female. I'm sorry, but I don't think so," said Lakeman.
>
> The hearing continues Jan 15.

Figure 3 "What Is a Woman?" Article written by Tom Yeung and published in *Xtra West* Jan. 11, 2001. Reprinted with permission of Xtra West.

The Choice Words cabaret included a number of provocative performances that shocked some and amused others. Many were in the vein of Breedlove's performance: punk-inflected and speaking to a particular set of interests at stake in that historical moment, pushing the boundaries of race and sexuality in the context of contemporary feminist politics. But there was another important moment for me that night, which challenged the audience in a completely different way. Earlier in the show, singer Mary Sue Bell introduced her set by talking about the right to choose to have a "baby," and that pro-choice women should also lobby for daycare and other support services for women who choose to give birth. She then played a song with the refrain of "All good things come from God" (Marin). Based on the looks of confusion and outrage that I could see from my vantage point backstage, I think more people in the audience were distraught over a song about God in a feminist cabaret and a performer who used the word "baby" at a pro-choice event than were offended by Breedlove's performance later on. Although I received earfuls about both performances, even from the festival organizers (for whom Bell's performance represented a weird interjection into the secular flow of the night), I was rather proud of myself. I figured that controversy was the sign of a successful cabaret. However, the only records that I have of this controversy are my own story and the vague recollections of Denise Sheppard, who was recovering from a concussion at the time, and so has significant memory gaps, especially during busy periods like the Rock for Choice festival. Sheppard remembers that Bell's performance "took me by surprise a lot. I remember standing there and just feeling frozen, and then racing to find Meegan and then I think we probably came to find you" (personal interview). The only blog account I have found that addressed that night, by *Soapbox Girls*' Lauren

Bacon, is not much help in confirming the audience response to Bell's performance, since Bacon did not see that part of the show: "Mary Sue Bell is the one performer we missed, 'cause we had to have a pee break." However, Bacon's response to Breedlove does help to confirm the conflicted response that I observed among the crowd in general:

> Lynn Breedlove, whom I'd never seen or heard before (Bad feminist!), shocked me in ways that made me love her. I don't know how else to describe it. I've been thinking about how intense it is when women become violently angry, and how positive that energy can be despite the fear it inspires—anyway, she brought that home in a big way. Part of me was all, "Oh, she's degrading people," but I couldn't deny that getting a guy from the audience up onstage to suck her dick while she read was so freakin' hot.

I retell and expand my version of this cabaret for three reasons. First, I believe that this show embodies many of the important aesthetic and political values that characterize what I have come to understand as a critically neglected, but nonetheless important cultural form: the feminist cabaret. Second, as a feminist cabaret, Choice Words exists as a repertoire of women's writing and performance as well as feminist politics, social life, and cruising; in general, it exists as an enactment of what I think of as a "feminist scene."[5] A show like this one, to my mind, must be considered in the context of this scene and can also be understood as an archive-in-motion of it. Third and finally, I tell this story because my story and others are virtually all that remain of the show. One might think that, as the organizer of the event, I am the ideal resource to provide information, able to recreate it, closely read the individual performances, and reconstruct the process of production, but I have lost all of this material. All I have is the story I just recounted, and a few other fuzzy recollections about the night. My immediate archive is entirely anecdotal, which, through the course of my research on this cabaret, has led me to consider the importance of anecdote in writing a rhizomatic historiography of the feminist cabaret specifically, but more generally, about feminist and queer community-based, or grassroots, performance.

For this essay, I theorize the cabaret as a repertoire of the writing and politics of contemporary feminist scenes. In order to do this, I must acknowledge the status of the cabaret's repertoire itself. That is, the presences and absences of knowledge about this event/these events are themselves in need of theorizing. In the context of this book on women's archives, I grapple with the problem of information-gathering and pose the following questions: Can I gather enough information about the Choice Words cabaret to gain a convincing sense of *knowing* or set of knowledges about it to make my first point about how the cabaret is a repertoire of contemporary feminist scenes valid, or at least convincing? What constitutes "proof" enough to determine that I *know* what went on that night? What and who are legitimate sources, and what do these sources *know*? Ultimately, this essay mobilizes the anecdote as the primary archival and epistemological source of what I call "repertoire knowledges"—that is, knowledges that emerge, amorphous and in motion—through the embodied practices of performance and event-making, and through the half-forgotten remainders/reminders of these performances and this event. These remainders/reminders are always both excessive and inadequate.

The Feminist Cabaret as a Social-Political-Aesthetic Formation

The cabaret, or "variety show," has been and continues to be a central form in contemporary feminist scenes, and in fact it can be argued that it is the place where the "feminist scene" becomes materialized in an apparent way.[6] Rock for Choice shows, May Day shows, lesbian and queer cabarets at Pride celebrations, and shows organized as women's/feminist events in the context of Asian History Month, Black History Month, and National Aboriginal Day, as well as December 6th and International Women's Day Cabarets, for example, are places where oftentimes diverse feminist performers and audiences come together, ostensibly for a good cause (usually produced as benefit shows, the proceeds of a cabaret generally go to a feminist or queer organization). These shows typically feature a range of artistic performances, including poetry and fiction readings, singer/songwriter and spoken word performances, performance art, comedy, dance, film, and video. These are frequently focused on a particular theme: Choice, Labour, Pride, and so on. The cabaret will also usually showcase performances by artists from a "diverse" range of identity positions based on race, class, ethnicity, sexuality, and ability. The cabaret is, arguably, one place in feminist social and political scenes where identity politics is still an organizing principle. Importantly, cabarets are, by their very nature as "variety" shows, tokenistic. The emphasis on "variety" in cabaret makes it the ideal form for a feminist politic seeking to ensure that many different kinds of voices share a stage at every event; the cabaret is also certainly a political/aesthetic/ organizational practice that exposes the ideological weaknesses and inevitable failures of these often solemn efforts. As Shane Vogel has observed, the cabaret has the capacity to produce "feelings of belonging and connection as well as alienation and interruption" (*Scene* 73) in a local scene.

A cabaret in the context of a feminist politic of inclusivity must include not only a variety of artistic forms but also artists from a range of backgrounds, identity locations, and so on. The cynical interpretation of a widely diverse cabaret is that each performer allows the organizer(s) to make a checkmark on the (imaginary?) Good Feminist Rules of Engagement List: Comedian (√); Musician (√); Dancer (√); Black Woman (√); Indigenous Woman (√); Trans*person (√). The content of the show is not the only way that the feminist cabaret becomes "diverse"; the shows are also generally advertised through a network based on social and political affiliations that includes (and it changes as new modes of social networking emerge) email, Twitter, Facebook, and MySpace lists; phone trees; posters and handbills at key independent and allied bookstores, coffee shops, bars, schools, and other public places with high feminist traffic; and public service announcements (PSAs) and featured spots/interviews on feminist and queer-themed radio shows on campus and community radio stations.[7] Furthermore, although it is not always the case, the general rule for a multi-artist event is that you can expect each performer to bring at least a few of her friends to the show. The "variety" of performers in any given show, as well as the "variety" of promotional strategies will ultimately be reflected, at least somewhat, by the "variety" within an audience.

Like other cabaret cultures, the feminist cabaret is both a form of entertainment and a space itself. The cabaret form is, at its most basic, a variety show with a host or MC (in the French tradition, a *conférencier*) who introduces each act by directly addressing the audience with no regard for theatre's fourth wall, moving the night along, usually with some panache. The cabaret as a space is a club that serves alcohol along with a nightly show; usually, a cabaret space is set up with tables and chairs rather than theatre-style row seating. The seating arrangement of a traditional cabaret setting facilitates conversations among audience members, and, perhaps more importantly, provides each person in the room a view of everyone else there. As Vogel writes in an article on the phenomenon of the queer cabaret (in particular, the *Kiki and Herb* shows), "people came to the cabaret to be seen, and the performances began long before the official show.... The conventions of cabaret presumed an ambivalent relationship between performer and spectator, fostering a space that was intimate and improvisatory" ("Where" 35). Although the seats that night at The Cultch were not arranged in cabaret style, but rather in permanently installed theatre-style row seating, there was a lot of coming and going from the main performance space to the bathrooms, and to and from the bar in the front foyer; the movement thus facilitated the sense that each person walking in and out of the room to go the bathroom, or those standing in the bar lineup in the front foyer, was both watcher and watched, spectator and performer. In a locally based feminist cabaret, not only is there a lot of "performing" going on in the lineup for the bar, the ticket booth, the bathrooms, and in the seats, but the people performing *onstage* are often part of the local feminist scene. The latter are thus often familiar enough to audience members to function also as gossip mill fodder—as the former or current lover of so-and-so, or the woman who got the job (or lost the job) at the rape crisis centre, or the person who was uncharacteristically drunk at the bar last week, or the editor of a zine, blog, or newsletter, or the girl who works in the bookstore, or the waitress at that restaurant, or the coffee shop manager, and so on. The performers, then, are often strangers neither to each other nor to the audience; they are part of a scene where they are known beyond their stage(d) personae.

In addition to the essential lack of distinction between performer and spectator, the cabaret has an important history that lends itself to the feminist benefit show. The "variety" element makes cabaret a form uniquely conducive to political entertainment. As Freidrich Hollaender, owner of the Tingletangle Cabaret (which, as Vogel notes, was "the model for Marlene Dietrich's cabaret in the 1930 film *Blue Angel*"), observed about the political possibilities of cabaret performance,

> The effect achieved by the contrasting moods in cabaret is truly not to be outdone; if one considers that eight hundred people out of a thousand regard the cabaret as an innocent amusement and attend it in this spirit, then it becomes possible to assess the healthy jolt to the psyche that a socially minded *chanson* fired off between two amusing parodies can occasion. Under the cover of an evening's relaxing entertainment, cabaret, like nothing else, suddenly dispenses a poison cookie. Suggestively administered and hastily swallowed, its effects reach far beyond the harmless evening to make otherwise placid blood boil and inspire the sluggish brain to think. (Vogel "Where" 37; Holleander 566–67)

My argument here is that, in the spirit of "diversity" and "inclusivity," a feminist cabaret will often showcase performances from a range of performers (so, for example, in the Choice Words cabaret, we had Breedlove and Bell sharing a stage), and thus a range of audiences. One can imagine, for the sake of argument, Breedlove's performance as the "poison cookie," perhaps for Bell's friends, and vice versa. Feminist cabaret draws together different audiences from within a city's (or town's) often conflicted, inclusive/tokenistic, exclusionary, rigid, passionate, sexually confused, well-intentioned yet often-misguided feminist scenes. It is a political form because it forces different constituency groups to listen to the writing and to participate in the performances of folks with whom they don't agree or would otherwise have no contact with. It is, I contend, in the spaces of feminist cabaret that issues like racism, trans politics, ablism, class privilege, homophobia, biphobia, heterophobia, xenophobia, S & M phobia, sex worker's rights, and so on, get broad airplay. These are the places where mutual understandings and even respect begin to happen, where emerging and established artists share spaces and make connections, where many women writers and performers develop their first fans, and audiences come into contact with new writers/writing and performers/performances.

The Cabaret as Repertoire of Feminist Knowledge

Rather than idealize the cabaret as a feminist/queer utopia, or dismiss it as an exercise in tokenism that also tends to be divisive, antagonistic, and cliquish, I want to foreground this cultural form as a site of feminist writing and performance as public culture, a form that is produced by, and produces, feminist scenes. Feminist cabarets draw together feminist and queer writing and performance with explicit and subtle enactments of feminist politics and social and sexual life. Because they happen over a short period of time (several hours at most), one might expect each cabaret to exist as a manageably encapsulated representative event that we can study in order to come to a greater understanding of the ways that feminist scenes work, and, most basically, in order to historicize more fully feminist activism and cultural production. However, in order to make a cabaret do the cultural memory work of a broader political and social scene, before one can make an argument about the status of cabaret as a repertoire of feminist writing and knowledges beyond very generalized observations like those I have made above, one must first do the work of remembering the cabaret itself.

The "repertoire" as I use it here references Diana's Taylor's mobilization of the term vis-à-vis its alternate, the "archive." Taylor notes that while the archive is made up of "supposedly enduring materials (i.e., texts, documents, buildings, bones)," the repertoire is a "repository of embodied practice/knowledge (i.e., spoken language, dance, sports, ritual)." Taylor's point is to argue that the study of performance allows us to "take seriously the repertoire of embodied practices as an important system of knowing and transmitting knowledge" (26). I follow Taylor here with my rendering of the feminist cabaret since, as an ephemeral form that rarely leaves behind any "official, enduring" trace, it is such a repertoire. In this context, several necessary questions emerge: How do we know, or come to know, what we do about feminist cabarets? How does one engage with this repertoire for the purposes of studying the scenes of feminist cabaret? What is the object of study for these events? Is it the performed texts? The audience's reception? The documentation of the event? The physical space of the theatre, bar, or café where the event takes place? Given the dearth of documentation about feminist cabarets, I ask myself: Is it possible to know *anything* about these events without knowing *everything*? Are the absences productive, and if so, how?

Why Don't We Keep Our Shit (er, Memorabilia)?

As I dug through the dozens of boxes that constitute what I consider my personal "archive" (or, as friends who have helped me move one of the nine times I have relocated since 2001 call them, my "unopened boxes of heavy shit"), I realized that I no longer have any of the "material" from the Choice Words cabaret. I could not find the poster or the set list, and all correspondence about this show happened via an email account whose cache was purged by some fly-by-night server many years ago. Since expanding my research of the Choice Words cabaret beyond my own basement, I have unearthed a few traces of the event. Perhaps the most useful and fantastically thorough is Lauren Bacon's account of the event on the blog *Soapbox Girls*. However, this blog entry is no longer available online because the blog was shut down and the archive is not publicly accessible. I got the entry from the author because (a) I remembered that she had published something about the cabaret, (b) I know her, and (c) I knew how to contact her. Sometimes research is about who your Facebook friends are.

Because I no longer have any files from the show, it was from this blog entry that I first got a complete list of performers from the night. There is also a performer list, it turns out, in the Literary Events section of the *Georgia Straight* from the week before the show (see Figure 4). After looking through all the local papers, I found three listings (but no advertisements), one article that featured Meegan Maulstaid, the founder and one of the organizers of Vancouver's Rock for Choice festival (see Figure 2), and one review of the show in the University of British Columbia student newspaper, *The Ubyssey*. There is also a short video shot and produced by Nikola Marin, a local video activist, which was broadcast by *Working TV*, and which remains online. If you Google "Choice Words Cabaret 2001," you can find this video clip. On most days, it is the only trace of this event picked up in a Google search. The video, nearly six minutes long, includes interviews with a few local performers, and very short clips of individual performances by these Vancouver-based artists (and no interviews with nor clips of the out-of-towners). The video also provides a humiliating reminder of my bright red bowl cut and not *a single* shot of my motorcycle boots. In the course of my research, I contacted Marin to find out if she still had the raw footage of the show and interviews. She did not. In addition to the published/broadcast materials related to Choice Words, I have, after soliciting "memories and stories" via email and Facebook from all of the cabaret performers I could find, received several anecdotal responses. I have also conducted an interview with Denise Sheppard, the other organizer of Rock for Choice. I have asked everyone I contacted whether they have a show poster or festival program; so far, none have been found. In

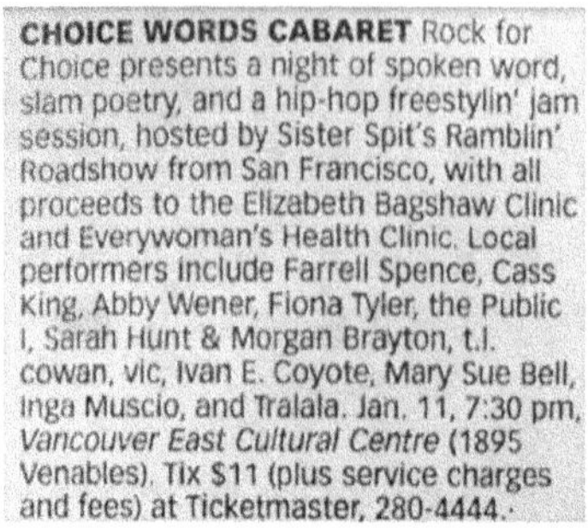

> **CHOICE WORDS CABARET** Rock for Choice presents a night of spoken word, slam poetry, and a hip-hop freestylin' jam session, hosted by Sister Spit's Ramblin' Roadshow from San Francisco, with all proceeds to the Elizabeth Bagshaw Clinic and Everywoman's Health Clinic. Local performers include Farrell Spence, Cass King, Abby Wener, Fiona Tyler, the Public i, Sarah Hunt & Morgan Brayton, t.l. cowan, vic, Ivan E. Coyote, Mary Sue Bell, Inga Muscio, and Tralala. Jan. 11, 7:30 pm, *Vancouver East Cultural Centre* (1895 Venables). Tix $11 (plus service charges and fees) at Ticketmaster, 280-4444.

Figure 4 Choice Words Cabaret Literary Events Time Out listing from the *Georgia Straight*, January 11–18, 2001. Reprinted courtesy of the *Georgia Straight*.

addition to the things I have been able to get, thanks to Abby Wener Herlin (formerly Abby Wener) who kept them, I now also have two copies of emails from that time: the first is a promotional email sent out to a long list of recipients, and the second is a "thank you" email sent to the performers ten days after the show.

Bacon's blog entry and the event listings filled in some of the blanks for me about who was on the bill that night, and even provided the exact date of the show. Her anecdotal response, which includes a list of the performers and a brief description of, and response to, each performance, ranges from urbane culture vulture snippets,

> Farrell Spence did this Marilyn Manson thing (I think...I'm not good with rock/alternative references)—"...the wrath of my vaginaaaaaaaaaaaa"—with a huge black wig and big-ass boots and fishnets and the piece de resistance—a rubber fake pussy strapped over her outfit. Holy shit! She was incredible, as usual. Very Diamanda Galas, if Diamanda Galas was funny as hell. (Bacon)

to confessions of the emotional impact of some performances,

> Renee [Rene] Van, whose name I hope I'm spelling correctly, made me cry. Bear in mind that this evening was so full of moving, intense performances I figured I'd either be a mess all the way through or I'd keep it together throughout. Wish I could tell you what it was that did it. Lovely.

> Nomy Lam[m] has been a heroine of mine (and lots of other folks) for a long time now, but I'd never seen her in person. Now I love her even more, because although I'd read her writing and read interviews and all that stuff, I had never experienced her singing voice. The woman is a goddess. Her singing is so visceral, deep, and pure, I was completely overwhelmed. (Bacon)

The language of Bacon's blog is one of affective and embodied engagement with these performances. Words and phrases like "powerful," "surprise," "inspiring," "courage," "cute," "punch in the gut," "intense," "shocked," "made me cry," "visceral," "overwhelmed," and "staggering" combine with her introductory notes, which explain that although she will "try to be brief" in her description of each performer/performance, "I can't be too quick or you'll lose out on the flavour of sitting still for five freaking hours with your knees and ass aching but not wanting to get up 'cause you can't bear to miss any of it." This blog entry represents to me the meeting of what Ann Cvetkovich calls a "radical archive of emotion" (241), and Taylor's repertoire of embodied knowledges.

The stories provided by the performers are also primarily reflective/reflexive of sensual, visceral, and emotional memories from the night. For example, Abby Wener Herlin's note recalls,

it is one of my most memorable performances...

i remember feeling alive that night, part of a community
i remember you introducing me saying i had a great ass, and i blushed
i was wearing leather pants
i remember with regard to my performance that i felt sturdy and solid
remember how black it was, not used to not seeing audience faces
i remember back stage felt a bit cliquey, as i didn't know many people except for you lovely and ivan
was [as] always blown away by sini and michelle tea[8]
yeah, was kinnie starr there too[?] or was that another show?[9]

i remember also amber dawn, doing a piece of striptease and i loved the variety of each women's words and stance, take, display. (Herlin)

Ivan E. Coyote's anecdote is also a series of emotional "facts":

I remember back stage was a little bit nuts and there was bands and gear and people everywhere. I remember Sini and Tara and Breedlove blowing me away. I had never heard anyone speak to class in such a powerful way as Tara Hardy did that night. I don't remember what piece it was exactly, but I do remember thinking "she totally gets it." I wanted her to know that we were from the same people. I think the first words I ever said to her were "My daddy is a welder." And she just looked straight at me with that look, you know, that Tara Hardy no fucking bullshit going on outta this mouth look of hers, and I knew she knew exactly what I was trying to say.

I remember Breedlove hauling out a dildo (was that just a dream??) and watching the beautiful interplay between Sini and Michelle Tea. Wasn't Inga there that night too, or am I confusing it with another gig? That was one stellar fucking lineup though, I tell you that much. I remember a very visceral feeling of meeting more of my people. (Coyote)[10]

Similarly, Sook C. Kong's recollections (see the epigraph at the beginning of this essay) explicitly have "to do with feelings and emotions." Lynn Breedlove's anecdotes, prompted by "interview" questions posed by Tara Jepsen, reveal that memories about a show don't necessarily have to do with that show in particular, but with an ongoing performance politic:

> TARA: LBL!! I remember when we went up to Vancouver to host and perform in Rock for Choice. Do you?
>
> LYNN: barely. remind me.
>
> ....
>
> TARA: Remember hollering at some of the doodz in the audience to get on the dyke agenda while you performed? I'm sure plenty of them were down, but you were sure that no one was left in ignorance or hatred by the end of the show. I complimented you later, but you were like, "whatever, I've been doing that for ten years" or however long you said. You said it was your job to bring the straight male community closer to the dyke community.
>
> LYNN: nope. but that sounds like something i believed in then. and yes, i was always harassing straight, white non-trans guys. i felt they were the last fair game and could and should take plenty of abuse, being at the top of the food chain. and look, i have succeeded in bringing the straight male community closer to the dyke community. now all the dykes are straight guys. myself included. except you, tara. get with the straight male agenda, will ya? (Breedlove and Jepsen)

Ultimately, Breedlove's anecdotes are about a number of events that happened around the show, all which contribute to the repertoire-knowledge of this event, as it is connected to other events.

> TARA: Remember how you and Sini and I stayed at "A Place at Penny's"? We were put up there, I think, by the person organizing the festival who was in a band called Che Chapter 127. They believed strongly in the likes of Che Guevara. It was a small room with two beds, and you and Sini smoked and smoked your cigarettes. Inside. Did you think I was going to live too long? I do concede it was fucking freezing outside.
>
> LYNN: hmmmm. i do remember meegs, who identifies as a pitbull and is the gnarliest lil' skater punk lead yeller in the world who puts fear in the hearts of linebackers. i do remember i used to smoke and it was one of my favourite things to do with sini. and like the narcissistic, desperate addicts we were, we didn't notice people choking in the corner on our exhaust. also

> i remember smoking in the snow in ottawa outside a dyke bar where they wouldn't let a trans guy in to my show and i was all hey, he's more my people than you bitches. and i was lonesome and cold outside, sucking morosely on my American Spirit, although i felt really healthy and cool about my brand choice. so i probably really was happy to be smoking inside with sini. sadly i don't remember a place for penny's, altho i wish i did cuz i googled images of it and it is sweeeeeet. but i do remember a funky motel where sini took her sox off and commented on how she was gonna get all these warts surgically removed from the bottom of her feet, and then on the way home, she fell asleep and drove across the freeway and narrowly missed killing both of us and when she got home that day the warts were gone. it was magic. (Breedlove and Jepsen)

Breedlove's "memory" of the show is informed by the personal, visceral stories that surround it (the smoking, the warts) and the politics of the time (harassing straight white non-trans guys, being frustrated that a dyke bar wouldn't let in transfolk). Although Breedlove's stories do not tell us anything directly about the Choice Words cabaret, they tell us about the social and political atmosphere of the time, an atmosphere that informs our understanding of the show.

After all of this, a number of questions remain: What knowledge can be produced by the material I have collected about the Choice Words cabaret? Can we draw any conclusions about its cultural work? Do I have enough information? The repertoire-knowledges provided by Lauren Bacon's blog and the performers' stories and memories (or lack thereof) might be understood to serve a particular anecdotal function; that is, by referencing the specific (however inaccurately), they call attention to the knowledges that remain after almost a decade, and for most of the performers, after hundreds of other shows have passed. The misrememberings, especially the fact that both Wener Herlin and Coyote remember Michelle Tea being at the show when she wasn't, for example, recalls the importance of situatedness and indicates that both Wener and Coyote were familiar enough with Sister Spit's usual co-hosting team to expect that this show was like others. The blending of the specific—Wener remembering her leather pants, Coyote remembering what she said to Tara Hardy—with the generalized recollection of a usual Sister Spit show, enables this set of repertoire-knoweleges to extend beyond this single cabaret, and connects it rhizomatically to others. The lack of "official" documentation of this event allows for fissures that produce new affective and embodied knowledges of feminist cabarets, and feminist scenes more broadly.

It turns out that not keeping our shit enables, out of necessity, the creation of an archive that straddles the specific and the non-specific. This could be an archive that, like Jane Gallop's (via Derrida) understanding of the anecdote, is "exorbitant" in its preoccupation with "the moment" (6, 3) and both excessive and inadequate. The anecdotal repertoire of Choice Words tells us about the physical and emotional responses of spectators and performers about this and (in the case of Breedlove) other shows, but not, particularly, the content of the performances. We have no texts, no scripts, no concrete sense of *what* it was that inspired these responses. The anecdote as repertoire-knowledge tells us too much and not enough.

The Archival Spectre of the WOW Cabaret at the Lesbian Herstory Archives; or Why I Wish Joan Nestle Was Canadian

I want to conclude by reflecting on the problem I present several times throughout the course of this essay: without much "official" material pertaining to the Choice Words cabaret, and in anticipation of insufficiently detailed, content-specific information about other feminist cabarets in Canada over the past twenty-five years, how do I proceed with a theory of the cabaret as a cultural form that both produces, and is produced by, past, present, and future feminist scenes? It strikes me, based upon the "power" of Choice Words, that cabarets have the political, aesthetic, and affective capacity to reflect or engage with feminist pasts and presents, while simultaneously rehearsing a variety of feminist futures.[11] Performances like Rene Van's, which told the story of a brutal assault on a butch dyke and her femme lover in the 1950s, and my own, which paid tribute to the pro-choice activists of the 1980s, brush up against Breedlove's gender-bending blow job and Trala La Farsi Sentiamo's "intense dance-slash-performance-art piece with another dancer whose name wasn't in the programme" (Bacon). The latter was (as I recall) an activist piece reflecting the hostility and violence of feminist responses to sex workers. The combination of these elements, perhaps, provokes what Aristotelians would call a feminist and queer catharsis.

As Kate Davy describes in her chapter in the collection *Beyond the Archives: Research as Lived Experience*, archival material that documents the content of feminist cabarets provides the tools necessary to take corrective historiographical measures. Davy's research on the early years of the WOW cabaret in Manhattan's East Village was bolstered by a treasure trove: cardboard boxes filled with WOW ephemera. I can't hide my longing for such material, and my jealousy of Davy's luck. Davy describes her discovery, which she made in the Lesbian Herstory Archives (LHA) of "a few boxes marked 'WOW' or 'Women's Theatre' into [which] had been tossed, in no particular order, press releases, programs, scripts, copies of opening night reviews, videotapes of some productions, and a smattering of photographs." Even with this treasure trove created by "[s]omeone (or a few someones) [who] had the foresight to clip these articles at the time and subsequently deposit them in the archive," Davy still laments that "the dynamics of archival work threw into relief the very nature of cultural memory, revealing painful erasures that ensue from an inevitable, ongoing process of forgetting." However, she notes that the archive, "[l]ike lived memory... was incomplete; taken together, however, a whole began to take shape" (130).[12]

Importantly for my purposes here, Davy describes the ways in which memory and archives take shape around these events: "I sensed something important but amorphous coming into focus; it was visceral. Like an archaeologist, I was beginning to unearth pieces of what was so deeply buried in the memories of participants" (131). Rather than attempting to formulate a theory of feminist cabarets broadly, Davy's task becomes "to rediscover feminism's lost genealogy and resurrect those instances of cultural production that reverse a slight-of-hand that made of *all* feminists '*the* feminists'" (132–33). Her project, then, is to claim for WOW and its scene an exemplary status, to re-remember these performances and rewrite "the reductive, simplified version of feminist history" that does not make room for the what Davy calls WOW's "anomalous performances." The process of cultural forgetting, she argues, "ultimately serves to support claims of originality for certain, sex-positive cultural developments in the 1990s. WOW's festivals belie this trajectory, providing evidence of a funny, parodic, eroticized, gender-bending aesthetic with roots firmly grounded in feminism." (133)[13]

The archival material collected about WOW makes it possible for Davy to do this re-remembering, or remembering differently. However, it occurs to me that the absence of these kinds of materials, documenting feminist and queer cabarets like Choice Words creates an opportunity for scholars like me who feel that tug of envy when reading about Davy's archival discoveries. Instead of lamenting the loss of most of the documents associated with Choice Words, this archive that never materialized, the challenge will be to work in the realm of repertoire-knowledges, to consider what we can know from what we have, as, for example, from anecdote. Gallop notes that a theory of the anecdote requires recognition of an inherent contradiction:

> An anecdote is the account of a single incident, a single moment. But as narrative, anecdote may also tend to elicit an urge to embed the incident in a larger story. Such an urge would lead us away from contact with the singular moment into all-too-familiar directions—conventional narrative arcs, standard plots. This contradiction between capturing the singular moment and a drive to insert the moment within a familiar plot may not be just a problem for this particular story but a tension intrinsic to the anecdote. (85)

Obviously, my impulse to generalize is palpable throughout this essay. What I have learned, though, in the course of writing, is to think of the anecdote as a bearer of inexplicit knowledges, and to consider the possibility of writing a historiography of feminist cabarets in Canada that relies less on an obsession with data, documents, and details, and more on a preoccupation with the repertoire-knowledges that explain less about who, what, when, and where, and more about *how* we, as members of feminist and queer scenes, come to know what we know about our shared events.

Acknowledgements

I would like to acknowledge the support of the Killam Postdoctoral Fellowship at the University of Calgary and a Visiting Research Fellowship at the Calgary Institute for the Humanities: without the financial and space resources offered by these fellowships, this work would have been impossible. Additionally, I would like to thank Linda Morra for pointing me in a useful direction, Julius Fisher for burning me a copy of the *Working TV* video, Michael Smith at the University of Calgary IT support desk for his patience in retrieving yet another batch of deleted emails, and Lauren Bacon, Lynn Breedlove, Ivan E. Coyote, Tara Jepsen, Sook C. Kong, and Abby Wener Herlin for their great stories, along with all of the performers who were part of the Choice Words Cabaret for a memorable night.

Notes

1 See my essay "Punk Rock Clit Lit."
2 I've theorized this scene and the word "dick" in relation to this and other dyke/queer/trans performances in "Punk Rock Clit Lit" (103 and 114).
3 See, for example, Cvetkovich (84–87) and Fuchs.
4 Although it is possible that some readers may interpret this anecdote as *mere gossip*, I think of this kind of gossip-knowledge as having at least two kinds of reception. As Code has convincingly argued, gossip as a "situated discourse...attuned to the location, the historical moment and the circumstances that generated it" (231) can be a valuable and even subversive form of knowing/knowledge, and depending on the gossiper-audience relationship, it can serve different purposes: "In a climate of trust, people gossip to think aloud about themselves and one and other, to work through extraordinary events, to know one and other better, and to establish community. In a climate of distrust, gossip is often malicious, playing with reputations, circulating truths better concealed, or half-truths elevated to the status of truth" (231). I imagine that readers' perceptions of whether my anecdote/gossip here is situated in a climate of trust or distrust will be determined by where they were sitting on the issue of trans-inclusivity in 2001, or indeed, where they sit on the issue today.
5 I am calling Choice Words a "feminist cabaret" in order to connect it to a long tradition of women's events that span many generations of feminists. However, Choice Words was also, obviously, very queer and it is connected to the long tradition of queer cabaret that I explicitly engage in other papers, though not here. Not

all feminist events are queer and not all queer events are feminist, but this event was certainly a feminist/queer event, and it marks a moment when these configurations/communities/identities/affiliations merged and clashed simultaneously. For an initial discussion about contemporary queer cabaret in Canada, see Cowan, 2010.

6 Certainly, feminist and lesbian gatherings of the early twentieth century were also structured around performance spaces (that is, the speeches of the suffragettes, and salons like Natalie Clifford Barney's *Acadèmie des Femmes* are famous examples); however, as a tool of transformational feminist politics, I think the cabaret form or variety show is a product of a particular set of feminist relations which emerged through critiques of the white hetero predominance within the North American feminist movement of the late 1970s and early 1980s which continues in feminist and queer scenes today.

7 It turns out that even *research* on feminist and queer cabaret can attract the attention of these radio shows. The fact that on December 14, 2009, this research project was featured on *Dykes on Mykes* (DoM) at McGill's CKUT reconfirms for me that feminist and queer media, performance, and research are mutually constitutive, informing, and sustaining. The website of the Montreal-based journal *No More Potlucks* podcasts DoM, so my discussion with DoM host and long-time cabaret performer, Dayna McLeod, is both archived and part of the repertoire of anecdotes about feminist and queer cabaret in Canada (Cowan, "T. L. Cowan!").

8 Michelle Tea, the co-founder of Sister Spit, was not performing that night and did not come to Vancouver for this show. Tea and Sini Anderson generally co-hosted Sister Spit shows; for this show, however, Tara Jepsen co-hosted with Sini.

9 As far as I remember, Kinnie Star did not perform at this show.

10 Inga Muscio did perform. In fact, although she does not remember, I recall that, as the last performer of the night before the hip-hop jam which closed the show, Inga managed to keep the crowd—already sitting for five hours—charmed and captivated, even though at one point during her performance she realized that she was missing pages to her text and ran backstage to find the rest of her story.

11 These cabarets might be understood to perform "temporal drag" similarly to the ways that, as Halberstam has observed, "[m]any contemporary queer performers like Tribe 8, The Butchies, and Bitch and Animal reference themes of gender-bending and sex play while also exploring their proximity to and distance from the women musicians who paved the way for an independent dyke music scene" (180). Furthermore, with its simultaneous performance of shared and contested pasts, presents and futures, and considering the sheer durational quality of its over-programmed length—Choice Words ran *over* the *five-hour* mark—the typical feminist cabaret disrupts what Elizabeth Freeman (who first coined "temporal drag") refers to as "chronormativity," or "the use of time to organize individual human bodies toward maximum productivity" (3). The feminist cabaret is a collective practice of the *anti-chrononormative*, which might be considered coterminous with other feminist practices like collectivity, the "go-round" or "checking-in" and consensus over efficiency.

12 In November 2009, I followed Davy's WOW trail and went to the Lesbian Herstory Archives in Brooklyn, looking for these boxes. However, even though there was a note in the WOW file folder indicating that there was more WOW material in two grey boxes "on top of the filing cabinet," I could not find them. Davy's "incomplete" archive was even more so on the day I went to the LHA; much like my

own memories and those of the other Choice Words performers, the remainders of performance housed in archives are vulnerable to forgetting, and can also be misplaced.

13 Dolan's chapter in *The Feminist Spectator as Critic* makes similar claims for the WOW cabaret as a queer performance scene that was lesbian- and sex-positive, unlike what she calls the "cultural feminist performance art [that] fails to take flight into the freeing fantasies that lesbian performance imagines" (81).

Works Cited

Bacon, Lauren. "choice words: You know what we did last night." *Soapbox Girls*. Jan. 12, 2001. Web. Received by email from author Aug. 11, 2009.

Breedlove, Lynn and Tara Jepsen. "tara jepsen interviewing lynn breedlove re rock for choice vancouver 200-something." Message to the author. Aug. 21, 2009. Email.

Code, Lorraine. "Gossip." *Encyclopaedia of Feminist Theories*. Ed. Lorraine Code. New York: Routledge, 2000. 230–31. Print.

Cowan, T. L. "'a one-shot affair': Cabaret as Curatorial Improvisation." *Canadian Theatre Review* 143 (2010). Forthcoming. Print.

———. "Punk Rock Clit Lit: Reading Toward a Punk Poetics." *Bent on Writing: Contemporary Queer Tales*. Ed. Elizabeth Ruth. Toronto: Women's Press, 2002. 103–21. Print.

———. "T.L. Cowan!" Interview with Dayna McLeod. *Dykes on Mykes*. Podcast posted on *No More Potlucks* Dec. 14, 2009. Web. Feb. 7, 2010.

Coyote, Ivan E. "Archiving Feminist Performance Through Your Stories." Message to author. Aug. 13, 2009. Email.

Cvetkovich, Ann. *An Archive of Feelings: Trauma, Sexuality, and Lesbian Public Cultures*. Durham: Duke UP, 2003. Print.

Davy, Kate. "Cultural Memory and the Lesbian Archive." *Beyond the Archives: Research as Lived Process*. Ed. Gesa E. Kirsch and Liz Rohan. Carbondale: Southern Illinois UP, 2008. 128–35. Print.

Dolan, Jill. "The Dynamics of Desire: Sexuality and Gender in Pornography and Performance." *The Feminist Spectator as Critic*. Ann Arbor: U of Michigan P, 1991. Print.

Freeman, Elizabeth. *Time Binds: Queer Temporalities, Queer Histories*. Durham: Duke UP. 2010. Print.

Fuchs, Cynthia. "If I Had a Dick: Queers, Punks, and Alternative Acts." *Mapping the Beat: Popular Music and Contemporary Theory*. Ed. John Sloop and Andrew Herman Thomas Swiss. Malden: Blackwell, 1998. Print.

Gallop, Jane. *Anecdotal Theory*. Durham: Duke UP, 2002. Print.

Halberstam, Judith. *In a Queer Time and Place: Transgender Bodies, Subcultural Lives*. NewYork: New York UP, 2005. Print.

Herlin, Abby Wener. "Archiving Feminist Performance through Your Stories." Message to the author. Aug. 13, 2009. Email.

Hollaender, Friedrich. "Cabaret." Trans. Don Reneau. *The Weimar Republic Sourcebook*. Ed. Anton Kaes, Martin Jay, and Edward Dimendberg. Berkeley: U of California P, 1994. 566–67. Print.
Kong, Sook C. "Re: Sook, here." Message to the author. Aug. 29, 2009. Email.
Marin, Nikola, prod. "Rock for Choice 2001: 'Choice Words' cabaret." *Working TV*. Episode 214. n.d. Web and DVD.
Sheppard, Denise. Personal Interview. Aug. 15, 2009. Email.
Taylor, Diana. *The Archive and the Repertoire: Performing Cultural Memory in the Americas*. Durham: Duke UP, 2003. Print.
Vogel, Shane. *The Scene of Harlem Cabaret: Race, Sexuality, Performance*. Chicago: U of Chicago P, 2009. Print.
———. "Where Are We Now? Queer World-Making and Cabaret Performance." *GLQ* 6.1 (2000): 29–60. Web.

"In the hope of making a connection": Rereading Archival Bodies, Responses, and Love in Marian Engel's *Bear* and Alice Munro's "Meneseteung"
Catherine Bates

Prologue: Personal Encounters with the Archive

Two personal encounters with archives influence my emotional and intellectual relationship to them. The first occurred in August 2001, while working at the University of Leeds Library: I was given the task of moving the well-established but rarely consulted Liddle Collection to accommodate the Feminist Archive North, which had grown too big for its previous Yorkshire home. Our job was to consolidate the Liddle collection into a smaller space—a strange task, since this was a collection of First World War memorabilia. The material we were moving was not the large amount of documents that constitute the lion's share of the collection, but instead the weaponry and clothing, donated by relatives, which I was told had once played an important part in bringing to life the First World War for local schoolchildren. It had lain on the shelves, untouched and gathering dust, for some years. This neglect could have resulted from the difficulty of cataloguing such material and publicizing its existence; it could have been because there are now other ways to bring the war to life through media technologies. Shifting the Liddle Collection made me realize the existence of a prevalent archive nightmare: the large amount of material that lies in the archives untouched and unexamined, saved but forgotten.

I also sensed some tension about and antagonism toward the imminent arrival of Feminist Archive North. The more established special collections staff made clear to me that I was party to the ideological decisions made about archives that happen all the time. On the one hand, to put it crudely, there was a sense that the First World War was being scaled back to make way for the feminists; on the other hand, for me it seemed to be a positive step that the two could sit side by side and spatially perform the fraught but real relationship these histories have with one another. The move was a radical one, of which I was pleased to be a part. Moreover, it gave me a rare chance to be behind the scenes and browse the shelves of the protected, hidden books and memorabilia.

My second archival experience was a research encounter involving a trip to the University of Calgary Special Collections. I had secured funding from the Canadian government, and I needed two esteemed academics' references to authorize my access to the material. Inevitably this time, my excitement was generated as much by the trouble to which I had gone, and to which others had gone to for me, as it was by the interest in what I was consulting: the Robert Kroetsch fonds. The authoritative structures surrounding the archives controlling what goes in, who gets to see it, and when material could be viewed during the restricted opening hours of the special collections, were emphasized to me by the archival staff. So was the material's connection to money. I found out that some writers in Canada might qualify for a tax rebate for the material they include in the archives, although as Penn Kemp shows in this volume, the process is not always so simple. For my part, I needed funding to see these archives. Any analysis of the politics and economics of the archive, however, does not sit easily next to the messy intimacy that characterized my response to the wide range of materials I found therein. Personal correspondence, pizza menus, half-written conference papers, annotated manuscripts—all became equally fascinating, even as it was disruptive of my attempt to build up a coherent research narrative. For example, the pizza menu did not simply constitute a piece of source material for Kroetsch's novel, nor remain a catalogue of consumable take-away food. In my distracted and curious rereading, it became both a piece of Kroetsch-abilia and a reminder of his need to eat. I was increasingly loving Kroetsch's work, and his modes of personal communication.

These encounters show archives to be both ordered and arbitrary, formal and informal, legitimizing power and undermining power. Through these personal encounters, I have begun to realize the need for a steady renewal of the archive. We need to rethink our relationship with it. As I will show, Marian Engel and Alice Munro's rereadings of the archive allow for such a renewal; they encourage the archive-reader and archivist, enabled by the messy intimacy of the loving body, to move beyond authoritative restriction.

Archive Stories
I see how Marian Engel and Alice Munro expand the archive's possibilities through their fiction. Their work develops alternative, ethical strategies of reading and living with the archive. My turn to fiction as a way to contemplate a renewal of the material archive is allied with Michel de Certeau's understanding of the nineteenth-century novel as constituting an archive for messy dailiness: "[an] index of particulars—the poetic or tragic murmurings of the everyday...which science does not know what to do with" (70). Here, de Certeau reads novels as a kind of "counter-archive," a way to disrupt the archive's drive to catalogue; I read Engel and Munro's work as meta-archival stories. Both *Bear* and "Meneseteung" disrupt stories of the archive by addressing its materiality. They invite us to consider how the archive is constructed, who decides what goes in it, and how it is then read. They encourage a meta-archival awareness. Engel and Munro also suggest that time spent in the archive involves an interrogation into what materials are made available, who has been involved in this construction, and what ordering system has been deployed. They invite us to question what research the story is dictating to the archival search, and why.

In *Bear*, Lou begins as an archivist who is buried within others' objects and manuscripts, and she catalogues these objects and papers according to the rules of her Director and the Institute. When she is sent to assess and catalogue the remaining estate of Colonel Jocelyn Cary, her encounter with a resident bear leads her to develop a more serendipitous, improvisatory relationship to the archive. Her love for the bear directs her to move beyond the archive-like research notes the colonel has made *about* bears and to develop her own relationship *with* the bear. She opts for what we might call a performative, experimental approach to research. This approach involves bodily knowledge and becomes changed by embodied memory: she physically explores the bear, shits with the bear, and becomes responsive to the bear, even as she acknowledges her need to project her own desires and stories onto him.

Alice Munro's short story "Meneseteung" is even more self-conscious in its figuration of the archiving process. We are told the story of a nineteenth-century "poetess," Almeda Roth, by a narrator who is interpreting archival material. This ostensibly consists of a poetry book (introduced by a small autobiography), a contemporary local newspaper, and a set of photographs. The unstable, improvisatory nature of the story told is highlighted by the narrator's obvious reliance upon and distrust of the gossip-motivated newspaper, the resemblance of the first section to a researcher's provisional musings, and the emphasis at the end of the story upon an archive researcher's desire and fallibility: "I thought there wasn't a person alive in the world but me who would know this, who would make the connection.... But perhaps this isn't so...I may have got it wrong" (Munro 73). This conclusion compels a *rereading* of the story, involving a closer consideration of the narrator's inclusion of details she admits to adding. The story's conclusion has led numerous critics to the archives themselves, to try and gauge just how much Munro based the story on archived, verifiable source material. "Meneseteung" is a story about reading the archives, which leads the interpreters of the story to go back to the archives; consequently, the readers of this critical mass about Munro's creative work are introduced to a variety of previously underexposed female writers. The story demonstrates the symbiotic relationship between archives and fiction, but it also needs to be theorized if we are to question the archive's hegemony *and* fully appreciate the myriad of possibilities to be found and produced within it if read creatively.[1]

Antoinette Burton expresses concern about the "sacrilization of the archive" and observes that the most "popular archive stories of the new millennium are shaped by a belief in the capacity of material evidence to create and sustain tests of verifiability" (5). Invoking Jacques Derrida's *Archive Fever*, she questions the passion for origins and genealogies that turns the archive into a repository of trusted evidence, which the authorized researcher can dig into to produce facts. Diana Taylor shares Burton's concerns and identifies three prevalent myths attending the archive: that it is unmediated, resists change, and is capable of providing "official" state and national histories (19). Both critics question the archive's perceived authority and impel us to acknowledge the ways the archive is "selected, classified, and presented for analysis" and interpreted to produce "stories" with ideological agendas and biases (Taylor 19). Received notions of the archive's authority and its status as an accepted receptacle of truth have serious implications for those whose stories are not stored in official collections or whose voices cannot be heard. As Michel de Certeau's work on orality and the everyday establishes, part of the problem is the archive's reliance upon and privileging of written documents and the consequent denial of lived voices and bodies. As theorized by Taylor, moreover, the archive is both dependent upon bodies and unable to contain them. Taylor favours the notion of "repertoire" as a more inclusive communicator of public and private memory, able to enact through embodied performances "gestures, orality, movement, dance, singing...acts usually thought of as ephemeral, nonreproducible knowledge" (20). Rather than replace the notion of the archive with another concept, as Taylor productively does, I make use of de Certeau's readings of the archive as potentially resistant. At his most optimistic, de Certeau argues that the voices of the marginalized can be heard through the documents that try to hide them. In other words, rather than looking for the body elsewhere as Taylor does, he finds it in the archive. Both theorists assert the need for a bodily invasion of the archive, which would enable it to yield more flexible, ethical possibilities.[2] Burton also gestures toward this invasion in her emphasis on the *desire* crucial to the constitution of the archive and its research production. The acknowledgement of the desire of the collector *and* the researcher leads us to realize that archives are already bodily stories: their telling involves "selective disclosures, half-truths, and partial pasts" necessarily complicated by bodily reactions and affective responses (however repressed they are) (20). An acknowledgement of this disruption of the archive by bodies necessarily expands the possibilities of archival communications.

Reading for the Archive's Agenda
Any straightforward notion of the archive as a receptacle of facts needs to be troubled. Dominick LaCapra cautions against an uncritical approach to the archive that makes it become a "fetish...a literal substitute for the 'reality' of the past which is 'always already' lost for the historian" (92). Ann Laura Stoler notes the interrogation of traditional ways the colonial archive has been read for the "last fifteen years" and urges others to read "against the grain" (99). However, the archive is still very much romanticized in the popular cultural imagination. As Suzanne Keen observes, "perhaps the most readily recognizable version of a fictional researcher is the detective who pores over scraps of paper for clues, finds the hidden or overlooked significance in documentary evidence, and uses brainpower to reveal the truth and solve the mystery of what *really* happened" (4). This teleological archive story gives the archive status as a valuable repository of "true" information, and the researcher the role of explorer-detective who solves the case.

The power of the official archival collection is characterized in useful terms by Margaret J.M. Ezell: "To have a place in the archive is to ensure that the document will be preserved, that it will be become part of a gathered cultural memory, that it will move from being a private textual object into a public context" (2). This importance of the archive in verifying and defining communal identities and producing heritage was further highlighted in the recent anxiety about the retention of Canadian soldiers' First World War medals, which were nearly sold to a private buyer. The fact that they were finally secured by the Canadian War Museum at great cost is testament to the symbiotic relationship between the imagining of a nation and archiving.[3]

There is an agenda controlling the production of an archive, associating it with official power structures. In *Bear*, Lou-as-archivist needs to secure the house for the Institute and ensure state funding for it. To do so, she must show that it constitutes an important piece of the region's story, providing a unique, explanatory perspective. We are told that

> while the Director wangled legal assistance at the Provincial Government's expense (for the Institute had gradually been taken over), Lou dug and devilled in library and files, praying as she worked that research would reveal enough to provide her subject with a character... it was up to her to find out how unusual he was, and in the meantime to pray to whatever gods, muses and members of Parliament overlooked the affairs of the Institute that enough would be revealed to develop the dim negative of that region's history. (14)

The Institute is now controlled by the provincial government; any archiving work to be done will be funded by this ruling body. Consequently, Lou needs to find a "character" unusual enough to elicit interest and play a central role in the telling of that region's history. The fictional and photographic metaphors used in this passage signify a move away from the archive-as-objective. We might assume the provincial government wants hard, solid facts to prove the need to spend money securing the house for the Institute, but we find that these facts need to be packaged into a sanctioned narrative to add to the imagined identity of the region. The right photograph needs to be developed to make it seem unusual, unique, and so somehow "authentic." The funding bodies, then, are subscribing to the romance of the archive which figures it as the place for exciting truths to be discovered by heroic researchers.

Engel highlights the performative nature of the archive. Just as Derrida suggests that Freud is writing *for* the archive, rather than producing material in some kind of "natural" way that is then judged as archive-worthy, so Lou is producing and fictionalizing, rather than simply finding the material to put in the archive.[4] And just as Foucault argues that the archive *is* "the system that establishes statements as events and things" (79), with respect to the colonial archive, Thomas Richards and Gayatri Spivak remind us of the political importance of paying attention to this performativity. Richards sees the imperial archive not simply as a collection of British libraries and museums posted around the globe, but rather as "a fantasy of knowledge collected and united in the service of state and Empire" (6). Meanwhile, in her examination of India's colonial archives, Spivak notes how the distinction between imperial literature and imperial archives becomes blurred as each feeds off the other (198). Spivak urges us to read beyond the "misreading" of an archive fiction which attempts to perform "reality" successfully, and recognize the story produced by the colonial archive as a simulacrum. For Spivak, this process necessarily involves recognizing that the colonizer-as-archivist defines himself through the production of the archive-colony.

Spivak's insights help us understand Lou's reluctance to produce the archive story desired by the provincial government and her director. By trying to avoid telling this story, she also avoids inscribing herself into a problematic, epistemologically violent archive story that would write the settler story over the other voices. Granted, she plays the system: she finds evidence to secure the funding to "research and discover" the years Colonel Cary had spent on Cary Island, funding that allows her to "inspect the property" (Engel 16). Once she is there, however, she finds the time to read, defers her archiving tasks, and becomes distracted. The Institute has asked her to become complicit with an archival story that privileges the settler history of northern Ontario. However, she refuses such complicity when she begins to card and classify, and finds a library that seems to signify Cary's English reading habits rather than his Canadian-ness:

> The Colonel's will specified that the books were not to be separated from the house. She and the Director had plotted to found a summer Institute, if the property was suitable. Now it looked to her as if the material he owned was all imported. The use of the building by scholars would only be justified if there was local history involved. You do not come to northern Ontario to study London in 1825.
> Or do you? she wondered mischievously. (46)

Lou questions the packaging of place within a particular research narrative. The house and the books are imported, but to exclude these from a story of northern Ontario would be to try either to claim an original Canadian-ness for Cary which does not involve his English past, or to maintain a story of the northern Ontario landscape that does not involve nineteenth-century Britain. Moreover, the emphasis on the playfulness of Lou's questioning signals a suture in cataloguing. She has not completely bought into the process. Her performance of cataloguing is signalled through her continual recognition that she should be seen as taking her role seriously. She continues to disrupt any notion of her role as constituting a kind of "truth organizer," or "arranger of benign materials." After a break exploring the island, "she [goes] upstairs to work. She was, after all...a reliable person. She sat down at her desk and proceeded to record what there was to record. Then, somehow, because she wondered how he would react to snow, she began to think about the bear" (47). The archive material begins to take a backseat, just becoming "what there was to record." Lou's *performance* as a "reliable person" is instead foregrounded; the free, indirect discourse indicates Lou's ironic stance toward her own work. This foregrounding highlights the danger posed to the performance from more wondering, this time about the bear.

The bear infiltrates the cataloguing process and invades the story. Lou's subsequent intimacy with him is anticipated. Their first physical love scene takes place in the library. By this time, she has let the bear in but is still trying to perform her role as the "reliable," committed archivist (89). Lou's thoughts digress to consider her journey to becoming an archivist. She moved from journalism to "the least parasitic of the narrative historical occupations," ostensibly to fulfill her "perverse desire, which she [had] suppressed, to reveal truth" rather than dealing with arbitrary deadlines (Engel 89). There is a sense of purity attached to the archives, labelled the most "non-parasitic." Archives are often associated with necessary original research in opposition to theoretical or critical work. Significantly in *Bear*, however, this sense of purity is associated with a "perverse desire," denaturalizing and de-familiarizing the archival impulse, instead of choosing to romanticize it. This revelation directly precedes her complete absorption in her work, which has become about finding Canadian books among Trelawny's collection. These books will consolidate his Canadian-ness, and thus justify the government funding. At this point she pays no attention to the bear, standing full height at the top of the stair. First, she finds an autographed first edition of *Wacousta*, which establishes Cary as a Canadian somebody after all, and her jubilant, relieved reaction confirms that her funding application is an alibi, only justified now.

In her imperative statement to "[l]ie down by duck, my beau" (Engel 90), it is unclear whether she is talking to the bear, Cary, or the book. All are possible, and all seem inappropriate addressees for an archivist. In its ambiguity this comment conflates all three, if only for a moment. The bear is on the brink of becoming her physical beau, and he does lie down, as if obeying her. But the book may have become more than a fetishized object; as a valued object, it garners respect, and she decides not to open it. Its Canadian-ness justifies her stay in the house but also enables her new, different lifestyle. The book also metonymically stands in for its owner, Cary, so she could be addressing him. Moreover, this ambiguity and uncertainty comes at the point when she is not "revealing truth," according to the traditional archive paradigm which figures her as either benign collector or victorious explorer. Instead she is becoming involved with the book/Cary/bear in a way which makes no easy separation between affect/intellect, book/owner, and object/person/bear possible. The flexibility of the archiving act at this stage sees Lou deconstructing herself, even as she deconstructs the notion of the archive.

The idea of deconstruction, however, still relies upon the notion of a structure that is taken apart. It seems less that she is taking something apart, than making her archiving performance more supple. She seeks to reach beyond the original archival boundaries—signified by Greek etymology of *arkhe* as "beginning" and "public building"—toward something else. This "something else" is messy, and cannot be contained within the security of architectural, psychological, intellectual, or bodily walls. She reads the next book on the shelf, Trelawny's remembrances of Byron and Shelley. As opposed to the historically significant and valued Canadian *Wacousta*, she finds this book fascinating in its "rubbish-ness":

> She began to read, enthralled. She had never read this book before, though the subject interested her. Why? Someone, some scholar, had told her it was a pile of rubbish. Most autobiography is rubbish, she thought. People remember things all wrong. But what amusing rubbish this is! What a man! Big. Abusive. A giant. A real descendant of the real Trelawny, the one about the twenty thousand Cornishmen. Oh, I'll believe he's a liar.
>
> Look at the bear, dozing and drowsing, like a groundhog, like a man: big (Engel 90–91).

"Rubbish" moves from being a blank dismissal to a kind of writing with the potential to entertain and provide pleasing contradiction, giving the reader (in this case, Lou) some agency; she decides to *believe* he is a liar. The expansiveness of this writing becomes again associated with the bear, forming an invitation for Lou to get involved with the writing, rather than to judge the book by its cover. She declares her thoughts aloud, and she gets down on her knees next to the bear. Kneeling and speaking become part of her active interpretation, an inevitable consequence of wondering what had earlier disturbed her cataloguing. Her excited reading is now a search for "some connection, some unfingerable intimacy among them [Trelawny/Cary/bear], some tie between longing and desire and the achievable" (91). Interpretation becomes speculative connection. An objective account, drawn from the archival materials (however degraded its form) is impossible. Lou does not, then, become subsumed within the colonial discoverer's dream where she situates her reading of Cary (92). Rather, her view of Cary becomes defined entirely by her own current loneliness and need for care. The present reading contextualizes the past material in a way that we would do well to remember in our own encounters with archives.

The bear, yet again, intervenes. He has moved closer to her, and as she runs her foot through his fur, she realizes her loneliness (92–93). She begins to masturbate, and the scene culminates with the bear "persevering to give her pleasure" with his tongue, before licking away her tears (93). The connection she finds here figures the bear licking her into a new possibility of existence, literalizing the mythical notion of the mother bear who shapes her blind and formless cubs with her tongue. The bear becomes the loving-creator, connecting her to a discourse in antithesis to the non-caring fetishization of the archived object.

This fetishization recalls Adorno's evocation of the *museal*, "a German word [that] describes objects to which the observer no longer has a vital relationship and which are in the process of dying" (173). Characterizing the museum as a place where objects go to die, Adorno invokes the alienating effect of the glass cabinets. Meanwhile Lou, with the help of the bear, revitalizes an object once designated as rubbish, and through the process of her identification with that object, revitalizes *herself*. She finds that the rubbish book provokes thought, that the archivist has the possibility of becoming an interactive reader, and that reading necessarily becomes a bodily performance.

Archives, Rubbish, and Responsibility

I will follow up my reading of this risky and fundamental scene, crucial for our rethinking of the archive, in two ways: first, by considering the relationship Munro and Engel insist upon between archive and rubbish; and second, by demonstrating how Munro and Engel do not deconstruct the archive so much as they reread it. The archive and the rubbish dump are closely connected. Both hold stuff, one the material we want to save, the other what we want to get rid of or wish to be dissociated from. Both signal the metonymic relationship objects have with us. Engel and Munro encourage us to make this connection between the archive and waste, and demonstrate the fragile border that is usually built between the two.

The threat of waste infiltrating order and the veneer of respectability is a constant worry in the newspaper descriptions from the *Vidette* that form part of "Meneseteung." Almeda Roth's house "faces on Dufferin Street, which is a street of considerable respectability," but her back windows overlook Pearl Street, which is "another story." Pearl Street "deteriorates" into the Pearl Street swamp, where nobody but "the poorest people, the unrespectable and undeserving poor" live. Here, people live in makeshift shacks surrounded by "piles of refuse and debris and crowds of runty children, slops are flung from doorways. The town tries to compel these people to build privies, but they would just as soon go in the bushes" (Munro 55–56). The people living here are described by the *Vidette* as literally living in their own waste; indeed, they become figured *as* waste, something to be actively avoided. It is significant that it is Almeda who is both the archive-subject and the ostensible subject of Munro's story, because she is a respectable citizen who has never ventured this far down the street. The boundary between the archive and the rubbish is clear then, but rubbish infiltrates this description of Almeda's living space. Moreover, Almeda does not regard the swamp view from her bedroom at the back of the house as dangerous and rubbishy. Instead, she finds the swamp presents a fine sight at dawn: "From her window she can see the sun rising, the swamp mist filling with light, the bulky, nearest trees floating against that mist" (56). Her version of the swamp is seen at a liminal time, on the day's threshold. Dawn provides the necessary uncertainty which allows Almeda an alternative vision, a chance to see beyond the boundaries imposed by the *Vidette's* reports. "It is said that even the town constable won't go down Pearl Street on a Saturday night" (56). The light of dawn deconstructs the deterministic value system that might project an inflexible, sealed archive in which we could neatly separate the respectable landscape from the morally corrupt.

Rubbish infiltrates "Meneseteung's" conclusions about researchers' motivations. The researcher/narrator ends her story with the realization that any "discoveries" she has made in the archive may not be discoveries at all. She writes,

> I worked away and got the whole stone clear and I read the name "Meda".... That was all the name there was—Meda. So it was true that she was called by that name in the family. Not just in the poem....
>
> I thought that there wasn't anybody alive in the world but me who would know this, who would make this connection. And I would be the last person to do so. But perhaps this isn't so. People are curious. A few people are. They will be driven to find things out, even trivial things. They will put things together. You see them going around with notebooks, scraping the dirt off gravestones, reading microfilm, just in the hope of seeing this trickle in time, making a connection, rescuing one thing from the rubbish. And they may get it wrong, after all. (73)

This final section of the story reveals much about relationship between "archive fever" and the fear of the fickle distinction between treasure and trash. The poem she finds in the archives, along with the biographical information it contains, leads the narrator eventually to find corroborative physical evidence in the graveyard that finishes the story. The archive becomes a place to find a life, but the graveyard is the place to both find its end and memorialize it. The graveyard becomes an extension of the archive. In fact, ending an archive journey in the graveyard has become something of a cliché, which connects archiving to detective work and death;[5] it is self-consciously rendered here, where a grave becomes not the final evidence, but the catalyst for the researcher's realization of her *desire* for it to be the final evidence. If the archive is about remembering, it is also about finding things out and putting them together.[6]

The urge to discover and make connections recalls the seduction of the archive and the desire many feel for it, which can lead to an *illusory* sense of achievement, a sense of closure upon which, perhaps, the traditional search through the archive is predicated. It also connects this desire to search with a sense of responsibility to the past, the trace, the other. The wish to make a connection and rescue one thing from the rubbish is arguably the desire to connect with the other, rather than shutting it out, like Lou's relationship with the bear. It is also a desire which asks us to consider what the rubbish is in this context. Does rubbish become, according to this logic, any stuff that is not cared for, that is, disconnected or unarchived? Munro urges us to consider how we decide what to rescue from the rubbish and how we connect with that which we rescue and assemble. de Certeau's present but absent voices do, perhaps, begin to make themselves heard in this questioning.

Bear also highlights the archive's relationship to rubbish. Lou as archivist, rather than researcher, is described at the beginning of the novel as "buried deep in her office, digging among maps and manuscripts," and surrounded by "things people brought her because she would not throw them out," such as "a Christmas card from the trenches with a celluloid boot on it, a parchment poem to Chingacousy Township graced with a wreath of human hair, a signed photograph of the founder of a seed company long ago absorbed by a competitor" (Engel 2). The archive is placed in the same discursive system as the rubbish dump. The archive is the one place/institution that saves the "things" (and the people they metonymically represent) from becoming garbage. It is one of the responsibilities of the archive to memorialize people and contain the potential for them to have been "more of a somebody than we thought." Indeed, the donors who give Lou "things" want their relatives to be remembered as important "characters." The research-discoverer of Munro's story thus becomes necessary; otherwise, the archive threatens to be conflated *with* the rubbish dump. However, for Lou, these "things" also remind her of an existence beyond the archives, which, as Derrida says, always "signifies its own exteriority" (17). The things put in the archive are not rubbish *because* Lou does not throw them out, and she does not throw them out because they signify a time before they were in the archive. To a certain extent, however, they are rejected objects that accumulate and vie for Lou's attention. Arguably, they are a constant reminder that without care and attention, objects—and people, as Munro and Engel remind us—can become obsolete, unwanted.

These stories also render the binary between archive construction and archive research problematic. "Meneseteung's" narrator extends the Almeda Roth archive through her reading, by moving to the graveyard. In *Bear*, Lou organizes the books, papers, and objects in Cary's library in her official position as archivist, and while doing so, decides the collection's worth and evaluates the landscape that somehow provides a context and coherence for this archivable material. Although both texts make us realize that our reading of the archive necessarily involves a construction of it, which in turn is based on our reading, they potentially suggest something more radical: that the archive only comes into being *through our reading* of it. This realization impels us to move beyond a notion of the archive as preknowledge, as raw material. To dislodge the archive's powerful, hegemonic status, we must not just read against the grain; as Stoler reminds us, we need to move beyond "archives-as-source...to work within the logic of archives-as-subject" (99). These archive fictions help us do this, and make it clear that each archival *re*reading contributes to the constitution of the archive itself.

Rereading the Archive
I am ultimately concerned with questioning the traditional ways the archive has been read as a benign part of the reconstruction of past stories and has been used as part of the constitution of state authority. Munro and Engel figure the archive as something more porous and symbiotic. Arguably, romances of the archive encourage us to see it is an unproblematic saviour. If we take this view, however, we do not get beyond the troubling notion of "archive-as-source," which encourages us to read through any objects/voices/people we find therein, effectively consuming, rather than engaging with them. Munro and Engel, by rereading the archival situation, allow for a loving engagement with the archive.

Both of their texts express anxiety about invasive, teleological readings which potentially other and so objectify their subjects. Lou, in *Bear*, distinguishes between a love which seems predicated upon a recognition that there is "a depth in [the bear] she could not reach," and a type of reading and analysis which she would potentially use—if it was possible—to "probe with her intellectual fingers" and "destroy" (Engel 119). The love is possible then, because she is unable to destroy the bear through analysis, but has learnt to appreciate there is a mystery to him that cannot be explained. She learns that the kind of critical analysis motivated by a need to pick something apart is ultimately destructive.

Lou's relationship with the bear is developed through the ways she interacts with and reads him. These two modes of being involved with him become intertwined: ultimately she reads him interactively, avoiding deterministic defining. We can see this in her continual renaming of him, along with her rejection of comparisons she could make between him and fictional bears, and him and Trelawny. In one of these first attempted and rejected renamings, it is his status as something beyond archival logic which she recognizes through her mistaken connection.

> Once and only once, she experimented with calling him "Trelawny," but the name did not inspire him and she realized she was wrong: this was no parasitical collector of memoirs, this was no pirate, this was an enormous living creature larger and older and wiser than time, a creature that was for the moment her creature, but that... could return to his own world, his own wisdom. (Engel 119)

Within this passage, which lovingly if problematically idealizes the bear, we find him to be even less parasitic than an archivist and figured in opposition to Trelawny. He is un-archiveable, beyond time and ownership. The logic of the archives is arguably a temporal logic. She reminds us of this when she catalogues Cary's bear notes by time, place, and date. The bear represents the excess of the archive, and her reading of him involves bodily response, making the naming of him inadequate. I emphasize the bodily response because this is how Lou's relationship with the bear begins. She is told by Lucy Leroy, "an old Indian woman" who has long been in an intimate relationship with the bear, that she should "shit with the bear" in order for him to like her (49). She follows the advice and their relationship slowly progresses, from swimming and exploring together, to engaging in sexual relations. It is useful to understand this way of being with the bear as a necessary alternative to the notes Cary makes, which disrupt Lou's cataloguing of his books. The notes place the bear in different cultural mythologies, perhaps in an attempt to read him. They provide one archive of the bear made through story. They emphasize a need to understand landscape, people, animals, and things through specific narrative frameworks, but they do not work for Lou. While she catalogues them, she ultimately cannot use them to relate to the bear. Shitting with the bear, however, involves being present with it and coordinating bodily movements. In this way she can move away from trying to categorize it, or place it in a catalogue, and create a different kind of bodily archival reading. In the final pages of my discussion, I would like to consider this a fantasy ideal of being with, rather than just plundering, the archive. In other words, I want to explore loving within the archive.

"Meneseteung" highlights the problems of reading someone within a critical framework which explains, even probes, the person into nonexistence. They can no longer *be*, and so cannot be *loved*, instead they can only represent and so be channelled through. This experience of being read happens first to Almeda Roth, through the reading we get of her from the judgmental pages of the *Vidette* newspaper. The ultimate consequences of these reductive reading practices are shown through Jarvis Poulter's disposal of the unnamed woman's body, and the ultimate alternative to *this* disposal is again a utopian reading experience in which Almeda tries to be with, rather than understand, the things surrounding her.

The *Vidette* plays a complicated role in "Meneseteung": from the very beginning it is both cited as a key source for the story and as a text which needs to be undermined *by* the story. The narrator-researcher contextualizes her own attempt at an objective reading of Roth's archival materials with the *Vidette's* clearly biased reading: "*Offerings,* the book is called. Gold lettering on a dull-blue cover. The author's full name underneath: Almeda Joynt Roth. The local paper, the *Vidette,* referred to her as "our poetess." There seems to be a mixture of respect and contempt, both for her calling and for her sex—or for their predictable conjuncture" (Munro 50). The shift between an attempt to *convey* what is found—the details of the book's physical nature—and to *interpret* what is found immediately gives the *Vidette* an authority, while simultaneously taking it away. It is clear that while the newspaper's writer was in some kind of temporal and perhaps physical context with Almeda, judgments (as Munro's narrator emphasizes) reduce her to a novelty item about town, owned by the journalists and their intended audience (*our* poetess). This reductive reading of Almeda is figured as inadequate, but is needed by the researcher along with the other items in the archive through which the story of Almeda is channelled and through which the narrator's own reading of her appearance is performed.

> The poetess has a long face; a rather long nose; full, sombre dark eyes, which seem ready to roll down her cheeks like giant tears; a lot of dark hair gathered around her face in droopy rolls and curtains. A streak of gray hair plain to see, although she is, in this picture, only twenty-five. Not a pretty girl, but the sort of woman who may age well, who probably won't get fat. (Munro 50)

Almeda has again become "the poetess." The Almeda in the photograph performs the role of the poetess, and the narrator performs a reading with the agenda of finding the poetess. This reading, like *Vidette's*, is inflected with gender concerns, moving from Roth-as-poetess to Roth-as-woman, with the potential to be an attractive mate. The necessity to read beyond the archival materials and create a new text is apparent here. We can glean that the narrator wants to move past the respect and contempt, but is reading within the *Vidette* framework first, making clear what she is responding to and resisting. The archive story that emerges is not one in which materials are being interpreted so that a discovery can be made. Instead, the materials are becoming part of a conversation in which the researcher, making us aware of the gaps between reading and interpretation, archive and truth, begins interpreting the archive materials as they interact with one another. Moreover, the researcher becomes part of that interaction. She tries to get inside Almeda's skin by getting into the language of the *Vidette's* judgment.

Almeda reads beyond the judgmental logic of the *Vidette*. The culminating moment of the story consists of a radical reading moment, brought on by a brief trauma which jolts her out of the logic espoused by the *Vidette*. Every Sunday she and Jarvis walk home together from church, a habit the *Vidette* noted approvingly. (She is a single woman who, having aged well, would still make a good wife. He is a businessman, respectably well off, good husband material.) The story implies, however, that they fail to gain the kind of intimacy which would lead to Jarvis calling for her before church, until the savageness of Pearl Street crosses the boundary, and a drunken fight which culminates outside Almeda's house disturbs her sleep one night. Failing to gather the courage or energy to get up and intervene, Almeda wakes up guiltily in the "early light," and goes to investigate. Believing the woman's body lying in a heap by the fence to be dead, she runs "barefoot, in her nightgown and flimsy wrapper" to Jarvis Poulter's house to get help. He goes back with her to investigate, and proceeds to "nudge the leg with the toe of his boot, just as you'd nudge a dog or a sow." He then pronounces that the woman is "far from dead." As if in response, she bangs her head "hard and rhythmically, against Almeda's picket fence...and lets out an open-mouthed yowl" before Jarvis yanks her up by the hair, shouting at her to go home (66). The scene concludes with Jarvis feeling "sufficiently stirred" by Almeda's "foolishness" and "need" to take the next step in courting, and he states his intention to call on her to walk to church (67). However, Almeda's bodily reaction to the event (nausea and "an accumulation of menstrual blood that has not yet started to flow" [68]) precludes this momentous occasion in their courtship and, leaving a note on the door to stop Jarvis from calling, she locks herself in, and spends her first full day in her nightgown, indoors. Although she does not consciously relate to the woman as Lou does to the bear, her body seemingly connects with her. Jarvis remains disconnected.

Jarvis's behaviour, which turns the woman into an object out of place, an intrusive piece of rubbish, brings on a kind of contemplation for Almeda. Her form of reading, privileged in the story, supersedes Jarvis's empirical, logical way of reading the woman's body, and points to the possibility of something new, in excess of conventional archive logic. The objects in Almeda's room, for instance, like those in Miss Havisham's, become part of her *museal* existence: they are not used, but rather are symbolic of her decision to keep herself in a kind of continual stasis (69).[7] Almeda's stasis is brought on by laudanum, which she takes to deal with the trauma of seeing Jarvis treat the woman like a piece of waste, and it also recontextualizes the objects. Her reading of them seems full of possibility. It is non-intrusive, the result of an "unresisting surrender to her surroundings," rather than a penetrating analysis. She sits within her own archive of things, beginning to read them interactively, and through this process she begins to understand them for their own possibilities beyond any intellectual, empirical interpretation. To join this moment of reading to Lou's shitting with the bear is to bring the body into the archive, and to acknowledge a possibility of interaction with the archive that goes both ways. Our rereadings of the archive potentially change it, but only if we allow it the possibility to change us.

Conclusion: Intimate Archival Encounters

I acknowledge that, in attempting to find love within the archive, I risk being considered inappropriate, unscholarly, and idealistic. However, I think legitimating that moment when a personal, intimate engagement is made with an archival thing can help us keep in mind the ethical imperative to touch (rather than read through) things, to listen for the present-absent voices, to question archival documents, converse with them, and to allow for an embodied experience of research. In this way, we can continually move beyond the kind of reductive thinking associated with the doctor who prescribes Almeda's laudanum rather than engaging with her difference, and Lou's boss, who only sees his own frustration in her body. But we can also understand Lou and Almeda, ostensibly fictional characters, as something more than fictional, as actual beings affecting readers, allowing them to become archival researchers. Aritha Van Herk argues for the excitement of a literal reading of *Bear*, and further informs us that "Engel said she wanted to write a love story and when she opened the door for the lover, a bear lumbered into the room" (144). This vision of the writer's room/head being invaded by the bear has enabled personal, intimate responses to the novel in which, as Van Herk implies, women develop the confidence to explore their own bodies as a way to develop writerly, political agency. "*Bear* makes everything literal. One cannot love satisfactorily without first loving oneself. And the bear, for all its physical bearishness, is a mirror to the woman, Lou, just as she, in her animal humanness, is a mirror to the bear" (144).

Most critics find it crucial in their analyses of "Meneseteung" to try and establish whether Almeda Roth is based upon a real nineteenth-century poetess. Some decide she is definitely fictional. Magdelene Redekop, for example, labels Munro's work a "mock historical story resembling an elegant practical joke." She continues, "Perhaps I can illustrate the joke best by confessing that I consulted various sources and got several librarians sleuthing for me in order to prove to myself that Almeda Joynt Roth is a fiction" (216). Redekop's critical certainty is odd to read alongside Coral Ann Howells's conviction that Munro did base Almeda upon a real person. Howells reads the story as a playful mixture of fact and fiction, and states, "I believe that Almeda's 'partly real'...I would suggest that Almeda's shadowy parallel may be found in the forgotten nineteenth-century poet Eloise Skimings (1836–1921), a native of Goderich and known locally as 'the poetess of Lake Huron'" (108).

In order to perform these readings, both critics create a research community for themselves. Redekop has her sleuths, and Howells thanks "Patricia Hamilton, Curatorial Assistant, Goderich County Museum" and "Dennis and Mary Ann Duffy" for providing her with archival material (166). Both become involved in returning other nineteenth-century women to some kind of discursive and personal existence. The gap between these readings again keeps the archive itself as part of a critical conversation. The stories held by the archive inspire two different readings in this case, but also potentially allow infinite women's voices to be reimagined and listened to. The voice that haunts and arguably transforms Almeda, that changes her bodily experience, is one rendered abject by Poulter. The danger is that this woman becomes a symbol, a way of reading Almeda. The difficulty becomes reading *her* and hearing her as literally as Van Herk reads the bear sex encounter. As de Certeau aims to do, however, we must try to hear this other woman, as much as we know we will fail. To hear her present absence is to make the archive loving.

Notes

1. Highmore points out the distinction de Certeau makes between "The Archives" and "archives." "The Archives" are "an impulse that has fashioned 'the west and the rest,' the epistemological violence that has yoked the diverse, dynamic actuality of life to a chain of signification from which there is no escape." "Archives" are "messy or ordered collections, wild or streamlined depositories that can be read variously: for the official line, or for anecdotes of 'native' insurgency, for instance" (86).
2. In *The Practice of Everyday Life*, de Certeau states "I am trying to hear these fragile ways in which the body makes itself heard in the language, the multiple voices set aside by the triumphal *conquista* of the economy that has, since the beginning of the 'modern age'... given itself the name of writing" (131). He argues that while you cannot hear the voices that have been written out or over, you can hear the sound of their absent presence. He further notes that, "the voices that are expelled have the potential to alter the expeller (even if momentarily) and to unbind the archival impulse, and it is through this alteration... that lost voices can be heard... orality insinuates itself, like one of the threads of which it is composed, into the network—an endless tapestry—of a scriptural economy" (132). In other words, the voices—through their expulsion—are there because of the effect they had upon the archivist.
3. I refer here to a set of nine medals, including the Victoria Cross, "awarded to Lt-Col Robert Shankland, a member of the 43rd Infantry Battalion of the Cameron Highlanders of Canada based in Winnipeg, after he led attacks against the Germans at Passchendaele, Belgium, during the First World War. The story of this great Canadian and his contribution to our history deserves to be preserved in our national military museum," Mark O'Neill, the museum's director general, said in a release ("Medals").
4. For example, while Derrida is writing, he identifies an anxiety within Freud that his work—*Civilization and Its Discontents*—will not be archive-worthy. He imagines him asking, "Is not what [I am] preparing to deliver to the printers so trivial as to be available everywhere?" (8).
5. For example, Robert Kroetsch's archivist Raymond tells us, "To take poetry into one's hands is to take one's life into one's hands. Surely Rita understood this when she asked me, late one evening, if I would, should the occasion arise, organize her papers and have them deposited in the vaults of the University of Calgary Special Collections Library. When I told her next morning that, yes, I would be happy to make her remains secure, she asked me what I was talking about" (45). For more on this connection between archiving and death, see Bates 12–15.
6. Ricouer understands the archive's "debt to the dead" (67) to be its most important function, whereas Merewether points to Freud's understanding of memory as a process of inscription, symbolized by the archive (11).
7. This reading of *Great Expectations*' Miss Havisham is heavily influenced by Wynne's work, presented in the paper "Museal Dickens." It is useful to put Almeda Roth within this context of women disrupting their expected status as objects of exchange, and inhabiting a "room of their own."

Works Cited

Adorno, Theodor W. 1967. *Prisms*. Trans. Samuel and Shierry Weber. Cambridge: MITP, 1983. Print.

Bates, Catherine. "*Messing* with the Archive: Back Doors, Rubbish and Traces in Robert Kroetsch's *The Hornbooks of Rita K*." *SubStance* 37.2 (2008): 8–24. Print.

Burton, Antoinette. *Archive Stories*. Durham: Duke UP, 2005. Print.

de Certeau, Michel. 1984. *The Practice of Everyday Life*. Trans. Steven Randall. Berkeley: U of California P, 1988. Print.

Derrida, Jacques. *Archive Fever: A Freudian Impression*. Trans. Eric Prenowitz. Chicago: Chicago UP, 1996. Print.

Engel, Marian. 1976. *Bear*. Toronto: McClelland and Stewart, 1990. Print.

Ezell, Margaret J. M. "Paraplex: Or, the Functions of the Angels in the Archives." *Women Writers Project*. Women Writers Project Conference: "Women in the Archives." Mar. 7, 2009. Web. Oct. 15, 2009. (http://www.wwp.brown.edu/about/activities/wwp20/papers/ezell.html).

Foucault, Michel, *The Archaeology of Knowledge*. 1969. Trans. A. M. Sheridan Smith. London: Tavistock, 1972. Print.

Highmore, Ben. *Michel de Certeau: Analysing Culture*. London/New York: Continuum, 2006. Print.

Howells, Coral Ann. *Alice Munro*. Manchester: Manchester UP, 1998. Print.

Keen, Suzanne. *Romances of the Archive in Contemporary British Fiction*. Toronto: U of Toronto P, 2001. Print.

Kroetsch, Robert. *The Hornbooks of Rita K*. Alberta: U of Alberta P, 2001. Print.

LaCapra, Dominick. *History and Criticism*. Ithaca: Cornell UP, 1985. Print.

"Medals including the Victoria Cross sold to the Canadian War Museum for $240,000. *CBC News*. Mar. 5, 2009. Web. Jan. 7, 2010. (http://www.cbc.ca/canada/story/2009/05/25/toronto-medal-auction.html).

Merewether, Charles. Introduction. *The Archive*. London: MITP, 2006. Print.

Munro, Alice. *Friend of My Youth*. London: Vintage, 1990. Print.

Redekop, Magdalene. *Mothers and Other Clowns*. London: Routledge, 1992. Print.

Richards, Thomas. *The Imperial Archive and the Fantasy of Empire*. London: Verso, 1996. Print.

Ricoeur, Paul. 1978. "Archives, Documents, Traces." *The Archive*. Ed. Charles Merewether. London: MITP, 2006. 64–68. Print.

Spivak, Gayatri Chakravorty. *A Critique of Postcolonial Reason: Towards a History of the Vanishing Present*. Cambridge: Harvard UP, 1999. Print.

Stoler, Ann Laura. "Colonial Archives and the Arts of Governance." *Archival Science* 2 (2002): 87–109. Print.

Taylor, Diana. *The Archive and the Repertoire*. Durham: Duke UP, 2003. Print.

Van Herk, Aritha. Afterword. *Bear*. Marian Engel. Toronto: McClelland and Stewart, 1990. Print.

Wynne, Deborah. "Museal Dickens." Keele English Research Seminar. Keele University, Oct. 14, 2009. Conference Paper.

An Archive of Complicity: Ethically (Re)Reading the Documentaries of Nelofer Pazira
Hannah McGregor

Introduction: Archiving Afghanistan

In the Afterword to *Working in Women's Archives*, Marlene Kadar outlines six goals for the recovery of women's archival material. The final goal, which informs the previous five (and indeed the entire anthology) is "[t]he ongoing project of rescuing women's lives and cultures from the 'anonymity of history'... so that they are understood as part of our history and our present" (116). This understanding of the ethics of feminist archival research begins from the assertion that women have been systematically excluded from official (literary) histories of Canada. As such, one of the primary ethical imperatives of the feminist scholar, as Helen Buss notes, is to "deconstruct the narrow boundaries in which established culture has bound us and [to] prepare space for others who have been similarly excluded" (Introduction 5). While acknowledging the ethical, political, and scholarly importance of this feminist project of deconstruction and reclamation, in this paper I approach the interrelation of women, archives, and ethics in contemporary Canada from a markedly different perspective.[1]

My perspective in this paper is directly inspired by the praise and critique that the films of Afghan-Canadian filmmaker Nelofer Pazira have garnered. Pazira fled Afghanistan in 1989 with her family and eventually immigrated to Canada, where she studied journalism and began making documentaries, first about Iran and eventually about her homeland. Her rise to fame came in 2001, when she starred in the fictional documentary *Kandahar*, directed by Mohsen Makhmalbaf. *Kandahar* is a fictionalized account of Pazira's quest to re-enter Afghanistan in order to find her childhood friend Dyana, who she worries may have committed suicide. Two years later, after the fall of the Taliban, Pazira was able to undertake the actual journey that *Kandahar* imagines; it is this journey that *Return to Kandahar* (2003) documents. Pazira followed up these films with a memoir, *A Bed of Red Flowers: In Search of My Afghanistan* (2006), and another short documentary also set in Afghanistan, entitled *Audition* (2008), in which she reflects on the place of film in contemporary Afghan culture. Her most recent film, *Act of Dishonour* (2010), returns to the fictionalized documentary genre of *Kandahar*. In a 2004 interview, Pazira describes her genre-crossing documentary filmmaking as the work of "a silly idealist who likes to break all the barriers and tries to create a way of just floating in between" (French 33). Pazira's body of work reflects this liminal approach with its increasingly experimental and self-reflexive tone, refusing to remain static but continually pushing the boundaries of representation through techniques ranging from the blurring of genre to meta-filmic commentary. Her films merge the visual pleasure of the landscapes and cultures she documents with the intellectual pleasure of challenging and provocative takes on the now-familiar subject of Afghanistan.

This reading of Pazira, however, is not the common one. Opinions of her work vacillate between extremes of praise and censure: she is praised by the media and popular reviews for her realistic depictions of Afghanistan in the midst of a political climate that makes this information pertinent, but she is critiqued by feminist scholars for her complicity with Canadian discourses of "saving" Afghan women that have been used to justify the War on Terror.[2] What for the public media is a useful archive of information about Afghanistan is, for feminist scholars, an archive of complicity. In post-9/11 Canada, the woman of colour has become not so much excluded from discourse and official history as marked, coded, described, curtailed, and discursively bounded by narratives of humanitarianism and security.[3] These official and hegemonic narratives employ Afghan women as symbols of Islamic patriarchy and Canadian benevolence. The relation between the erased histories of some Canadian women and the public fetishization of others suggests, as Ann Laura Stoler argues, that archives not only shape "what stories [can]not be told" (91) but also determine "what accounts [are] authorized" through the production of official history (93).

In this essay, I set out to question both of these narratives of Pazira's work. In order to do so, I differentiate between Pazira's artistic archive, including films and memoir, with its invitation to critical and reflexive reading and its problematization of representation, and the official Canadian archive of publicly disseminated information about Afghanistan into which Pazira has been absorbed as a public figure, chiefly through critical and popular discussion of her film *Return to Kandahar*. Neither of these archives are exclusively material, and they include various discursive components; they are nonetheless shaped by the material conditions of production and dissemination. I begin with an analysis of these conditions in relation to Pazira's work. Then I consider the ways in which both the popular media and feminist critics have responded to *Kandahar* and *Return to Kandahar*. It is possible—and indeed desirable—to read Pazira's documentaries against the grain of the archive in which they have been situated both by the Canadian media and by critics like Yasmin Jiwani and Sunera Thobani. Stoler insists that "[r]eading only against the grain of the...archive bypasses the power in the production of the archive itself" (101), a critical omission that I hope to avoid by paying closer attention to what constitutes the archive in which Pazira's documentaries arguably participate. I then move on to a close reading of Pazira's work, and focus on *Audition* and *Return to Kandahar* in order to demonstrate what I consider the ethical importance of liberating Pazira's artistic archive from the archive of Canadian-produced and publicly disseminated information about Afghanistan. I call this the Canadian archive on Afghanistan.

In his discussion of the emergence of the archive into the cultural imagination of the twentieth century, Michael O'Driscoll emphasizes the ethical responsibility to recognize the archive as not only a function of power but also, in its materiality, as a potential site of resistance to the very power that constitutes it (298, 288). For this reason, my attempt at an ethical counter-reading of two of Pazira's documentaries will focus upon the material conditions of documentary production, as well as the traces of dislocation and its trauma. I choose to focus on Pazira's documentaries in part because, as Ann Cvetkovich notes, documentaries "demonstrate the profoundly affective power of a useful archive...which must preserve and produce not just knowledge but feeling" (241). In challenging familiar readings of Pazira's work, both complimentary and critical, I intend to reread this archive of complicity as an artistic archive that engages seriously with issues of dislocation, representation, and cultural translation. My analysis of Pazira provides an opportunity to reread the process of archivization as a potential source of agency wherein the artist is neither irredeemably complicit nor a victim of hegemonic national narratives. Instead, the archive becomes an ambiguous site of negotiation between the ethical imperative to produce border-crossing work and the unavoidable realities of material production.

The Materiality of the Archive

Pazira's films are not exclusively a material archive; instead, her archive consists of a web of interrelated artistic productions, critical responses, and media representations. However, they are shaped by the material conditions of production and by the real, lived traumas of a diasporic subject. The independent diasporic woman filmmaker occupies a difficult position. She must deal with the standard difficulties of independent filmmakers (funding, distribution, and artistic compromise), while negotiating an identity at once marginalized and exoticized. Her subject position makes her films more vulnerable to critique from other post-colonial and feminist thinkers and, particularly since she's an Afghan-Canadian woman producing documentaries in the wake of September 11, more exposed to certain kinds of social and political coding. Because Pazira's Afghan background lends her documentaries an aura of cultural authenticity, they are both more prone to being read as the "truth" about Afghanistan and to being critiqued for complicity with this reading. An ethical reading of Pazira's films, however, will attend not only to how they have been received and the discourses that have circulated about them but also to how material conditions shape both the production and reception of films. Reading the materiality of this discursive archive provides a starting point of resistance against the ways in which it has been constructed both by critics and by the Canadian media.

Sunera Thobani asserts that the war in Afghanistan created a sudden demand in the mainstream media for Muslim women journalists and filmmakers and gave them unprecedented opportunities to represent Afghanistan and Islam ("Gender" 226). These opportunities can also lead to a particular burden of expectation borne by independent women filmmakers, as C. A. Griffith and H. L. T. Quan point out. In the face of an "increasingly monopolistic" mainstream media, women filmmakers are expected "to explore issues with more detail and attention to the layers of meaning, and to take up topics and perspectives which are often marginalized and silenced" (Griffith and Quan 43). These disparate expectations are evident in a critique like Thobani's. Thobani dismisses Sally Armstrong's reductive documentary about Afghan women, *The Daughters of Afghanistan*, as typical white liberal feminism, but construes Pazira's *Return to Kandahar* as more dangerous precisely because of Pazira's insider status (228–29).

At the same time as they are expected to fill in the gaps left by mainstream media, independent filmmakers are faced with the constant necessity to compromise in order to garner funding and make their films marketable (Naficy 49–50). In *An Accented Cinema*, Hamid Naficy points out how exilic and diasporic filmmakers experience interwoven moments of dependence and autonomy, particularly with respect to financial dependence and the autonomy of artistic expression (44–46). *Return to Kandahar* was funded and aired by the CBC. A corporate sponsorship of this kind influences the filmmaker's work almost by necessity; she will make decisions in keeping with both the nature of her funding body and the expected nature of her audience. Features of *Return to Kandahar*, including several deliberate references to Canada as a space of political freedom and a focus upon Pazira as a recognizable figure, suggest this level of influence. It is interesting to note that *Audition*, with its marked lack of slick production values and commodified, viewer-friendly appeal, was made only after Pazira's contract with CBC terminated, and was funded by a partnership between the University of Alberta and Kandahar Films, Pazira's own production company.

Naficy notes that academic institutions constitute a viable alternative market that generally exerts less content- or form-related pressures on the filmmaker (60). However, in a March 9, 2009, question-and-answer period following a screening of *Audition* at the University of Alberta's Festival of Ideas, Pazira expressed a continuing sense of the restraint required to produce this documentary, generated largely by concerns about the audience and accessibility. She had originally intended to provide no voiceover for *Audition*, but was concerned that her audience would be unable to connect to the film without some sort of continuous narrative being provided. In its present form, the film is still experimental in nature, with Pazira allowing interactions and unexpected circumstances to shape the story instead of fitting images into a predetermined narrative. *Audition* thus reflects the increased, if not complete, autonomy of the filmmaker, an autonomy informed by modes of production. Pazira's relationship with the CBC gave her opportunities, in the form of funding and distribution, which would have otherwise remained unavailable at that early stage of her career. If she did "attempt to get ahead by cashing in on the newsworthiness" of Afghanistan (Naficy 53), she accepted a level of dependence in order to realize more fully the autonomy of artistic expression.

Pazira's partnership with the CBC not only influenced *Return to Kandahar* at the level of production. The relationship also shaped the transmission and reception of the documentary in particular ways through the CBC's self-construction as Canada's source of information about the world. After 9/11, independent documentaries about Afghanistan and the

War on Terror "enabled [the CBC] to implicitly foster nation building by reinforcing the recasting of the nation as once more engaged in a civilizing mission" (Thobani, "Gender" 237). On the webpage dedicated to independent documentary filmmakers, the CBC employs precisely this rhetoric of nation-building, making it clear that access to information about other cultures is central to Canadian national identity:

> And we know what Canadians want—we want to be entertained, we want to be compelled, we want to know more about the world and sometimes just escape from it. We identify with universal stories and characters that we can relate to but we're also interested in getting a glimpse of a world we wouldn't otherwise know. We are smart, creative, inquisitive and diverse. We are uniquely and patriotically Canadian! ("Independent Producers")

This rhetoric is an example of what Stoler calls "the legitimating social coordinates of epistemologies: how people imagine they know what they know and what institutions validate that knowledge" (95). The CBC is an institution that claims the legitimacy to produce knowledge about Canada and the rest of the world *for* Canadians. Pazira's association with the CBC thus shapes *Return to Kandahar* in ways that have more to do with its public reception than with the actual content of the film.

An independent, diasporic woman filmmaker like Pazira may experience moments of privilege brought about by particular political contexts, but ultimately this privilege only adds another layer of difficulty to an already troubled position: the difficulty of negotiating the expectations of post-colonial and feminist critique without losing sight of concerns like marketability. At the same time practical material considerations, such as funding, may have larger repercussions, particularly in terms of the absorption of Pazira's work into a Canadian public archive on Afghanistan.

Pazira in the Canadian Media

While Pazira's films form one kind of artistic archive available to multiple readings, the information that has built up around them has formed a different archive. This archive consists not only of a certain reading of Pazira's films but also of the media coverage that has risen up around them and Pazira herself. It can thus be read as an example of archives as "sites of...knowledge production [and] monuments of states" (Stoler 90). The films *Kandahar* and *Return to Kandahar* can both be read as using the rhetoric of Afghan women's liberation to justify the war in Afghanistan. When *Kandahar* premiered at the 2001 Cannes film festival, it was largely ignored. However, in the wake of September 11, 2001, public attention latched onto this film as what Thobani calls a "presentation of the unvarnished 'truth' about Afghanistan and its women.... Astonishingly," she points out, "President Bush was reported to have made a request to see the film in order to 'help him understand the situation in Afghanistan'" (237). Although *Kandahar* is a fictional film that deliberately employs the form of a documentary, it does not attempt to conceal its fictional status. The propensity for writers, journalists, and even politicians to mistake the film for a transparent representation of reality (when even a documentary lacks representational transparency) suggests the aura of cultural authenticity that was built up around the film. This authenticity drew particularly on the figure of Pazira as a liberated Afghan-Canadian woman.

The sense of both films as vehicles of authentic knowledge about Afghanistan is evident in reviews. A *Time Canada* article on *Kandahar* explicitly describes it as "contribut[ing] to the understanding of the Afghan predicament" ("Cry" par. 3) and claims that it "help[s] [to] educate the world—and set [Pazira's] fellow Afghans free" (par. 4). *Return to Kandahar* was similarly lauded for its unvarnished depiction of the truth of Afghan women's lives under the Taliban regime. David Johnson's 2003 review for *Maclean's* is an excellent example of the ways in which both the documentary and Pazira as a public figure have been coded. It emphasizes the purported transparency of the documentary genre when it calls the film "an unalloyed documentary" that "takes us deeper into Afghanistan than all those endless hours of CNN" (pars. 15, 17). Despite being credited as a director of the film—and having professional training as a documentary-maker—Pazira is described as an aestheticized icon of Western liberated womanhood: "When male students challenge her right to interview their female classmates, this woman who refuses to hide her beauty, or intelligence, behind a burka demolishes them with fierce, indisputable words" (par. 16). Although this scene in the documentary can be read as empowering, Johnson's description reduces it to an example of liberal rhetoric that contrasts Afghanistan as the site of Islamic patriarchy with Canada as the site of freedom and gender equality. This binary is not only reductive and misleading, it is also a major component in the Canadian justification for military intervention in Afghanistan.

The Canadian archive on Afghanistan is in fact made up of multiple overlapping archives, including scholarly articles, documentaries, and media coverage. Different modes of research make different archives available. To get a sense of how Pazira circulates as a public figure in the Canadian media, I performed a search of the Factiva database for Pazira's name, thereby approaching it in a manner that Cecily Devereux explores within this very volume. As of December 2009, the search yielded hundreds of references to Pazira in mainstream print media, including twenty-six references in the *Globe and Mail* and twenty-eight in the *National Post*.⁴ Notably, these articles, reviews, and interviews begin to proliferate in October 2001. Before that date, Pazira had little cultural capital within Canada. Although there is not space here to analyze fully the range of media references to Pazira, I will highlight a few indicative examples. Liam Lacey's *Globe and Mail* review of *Kandahar* is titled "Heart of the Afghan Darkness," and it constructs Afghanistan as a site of barbarism and Pazira as an intrepid adventurer. Lacey overtly states that "[s]ince Sept. 11, *Kandahar* has moved into the essential-viewing category" ("Heart"). Jeet Heer of the *National Post* also frames the fictional film—which he calls "lightly fictionalized"—as a source of information about Afghanistan: "Even the best informed citizen knows next to nothing about Afghanistan, the central battleground in the war against terrorism.... The film works best as an informative guide to a part of the world we need to better understand" ("Necessary"). In fact, Heer denounces the film's artistic value in favour of its status as an educational document: "*Kandahar* is so necessary an introduction to the realities of Afghanistan that it would seem churlish to criticize it on esthetic [*sic*] grounds. Yet it has to be said that the movie is better as a work of information than a work of art" ("Necessary"). As Stoler points out, it is the archive system itself that determines "what can and cannot be said" (96) and establishes "what kinds of truth-claims lie in documentation" (94). Thus, the Canadian archive on Afghanistan turns the experimental and fictional film *Kandahar* into a pedagogical tool about the realities of Afghanistan, a truth-claim that adheres even more strongly to *Return to Kandahar*, a self-proclaimed documentary.

The Archive as Knowledge Production
Pazira has become a component in the Canadian archive on Afghanistan, with or without her approval. Her own body of work, including her films and memoir, constitute an artistic archive that invites participatory and self-reflexive reading. But the Canadian archive on Afghanistan deploys Pazira and her artistic production as part of a national body of knowledge that reinforces certain myths about Canada, while also justifying the war in Afghanistan with discourses about the need to "save" Afghan women. Drawing on Stoler's definition of the archive as "a strong *metaphor* for any corpus of selective forgettings and collections" and a set of "intricate technologies of rule" and knowledge production (94, 87, 90), I argue that Pazira's films can be read as complicit with the Canadian archive on Afghanistan. That reading is not, however, the only one to which they lend themselves.

Several Canadian feminist scholars have drawn attention to the way in which news coverage of and documentaries about Canada's international affairs participate in nation-building projects. Sherene Razack, for example, analyzes the archive of documentaries produced by both the CBC and the Canadian military about the Rwandan genocide. She argues these documentaries produce a certain image of Canadians as "citizens of a compassionate middle power who is largely uninvolved in the brutalities of the world" (376). The documentaries constitute a "public narrative of Rwanda" that relies upon affect not only to produce knowledge about Canada as a nation but also, in so doing, to produce discursively the nation itself (Stoler 98). Cvetkovich's argument that documentaries are better able to communicate the "profoundly affective power of a useful archive" (109–10) is liberating in the case of a historically erased archive like that of lesbian feeling. Affect, however, can become ethically problematic when it is produced by the consumption of others' pain (Razack 375–76). Razack reads documentaries as part of the technology of nation-building, and affect as a key component in the creation of an archive of information about Canada. This sort of archive does not represent reality, but produces as much as it records the realities it is only supposed to describe, following Stoler (103).

Yasmin Jiwani takes a similar approach to her study of depictions of Afghan women in the Canadian press between 2001 and 2007. Using the *Globe and Mail* as her sample archive, Jiwani "demonstrate[s how] constructions of Afghan women as quintessential innocent victims requiring rescue" function as a masculinist justification for Canadian military intervention in Afghanistan (729). Jiwani focuses upon how this instrumentalization of Afghan women operates in a Canadian context, whereby the national imaginary is built upon "discourses of care, compassion, and rescue" (729). The knowledge produced about Afghan women therefore emphasizes their status as victims of Islamic misogyny (731–32), and once again draws upon affect to summon "feelings of identification and empathetic, if not sympathetic, sentiment" for these women whose only crime is "being women" (Jiwani 735). This discourse also relies upon narratives of heroic Afghan women that emphasize their "worthiness" of Canadian liberation, and stories of diasporic Afghan women that construct Canada as the site of liberation and agency (737–38). Jiwani explicitly includes Pazira in the latter category, a public figure who reinforces Canada's image of Afghanistan by describing the dangers she encounters when returning to her homeland. Pazira's public statements about her willingness to die if it means helping "those little Afghan girls" function, according to Jiwani, "as a form of ventriloquism, echoing what 'we' as the audience would expect of her" (738). What Jiwani implies is that Pazira functions, for a Canadian audience, as a native informant.

The native informant, as Stoler notes, "draws our attention to the relationship between archiving, experts, and knowledge production" (96). Pazira's documentaries are absorbed into the Canadian archive on Afghanistan because her relationship to Afghanistan and her gender empower her with a level of authenticity that Thobani refers to as transnational cultural capital. Pazira's knowledge of the language and customs of both Afghanistan and Canada allow her to function as a two-way cultural translator, and thus to explain Afghanistan to her Canadian audience and Canada to her Afghan interlocutors (Thobani, "Gender " 227).[5] In her article, "Gender and Empire: Veilomentaries and the War on Terror," Thobani analyzes Pazira's *Return to Kandahar* and Sally Armstrong's *Daughters of Afghanistan* to emphasize, like Jiwani, how the production of knowledge about Afghan women functions as a means of justifying and even promoting Canadian military intervention in Afghanistan, and of discursively producing Canada itself. She describes these documentaries as a form of governance that produces subjectivities ("Gender" 222). Canadian and Afghan identities are invented and naturalized by these documentaries; Pazira, as a diasporic Afghan-Canadian, occupies a space somewhere between the two. This liminality is why, according to Thobani, Sally Armstrong can comfortably adopt the position of the benevolent white feminist, whereas Pazira must struggle "to put social and cultural distance between herself and the locals" ("Gender" 229).

Thobani's critique demonstrates a remarkable lack of sympathy for the difficult position from which Pazira, as a diasporic subject, produces her documentaries.[6] It also fails to acknowledge the potential ethical value of cultural translation. Although Thobani acknowledges that Pazira's complicity with Canadian knowledge production may be happening "despite [her] best intentions" (239), Thobani's frequent references to intentionality, including her emphasis on Pazira's "*strategy* of auto-Orientalizing," imply that she believes Pazira is using a *deliberate* representational strategy ("Gender" 227; emphasis mine). Deliberately or not, *Return to Kandahar* lacks the level of self-reflexivity necessary to counteract Western discourses of saving Afghan women. This lack becomes particularly apparent when reading *Return to Kandahar* against *Audition*, as the latter forces the viewer to consider the very nature of the documentary and to question its ability to represent reality. Thobani's critiques are valid, particularly from the perspective of the circulation and reception of Pazira's work. What concerns me is what is left out of her reading of Pazira's work, namely the complex and beleaguered position of the diasporic woman filmmaker, and the importance of the artistic archive formed by Pazira's films and memoir.

Reading *Audition*

The 2008 experimental documentary *Audition* can, in fact, be interpreted as providing a model for an ethically resistant reading approach for her archives. The problem with Thobani and Jiwani's readings of Pazira, as much as with the latter's political coding in articles and reviews, is that both perspectives appropriate Pazira's work in the interest of making an argument or supporting a political position. Helen Buss points out the critical imperative to understand a woman's subjectivity on the terms in which it was experienced, rather than "deform[ing] the account by reading from above, from a class position as an academic that appropriates rather than explicates" ("Constructing" 34). To appropriate Pazira's work repeats the discursive violence of turning her documentaries into an archive of knowledge production about Afghanistan. This appropriation is the critical danger of a critique like Thobani's, which reads Pazira's work on the terms set by the archive, an important exercise, but one that cannot, and should not, be the final critical word on Pazira. *Audition* can provide a model for reading Pazira's other documentaries, particularly *Return to Kandahar*, in terms of her own problematization of her iconic status and her desire to denaturalize the representational strategies of the documentary film. It also suggests the importance of reading her body of work as an archive-in-process.

Audition draws attention to Pazira's self-reflexivity and her understanding of the social responsibility of the filmmaker. In fact, the self-conscious way in which the film seems to respond to many of Thobani's critiques—namely, that Pazira exhibits a dangerous complicity with the archivization of her documentaries—suggests a dialogic relationship between the filmmaker and the processes by which her films have been incorporated into official narratives of Afghanistan. It is worth noting that this film has received substantially less public attention than either *Kandahar* or *Return to Kandahar*, perhaps because of its reduction in commercial appeal and experimental tone. The film reveals a changing approach to documentary-making that resists both the fetishization of Pazira herself and the possibility of reading documentaries as transparent representations of the reality of Afghanistan.

Audition plays on both the definitions of its title, meaning either "the action of hearing or listening" or "a trial or performance of an actor, singer, etc." (*Oxford English Dictionary Online*). The latter is more obviously applicable in the context of this documentary, which accumulates audition footage alongside interviews and archival images of popular Afghan films. The former, however, also accents the documentary's focus on a multiplicity of voices, and its interruption of the primacy of the gaze through its emphasis on dialogue (Kaplan 219). *Audition* is full of Afghan voices, and makes great demands on viewers in terms of reading subtitles. This uncompromising emphasis on the audible self-representation of her interlocutors demonstrates Pazira's focus on speech as a form of agency and on the ethical dimensions of attentive listening/reading.

The title also disrupts the purported transparency of representation in the documentary genre. Thobani points out the tendency for documentaries, particularly those that provide information about other cultures, to be "treated as having a greater proximity to 'reality' and 'truth'" ("Gender" 237). *Audition* constantly highlights the constructed nature of the film and draws critical attention to the presence of the camera and its effect on people. Early in the film, while an assembled group watches one of Pazira's previous documentaries, her voiceover comments that "they watched the film as our cameras watched them." Particularly interesting is a scene in which she films a group of women at a shrine. After objecting to the camera, one of the women shouts out, "Go get the camera and turn it on her." After they do so, Pazira considers the "intrusive eye" of the camera "recording our awareness of its presence" (*Audition*). Moreover, the entire documentary is structured around a deliberately misleading use of images. The opening scene, in which a group of women washing clothes object to a man taking pictures of them, is revealed in the final scene to be a performance, acted by the women and directed by Pazira. By playing with viewer expectations, Pazira forces viewers to critique the assumptions with which they approach representations of Afghanistan, including assumptions about cultural fear of images and technology. The film similarly obliges viewers to question the truth-status of the archive as a whole. Neither the document nor the documentary is a simple receptacle of current or past realities. Pazira's archive demands reflexive and critical reading, in contrast to the Canadian archive on Afghanistan, which produces and reproduces hegemonic truths.

Along with frequent shots of Pazira's presence behind the camera, these scenes serve to foreground the constructed nature of the documentary and the performance of identity that inevitably takes place in the presence of a camera. Pazira is aware that what she can capture on film will never be "authentic," it can only be the response of subjects to the very act of filming. This destabilization of the truth-value of the documentary similarly calls into question the image of the archive as a receptacle of objective fact, encouraging viewers to interrogate the contexts and power dynamics of archivization. Considering this decentring of truth and authenticity, it makes sense that much of the documentary takes the form of auditions, in which people are invited to perform for the camera, disposing entirely with the illusion of natural behaviour. Clearly conscious of the propensity of Afghanistan images to be absorbed into an archive of reductive Orientalist discourses, Pazira continually evades such an absorption by problematizing the possibilities of representation and cultural translation. At the same time, she highlights the necessity of attempting representation with her arguments about the subversive potential of film, and its ability to act as a mirror for society. "Cinema," she tells a group of young Afghan men, "reflects the inner shortcomings of a society. And when we see those issues reflected in a film and understand them, we can then attend to those shortcomings...I am trying to achieve that reflective mirror for this society" (*Audition*). Pazira's understanding of the social role of film suggests a different reading of her archive, not as a collection of documents reflecting a hegemonic truth, but as an artistic collection demanding reflexive and critical reading.

(Re)Reading *Return to Kandahar*

Audition, I have argued, provides a potential model for a resistant reading of *Return to Kandahar*. There are two aspects of *Return to Kandahar* that I would like to examine in detail in order to give a clearer sense of what I mean by an ethical rereading of Pazira's work, one that does not focus exclusively on reception or read each work in isolation. The first is the arrival scene, where Pazira travels with her crew through the streets of Kabul trying to find her childhood home. Mir Hekmatullah Sadat's study of the Afghan diaspora points out how difficult it is for those who have lived abroad to return home; they are often considered "foreign Afghan[s]," and treated with distrust (331). The potentially traumatic nature of homecoming is also apparent in Naficy's description of exilic filmmakers. Unable to return to their homelands, they "memorialize the homeland by fetishizing it" (12). Pazira's initial return home, after thirteen years of exile, is understandably a traumatic experience, and the trauma of realizing that the homeland has been unrecognizably altered is expressed by Pazira through her anxiety at not being able to find her old house, and then her distress about its ruined condition when she finally recognizes it. Thobani, however, interprets this scene as a threat to Pazira's status as a native informant who is expected to guide her crew through the unfamiliar landscape. Pazira's panic, she argues, emerges from the filmmaker's awareness that any failure to recognize her home or homeland will be interpreted as weakness and inauthenticity ("Gender" 229). What is read by Thobani as a reinforcement of Pazira's self-construction as a possessor of cultural authority can be reread through a different lens as an evocation of the troubled relationship between a diasporic artist and her homeland. Of course, the ambiguity of the scene leaves it as open to Thobani's interpretation as it is to my own. Such is the value of the artistic archive that invites multiple readings. The danger of Thobani's reading, however, is that it fails to move beyond Pazira's potential complicity with her own status as native informant, and thus does not consider either the possible ethical value of cultural translation or the importance of reading Pazira's films against the grain of the Canadian archive on Afghanistan.

Thobani also identifies Pazira's focus on the burka as a particularly problematic aspect of *Return to Kandahar*, whereas I am more interested in the complex treatment this contentious image receives in Pazira's different works. The burka features as both a frequent visual trope of the documentary, with Pazira symbolically lowering one over her head before entering Afghanistan, and as a source of frustration in her search for her friend Dyana, because the burka obscures the identities of all the women around her. Much has been written about the Western fascination with the burka as a visual symbol of the Orient and the misogynistic repressiveness of Islamic societies.[7] For Thobani, "[t]he veil operates as a signifier of the passivity and silence of [Muslim] women, victims of their culture, religion, and communities" ("Gender" 219), and leads to a construction of Afghan women as the victims of Muslim misogyny with which Pazira's film is complicit. However, in her memoir *A Bed of Red Flowers* published in 2005, three years *before* Thobani's article, Pazira reflects on her own changing understanding of the burka. She describes a moment during the filming of *Kandahar* when a young woman named Gulolay asks to be paid for her work on the film with a burka instead of money: "I want it for the night of my wedding," she tells Pazira, "It makes the bride more mysterious and desirable" (311). Pazira's first instinct is to refuse. Although she once understood the burka as a source of safety, she confesses that "since the Taliban made the burqa mandatory, I have begun to despise it, concluding that it is one of the worst symbols and tools of women's oppression" (310–11). She confronts Gulolay, and she compares wearing the burka to being in prison. Gulolay replies, "Why should it be a prison when you want it?" Her comment makes Pazira wonder if perhaps she does not understand the woman's perspective (313). This interaction with Gulolay, and the accompanying history of the burka, which emphasizes themes of agency and mobility, suggests Pazira understands that beneath the burka is an alternate space "for human flourishing" (Ansari 56). It is difficult to say why this nuanced treatment of a complex issue does not appear in *Return to Kandahar*, although the earlier-discussed questions of production should enter into consideration here. It is certainly carried through in Pazira's most recent film, *Acts of Dishonour*, a fictionalized account of the interaction described in *A Bed of Red Flowers* that interrogates the multiple meanings of the burka for Afghan women and for outsiders, with the latter imagining themselves as "saving" Afghan women from their own culture. Reading *Return to Kandahar* in conjunction with *A Bed of Red Flowers* and *Acts of Dishonour* serves as a reminder that, as E. Ann Kaplan points out, a "subjectivity-in-between...needs to be worked through in the process of making art" (237). Pazira uses her art as a medium for working through her understanding of both Afghan and Canadian culture, and her relation to them.

Conclusion: Cultural Translation in the Archive

There are various ways in which to read the archive constituted by Pazira's films and memoir. Through public media response they can be incorporated into the Canadian archive on Afghanistan, and through the frame of feminist critique they can be viewed as an archive of complicity. The archive that has yet to be acknowledged, however, is the artistic one that both evokes the trauma of dislocation and diaspora and demands a more critical and reflexive reading process. For this reason, I propose rereading what Thobani calls Pazira's "strategy of auto-Orientalizing" ("Gender" 227) instead as a *tactic* of auto-Orientalizing. Smaro Kamboureli draws on Michel de Certeau to differentiate between a strategy and a tactic: the former is an "instrument of the dominant order" that reinforces that order, operating much like the Canadian archive on Afghanistan, whereas the latter deliberately reveals the workings of discourse in order to denaturalize its productions (940). What this means is that, depending on how Pazira's documentaries are read, they can be interpreted as reinforcing Canadian constructions of Afghan women as victims who justify military intervention into Afghanistan, or as an Afghan-Canadian woman embracing her liminal cultural position to attempt the task of cultural translation.

Cultural translation, according to Sandra Bermann, provides "hope for insight, reciprocity, and therefore creative negotiation, if never perfect resolution" (8). It is for this reason that Henry Staten describes it as "fundamentally an ethical task" (113). Is it possible for Pazira's films to constitute an archive of cultural translation between Afghanistan and Canada without falling into the trap of complicity with Canadian knowledge production? Such a possibility depends on how the archive is read. The reading I have offered above is an attempt, while acknowledging the other available readings, to suggest an alternative understanding of Pazira's archive as a way to work through a liminal subject position and constantly push the borders of representation.

The possibility of reading Pazira's work against the grain of the archive does not obliterate the archive itself, nor does it entirely erase its complicity. However, a good reading "can hold many possibilities of subjectivity without resorting to narrative closure as a release from the demands of multiplicity" (Buss, "Constructing" 34). An ethical reading of Pazira's work will therefore make space for the many possible readings without demanding a single definitive truth. An ethical reading resists the premature imposition of absolute meaning upon the work of art or document. From this perspective, it is the ethical imperative of the feminist critic not to produce a definitive feminist reading of Pazira's work, but to refuse the closure of meaning, both from within the archive and without.

Notes

1. I would like to thank Daphne Read for her enormous support and encouragement in working through these ideas, Smaro Kamboureli for helping me to reformulate my understanding of the archive, Robert Zacharias and TransCanada Institute for the venue to present this paper at an early stage, and Linda Morra and Jessica Schagerl for this tremendous opportunity and much editorial advice.
2. The death of Osama bin Laden in May 2011 aligns with a more general shift of public attention away from Afghanistan as the primary site of terrorist threat and toward a more diffuse network of countries, including Pakistan, Yemen, and Somalia. In the immediate wake of 9/11, however, media fixation on Afghanistan as the home of the al-Qaeda led to a fascination with the country that produced a bevy of films, books, and television specials.
3. See the *University of Toronto Quarterly* special issue, *Discourses of Security, Peacekeeping Narratives, and the Cultural Imagination in Canada*, edited by Härting and Kamboureli.
4. See Devereux in this volume for an understanding of how the Factiva database, like eBay, might be approached as an archive.
5. In her most recent film, *Acts of Dishonour*, Pazira plays the role of an Afghan-Canadian translator working with a Canadian film crew, another example of the filmmaker's self-reflexive positioning.
6. The story of Thobani's October 1, 2001, speech at the conference of the Canadian Association of Sexual Assault Centres and the ensuing uproar (which included an RCMP charge of inciting hatred against the United States) provide an important perspective on Thobani's own experience of being a woman of colour in post-9/11 Canada. They also shed light on why she might judge Pazira so much more stringently than she does Armstrong. See her conference address (http://www.casac.ca/english/conference01/conf01_thobani.htm) and her response to the ensuing scandal, "War Frenzy," (http://www.casac.ca/english/conference01/thobani_response.htm).
7. See, for example, Jiwani's "Helpless Maidens and Chivalrous Knights," Ansari's "'Should I Go and Pull Her *Burqa* Off?'" and Abu-Lughod's "Do Muslim Women Really Need Saving?"

Works Cited

Abu-Lughod, Lila. "Do Muslim Women Really Need Saving? Anthropological Reflections on Cultural Relativism and Its Others." *American Anthropologist* 104 (2002): 783–90. Print.

Ansari, Usamah. "'Should I Go and Pull Her *Burqa* Off?': Feminist Compulsions, Insider Consent, and a *Return to Kandahar*." *Critical Studies in Media Communication* 25 (2008): 48–67. Web. Mar. 14, 2009.

Audition. Dir. Nelofer Pazira. Kandahar Films Inc., 2008. Film.

"Audition." Def. 1a, 1b. *The Oxford English Dictionary Online*. n.d. Web. Apr. 19, 2009. (http://oed.com/).

Bermann, Sandra. Introduction. *Nation, Language, and the Ethics of Translation*. Ed. Sandra Bermann and Michael Wood. Princeton: Princeton UP, 2005. 1–10. Print.

Buss, Helen M. Introduction. Buss and Kadar 1–5. Print.

———. "Constructing Female Subjects in the Archive: A Reading of Three Versions of One Woman's Subjectivity." Buss and Kadar 23–34. Print.

Buss, Helen M., and Marlene Kadar, eds. *Working in Women's Archives: Researching Women's Private Literature and Archival Documents*. Waterloo: Wilfrid Laurier UP, 2001. Print.

"Cry, the Beloved Country." *Time Canada*. Dec. 3, 2001. Web. Dec. 12, 2009.

Cvetkovich, Ann. "In the Archives of Lesbian Feelings: Documentary and Popular Culture." *Camera Obscura* 49.17 (2002): 107–47. Dec. 18, 2009. Web.

French, Michelle. "Woman with a Focus." *Herizons* 18 (2004): 32–33. Web. Apr. 15, 2009.

Griffith, C. A., and H. L. T. Quan. "The Many Faces of Globalism and the Challenges of Documentary Filmmaking." *Meridians* 2 (2001): 42–57. Print.

Härting, Heike, and Smaro Kamboureli, eds. *Discourses of Security, Peacekeeping Narratives, and the Cultural Imagination in Canada*. Spec. issue of *University of Toronto Quarterly* 78.2 (2009): 659–820. Print.

Heer, Jeet. "Necessary Glimpses of the Real Afghanistan." Rev. of *Kandahar*, dir. Mohsen Makhmalbaf. *National Post* Oct. 26, 2001. Web. Dec. 12, 2009.

"Independent Producers." Canadian Broadcasting Corporation. *CBC.ca*. n.d. Web. Apr. 17, 2009.

Jiwani, Yasmin. "Helpless Maidens and Chivalrous Knights: Afghan Women in the Canadian Press." Härting and Kamboureli 728–44. Print.

Johnson, Brian D. "In the Aftermath of Love and War." *Maclean's* Mar. 31, 2003. Web. Dec. 12, 2009.

Kadar, Marlene. Afterword. Buss and Kadar 115–17. Print.

Kamboureli, Smaro. "The Limits of the Ethical Turn: Troping towards the Other, Yann Martel, and *Self*." *University of Toronto Quarterly* 76.3 (2007): 937–61. Print.

Kandahar. Dir. Mohsen Makhmalbaf. Perf. Nelofer Pazira. Avatar Films, 2001. Film.

Kaplan, E. Ann. *Looking for the Other: Feminism, Film, and the Imperial Gaze*. New York: Routledge, 1997. Print.

Lacey, Liam. "Heart of the Afghan darkness." Rev. of *Kandahar*, dir. Mohsen Makhmalfbaf. *Globe and Mail* Oct. 26, 2001. Web. Dec. 12, 2009.

Naficy, Hamid. *An Accented Cinema: Exilic and Diasporic Filmmaking*. Princeton: Princeton UP, 2001. Print.

O'Driscoll, Michael J. "Derrida, Foucault, and the Archiviolithics of History." *After Poststructuralism: Writing the Intellectual History of Theory*. Ed. Tilottama Rajan and Michael J. O'Driscoll. Toronto: U of Toronto P, 2002. 284–309. Print.

Pazira, Nelofer. *A Bed of Red Flowers: In Search of My Afghanistan*. New York: Free P, 2005. Print.

Razack, Sherene H. "Stealing the Pain of Others: Reflections on Canadian Humanitarian Responses." *Review of Education, Pedagogy, and Cultural Studies* 29 (2007): 375–94. Print.

Return to Kandahar. Dirs. Paul Jay and Nelofer Pazira. Icebreaker Films & j film, 2003. Film.

Sadat, Mir Hekmatullah. "Hyphenating *Afghaniyat* (Afghan-ness) in the Afghan Diaspora." *Journal of Muslim Minority Affairs* 28 (2008): 329–42. Web. Apr. 3, 2009.

Staten, Henry. "Tracking the 'Native Informant': Cultural Translation as the Horizon of Literary Translation." *Nation, Language, and the Ethics of Translation*. Ed. Sandra Bermann and Michael Wood. Princeton: Princeton UP, 2005. 111–26. Print.

Stoler, Ann Laura. "Colonial Archives and the Arts of Governance." *Archival Science* 2 (2002): 87–109. Web. Dec. 18, 2009.

Thobani, Sunera. "Gender and Empire: Veilomentaries and the War on Terror." *Global Communications: Toward a Transcultural Political Economy*. Ed. Paula Chakravartty and Yuezhi Zhao. Lanham: Rowman & Littlefield, 2008. 219–42. Print.

———. "Sunera Thobani's Speech." *From Victimization to Criminalization Conference*. Canadian Association of Sexual Assault Centres. Oct. 1, 2001. Web. July 14, 2009. (http://www.casac.ca/english/conference01/conf01_thobani.htm).

———. "War Frenzy." Canadian Association of Sexual Assault Centres. Oct. 15, 2001. Web. July 14, 2009. (http://www.casac.ca/english/conference01/thobani_response.htm).

Psyche and Her Helpers, under Cloud Cover
Penn Kemp

> We used to live in the imaginary world of the mirror, of the divided self and of the stage, of otherness and alienation. Today we live in the imaginary world of the screen, of the interface and the reduplication of contiguity and networks. All our machines are screens. We too have become screens, and our interactivity has become the interactivity of screens. Nothing that appears on the screen is meant to be deciphered in depth, but actually to be explored instantaneously, in an abreaction immediate to meaning—or an immediate convolution of the poles of representation.
> —*Baudrillard, 7*

> [Archives] are a cloud of witnesses about our society.
> —*Cox, xi*

The urge to sort is at least as old as the myth of Psyche. To regain her beloved god-husband, Eros, Psyche had to placate her mother-in-law, Venus, by overcoming several challenges. In *The Golden Ass,* Apuleius tells us how Psyche must "separate all the grains in a large basket of mixed kinds before nightfall. An ant takes pity on Psyche, and, with its ant companions, separates the grains for her" ("Cupid and Psyche"). For me, these insect helpers represent instinct, the synchronicities of seemingly random choice. For completing her tasks, Psyche is rewarded with a precious box of beauty as a way of assuring her own immortality.

An archive, in some small measure, is a synecdoche for that box of beauty, a soul's work. It has a living quality of its own that draws one in. It includes the activity of a mind/spirit, that larger container for the brain. An archive is not just a dead body of material but also a repository of a life's creative process. Researchers replicate the process of Psyche's sorting in choosing the material that calls out to them. Out of the fragments of material available, they make their own whole through their interaction with the work, just as readers in part create the piece they are reading.

History as a search to delineate the many facets of truth fascinates me. I believe in documentation as a resource, as a memory bank: "these fragments I have shored against my ruins," as Eliot wrote in "The Waste Land" (l. 431). What I don't understand now, I may learn to comprehend later. So I gather information, thoughts, ideas, and collect them in metaphoric heaps until the piles find their own form. Slowly, they take shape and begin to make sense. An archive is more associative than linear for me; it is a spiral of possible interpretations with a historical through-line.

When I was approached to write a short essay for this volume, the editors asked me to reflect on the nature of women, archives, and creativity. "How do you archive creativity?" I was asked. "Can you even claim to do so? Or is it only possible to archive creative output? What does that process mean for someone who wants to research a creative mind?" Creativity, I believe, is less about genius than it is about character: discipline and perseverance. A mind like mine works laterally; the poet in me delights in the pleasure of found surprise. It chafes at logical systems like the archive, even while my inner academic finds agreement in order, the neat completion of years of work. The numerous parts of the brain concur when I perceive the archive as offering a marriage of form and content.

There's a real pleasure in knowing that my work, rough or polished, is stored in a library and available to me—although my archive up to 2010 is in the Rare Book Library at McGill, hundreds of kilometres from London, Ontario, where I live. Though the work is not to hand, it is not lost, either; it is safely stored. Knowing that the work is protected somehow eliminates a false nostalgia that would have stood between me and earlier documents. I'm not distracted by a sense of loss for incomplete work or abandoned files. Projects I have deposited but not completed may always be retrieved. That knowledge frees me to remember more clearly what has been deposited in the archive, without emotional resistance or regret. The archive catalogues most aspects of my life, from first diaries to my own children's drawings as they related to my work. My poetic self always has access to my computer.

It delights in the serendipity of finding files at random, even though I am occasionally frustrated when I can't immediately find what I'm looking for. The trail back home is marked by bread crumbs that won't soon disintegrate in their protected environment.

In 1983, a librarian friend, Bill Rolph, and I initially devised a system of our own to deal with all the different sectors of my work. There was a section for everything, and allowance for all the new projects I could conjure. I was able to maintain this system of filing for the next two decades. Even so, my physical archives are at McGill by happenstance. The archivist who was first interested in collecting my work, Dr. Bruce Whiteman, moved from McMaster to McGill before my first deposit in the mid-1980s. From then on, every five years or so, I made arrangements to take five to ten boxes that had been evaluated down to Montreal. There are about sixty boxes in all. The papers were evaluated by the very knowledgeable book collector Nelson Ball; he took precise notes on their contents, measuring them with his ruler. In 2011, I am delighted to report, my alma mater Western University acquired my archives of the last decade, so now they are only a few blocks from my home.

In the beginning, I presented the material with an eye to beauty as well as notation, then I learned that my carefully marked folders were tossed, replaced by McGill's own organizational system. So now my papers are loosely arranged in manila envelopes, preferably the ones that open along the length so that they can be stuffed and sorted more easily. Until 2001, I was constantly travelling. For years, boxes would accompany me on voyages to my different temporary homes. It was a great relief to ship this history off to a safe place where I was no longer responsible for water damage, mouse droppings, and all the vicissitudes of a life on the move. My need for security is allayed now that I have a house. Because the basement has room, I hadn't deposited in the archives for ten years. I deposit archives in those rare years when I am actually making enought money as a writer to pay taxes, and therefore can claim a percentage of the evaluation as a tax writeoff. But my material is accruing, and I am procrastinating. My excuse is that I might want to access the material piling up in file cabinets downstairs. However, now we are settled (in the house I grew up in!) and even the house contains its own material history extending over sixty years. The walls are lined with my father's paintings, friends' art, mementoes from exotic travels, even a year-long mask-making project. What objects belong to the next shipment to the archives? Could they even deal with this material history, which certainly manifests facets of my creativity? What is still needed for inspiration or comfort? It always comes down to choice, and the consequences of choice. One of the problems with my archive is deciding what to include: books, anthologies, and magazines in which my work has been published, but for which I received only one copy. Books dedicated to me, signed books, or books I have written blurbs for. What do you give to the archive, and what do you keep? What might be needed as a reference, as a record?

What my evaluator is most interested in is the documentation of the creative process. He is suspicious of computer archives, because he argues that they do not track the manuscript changes once made by hand, the emendations and additions that are so interesting to follow. A traditional paper archive allows a researcher to trace creative output systematically, with a tactility that an electronic archive cannot offer. A depth of personality surfaces in the particularities of a print edit: heavy or tentative pencil corrections to a manuscript grant the researcher apparent access to specific creative processes. As by palimpsest, you can glimpse the mood and mind of the author in the tracings of an edit. But I keep different drafts of work, so the creative process can be traced. Digital archives may be as thorough, since every edit might be saved, but they are limited to two dimensions. They are also confined to specific technologies, which are in danger of becoming outmoded and indecipherable. I believe that's what evaluators find difficult about the electronic archives. As well, archivists have not been able to determine a way to evaluate my email archives, as the digital formats keep changing. Will researchers be able to see/read/hear my digital archives in ten years, in twenty?

Documentation through electronic archiving is invaluable in its ability to link one piece to the next by date, size, theme, and subject. My email archives are extensive, sorted by such categories and more. Psyche has her helpful ants, not instinctual this time, but technological. My interviews and performance archives are available in their current format of reel-to-reel, cassette, CD, CD-ROM, video, and DVD. Who knows whether those media will continue to be accessible? In the case of sound archives, there are even more options. Musical, spoken word, and sound poetry are usually stored in standard formats; performances can be stored in various standard formats as well. The current MP3 format, for example, is an industry standard, and can therefore be considered non-proprietary. (MP3 files are compressed to various degrees. The least compressed files are very close to lossless, while offering compression of about 10:1.) Is this part of the way of the future? I need only recall that the first radio production of my work was recorded in 1973 on KRAB FM in Seattle; and my first book, *Bearing Down*, was performed with four voices and recorded on a reel-to-reel tape that was included in one of my first deposits at McGill.

Pendas Productions is a literary micro-publishing house run by my husband, Gavin Stairs, and me. Gavin is our designer, publisher, and in-house technologist. He explains all things digital. We operate from the position that poetry doesn't sell anyway, except from the stage. So why not make as much as possible available online? What is developed locally can go viral. I archive many sound operas and interviews on www.radio.com/talk/gatheringvoices, my Literature-on-Air show broadcast on Western University's radio station (CHRW). We are very active on Facebook, where I advertise frequently to literary contacts. On myspace.com/pennkemp we've had thousands of visitors, with excellent comments and name recognition. Online social networks like Facebook, Twitter, and MySpace have allowed writers like me to distribute their work, store material, and make our content widely available. However, such online archives are transient and arbitrary, beyond our control. Everyone who posts material online also needs to be very careful about privacy. In paper archives, you can limit what is available to researchers: some correspondence might be read only after death. So what is the trade-off? What happens to our online material? Google, for example, hopes to become the main depository of your digital life, enveloping all your transactions in their overarching cloud. In return, they argue, you will be able to access all data anywhere, anytime.

I'm not a digital native, but I'm learning a lot about the growing influence of the cloud on the Internet, what I call the cloud cover. I'm even archiving much of my work there. The Internet makes it possible to project your archives into virtual space. You stay connected to your readers. You are part of the shift. Like many other writers who live their lives under the digital cloud cover, I am a guinea pig in this new experiment. The cloud is a metaphor for a collective computing network. It is not one cloud but many, some of which are transient, such as the social networks. Others are more permanent, as they are, to a degree, stored under your control. In some ways, clouds are more permanent than personal storage, because the job of keeping the media and access current falls to the archivist, data collective, or corporation. In the current cloud metaphor, it should be the archive's job to transfer everything and to keep it current. A cloud model archive could be organized much as a backup service is now, with a widget in the client's computer which transfers data as it is created, with appropriate annotation, to a database at the archive. Or rather, which is the archive. That this archive would be large is a given—rather normal in these days, as large online databases are proliferating everywhere. They depend on cheap, redundant mass storage technology that can be quite easily replaced with no loss of data, and will ordinarily keep pace with technological advancements. Such an archive will be easily searched, collated, and analyzed using tools becoming more and more common.

So much has changed over the time I've been writing. As a child of the Cold War, I did not expect to live long, let alone leave such a documented trail behind me. Who could have guessed that I would leave such a substantial digital trail? A paper trail like mine, I assumed, would be vaporized by nuclear war. That fear did not deter me from committing words to paper—I wrote voraciously against the threat of total destruction—but it did instill an overshadowing sense of impermanence. As a Buddhist, I believe that all things are temporary, but in relative terms, the library is a hell of a lot better than an inferno. It is such a blessing to know that the work will be saved for longer than I would ever have imagined when I started out. It doesn't really matter to me if my archive is mulled over by graduate students, or ignored, or forgotten. I know it lives on in a physical place, more than a virtual reality. I am still happy to wave goodbye to boxes of my past lives, as if I were seeing kids off to school. Although my house collects "stuff" seemingly on its own, I continue to pare down, to simplify, to prioritize, even as the scope of my work widens into ever more projects. Contrary trends continue, enantiodromian, assuming different weights of importance and priorities over time, to which I may return. And I continue to record and amass. Even if I had had a safe place to store my work in decades past, the purging of papers would have been necessary every so often to prepare a clean slate, a new beginning.

Works Cited

Baudrillard, Jean. *Simulacra and Simulation*. Trans. Sheila Faria Glaser. Ann Arbor: U of Michigan P, 1995. Print.

Cox, Richard J. *Personal Archives and a New Archival Calling: Reading Reflections and Ruminations*. Litwin Books, 2009. Print.

"Cupid and Pysche." *Carnaval.com*. Carnaval, n.d. Web. Apr. 29, 2010. (http://www.carnaval.com/isis/gold/).

Eliot, T. S. "The Waste Land." *The Norton Anthology of English Literature*. 6th ed. Vol. 2. New York: W. W. Norton, 1993. 2147–60. Print.

II. Restrictions

Archival Matters
Sally Clark

I am a Canadian playwright. My first play, *Lost Souls and Missing Persons*, was produced by Theatre Passe Muraille under the direction of Clarke Rogers in 1984. I wrote several plays after that, including *Moo*, *The Trial of Judith K.*, *Life Without Instruction*, and *Jehanne of the Witches*, to name a few.

In the early 1990s, some of my writer friends were "selling" their archives to universities for "large sums of money."[1] They were urging me to do the same. It seemed too early. I associate archiving with taking stock. It's like clearing an attic. You get rid of old things so you can move on. But in order to do so, you must stop and reflect on where you've been. If you're still in the current, the last thing you want to do is stop. I felt that I was just getting started, that I didn't have time to stop and sort through my work. You can't create new work while you're archiving old work, and if your old work is only a few years old, then the act of self-reflection is bound to prevent any new ideas from strolling into your head.

I write in longhand, and when those sheets of paper start to pile up and look like they're going somewhere, I then type them into my computer and print out the pages. I use these sheets as my hard copy and edit or rearrange from there. As I work, the paper becomes a living entity. Even when the play is finished, the pages retain possibilities for other directions. I wrote a screenplay for *Lost Souls and Missing Persons* about ten years after I wrote the play. A screenplay is often radically different from the source material. For instance, there were scenes that had been taken out of the play because they were too filmic, and those abandoned scenes worked well in the screenplay. I found it extremely helpful to have the early drafts close at hand and not in some library halfway across the country.

For me, archiving one's work has a finality to it that puts it in the same category as making a will or getting married. Issues of disposing of one's property and accepting one's mortality come to the fore. It can take many years before I feel that I am "done" with a particular piece of writing. Once I am finished with it though, that pile of paper goes from being a wealth of possibilities to garbage. It is alive or it is dead; there is no interim stage for me. As I never had the time or inclination to spend an afternoon sorting through my papers to see which ones were really dead and which were playing possum, I simply put them into boxes and left them.

In 2007, I finally decided to try and donate or sell my archives. Since the 1990s, funding for universities has steadily dwindled, along with funding for the arts. When money is tight—and, for as long as I can remember, it has always been "tight" for the arts—then that great wealth of archival material becomes nothing more than a pile of mouldy papers. What distinguishes those papers from garbage? Seeking a buyer for one's archives is similar to brokering a marriage. A writer with papers is like a bride with her dowry, carrying the intrinsic risk of waiting too long to sell the goods. The negotiation is over what the dowry is worth and the unspoken factoring of what the bride is worth. There is the sense of being formally accepted in Society. Does someone think you're worth keeping?

What are you worth? Andy Warhol's prediction that everyone would have fifteen minutes of fame was uncannily accurate. I think of television stars who were worth a lot at the height of their careers, and are now forgotten. Should we be collecting their "stuff" for archives? Where do you draw the line at archival matter? When does someone go from being unimportant to being someone whose papers and ephemera are worth keeping?

I decided not to dwell any further on these fruitless ruminations and set myself to the task at hand. I was aware that the University of Guelph was collecting the archives of Canadian theatre artists. I asked Ric Knowles, who is a professor at Guelph, if he thought the library there would be interested in my papers. Ric put me in touch with Lorne Bruce, the Head of Archives and Special Collections at the University of Guelph Library. Lorne said that the university would be very interested in receiving a donation of my archival material. They would appraise it and issue me a tax receipt for the value. I asked Lorne if it would be all right for me to donate a portion of my archives, and reserve the rest for a later time. He said that would be fine, and in fact, that it was much wiser to do that than try and deposit everything at once.

I started to realize that I had made many erroneous assumptions about "archives," the first one being the belief that I had to hand over everything at once. For some obscure reason, I had assumed that selling one's archives was like selling a house. You couldn't sell the basement and keep the top two floors, you had to sell the whole house. My agent used to refer to my plays as properties, so I suppose that's where I got the idea. I also assumed that if you "sold" your archives, then you had to include your correspondence. This was another reason I hesitated to approach archives, because I felt that it would be wrong to expose my friends' letters to public scrutiny.

In my letters to friends, I often adopted a certain persona that was more a reflection of the receiver than of me. A gay friend and I used to meet for dinner on a regular basis. He would always launch into a story about the latest young man who took his fancy. Years later, in my letters to him, I unconsciously took on his persona and wrote as one gay man to another, exaggerating my experiences to make them more interesting for him. I suppose I was trying to recreate the sorts of conversations that we used to have. In letters to old friends, I reverted to being the person I was when I last saw them. For me, a letter is a personal matter between the sender and the receiver, so I don't think I have the right to sell or donate my friends' letters. I consider it an invasion of their privacy.

Computers have also changed the nature of personal correspondence. One sends a letter with the assumption that no one, other than the receiver, will read it. Because emails can be widely disseminated, one's guard is up when composing them. I hope that my email will remain with the person to whom I sent it, but I don't assume that it will. Email is, by its very nature, public. My emails are different from my letters, less intimate. Forewarned or not, I still wouldn't hand my friends' emails to an archive.

One can choose, of course, to ignore correspondence altogether. Lorne sent me a list of items that could be considered, and I was surprised to discover that it was quite extensive: production files, manuscripts and scripts by others, theatre programs, clippings and printed material, art material, posters, videotapes, financial material, and so on. The inclusion of "financial material" surprised me. Years ago, I had merrily thrown out all the accumulated bills and financial records for a production of *Saint Frances of Hollywood* in Toronto in 1994. Hrant Alianak was the "real" producer of the show. He kept meticulous records. When I found out about the archival list, I called Hrant and said, "Keep your financial records of all those shows you produced. They're actually worth something." He had already consigned them to the dumpster years ago. Who knew? Neither of us considered drafting a budget and managing the bills to be a collectible asset, but then with the 2009 stock market crash, we've all seen just how creative accounting can be.

As I was sorting through my "material," I realized that I had several binders documenting my own "archival" research for the plays. I've written quite a few plays based on historical incidents, and have often made use of university libraries and archives. I usually begin with a vague idea of a subject that intrigues me. I like to spend a few months reading books about it, and looking for that hook that will propel me into action. Once I find it, I have to act fast. I collect the information as quickly as possible; I can't afford to get bogged down in details. I remain true to the historical facts, although my interpretation of those facts is usually radically different from the accepted history. I prefer to write about stories for which the information is murky, such as the relationship between Joan of Arc and Gilles de Rais. I write plays, and the very nature of the word should suggest that I am "playing" with the subject and inviting the audience to do likewise.

In 1986, I started to write a play about Artemisia Gentileschi. I had first encountered her story in Germaine Greer's book on women artists, *The Obstacle Race*. Artemisia's paintings are bold and horrifying; no delicate flowers in vases for her. Several of her paintings depict Judith chopping off the head of Holofernes. The male artists of her time usually portray Judith holding a sword and a basket and sporting a secret smile, hinting at the contents of the basket. Artemisia shows Judith hacking away at Holofernes' neck as if she were slaughtering an ox, blood spurting out—a messy business. Artemisia's father Orazio was a well-respected painter who was a follower of Caravaggio. Although Orazio had three sons, he trained his nine-year-old daughter Artemisia in his craft—a highly unusual act. When she was fourteen, he asked his best friend, Agostino Tassi, a known womanizer and suspected murderer, to teach Artemisia "perspective." At her first lesson, Tassi raped her. The irony of the lesson, and the expedient manner in which Artemisia recovered from the rape and became absorbed in producing her ferocious paintings fascinated me. After the rape, Artemisia and Tassi became secretly engaged. Later, Tassi stole some of Orazio's paintings and claimed them for his dowry. Orazio was furious with him, so he sued Tassi for theft and, as an afterthought, rape. In the ensuing court case, Tassi denied the engagement and claimed that he had never met Artemisia.

When I first had the idea for the play (1986), I could find no books written in English about Artemisia Gentileschi. I found university theses and journal articles, but most of the authors focused on Orazio's work. There was little mention of his personal history, or the court case. There were probably books written about her in Italian, but I couldn't afford to hire someone to translate them. I desperately wanted to find a copy of the trial, but it, too, was available only in Italian. Then I had a stroke of luck. I found Roland Barthes's book, *Une acte de viol in 1610,* which was an analysis of the relationship between Artemisia, her chaperone Tutia (who was curiously absent for the first lesson), Orazio, and Tassi. The book included the trial documents as an appendix. I couldn't find an English translation of Barthes's book, but I knew enough French to take on the task of doing my own translation. After I had completed the play, Mary Garrard's comprehensive biography on Artemisia Gentileschi was published, in English, of course. In many ways, I relished the challenge of having to track down Artemisia's story. It made her struggle more alive for me.

In 2001, Michael Clark, then Artistic Director of Nakai Theatre, commissioned me to write a play about the Yukon. I was having difficulty with the commission. I had read many recent books about the Yukon, but hadn't yet found my story. I was given an opportunity to stay at Berton House in Dawson City for the winter. The library there had many autobiographies written by people who had lived in the city through the gold rush era. These books had been out of print for at least fifty years. They were a treasure trove: idiosyncratic, full of lies and tall tales, they conjured up a vivid sense of how life was back then.

One book that particularly interested me was divided into two volumes. The first volume was written by a prospector named Ed Lung, the second by his wife, Velma. The contrast between the two accounts was quite hilarious. Ed was congenitally unlucky, always in the wrong place at the wrong time, always missing the gold. He thought of Velma as his lucky star and, in truth, she was. She managed to steer Ed in the right direction, and eventually they found their gold, a modest claim that gave them some money. Most of the book was devoted to the struggles to make their fortune. As an afterthought in her memoirs, Velma mentions that their sled dog, Rover, was highly intelligent. Inclement weather forced Ed and Rover to stay in a cabin alone for one month. To pass the time, Ed taught Rover to laugh, and then to talk, and finally to walk around on his two hind legs and pretend he was a person. According to Ed, Rover had quite a large vocabulary, his favourite phrases being "Hello Daddy" and "When's dinner?" It didn't seem to occur to Ed or Velma that Rover's ability to talk was unusual behaviour. They probably could have made a small fortune touring the States with their talking dog. Instead, they remained in Dawson City. Rover was given an honourary membership in the Dawson City Athletic Society, and performed at their functions on occasion. Are the tales about Rover true or false? After spending so much time reading these memoirs, everything seems likely.

The inspiration for my play *Wanted* came from a gruesome account described in Kathryn Winslow's book *Big Pan-Out*. In 1898, one of the saloons had a special act. A man would mount a realistic scaffold, allow his arms to be tied behind his back and a noose placed around his neck. "The platform was then pulled out from under him and he dropped into space to dangle until his face turned purple. At that point, the curtain was drawn. A different man was recruited every night so the customers could not be sure whether the hanged man lived through the ordeal. It added to the horror of it for them to remain in doubt" (Winslow n.p.). When I read about this "entertainment," I felt compelled to write a scene around it. Three characters dominated my scene: the hanged man, his female lover, and the man who arranged the hanging. I wrote the hanging scene first, and then wrote the rest of the play to discover who these characters were.

Of all this material, what will be considered archival in the future? The nature of archival material has changed enormously. Over the last century, typewritten pages have managed to acquire the same fetishistic allure as longhand. In 1980, a first draft would be handwritten pages or a hand-typed draft; it had more value because it was unique. It was a fetish: the original One. With computers, the One is reduced to a blip on a CD. It can be printed out, and who would know one copy from another? There's no texture, no impact of typewriter keys on the pages, no tear stains, or scotch spills—just bland, printer-perfect pages. I suppose, if you're feeling enormously generous, you could throw in a very old computer printout for the archives, something with a trace of mould around the edges or a rusted stain where the paper clip that held it together used to be.

Can a floppy disc ever hold the same appeal? Is it even collectible? "Here's the floppy that my novel was on" simply doesn't have the same panache as "here's my manuscript." DVDs are particularly alarming when you discover your entire life's work consists of one fraction of its disc space. It's all over in the blink of an eye. In the grand scheme of things, that's all one's life is. A blink of an eye.

Note

1 Selling one's archives actually meant that one "donated" one's archival material, which was then assessed, and the university or library then issues the author a tax receipt.

Works Cited

Barthes, Roland. *Actes d'un procès pour viol en 1612.* France: Editions des Femmes, 1984. Print.

Garrard, Mary D. *Artemesia Gentileschi.* Princeton: Princeton UP, 1991. Print.

Winslow, Kathryn. *Big Pan-Out.* New York: W. W. Norton & Co., 1951. Print.

Keeping the Archive Door Open: Writing about Florence Carlyle
Susan Butlin

Doing archival research on Canadian women's history presents particular research and methodological challenges. Because of the especially fragmentary nature of the archive on pre-1920s women in Canada, it is necessary for researchers to see beyond classifications and canon, and to be open to the unexpected. In her article "'A Dusting Off': An Anecdotal Account of Editing the L. M. Montgomery Journals," Mary Rubio speaks of the problems of writing about a well-known subject and points out that a new look may go against the grain and make fans unhappy. This problem occurs not only in writing about a familiar subject. In my own historical research about the Canadian artist Florence Carlyle (1864–1923) for my book, *The Practice of Her Profession: Florence Carlyle, Canadian Painter in the Age of Impressionism*, I found that archives and recent writings about her tended to edit her production and interests to a uniformly narrow shape.[1] She was presented as a painter; however, her production was identified as portraiture, landscapes, daily life and the domestic, otherwise known as "genre"—that is, subject matter in the "high art" category. Indeed, most of the archival materials in specially organized artist's files kept at important national institutions overwhelmingly supported this view of her work. As I came to know my subject and her production better, however, I realized that much was not being said about her canon, and some of her works were not admitted to it. In fact, Carlyle's career, production, and life were much more eclectic than the archive or previous writing about her has dared to admit.

My recent work on Canadian women artists active in the period prior to 1914 shows that scholarship in this area has tended to be erratic and narrow in focus for most of these women ("A New Matrix"). Many of the careers and achievements, and much of the production by Canadian women artists of this period have been lost to art history. A number of these artists, including Florence Carlyle, were well known during their lifetimes, but subsequently marginalized by the art history canon. This essay explores the research trajectory I followed and addresses questions and difficulties I encountered while writing my book on Carlyle; it reveals the special challenges that one faces when writing about women in this period because, in part, of the scant material that survives about Canadian women in pre-1920s archives.

There are many challenges inherent in writing biography, and the researcher would do well to accept that historical sources are potentially flawed and unreliable. Historical formulations of identity are continuously negotiated, a process that is never complete. "All representation has a politics; it also has a history," Linda Hutcheon asserted in *Remembering Postmodernism*, "[i]ssues of gender, class, race, etc. are now part of the discourse of the visual arts/ literary arts. Social history cannot be separated from the history of art: in both, memory is at work" (129). Thus, research in women's archives begs a special awareness of the limitations and potentially misleading biases that may occur as a result of incomplete collections or partial survival of archival materials; in particular, the researcher needs to be sensitive and open to historical and personal contexts.

Indeed, researchers need to take an expansive approach to the careers of nineteenth- and early-twentieth-century women artists and writers. A broader context for the work of women artists reveals both the range and diversity of their artistic production and their entrepreneurial skills and leadership. Often, such an approach reveals these women's connections with colleagues in the arts, editors, dealers, and clients, and includes critical reception, because critics' opinions could also have an impact on sales and profit. I employed this expansive approach in *The Practice of Her Profession*. When conducting my primary research for the book, I patiently trailed after Florence Carlyle through the archives, books, articles, and catalogue essays. I interviewed her relatives, read her letters, and looked at her paintings. Here, in this world of creaking filing cabinets and dimly lit closet archives, hundred-year-old scrapbooks pasted with valuable ephemera threatened to crumble to dust as I turned the pages. Paintings jiggled in their frames, held there only by the efforts of a rusty nail or two. I read about her production that is not extant. Looking for any mention of her or her work, I searched through microfilmed newspapers for exhibition reviews, and for art and social columns. I thought about her personality and relationships, intimate and otherwise. I studied the artist in photographs, toured the house in which she grew up (introducing myself to the present owner), and imagined the events she attended, going so far as to recreate one of these in a semi-fictional account. These efforts helped to build a context, and ultimately I made connections between Florence Carlyle, her colleagues, and what was hidden about her life and production. It led to more questions.

Since I was living in Ottawa at the time, my initial research began with the artist clipping file on Carlyle, and curatorial files relating to her two paintings in the collection of the National Gallery of Canada (NGC) in Ottawa. I gathered from these that she was a painter and that she had exhibited widely on a national scale, and to a limited extent, abroad. I also learned that her work was admired sufficiently in the years prior to 1914 such that two of her paintings had been purchased by the NGC. The fact that they were not on view in the Canadian galleries, however, and have not been for some time, led me to speculate that she was not deemed an important artist within the national canon of art.

One of the goals of my research and the subsequent book on Carlyle was to rectify the gaps and omissions in our art historical knowledge about women artists in order to reinstate artists like Carlyle and their production in the art historical canon. This task is ongoing. In Canada, as elsewhere in the world, restoring the archives is as challenging as reinstating women in the canon of art history. As Griselda Pollock asserts, the task of revising the canon, that which sanctions what art we should study, also involves grappling with the terms that caused the neglect of women artists, and an analysis and critique of the hierarchy of gender (23–29). The canon is divided between high art and craft art forms. The former, painting and sculpture, has been seen as creative, whereas the latter—textile arts, illustration, and jewellery design—has traditionally been viewed as merely decorative, dexterous production. This devaluation came about, in part, because such work was associated with traditional production by women, and so was classed as quintessentially "feminine." Such production thus lacked status, and could not be accommodated by the "high art" classification. This division has been challenged on behalf of Western women and non-Western cultures in general by feminist art historians, who have exposed the capriciousness of the entire value system and have argued that such valuations of art by the canon are culturally biased and influenced by gender, not based on excellence (Pollock 25).

What I had found in the NGC files on Carlyle was quite limited. Although I did not know it at the time, the artist and the diversity of her production had been edited by those whose value system diminished her to something akin to a ten-line entry in a catalogue. Clearly, this initial foray was only going to take me so far. These humble beginnings and my encounter with Carlyle's archival holdings in other large institutions left me little choice but to pursue out-of-the-way archives and, eventually, private holdings. I was obliged to conclude that it is not consistently the archive of the largest size or those within national institutions that may hold the most complete or helpful collections on historical Canadian women. I discovered that small and more obscure archival deposits can offer a diversity, depth, and wealth that brings the subject into much sharper focus. Although there is a risk, in spending the time and effort to search out and visit small archives, that one may come up with nothing, this has rarely been my experience. Instead, archival holdings close to where the subject was born, grew up, or worked, or those in close proximity to where the extended family lived sometimes possess unique or more extensive material, because the collecting habits and goals of these archives often differ substantially from those of the larger national institutions.

In Canada, the collections policy of national institutions appears to privilege the stars of the Canadian art history canon. By contrast, small archival holdings on a local subject may have been in existence for a longer period of time, perhaps even before the person was known in the broader context. These holdings are rarely edited for content as the national ones may be, so that virtually everything connected with the subject goes in. Small archives of this sort include, for example, regional history collections in local public libraries, archival holdings in local museums and small galleries, or regional county archives. These archives collect materials about local artists or writers and see them within a context of place, family, colleagues, and the local artistic milieu or history. The material about the subject is often waiting there to be perused; it has not been edited out as unimportant or extraneous. Personal details are also frequently retained in the local archival collection: minutiae about the subject's production and professional practices, her habits, those she knew, and anecdotes about her are often kept and valued as personal connections to a local subject.

Florence Carlyle grew up in the town of Woodstock, Ontario, and lived there in the 1870s and 1880s. She left in 1890 to study in France for five years, but returned in the late 1890s to open a working studio in Woodstock and a teaching studio in nearby London. Natalie Luckyj, who had spearheaded research into historical Canadian women artists in the 1970s, suggested that I visit the small art gallery in Woodstock, since they had a number of Carlyle paintings.[2] Indeed, the gallery turned out to be an important source of archival material for Carlyle and her work. The curator kindly gave me access to all of her paintings and to the two metal filing cabinets that held photographs, newspaper clipping files, and Carlyle's letters and family memoirs, including one by her cousin Helene Youmans, who had accompanied the artist to New York City as a model for the Osborne Calendar Company commissions.[3] The gallery staff introduced me to the artist's niece, Florence Carlyle Johnston, who invited me to lunch at her apartment, where her collection of inherited Carlyle paintings was hung salon style, covering the walls from floor to ceiling. Most of these works were donated to the Woodstock gallery after Mrs. Johnston's death several years later.[4] While in Woodstock, I located and photographed the artist's home on Wilson Street and looked for evidence of the "red barn" behind the house which had served as her studio between trips to New York. The house, while still standing, had deteriorated and lost both its elegant front porch and the barn behind it. Sadly (though perhaps not surprisingly), the house had not been identified as a historical or heritage landmark.

The research trip to the Woodstock Art Gallery met my hopeful expectations. It proved to be a key source of material. More serendipitous discoveries awaited me on later research trips to Toronto. These findings taught me to understand that, as a researcher, I could not consistently plan for what I would encounter but must be open to hints and clues. The research trips started out predictably enough. Located adjacent to their historic buildings on the Toronto waterfront, the archives of the Canadian National Exhibition (CNE) gave me access to their collection of annual art department exhibition catalogues. This allowed me to chart the artist's exhibition history in relation to this important venue. Carlyle's art activity with the CNE dated from 1880, when Princess Louise (1848–1939), a daughter of Queen Victoria and the wife of the Governor General, had toured the exhibition displays, and bought one of Carlyle's paintings.

Another research trip led me to London, Ontario, where Carlyle had a teaching studio for several years, from about 1904. I hoped to find some information on her clients, answers to the question of where and to whom she sold her work, or other evidence of how she conducted her professional life. When I visited the archive at Museum London, much to my disappointment, the artist file on Carlyle was almost literally paper thin. But it did contain a letter dated December 6, 1922 from Carlyle to a Mr. O. B. Graves, who turned out to be a dealer in art and the owner of a commercial gallery in London, Ontario that sold paintings, wallpaper, and paint and artists' supplies.

Then, as now, artists had to think in terms of profit and loss, and of income in relation to expenses. In addition to selling work in public exhibitions, Canadian women artists of Carlyle's generation regularly exhibited and sold work through commercial galleries.[5] The language of the time, however, reflected women's partial inclusion in the Canadian art scene. Although there was a growing presence of female entrepreneurs in Canada in the years prior to 1914, there was also social resistance to women running businesses. Such resistance even manifests itself in the fact that there was no vocabulary to describe them. By the 1910s, the term "business woman" was commonly used, but it referred to a stenographer, typist, or clerk, not to entrepreneurs such as Carlyle (Deutsch 117).

Yet many women artists in the period saw new applications for their skills as cultural professionals and exploited them: artists such as Estelle Kerr (1879–1971), who edited arts columns as a sideline to her painting and illustrating work; or Harriet Ford (1859–1938), who branched out into domestic mural and furniture designs; Elizabeth McGillivray Knowles (1866–1928) organized and advertised exhibit tours of her work in commercial venues, such as department store galleries at Eaton's or Simpson's, rooms in hotels, or her own studio.[6] Women artists learned to be entrepreneurs and to run their art practices as businesses, for without a private income, the business would not survive.

As I read and reread Carlyle's letter to her London, Ontario, dealer, I realized that it contained significant details about how women artists marketed their art production.[7] In addition to revealing her friendship with Graves, it also showed her business acumen. At the time she wrote the letter, Carlyle, who was living in England, was on holiday in Canada and staying in Toronto with her sister, Maude. The artist had previously sent some older paintings to Graves to exhibit and sell in his store. In this letter, she invites him frankly to make her an offer for the unsold works. She negotiates their value with a fined-tuned business sense. There is evidence of the closeness of their relationship, as she confides to him that she is not well. "My health is such that my people are packing me off to England at once.... you have always been a friend—please stand by me again. Make me an offer for the pictures—will you?... I sail from New York next Thursday. Do you think I can have the cheque by then, Mr. Graves?"[8] Carlyle leaves Canada and dies at her home in Sussex, England, five months later. This letter, one of her last, is likely her final professional correspondence.

This rare and fragile letter that survives in the Museum London archive is important for the light it sheds on how Carlyle, and by implication,

Canadian women artists of her generation engaged with the business world as professionals and negotiated fair prices for their art production. Yet more evidence was to emerge that revealed the extent of Carlyle's success in guiding her professional career with respect to commercial and business activities.

About this time, I arranged to visit the archive of the Women's Art Association of Canada, located in a white Victorian house situated in park-like grounds on a quiet side street in the area of Yorkville in Toronto. Carlyle's colleague, Mary Ella Williams Dignam (1857–1938),[9] had founded the Women's Art Club in Toronto in 1887. This Canadian women's art institution was incorporated in 1892 as the Women's Art Association of Canada, and played an important role in sustaining women artists in this country in the years prior to about 1914. Although I had expected the building to be a kind of museum dedicated to the Women's Art Association's history, I was surprised to find that the association remains active and holds art lecture series and exhibitions for its female membership. The archive holdings appeared to be a relatively unimportant aspect, as evidenced by their location at the time in a small closet of an upstairs reception room. However, the dedication to chronicling the activity of the association and its members, of which Carlyle had been one was there: it manifested in a rich yet fragile collection of scrapbooks, photographs, and catalogues extending back over one hundred years, from which they graciously allowed me to photocopy. As I was doing this, I had an amiable conversation with one of the directors who asked me, "Of course, you know the Florence Carlyle at the Granite Club?" In fact, I knew the whereabouts of very few of her paintings in private hands and holdings. I replied that, while I had heard of this historic Toronto curling club, I did not know anything about their art collection.

Armed with this information, I was able to visit the Granite Club and study a Carlyle painting generally unknown to the larger academic art world. The painting, *Summer*, was likely purchased by the club directly from the artist at an Ontario Society of Artists exhibition around 1901. Discovering that *Summer* had been bought by a private club confirmed that Carlyle's work was received with great interest in Canada by 1900; her work had been admired not only by critics but also by the Canadian public, including prestigious clients like the Granite Club and the National Club in Toronto. These discoveries rendered me sensitive to the sales aspect of Carlyle's art practice and, over time, helped me to see the business side of the professional art practices used by Carlyle and her female colleagues. They eventually led me to conclude that the artists themselves, in the production and marketing choices they made, effectively worked as entrepreneurs

Figure 5 *Summer*, ca. 1901, Florence Carlyle. Oil on canvas, 100 x 57.9 cm. From the Collection of the Granite Club, Toronto. Photograph by Dave Starrett, Toronto.

at a time when women were actively discouraged from involvement in the commercial and professional world.

The search for clues about Carlyle's professional art practice and production led to some surprising and frankly unwanted findings—at times, I did not know what to do with them. I had hoped to find information on her clients, the portraits that were commissioned, and wealthy private collectors. I did find these, but in addition I uncovered evidence of commissioned work she did for an American calendar company for which she regularly journeyed to her studio in New York during the winter months to paint popular subjects within a narrow field and strict timelines. These paintings were used as calendar art and, compared to the sporadic commissions and sales of her high art, the pay from the calendar commissions was regular and lucrative. I also found that she was trying to get a novel published. What had happened to my artist dedicated to high art? I set this material to one side, and looked at it out of the corner of my eye.

Encountering these unexpected discoveries raised the question about how they fit into the picture I was forming of Carlyle's life and work. Like most historical researchers, it had taken me a long time to come to grips with my subject. I discovered that the unexpected may be disruptive for the researcher, yet my feelings of dislike (for a time) for the unexpected material led to a greater understanding of my own subjectivity as a researcher and writer. I became acutely and uncomfortably aware of what was meant by researcher bias, because I had found it in myself.

Carlyle's calendar work with the Osborne Calendar Company of New York City, mentioned in newspaper clippings I discovered in a regional history archive at the London (Ontario) Public Library, gave me a sense of how lucrative these commissions were. With my newfound sensitivity to the business end of a woman's art practice at the turn of the twentieth century, I paid increasing attention. The reaction of Olaf P. Rechnitzer, a columnist in London, Ontario, even some fifteen years after the release of the Osborne calendars, gave contemporary and local opinion to this aspect of her production and art activity (17). Rechnitzer was an admirer of these New York calendar commissions, and did not denigrate them as simply popular art. The contemporary and regional reaction stands in stark contrast to the present-day attitude, which tends to devalue commercial calendar artwork commissions by "fine art" artists, because they are not seen as belonging to the high art category valued by the canon. Interestingly, nothing about Carlyle's calendar commissions was included in the archives of the large national institutions I visited.

It is important to point out that commercial and craft production by Canadian artists who are considered central to the canon of Canadian art stands a better chance of inclusion in archival collections and contemporary scholarship than similar work by artists such as Carlyle, who are situated on the margins of the canon. For example, Tom Thomson (1877–1917) and members of the Group of Seven, including J. E. H. MacDonald (1873–1932), worked at the Toronto commercial art firm Grip Limited. Commercial production and activity by members of the Group of Seven, while generally presented as secondary in importance to their high art paintings, is regarded as an integral part of their professional activity; this production has thus been included in scholarship on them.[10] Recent scholarship on Emily Carr (1871–1945), one of the few historical Canadian women painters of that generation to have attained iconic status today, does include discussion of her commercial and craft production.[11]

In comparison, while researching my PhD dissertation, in which I examined the careers of more than fifty of Carlyle's Canadian women artist contemporaries, I realized that this approach of reconstructing the artist into a narrow shape that admits only certain facts about her life and work is a disturbing recurrence ("A New Matrix" 261–64). I concluded from this analysis that the canon divides high art from craft art forms. I have also deduced that the lives and production of artists such as Carlyle, who may have been well known during their lifetimes but who are little known within contemporary art historical knowledge, are generally seen in narrow terms; their craft and commercial production often omitted from their oeuvre. By contrast, the value placed on the art production by canonical artists such as Emily Carr and the Group of Seven is very high, so high that their production in craft and commercial art forms is sometimes included in discussions of their lives and work, although, even in this context, it is often devalued and seen as peripheral to, or supportive of, their "high" art production.

Eventually, my research into Carlyle's work for the Osborne Calendar Company yielded an understanding of my own subjectivity and greater insight into Carlyle's life and work. These discoveries helped me to understand the broader context of an artist's life as an entrepreneur, and to value her production without hierarchical judgment, whether it was in the traditionally "high" art categories, handicraft, or popular commercial areas. My change in attitude to what was emerging in the archive helped me establish a new and complex picture of the artist. I no longer viewed Carlyle as just "spinning in her own orbit," but as part of a community of other artists, dealers, art critics, editors, and clients—whether private, state, or commercial. Her production demonstrated a startling diversity.

The inclusion of the entire oeuvre of historical women artists and writers, specifically incorporating this diversity of production, is important for what it contributes to the project of establishing a more comprehensive cultural history. This more inclusive practice raises questions about the dangers of "picking and choosing," of making decisions about what should be emphasized and included, or excluded, when writing about women artists and their production. Here, the theoretical insights of Philippe Lejeune are helpful in raising ethical issues relating to the distortion of archival remains, which include the imposition, by others, of a constructed identity on a subject (206).[12] Lejeune suggests that we should avoid an appropriation of the archival remains and work toward what might be termed an explication. Thus, I believe avoiding the imposition of our desires or subjectivities onto the archive is important. The rich diversity of the archival remains, while at times perplexing, should be allowed to point the way in our research.

Diversity was valued by cultural historian Raymond Williams, who wrote about the necessity of not overemphasizing the importance of one cultural element. He argued against valuing what he termed emergent cultural elements or "high" art forms over popular, or "dominant," cultural elements (qtd. in Tippett 556). Historians, he believed, should look at all the components that define activity in artistic culture rather than privileging one area of cultural production over another, because doing so may involve a value judgment. Williams's theories in this respect are applicable to the ongoing project of a more inclusive recovery of women artists' and writers' total art practice. Such a history would include Florence Carlyle's calendar paintings—but also similar material by Canadian artist colleagues. So, for example, such a history would take into account Mary Bell Eastlake's jewellery creations; Mary Riter Hamilton's work with textiles; Harriet Ford's writing, furniture, and jewellery work; and Estelle Kerr's textual production as a newspaper columnist ("A New Matrix" 228–70).

In researching women in the archives, I saw a problem with the inclusion of only high art production and activity, especially *in archival practices*, not just in exhibitions and writings. Such practices limit the ability to see anything beyond this high art production, for whatever reason. Sometimes in an archival collection, the message conveyed to the public and academy is that the inclusions are representative of the subject. Such a message suggests that little variation exists beyond what was collected; if material does exist but is excluded or devalued, as often happens with applied arts and crafts and "popular" cultural production, then the implication is that it is of minimal importance. These exclusions have resulted in a distorted view of women artists' and writers' professional careers and production, for as Bridget Elliott and Janice Helland point out, often the less valued parts of a women artist's oeuvre, the applied arts and crafts, are allowed to "deteriorate and disappear" by an art world that values and preserves only the paintings and other so-called high art production (10).

As Veronica Strong-Boag writes in her introduction to *Rethinking Canada: The Promise of Women's History*, "Asking who we are and may become involves questioning who we were" (1). This questioning should go one step further and extend to the entire production and activity of Canadian women artists to create a new historical narrative that encompasses what we ordinarily value as both "high" and "low" cultural production. Carlyle, for instance, engaged in the new age of the mass circulation media and managed a range of resources to support her diverse professional practice. She exemplified a new approach to the independent and active organization and promotion of her own career. She was a champion of a new ideal for women's working and private lives. The characteristics of her life were those of the era's New Woman. In a world governed by the conventions of patriarchy, she contributed to a new model of artistic professionalism in Canada and, significantly, her colleagues recognized her as an exemplar.

In 1914, Madge Macbeth spoke of Carlyle as a model for women in the arts, and specifically emphasized her work in illustration and commercial art in New York. She described Carlyle in glowing terms as someone "whose story should inspire any who may grow discouraged" (23).[13] In the same year, Margaret Bell's article "Women and Art in Canada" focused on Carlyle's gaining professional recognition through commercial art commissions. Bell asserted that Carlyle's achievements in this area "revolutionized popular art" (7).[14] Following this trail through the archives of women arts columnists, I discovered that respect for Carlyle's diverse production was also evident in a younger generation of women artists. Thirty-four-year-old Estelle Kerr was herself working in the field of commercial art in 1913 as an illustrator and cartoonist when she wrote of Carlyle in her column, "The Artist," for *Saturday Night*. Kerr's target audience was women, and the article's theme was how women could work as professionals in the field of art and achieve financial independence. She linked Carlyle's success directly to her commercial art activity and cited her career as evidence of women's ability to achieve an "extremely remunerative" living as artists (29).[15] Had I not followed the leads I found in the archive that had gestured toward this diversity and commercial activity in Carlyle's production and innovative professional practice, I would not have been aware of why the artist was considered by her female colleagues in the Canadian art scene as a model for an emerging generation of women. I learned from the process of researching historical women artists in the archives that researchers need to relinquish control of the subject and allow the material to lead. The journey took me from the initial feeling that I did not have a grasp of the subject, to thinking some time later that I knew the subject quite well. After, I emerged at a point where the material invited me to look further and resist the impulse to construct the subject, until I encountered and explored the unexpected, and sometimes undesirable, archival material. I learned that it is healthy to distrust your understanding of the subject, since this distrust may lead to useful additions and insights. When I accepted all the material I had found on Carlyle and embraced it, even the unwanted and unexpected, then I began to write.

Notes

1 This book emerged from my master's thesis on Florence Carlyle. See Butlin, "Making a Living." When the idea to turn the thesis into a book presented itself, I realized that there were many new avenues and questions I wished to consider. The subsequent book benefited from this broadening of scope and much additional research over a period of ten years in both private and public archives, and from my Doctoral research on a related subject.
2 Carlyle was included in the 1975 exhibition and catalogue *From Women's Eyes*.
3 The Curators Maria Ricker and Anna-Marie Larsen and the staff of the WAG have been extremely helpful and accommodating to me over the years.
4 I interviewed Florence Carlyle Johnston in August 1993. I also corresponded with Johnston throughout 1993 and 1994. See the Bibliography and Personal Sources in Butlin's *Practice of Her Profession*, 279.
5 For example, in January 1895, Carlyle's friend and colleague Louise Tully exhibited a number of wood carvings for sale at Roberts' and Son Art Galleries in Toronto,

after returning from art studies in London, England. Between 1914 and 1928, Elizabeth McGillivray Knowles held solo exhibitions in Toronto at the commercial art gallery in the Robert Simpson Co. Limited department store, and sold work at Johnson Art Galleries in Montreal. Sculptor Florence Wyle marketed her production through Eaton's gift shop in Toronto. See Butlin, "A New Matrix," 283–86.
6 See Butlin, "A New Matrix," 308–9.
7 See Carlyle's letters to Graves, December 6, 1922, and ca. December 1922.
8 Letter from Carlyle to Graves, December 6, 1922.
9 Mary Ella Williams Dignam was a painter of figures and landscapes. She has received scholarly attention for her involvement with the Woman's Art Association of Canada and the Canadian Handicrafts Guild. See McLeod, 36–40.
10 See, for example, Hill's discussion of the involvement of Group of Seven members with book illustration, mural painting, and set design (123–27). The Grip firm and their link with the group is discussed in Reid (142).
11 See, for example, Carr's textile and pottery creations in Hill, Lamoureaux, and Thom, (88–89, and 136–37).
12 See also Buss, "Constructing Female Subjects," in Buss and Kadar, 23–24.
13 Macbeth (1880–1965), a widow, juggled several careers to support herself and her two young children. She was a writer of fiction, an arts columnist, and a photographer.
14 Margaret Bell (Saunders) was an arts columnist.
15 Kerr (1879–1971) was a painter, illustrator, cartoonist, and arts and travel columnist.

Works Cited

Bell, Margaret. "Women and Art in Canada." *Everywoman's World* 3 (1914): 7, 15, 30. Print.

Buss, Helen M. "Constructing Female Subjects in the Archive: A Reading of Three Versions of One Woman's Subjectivity." Buss and Kadar 23–34. Print.

Buss, Helen M., and Marlene Kadar, eds. *Working in Women's Archives: Researching Women's Private Literature and Archival Documents*. Waterloo: Wilfrid Laurier UP, 2001. Print.

Butlin, Susan. "A New Matrix of the Arts: A History of the Professionalization of Canadian Women Artists, 1880–1914." PhD Diss. Carleton U, 2008. Print.

———. "Making a Living: Florence Carlyle and the Negotiation of a Professional Artistic Identity." MA thesis. Carleton U, 1995. Print.

———. *The Practice of Her Profession: Florence Carlyle, Canadian Painter in the Age of Impressionism*. Kingston: McGill-Queen's UP, 2009. Print.

Carlyle, Florence. Letter to O. B. Graves. Dec. 6, 1922. Artist Files. Museum London Archives, London, ON.

Deutsch, Sarah. *Women and the City: Gender, Space, and Power in Boston, 1870–1940*. Oxford: Oxford UP, 2000. Print.

Elliott, Bridget, and Janice Helland, eds. *Women Artists and the Decorative Arts 1880–1935: The Gender of Ornament*. London: Ashgate, 2002. Print.

Farr, Dorothy, and Natalie Luckyj. *From Women's Eyes*. Kingston: Agnes Etherington Art Centre, 1975. Print.

Hill, Charles. *The Group of Seven: Art for a Nation*. Toronto/Ottawa: McClelland & Stewart/National Gallery of Canada, 1995. Print.

Hill, Charles, Johanne Lamoureaux, and Ian M. Thom. *Emily Carr: New Perspectives on a Canadian Icon*. Vancouver: Douglas & McIntyre/National Gallery of Canada/Vancouver Art Gallery, 2006. Print.

Hutcheon, Linda. Afterword. *Remembering Postmodernism: Trends in Recent Canadian Art*. Ed. Mark Cheetham. Toronto: Oxford UP, 1991. Print.

Kerr, Estelle M. "The Artist." *Saturday Night* June 7, 1913: 29. Print.

Lejeune, Philippe. "Autobiography of Those Who Do Not Write." *On Autobiography*. Ed. Paul John Eakin. Trans. Katherine Leary. Minneapolis: Minnesota UP, 1989. Print.

Macbeth, Madge. "Canadian Women in the Arts." *Maclean's Magazine*, Oct. 12, 1914: 23–25, 105–8. Print.

McLeod, Ellen Easton. *In Good Hands: The Women of the Canadian Handicrafts Guild*. Kingston/Ottawa: McGill-Queen's UP/Carleton UP, 1999. Print.

Pollock, Griselda. *Differencing the Canon: Feminist Desire and the Writing of Art's Histories*. London: Routledge, 1999. Print.

Rechnitzer, Olaf P. "Nations Acclaim London Artists." *London Advertiser* (magazine section), Jan. 17, 1925: 1. Print.

Reid, Dennis. *A Concise History of Canadian Painting*. Toronto: Oxford UP, 1998.

Rubio, Mary. "'A Dusting Off': An Anecdotal Account of Editing the L. M. Montgomery Journals." Buss and Kadar 51–78. Print.

Strong-Boag, Veronica, ed. *Rethinking Canada: The Promise of Women's History*. 4th ed. Toronto: Oxford UP, 2002. Print.

Tippett, Maria. "The Writing of English-Canadian Cultural History, 1970–85." *Canadian Historical Review* 67.4 (1986): 548–61. Print.

The Oral, the Archive, and Ethics: Canadian Women Writers Telling It
Andrea Beverley

In 1988, while Daphne Marlatt was occupying the Ruth Wynn Woodward Chair of Women's Studies at Simon Fraser University, she organized a conference called Telling It: Women and Language Across Cultures. The promotional pamphlet for the event promised that it would feature Native, Asian Canadian, and lesbian writers "whose voices are too infrequently heard," in order to showcase their work and discuss their relationships with their respective communities, audiences, and publishers.[1] During the two-day conference, eight writers read excerpts from their creative work and participated in panel discussions on how their writing related to their particular politics, spiritualities, languages, and cultures. Workshops and discussions addressed such issues as alternative versus mainstream publishing, "interfacing" the oral and the written, and politically motivated writing. In addition to celebrating the work of the invited writers, Marlatt's specific intention was to create "a space for dialogue" and a "talking-space" (*Telling It* 12). She hoped particularly that the conversation would address "rift-lines, not the least of which are the rifts of race and sexual orientation...which have become so apparent in the women's movement" (*Telling It* 12). Transcripts, as well as published proceedings, reveal that the issue of difference within feminism did indeed surface, sometimes accompanied by palpable tension. Beyond the actual conference, these rift-lines also affected the publication that emerged from the event, a volume entitled *Telling It: Women and Language Across Cultures*. The book is subtitled *the transformation of a conference,* and in this essay I argue that a close reading of that "transformation" contributes to an understanding of the feminist politics of the event and its era. In this first section, I situate *Telling It* in its historical, feminist, and Canadian context, and I describe the editing process by which it became a published volume, despite the withdrawal of one of the original contributors. In the second section, I take a step back to consider my own research methodologies in light of the regulations and ambiguities of archival research. Ultimately, I suggest that issues of silence and voice are paramount in an evaluation of the feminist work in *Telling It*, just as silence and voice are the keywords that must inform my consideration of archival research methodologies.

As Marlatt explains, the rift-lines that she hoped to explore at *Telling It* were already apparent in feminist debates of the time (15–17). Yet within the Canadian literary context, *Telling It* may well have been, as Pauline Butling claims, "the first conference to address the intersections of gender, race, and sexuality" (33). Butling views *Telling It* as a watershed moment, and she includes it in her list of "important oral research sites of the past two decades" (33). She explains that she takes her definition of "research" from bpNichol, who defined a "research site" as a place of poetic investigation and experimentation (32). Like Butling, I became interested in *Telling It* as a ground-breaking "research site" where Canadian women writers grapple with issues of contemporary feminism, perhaps for the first time in this type of context. I am particularly interested in how the conference attendees struggled toward an anti-essentialist understanding of women that acknowledges differences of sexuality, class, and racial positioning while pursuing collaboration across difference. The fact that *Telling It* was an *oral* research site, as Butling specifies, did not strike me as particularly significant at the outset. However, as I delved into the archives, I became increasingly captivated by the complex process through which this conference had been transformed into a textual volume. I began to ask, how might a responsible historicization of this site address the differences between the original event (accessible through transcripts) and the published text? What does it mean to find silence—particularly the silence of a writer who chose to withdraw from the project—in the midst of this "oral research site"? What are the ethical issues that arise when archival research is brought to bear on an interpretation of this moment? Drawing on research at Library and Archives Canada (LAC), I address these queries in this essay. Ultimately, I argue that the editorial processes of *Telling It* are directly related to the feminist politics of the event and the era, and that the scholarly pertinence of this information must be weighed against issues of archival privacy.

Telling It took place in the late 1980s, when feminists were acknowledging the long-standing internal diversity of the women's movement and grappling with the implications of differences between women, especially differences of class, race, and sexual orientation (Devereux and Devereux 9; Crosby 131; Gunew and Yeatman xxiv). Of course, women of varying sexualities and racial backgrounds had always been involved in feminist work, but the time had come to question "the centrality of gender as a conceptual lens," and to assert the vast differences between women's experiences (Amos and Parmar 287; Gubar 117). By 1992, Christina Crosby claimed that "feminisms are marked by nation and race (Lorde's 'white american' feminism), by class, ethnicity, sexuality: black feminism, Latina feminism, lesbian feminism, middle-class mainstream feminism, and so on. It would seem that dealing with the fact of differences is *the* project of women's studies today" (131). Marlatt hoped that *Telling It* would participate in this project, and that attendees could discover "that women with dissimilar, even unequal experiences of oppression, might be able to speak openly and hear each other openly, might even (and this was a wilder hope) find some sense of shared ground" (13). Much discussion at *Telling It* did centre on women's multiple positionings and their varied experiences of diverse identity categories (Telling It 44, 52, 101, 129, 196). For instance, following a panel entitled "Across the Cultural Gap," Jillian Riddington commented, "This is about closing the gaps. There *are* differences in languages, there *are* differences in experience, and we need to talk about them, we need to understand each other so that those gaps that people try and make between women become bridged" (Telling It 47). The use of spatial and architectural metaphors of gaps and bridges is typical in such interventions. Through this imagery, and as Marlatt had hoped, attendees were struggling to understand the internal diversity of "woman" as a category, while still connecting and collaborating with one another.

The question of connecting despite differences was broached during conference discussions, and it is richly dramatized in the story of the *Telling It* edited volume. Following the 1988 conference, with sixteen hours of recorded material in hand, Daphne Marlatt invited Sky Lee, Lee Maracle, and Betsy Warland to form an editing collective with her. She chose these women in particular because it seemed geographically feasible (they all lived in Vancouver at the time) but also because they "represented each of the three communities featured at the conference" (*Telling It* 17). In a Canada Council grant application form, Marlatt explained that it was important to form such a collective "because editing can be a subtly political activity when it comes to deciding what to include or cut, or how much to shift an oral voice to the printed page."[2] The editing collective recognized that there was nothing neutral about their task; rather, the editorial decisions that they would make together spoke to issues of voice and representation. However, both Marlatt and Warland admit in the final publication that they were surprised by just how difficult it was to edit as a group. In her introduction, Marlatt writes that it was shocking to discover that items she took for granted (related to punctuation and grammar, specifically the implications of certain pronouns and capitalization) actually reflected her individual cultural values (Telling It 18). Warland states bluntly in her retrospective essay that "[t]his commentary has been the hardest thing I have ever written" (192).[3] In a letter from Marlatt to Maracle, written after an editing meeting that Maracle had been unable to attend, Marlatt writes, "[w]e seem to have, at least the three of us do, such different ideas of how to edit the discussions with the audience at the end of each panel."[4] When Marlatt wondered about Maracle's commitment to the editing collective, Maracle replied, "I realize that you wanted to do the project collectively, but we likely have a different concept of just what the collective process is all about."[5] Working collaboratively was a challenge for every participant, since each had divergent ideas on how to edit the proceedings, and on how to do so as a group. In a final report on the *Telling It* book project, Marlatt summed up the process this way: "Putting this book together was not an easy task for any of us—it required much soul-searching and some difficult collective decisions."[6] Obviously, the editing collective persevered and the hard work of their collaboration is palpable not only through the archives of their editing process but also in the text itself. Indeed, in her review of the book for *Books in Canada,* Erin Mouré says, "I felt the caring and thoughtfulness of the editing more strongly than the tensions of the actual event" ("Language").

Enthusiasm for the successes of their collective editorial work must be tempered by a strange silence manifest throughout the *Telling It* text. The original roster for the conference included eight creative writers, whereas only seven are evident in the text. An eighth author did indeed participate in the event, but she ultimately refused to be involved in the book project and asked for her comments to be removed from the published proceedings. In the section drawn from the first panel of the conference, a footnote refers to this absence.[7] The archives reveal this writer's official reason for pulling out of the project, sent to the editing collective after the conference: "I don't feel ethically comfortable to collaborate myself as a writer in such a collection which might be indirectly discriminating against certain groups of women writers."[8] The statement is succinct and mysterious: which "groups of women writers" are potentially being discriminated against? Is she suggesting (like Eileen Manion in her book review of *Telling It*) that African Canadian women writers should have been invited as well (28)? In fact, despite her official statement, there are numerous hints in *Telling It* and the archives that this author's reticence has its roots in a controversy that erupted during the first panel discussion, a controversy catalyzed by her own remarks. Although they could no longer publish what the eighth writer had said, the editing collective sought a way to "air the debate."[9] Hence, the eighth writer's comments are indicated by ellipses in the proceedings, while a footnote explains that she "questioned the inclusion of lesbian writers in the conference. She wondered how lesbians could constitute a culture since lesbians lack their own language" (Telling It 44). The subsequent debate seems to have been one of the most salient and memorable moments of the conference, judging by the editors' insistence on including it, the space that it occupies in the three retrospective essays, and the fact that it seems to have occasioned the eighth writer's withdrawal from the project.

How can we read the absent presence of this eighth author, especially when *Telling It* was ostensibly an event dedicated to building bridges between women in Canada's literary community? Is her withdrawal an example of a failure to connect across difference? Is she at fault for ultimately bowing out of the extended conversation? Or were her assertions too divergent, too potentially discriminatory, to figure into the feminist bridge-building of *Telling It*? There are several ways to think about her silence. In their retrospective essays, Lee and Warland reproach the eighth writer for withdrawing, and imply that her silence is an avoidance of a potentially beneficial debate: her silence is figured as a "gaping hole," an "unwillingness" and a refusal to connect (Telling It 188, 192). For Lee and Warland, the eighth writer's withdrawal is a disappointing absence, but it can also be read as a proactive choice on her part. In her final report on *Telling It*, Marlatt notes that this eighth writer "refused to give permission to include her statements, and indeed asked that her presence be erased, on political grounds. This was difficult for us."[10] This description alludes to the power that the eighth writer wielded when she decided to withdraw. Writing on silence in post-colonial contexts, Rajeswari Sunder Rajan reminds us that

> [s]ilence, by the same token that regards speech as the expression of the self, may become a barrier to a knowledge of the self, to its penetration by

> a perceiver. When this happens, the operation of silence becomes an operation of power rather than powerlessness. Silence as withheld communication produces mystery and enigma; it expresses displeasure. (87)

That is, the eighth writer's decision to fall silent may have been a calculated, self-preservative, and powerful move on her part, meant to frustrate her angry interlocutors. Of course, another unfortunate rationale for her silence must also be admitted: she may have felt unheard, disrespected, and forced to withdraw. The questions then become: what does it mean for a self-identified feminist to choose *not* to participate in a cross-cultural feminist dialogue? Or what does it mean if a self-identified feminist is made to feel that she cannot participate? These are pertinent questions for feminist movements that value inclusion and respect difference, especially because this situation emerges from an event intended to build bridges between differently positioned women.

* * *

Thus far, I have argued that the feminist politics of *Telling It* and its era play out in the microcosm of the collaborative process that brought this oral event to its textual incarnation. I have also suggested that the silence of the eighth writer speaks to these feminist politics because her controversial intervention was directly related to issues of diversity between women, and because her refusal to collaborate further dramatizes the difficulties of collaboration across differences. However, this admission requires addressing the complex ethical questions of my use of archival research. That is, the rules governing access to archival fonds shaped the way in which I read their content. Subsequently, I made decisions about the extent to which that content would shape my understanding and presentation of *Telling It*. These questions—about the regulation of archives, the weight of background material in literary interpretation, the privacy that should be accorded to an archive's third party—came to the forefront of my considerations of *Telling It*. As I explain below, these are also the questions that ultimately led back to the issues of voice and silence that troubled the *Telling It* editorial collective.

In her work on literary archives, Sara S. Hodson describes the difficulties of working with an author's papers, especially in light of the "competing ethics of providing access while protecting privacy" (131). Hodson states that literary archives present particular privacy-related challenges for archivists and researchers because the author might be a high-profile public figure; the archive often contains personal letters and manuscripts; copyright law can connect with issues of privacy; and there is a growing tendency to collect papers from authors who are still alive (138–48). One technique that archives might use to manage these delicate issues of privacy is to accept fonds which the donor (or another designated individual) only permits certain researchers to access, deciding who gets it on a case-by-case basis (Hodson 134). For instance, the Daphne Marlatt fonds at Library and Archives Canada, from which I accessed the *Telling It* transcripts, is a restricted collection, meaning that researchers must have Marlatt's permission before accessing it. Michael Ondaatje's and Jane Urquhart's fonds are similarly restricted, whereas others have no restrictions at all, or allow limited access only to certain documents within the archive.[11] Hodson is vehemently opposed to the strategy employed by Marlatt, Ondaatje, and Urquhart to manage their own archives. She argues that "selective availability not only contravenes the ethic of free and unfettered access that remains a cornerstone of the archival profession in a democratic society, it can also lead to trouble for both the donor and the curator" (135). However, Hodson is also aware of the growing incentives for repositories to collect authors' papers in their lifetime, thereby increasing the number of authors who insist on actively participating in the management of their archives (146). Marlatt is one of those authors who takes an active role in the management of her deposited material; I was grateful when she granted me permission to consult her fonds, but the ethical considerations surrounding my subsequent use of that material alerted me to the complexities of issues of privacy and archives.

Hodson emphasizes that the privacy issues of an archive's "third party" are often the most difficult and "worrisome" to resolve, and I found this to be true in the case of Marlatt's fonds (132). The most typical example of an archive's "third party" is a correspondent whose letters are contained within it but who did not participate in the disposition of those materials, and may not even know that his or her letters (or letters addressed to him or her) have been archived. For instance, I quoted above from correspondence between Marlatt and Maracle, Maracle being a "third party" of Marlatt's archive, where I read these letters. Of course, the most conspicuous third party of Marlatt's archive is *Telling It*'s eighth writer. Because the archive contains complete transcripts of the recorded conference material, the eighth writer's identity is revealed and her comments are recorded, along with subsequent correspondence concerning her withdrawal from the publication.[12]

To supplement my readings of *Telling It*, I could therefore provide a much more detailed account of the controversy catalyzed by her remarks. Thus far, however, I have chosen to refer to her anonymously, and I have quoted from only one archival document penned by her about one concern:

her official reason for withdrawing from the project. Is this inconsistent with my decision to quote from Maracle's correspondence with Marlatt? By what criteria do I decide that Maracle's letter and the eighth writer's official refusal are not private enough to censor, although I do not quote from the eighth writer's other comments, regardless of their potential pertinence? Apart from laws related to copyright or restricted access, Hodson concludes that there are very few guidelines for curators and archivists faced with dilemmas of open access versus the right to privacy. She laments the fact that "[t]here appear few even satisfactory guidelines for handling potentially sensitive letters and manuscripts" (148). In our Canadian context, Christl Verduyn's work on Marian Engel grapples with these same questions from the perspective of a literary scholar. "What to do," she asks, "when the interest of a person's private papers collides with her express wish that any attention directed toward her be placed on her published, public work?" (Verduyn 92). As one of her own sources asks, "How intimate is intimate?" and "How can one justify the intrusion?" (Coldwell qtd. in Verduyn 93). Both Hodson from the archivist's perspective, and Verduyn from the researcher's perspective, acknowledge the difficulties of these questions, and they emphasize the uniqueness of the ethical gray areas arising from each individual archive (Hodson 148; Verduyn 100).

The particularities of the eighth writer as a third party of Marlatt's archive relate to the very themes and debates that occasioned her participation in the conference and her withdrawal from the project. Consider the common theme of "voice" running through the topics of the conference, the editing process, and the archival issues. *Telling It* was concerned with the voices that are not sufficiently heard within the feminist movement and Canadian literature. Not only did Marlatt hope that *Telling It* would be a space wherein feminism's rift-lines would be examined but also she situated the conference in terms of Canadian publishing. She addresses this process in a grant application completed prior to the conference:

> Unlike the United States, which has a growing body of work by Native Indian, Asian American and lesbian writers as well as a growing body of theory around that work, women Native writers in Canada are just beginning to make their voices heard, as are women Asian Canadians, with the exception of Joy Kogawa, whose novel *Obasan* received critical acclaim.[13]

The eighth writer pulled her voice out of the conversations following the conference, and the editing collective sought a way to reconstruct the essence of the controversial debate without citing the instigating voice. These citations are available in a restricted archive but only as a third party, meaning that the writer had no say (no voice) in the matter. Item C2 of the

Association of Canadian Archivists' Code of Ethics states that archivists must "make every attempt possible to respect the privacy of the individuals who created or are the subjects of records, *especially those who had no voice in the disposition of the records*" (emphasis mine). On the one hand, the discussions and presentations at *Telling It* are based on the premise that all voices need to be heard in a just public sphere or social movement. On the other hand, the eighth writer's withdrawal and the guidelines from the archivists' association remind us of an individual's right to unconditional governance of her own voice. The difference between these two standpoints lies in the interplay between a speaker's intentions (does she want to speak?) and her access to dissemination (is she permitted to speak?).

There are also revealing parallels to be drawn between the positions of the Telling It Book Collective and scholars researching *Telling It*. Like the editing collective, I have tried to describe the stakes of the conference and "air the debate" surrounding the eighth writer within the confines imposed by her withdrawal from the project. There is a desire to remain faithful to what actually transpired at the 1988 event and a palpable frustration at the limitations imposed. My discussion of the tension between open access and privacy rights implicitly suggests that the whole truth lies in the archive but that it cannot be legitimately disclosed. This suggestion, however, is properly nuanced in the words of Canadian life writing expert Marlene Kadar, who reminds scholars that the archive is always an "incomplete site... part of what makes the archive a complex text is that it is a fragmentary piece of knowledge, or an unfixed and changing piece of knowledge" (115). An archive is incomplete in the sense that it is comprised of material selected by a donor or circumstances of history, upon which an archivist has imposed a specific kind of order, based on the selection and organization of the material; it may be added to in the future and it may be fraudulent; and its formation and interpretation are most certainly influenced by social and cultural processes that determine value (Kadar 115; Cox 240–47). As researchers, however, it can be difficult to operate according to this nuanced concept of archival truth. When I presented some of my thoughts on *Telling It* at the ACCUTE conference in May 2009,[14] one enthusiastic commenter expressed disapproval of and even anger about the fact that the eighth writer was impeding our potentially complete understanding of what happened at the conference. "Why should she keep us from knowledge?" was the sentiment. In response to this question, and in defence of my own choice to respect the eighth writer's silence, I turn to the strategy eventually adopted by the Telling It Book Collective. The book born out of the initial conference is "not so much a proceedings as it is the transformation of a conference.... [The] commentaries open discussion into a context that is at once more analytical and more personal" (9).[15] The eighth writer does not keep us from understanding *Telling It*, nor is our task to recreate the absolute truth of that event, as if that were possible. Keeping in mind Kadar's point about the inconclusive nature of archives, and following the textual *Telling It*'s transformed, analytical, and personal angle, we can acknowledge *this* discussion of ethics, archives, voice, silence, feminism, and politics as another "transformation" of that initial (now inaccessible) moment.

In her Afterword to *Working in Women's Archives*, Kadar lists "six operations" of women's archival research. One operation accomplished by such research is "the investigation...of how women's lives and works change how we think about reading" (116). Kadar adds that such research should contribute to "the continuing interrogation of 'women' as a fixed category of study in the academy" (117). In light of what the archives do and do not reveal, thinking through the process by which *Telling It* was transformed from a conference into a text contributes to both of these operations. The process may "change how we think about reading" because it encourages us to consider how our positioning as critics parallels the standpoints of archivists or editors, and it challenges us to articulate how archives can influence the way we read. It also reminds us to interrogate "women" as a fixed category because the process dramatizes the interpersonal diversity at the heart of a group of women striving to collaborate even as they acknowledge their profound differences. Cultural critic Ien Ang suggests that "moments of ultimate failure of communication should not be encountered with regret, but rather should be accepted as the starting point for a more modest feminism, one which is predicated on the fundamental *limits* to the very idea of sisterhood" (396–97). Using Ang's logic, the withdrawal of the eighth writer might therefore offer an instance from which to consider the challenges of anti-essentialist feminism. From a critical perspective, a similar attitude would regard the silence of the eighth writer not as an unfortunate impediment to research but rather as an invitation to reflect on the subtexts and implications of that silence and to re-examine the assumptions of the critical drive for mastery over an object of knowledge. An uninhibited account of all that I read in Marlatt's archive might lend a sense of authoritative thoroughness to these reflections, and it would undoubtedly be informative and productive. However, grappling with the limitations placed on my research has afforded an occasion to consider the processes of research and recognize the politics of the themes of *Telling It* at work.

Although I have focused on moments of difficulty in feminist collaboration, *Telling It* is much more than a site of frustrations and failed communication. To begin with, it succeeded in amassing a significant crowd of women interested in marginalized writers and anti-essentialist feminism.[16] One of the Native participants commented that the conference was the first of its kind in Canada,[17] and Viola Thomas, writing in support of funding for the *Telling It* volume, stressed that such a publication would be long overdue in Canada.[18] In terms of its methodology, reviewers of the publication have commented on the intense, admirable listening that took place during this dialogue. For instance, in her critique, Erin Mouré notes that the sense of "*listening*" is palpable in *Telling It*, and she sees it as a strategy that resists suspicion, blockage, fear, and refusals ("Language"; emphasis in original). In the final essay of *Telling It*, Betsy Warland discusses listening as a much-appreciated component of the *Telling It* experience (195–96). Ultimately, to remember both the commendable listening of *Telling It and* the silence of the eighth writer is to realize both the possibilities and vulnerabilities of cross-cultural feminist dialogue. The work of this essay has been to further an understanding of these possibilities and vulnerabilities in the context of Canadian women writers, and to bring issues of archival research to bear on this important discussion. Archives are complex sites of incompleteness and regimentation. In the case of *Telling It*, dealing with those complexities contributes to a more thorough understanding of the politics of the research site and encourages scholars to consider privacy restrictions not as hurdles to be overcome, but as invitations to rethink our own standing points.

Notes

1. *Telling It* promotional pamphlet and registration form.
2. Daphne Marlatt Canada Council Exploration Program grant application.
3. She goes on to ask, "Why? Primarily because I am writing beyond my own boundaries, beyond what I've said on paper before. There are other reasons. One is the fact that I am the only White woman writing a commentary and because of racism and the upheaval around lesbianism I have keenly felt my words being scrutinized. Throughout the course of many drafts I have received considerable feedback and criticism from the other editors. I have rewritten and rewritten this. Have said in my private, hopeless hours that I'm not going to participate in the commentaries—yet I know I must not censor myself" (*Telling It* 192).
4. Daphne Marlatt, letter to Lee Maracle, Nov. 17, 1989.
5. Lee Maracle, letter to Daphne Marlatt, n.d.
6. Daphne Marlatt, "Final Report on 'Telling It' Project."
7. The footnote reads, "Editors' note: A fourth writer who participated on this panel has chosen not to have her talk included in this book" (*Telling It* 21).
8. This statement, written by the author in question, can be found in the Daphne Marlatt fonds in the Library and Archives Canada.
9. Daphne Marlatt, "Final Report on 'Telling It' Project."
10. Ibid.
11. Literary Archives. *Library and Archives Canada*.

12 The eighth writer's name and comments were blacked out on certain copies of the transcripts but because the marking was inconsistent, and because the archives contain numerous copies of these transcripts, none of the information was successfully censored.
13 Daphne Marlatt "Simon Fraser University President's Research Grant Application," p. 3.
14 The Association of Canadian College and University Teacher's of English's 2009 conference took place May 23–26 at Carleton University as part of the Congress of the Humanities and Social Sciences. I presented on a panel discussing "Women's Writing in Canada" co-organized by the Canadian Literature Centre and the Association for Canadian and Québec Literatures.
15 One could certainly argue that all publications stemming from conferences are transformations of the original events. However, *Telling It* is notably self-conscious of its transformed status (note the subtitle "the transformation of a conference," and 10, 17) and does not profess to be a conference proceedings. In her Introduction, Marlatt notes that the editing collective "decided that we would not attempt to edit a proceedings of the conference—or at least that the proceedings would be only partial. What we were most interested in doing was furthering the discussion of issues that were raised at the conference" (17). In the context of Canadian feminism, the 1983 Women and Words/Les femmes et les mots provides an interesting precedent here, as the conference spawned both an anthology and a proceedings, which might be read as different types of "transformations" (Dybikowski; West Coast). Women and Words/Les femmes et les mots also connects to *Telling It* thematically, as Marlatt acknowledges (15).
16 In Marlatt's outline for her welcome speech at the beginning of the conference, she notes that the enrolment exceeded their expectations and they had been required to change room reservations to accommodate everyone.
17 Daphne Marlatt, "Simon Fraser University President's Research Grant Application," p. 2.
18 Viola Thomas, Letter of Appraisal for the Canada Council Explorations Program.

Works Cited

Amos, Valerie, and Pratibha Parmar. "Challenging Imperial Feminism." *The Feminist History Reader*. Ed. Sue Morgan. New York: Routledge, 2006. 284–94. Print.

Ang, Ien. "I'm a feminist but... 'Other' women and postnational feminism." 1995. *Feminism and 'Race'*. Ed. Kum-Kum Bhavnani. Oxford: Oxford UP, 2001. 394–409. Print.

Association of Canadian Archivists. *Code of Ethics*, 1995–2009. Section C2. n.d. Web. Oct. 10, 2009.

Butling, Pauline. "One Potato, Two Potato, Three Potato, Four: Poetry, Publishing, Politics and Communities." *Writing in Our Time: Canada's Radical Poetries in English (1957–2003)*. Ed. Pauline Butling and Susan Rudy. Waterloo: Wilfrid Laurier UP, 2005. 29–48. Print.

Cox, Richard J. *Ethics, Accountability, and Recordkeeping in a Dangerous World*. London: Facet, 2006. Print.

Crosby, Christina. "Dealing with Differences." *Feminists Theorize the Political*. Ed. Judith Butler and Joan W. Scott. New York: Routledge, 1992. 130–43. Print.

Devereux, Cecily, and Jo Devereux. "Feminism... What Are We Supposed to Do Now?" *English Studies in Canada* 31.2–3 (2005): 9–11. Print.

Dybikowski, Ann, et al., eds. *In the Feminine: Women and Words / Les femmes et les mots.* Conference Proceedings, 1983. Edmonton: Longspoon, 1985. Print.

Gubar, Susan. *Critical Condition: Feminism at the Turn of the Century.* New York: Columbia UP, 2000. Print.

Gunew, Sneja, and Anna Yeatman, eds. Introduction. *Feminism and the Politics of Difference.* Halifax: Fernwood P, 1993. xiii–xxv. Print.

Hodson, Sara S. "In Secret Kept, In Silence Sealed: Privacy in the Papers of Authors and Celebrities." *Privacy and Confidentiality Perspectives: Archivists and Archival Records.* Ed. Menzi L. Behrnd-Klodt, and Peter J. Wosh. Chicago: Society of American Archivists, 2005. 131–48. Print.

Kadar, Marlene. Afterword. *Working in Women's Archives: Researching Women's Private Literature and Archival Documents.* Ed. Helen M. Buss and Marlene Kadar. Waterloo: Wilfrid Laurier UP, 2001. 115–17. Print.

Literary Archives. *Library and Archives Canada.* May 12, 2009. Web. Oct. 31, 2009.

Manion, Eileen. "Fractured margins." Rev. of *Telling It: Women and Language Across Cultures,* by The Telling It Book Collective. *The Women's Review of Books* 8.12 (1991): 28. Print.

Maracle, Lee. Letter to Daphne Marlatt. N.d. MS. Daphne Marlatt fonds LMS-0119 1993-13 Box 21, f. 7. Library and Archives Canada, Ottawa.

Marlatt, Daphne. Author's statement requesting removal from *Telling it.* TS. Daphne Marlatt fonds LMS-0119 1993-13 Box 21, f. 7. Library and Archives Canada, Ottawa.

———. Canada Council Exploration Program grant application. TS. Daphne Marlatt fonds LMS-0119 1993-13 Box 21, f. 2. Library and Archives Canada, Ottawa.

———. Letter to Lee Maracle. Nov. 17, 1989. MS. Daphne Marlatt fonds LMS-0119 1993-13 Box 21, f. 7. Library and Archives Canada, Ottawa.

———. Outline for *Telling It* Welcome Speech. MS. Daphne Marlatt fonds LMS-0119 1993-13 Box 21, f. 4. Library and Archives Canada, Ottawa.

———. "Simon Fraser University President's Research Grant Application." P. 2, 3. TS. Daphne Marlatt fonds LMS-0119 1993-13 Box 21, f. 1. Library and Archives Canada, Ottawa.

———. *Telling It* promotional pamphlet and registration form. Daphne Marlatt fonds LMS-0119 1993-13 Box 21, f. 6. Library and Archives Canada, Ottawa.

Mouré, Erin. "Language in Her Ear." Rev. of *Telling It: Women and Language Across Cultures,* by The Telling It Book Collective. *Books in Canada.* April 1991. Web. Sept. 1, 2009.

Rajan, Rajeswari Sunder. *Real and Imagined Women.* London: Routledge, 1993. Print.

The Telling It Book Collective. *Telling It: Women and Language across Cultures.* Vancouver: Press Gang P, 1990. Print.

Thomas, Viola. Letter of Appraisal for the Canada Council Explorations Program. MS. Daphne Marlatt fonds LMS-0119 1993-13 Box 21, f. 2. Library and Archives Canada, Ottawa.

Verduyn, Christl. "Personal Papers: Putting Lives on the Line–Working with the Marian Engel Archive." *Working in Women's Archives: Researching Women's Private Literature and Archival Documents.* Ed. Helen M. Buss and Marlene Kadar. Waterloo: Wilfrid Laurier UP, 2001. 91–101. Print.

West Coast Editorial Collective. *Women and Words: The Anthology/ Les Femmes et les mots: une anthologie.* Madeira Park: Harbour, 1984. Print.

Halted by the Archive: The Impact of Excessive Archival Restrictions on Scholars
Ruth Panofsky and Michael Moir

The Scholar

In 1999, I was awarded a Professional Writer's Grant by the Canada Council for the Arts to support a study of the novelist Adele Wiseman.[1] The project I proposed would rely extensively on the Wiseman fonds held at York University. By 1999, I already had used Wiseman's papers in conjunction with two book projects, *Adele Wiseman: An Annotated Bibliography*, and *Selected Letters of Margaret Laurence and Adele Wiseman*, co-edited with John Lennox.[2] For the first project, Wiseman herself had given me full access to her private papers while they remained in her possession. On numerous visits to her Toronto flat in 1989 and 1990, I worked with material that she later deposited at York in 1991 as the first accession of the Wiseman fonds. On those visits, Wiseman offered up a seemingly chaotic arrangement of countless boxes from which I culled invaluable documents. The details of a life, from the minutiae of shopping lists to the original typescripts of her various works, remained intact in that remarkable collection of boxes. In an effort to develop a comprehensive bibliography, I worked furiously to record and annotate items that Wiseman had saved over the years. By the time of her death in June 1992, having been mentored by the woman whose writing I had so long admired and whose archive I had studied in the privacy of her home, I felt compelled to honour her with a special Wiseman issue of the literary journal *Room of One's Own*, which appeared in September 1993 under my guest editorship.[3]

Before her death, Wiseman granted me and John Lennox permission to use her side of the correspondence in preparing *Selected Letters of Margaret Laurence and Adele Wiseman*. For that project, when the first accession of her papers was not yet catalogued and stored in an archival vault of the Scott Library, Wiseman gave me ready access to the same cache of boxes I had consulted in her flat. Although she did not live to celebrate the publication of our work, a testimony to her forty-year friendship with Laurence, Wiseman sanctioned our editorial project by giving us unrestricted access to her archive. Following her mother's death, Tamara Stone, Wiseman's daughter and literary executor, showed a similar generosity by renewing permission to publish the letters we had been editing.

In 1996, four years after her mother's death, Stone deposited the second accession of the Wiseman fonds at York University. At the time, however, since she did not sign over the deposit of papers to York, the second accession was inaccessible to researchers. The first accession remained open for scholarly use, but permission to photocopy and cite from unpublished archival material had to be provided by Wiseman's literary executor.

In 1998, one year after the appearance of *Selected Letters*, I submitted an application to the Canada Council. The project I envisaged, a biographical study that would also attend to the writer's literary career, grew naturally out of my previous work on Wiseman. In March 1999, when I learned that my application had been successful, I planned a period of sustained research and was optimistic that my career-long devotion to Wiseman studies would result in a monograph. Since my relations with Tamara Stone remained cordial and open, I assumed she would continue to grant me access to the Wiseman fonds. The luxury of that access, however, was soon denied.

Barbara Craig, one-time archivist of York University and Professor Emerita in the Faculty of Information at the University of Toronto, acknowledges that the fundamental reality of archival "work is the record: its physical nature, its creation, its uses and its relationship to the values of our society" (140). She argues, however, that "[t]he document is not a stifling prison for data; the context and form of the document give additional meaning to the information contained within." Moreover, "[d]ocumentary information is unlike any other kind of data; access to it and use of it make a unique contribution to society." In fact, this "provides the ultimate justification for archives" (140, 136). In 2000, just as my work on Wiseman intensified, Stone refused to sign over the second accession of the Wiseman fonds, in effect restricting scholarly access to half the collection and, for all intents and purposes, turning the Clara Thomas Archives into a storage centre. Moreover, she no longer granted scholars permission either to reproduce or cite archival material. It appeared that Stone's overzealous regard for the archival record would come at the unfortunate expense of its use.

The reasons for Stone's decision to restrict access to the Wiseman fonds remained private, and for a time, in the immediate wake of refusal of access, I embarked on a futile campaign of appeals (both personal and through the offices of her lawyer, Marion Hebb) to convince her of my honest intentions and scholarly integrity. She did not entertain appeals, however, regardless of whether these were based on my past relationship with her mother, my previous work on Wiseman, or her former goodwill toward me. As literary executor, Tamara Stone was, and remains, formidable. Her wilfulness prevented the rise in scholarship that often follows the death of a prominent author. In fact, her actions appear to have countered Wiseman's personal hope that her papers be consulted by scholars. As the writer self-consciously quipped in a letter to Margaret Laurence, dated January 10, 1981, following the deposition of Laurence's own papers to York University, "[I]f one were only a letter writer of the scintillating kind, whose epistles were guaranteed to be Woolfed down by the hungry Canlit essayists of the future, with some little shocks of *pleasure*, it would allay perhaps the uneasiness of knowing this is scheduled for the 1981 file marked 'Writer Friends'" (Lennox and Panofsky 363). Although I had consulted the first accession of the Wiseman fonds and knew its contents, I had conceived of a large project that required access to the second accession. It soon became evident that the restrictions imposed on the Wiseman papers would affect the course of my research. After some time, however, once the initial shock of rejection had worn off, I reconsidered my project in light of available archival material and redefined its focus.

As a Canadianist with secondary expertise in publishing history and author–publisher relations, I recognized Wiseman's literary career—the composition, publication, and reception of her various works; her relationships with editors, publishers, and literary agents; her literary apprenticeship and later role as mentor to students and other writers; and her sustaining friendship with fellow writer Margaret Laurence—as potentially rich subject matter for a monograph. Moreover, having worked previously with the Macmillan Company of Canada fonds, housed at Hamilton's McMaster University (Macmillan published Wiseman's award-winning first novel, *The Sacrifice*, in 1956), I knew of the extensive and detailed correspondence that existed between Wiseman, her Macmillan editor Kildare Dobbs, and Macmillan president John Morgan Gray. When it became clear that I would not have access to the Wiseman fonds, I returned to the Macmillan archive.

My research uncovered an invaluable primary record of publication and the enduring connection between Wiseman and her first publisher. It also led to my further investigation of fonds likewise housed at McMaster: the McClelland & Stewart fonds; the Jack McClelland fonds; and the Clarke, Irwin fonds. Wiseman's second novel, *Crackpot*, was published in 1974 by McClelland & Stewart, and her memoir, *Old Woman at Play*, was published in 1978 by Clarke, Irwin. Preliminary work in these various fonds confirmed my impression that an original study of Wiseman's literary career could be written out of the primary material that existed outside the Wiseman fonds held at York. I proceeded with caution and determination to undertake further research and began crafting my project anew.

In truth, my work proceeded slowly. I worried that my newly narrowed focus would not produce the extended, comprehensive study I had hoped to write. More importantly, I was concerned for the accuracy and completeness of my project. Without access to the Wiseman fonds, I could not be absolutely certain of my claims, and the possibility loomed that future scholars, who might have access to those very fonds, could find fault with my work. These concerns, which shaped my approach to the project, as did Stone's injunction against access, may have accounted for my especially meticulous attention to available primary material and my careful use of citation.

I consulted a wide range of primary sources for my work, including several publishers' archives; the Margaret Laurence fonds held at York University; the Malcolm Ross fonds held at the University of Calgary and the University of Toronto; the John Morgan Gray fonds; and the Robert Weaver fonds, both held at Library and Archives Canada. In addition, I conducted interviews with individuals who had been connected with Wiseman and could comment on her literary career. Since I was restricted to citing only previously published material by Wiseman, I could not cite newly discovered archival resources. As a result, the voice of Wiseman that is heard in my study is not nearly as bold, dynamic, or nuanced as it might have been. Further, my research focused on Wiseman's public life, since I intuited that Tamara Stone might be provoked if it included much personal information. Although unwilling to antagonize Wiseman's literary executor, I was resolved to build on my previous work and make a further contribution to Wiseman studies.

Between 1998 and 2003, the staff of the Clara Thomas Archives sought repeatedly to contact Stone, who changed residences periodically and did not maintain contact with York University. Over the course of several years, a number of archivists—among them Barbara Craig, the late Kent Haworth, and more recently, Suzanne Dubeau and Michael Moir—tried to convince her of the need to assign the second accession of the Wiseman fonds to York and open the archive to scholars. Stone proved intractable.

One morning in early January 2004, however, she arrived unannounced at the Clara Thomas Archives and proclaimed her intention to make the second accession accessible to scholars, although they would still require permission to reproduce or cite material from the Wiseman fonds. When Suzanne Dubeau telephoned to give me the welcome news, she declared with unusual vigour, "Fortunately, I was in the Archives at the time!" It was fortunate for me as well. Since my work was nearing completion, I would not seek permission to cite from previously unpublished material, but I was able to return to the Wiseman fonds in time to make the necessary revisions to my manuscript. Not surprisingly, I was both reassured and relieved by my reading in the second accession, since it corroborated my general findings. Finally, I felt ready to submit my work to a publisher. In January 2005 I sent the manuscript, titled *The Force of Vocation: The Literary Career of Adele Wiseman*, to the University of Manitoba Press, whose director, David Carr, had expressed interest in the project. The monograph was published in 2006.

Were it not for the persistent archivists of the Clara Thomas Archives, Tamara Stone might never have found her way onto the wind-blown campus of York University in January 2004, and I would not have had the opportunity, snatched as it was at the last moment, to consult material that proved invaluable to my study of Wiseman. In an offhand manner and against its archival will, York University was for too long made into a storage facility for the Wiseman fonds. The belief of its archivists, that "[e]ach and every user should leave our institutions, not with a sigh of relief at having successfully negotiated an obstacle course, but with a genuine sense of satisfaction with his or her experience and an itch to return to continue this exploration" (Craig 137), drove the campaign—undertaken carefully, over a number of years—to make the Wiseman fonds accessible to researchers. I, for one, am grateful to all archivists who continue to lobby for access to their collections and who regard researchers as mutual "participants in the archival mission" (Craig 140).

The Archivist

Archives play a major role within the university's mission to preserve, pursue, and disseminate knowledge in order to achieve excellence in research and teaching. Unique research collections are the treasure troves that attract graduate students, faculty, and an international community of scholars.

Universities invest significant time, energy, and financial resources into acquiring archival collections and ensuring their preservation through the use of specialized supplies, through labour-intensive conservation treatments for select items, and by establishing environmentally controlled storage facilities. Educational programming, reference, and outreach services through on-site and virtual exhibits add additional costs that make it far more expensive to manage a linear metre of archival holdings than the equivalent amount of published material on a library's open shelves. A reasonable return on this investment can be achieved only through unfettered access to and use of archival collections. Why, then, did York University risk turning the Clara Thomas Archives into little more than a storeroom for the Adele Wiseman fonds for so many years? Why did its archivists put themselves in the unenviable position of denying Ruth Panofsky access to material that she had consulted before Adele Wiseman's death, thereby thwarting the pursuit and dissemination of knowledge that lies at the heart of the university's mission? The answers to these questions lie in the challenges inherent in dealing with donors and personal papers so closely connected to contemporary history, and in balancing the short- and long-term priorities of preservation and access.

As Robert Fulford noted in the *National Post*, most universities lack the financial resources to compete with the University of Texas's purchase of five hundred boxes of Norman Mailer's memorabilia for $2.5 million U.S. (AL 1). Instead, archivists rely on connections with authors made through faculty members, guest lecturers, honourary doctorates, book dealers, literary agents, previous donors, and serendipity to solicit the donation of literary papers to repositories such as the Clara Thomas Archives. Negotiations can take anywhere from a few weeks to several years to culminate in a donation, as an author or his or her heirs develop a relationship of trust with an archivist and a repository. Discussions are driven partially by financial considerations. Although it may once have been true that many Canadian authors could generate more income through the sale of their papers than through their published work, most transactions now revolve around the issuance of tax receipts that shelter the donor's taxable income over several years.[4] The need for tax relief can also drive regular accruals to fonds, as donors seek to donate material during particularly lucrative times in their careers. Periods of low income can stall the transfer of ownership until it becomes more viable economically. Financial issues, coupled with the challenge of contacting a donor who had moved out of the country, delayed the transfer of ownership of Adele Wiseman's second accession of papers to York University. This situation obstructed general access to the Wiseman fonds and had a negative impact on Ruth Panofsky's research.

Donations are not only financial exchanges; they also mark an author's standing within the Canadian literary community. Donors recognize that literary papers can support the critical study of the creative process and the business of writing and publishing. Wiseman, for example, was prepared to lay open a comprehensive range of personal and professional documents to the scrutiny of researchers. Other authors have been less forthcoming. JoAnn McCaig noted that Alice Munro was careful to transfer "only documents pertaining to the business of writing" when she gave her papers to the University of Calgary, and thus withheld personal letters and journals (xiii). Munro's approach is by no means unique. The papers of James Field, editor and publisher of the *Atlantic Monthly* and his wife Annie were similarly "sanitized" when they were acquired by the Huntington Library in 1922.[5] Munro's contract with the University of Calgary, however, took the filtering of sensitive material one step further: it obliged library staff either to remove or restrict access to personal or financial information during the processing of her papers.

This arrangement speaks to a long-standing relationship between donor and archivist in repositories that collect historical manuscripts, a practice distinct from that undertaken by archives devoted to public records. In the case of the former type of institution, Raymond Geselbracht has traced the gradual and casual development since the 1920s of donor-specified restrictions on access to collections in the United States. Although archivists have been outspoken in support of access to personal papers for research, they have "emphasized the duty of the repository to protect the confidences expressed in the documents" (Geselbracht 145–46). Archivists have spoken of proprietary relationships with donors and a fiduciary responsibility to preserve their privacy. Working within this perspective, repositories entered into agreements that allowed donors to screen researchers and prohibit access, and gave archivists the authority to review the notes of researchers and withhold permission to cite material of a personal nature that was not directly relevant to the subject under review. As recently as 1977, the Society of American Archivists sanctioned the review of reference notes, thereby perpetuating the role of archivist as censor, something that would not sit well with today's practitioners (Geselbracht 152).

The practice of reviewing a researcher's notes appears to have died out, but many repositories, including the Clara Thomas Archives, continue the tradition of allowing donors to control access to archival documents. For example, acclaimed writer Norman Levine sold the manuscript of his first book, *Canada Made Me*, to the University of Texas after it was rejected by McGill University because the latter lacked sufficient space. Since Levine was determined to find a Canadian repository for his literary papers, he finally settled on York University in 1971 at the suggestion of an antiquarian book and manuscript dealer in London, England. His biannual deposits of correspondence and manuscripts continued until 2003, with the understanding that researchers were required to seek Levine's consent to access and photocopy his archives; in the case of correspondence written to the author, it was also necessary for researchers to obtain consent from third parties whose letters form part of the fonds. Seeking permission could be a long and unpredictable process. Levine had lived in England for much of his life, and he eschewed the use of technologies that could expedite requests. Permission for access was sometimes contingent upon researchers submitting their work to Levine for review prior to publication; his support for projects was arbitrarily revoked on two occasions in the years leading up to his death in 2005. These access restrictions put York University's archivists in the uncomfortable role of gatekeepers, and impeded critical analysis of the writer's work. From the archivist's perspective, however, there is no alternative but to accept such arrangements, unless the repository is willing to forego future accruals to an author's fonds.

The current difficulties created by access restrictions are largely the result of changes in the types of documents collected by university archives and manuscript repositories, and researchers' increasing focus on contemporary figures. The tendency to collect the papers of people long dead and from a distant past permitted the casual development of access restrictions during much of the twentieth century, as Geselbracht notes. By the 1970s, however, the cultural landscape changed. The emergence of courses on Canadian literature at institutions such as York University, under the influence of professors like Clara Thomas, resulted in a growing interest in the papers of living authors. It was largely because of the friendship of Clara Thomas and Margaret Laurence, for example, that Laurence's papers were deposited at York in 1980, seven years before her death. Adele's Wiseman's papers followed in 1991 at the urging of Laurence, Wiseman's lifelong friend. York is not the only academic institution to acquire archival fonds in this manner. Sara Hodson, curator of manuscripts at the Huntington Library, has noted the increasing trend for repositories to collect the papers of living authors, the competition among repositories for these papers, and the desire of "those institutions to nail down a literary archive as soon as possible," which has increased the likelihood that repositories will come into possession of private and sensitive documents of recent vintage (209). At the same time, researchers have sought out these archives as the sources of such private details as one might read in the "increasingly frank biographies that became standard in the latter part of the twentieth century" (206). In view of this trend, one can understand why Stephen Joyce, the grandson of James Joyce, announced in 1988 at a conference honouring the Irish novelist that he had burned letters written by Samuel Beckett and Joyce's daughter Nora—much to the outrage of those in attendance—in an attempt to preserve the families' privacy (Hodson 204).

The exercise of copyright by authors and their heirs who have donated papers to archives is a more temperate response to the need for privacy, although it creates a significant hurdle for researchers working on the papers of contemporary authors. Ruth Panofsky has discussed the impact of Tamara Stone's refusal to allow her to reproduce or cite from the letters of Adele Wiseman, and she is not alone in her predicament. When Ian Hamilton attempted to publish an unauthorized biography of J. D. Salinger, the courts upheld the novelist's assertion that Hamilton's use of his letters (held in libraries at Harvard, Princeton, and the University of Texas) constituted an infringement upon the fair use conditions of copyright. Quotations or paraphrases were not permitted, and Hamilton's book finally focused more on his legal experiences than on the life of Salinger (Hodson 208). JoAnn McCaig encountered similar difficulties when attempting to write about the authorship and literary process of Alice Munro. She begins her book, *Reading in Alice Munro's Archives*, with the announcement, "This is not the book I wanted to publish." The preface then describes Munro's decision to withhold permission from McCaig to quote from or paraphrase archival documents—she judged the researcher's draft to be full of "bizarre assumptions" and "blatant disregard for fact"—and the impact that decision had on McCaig's work (viii–xvi). Such company will give little comfort to Ruth Panofsky, but it demonstrates that her experience at the Clara Thomas Archives is by no means unique.

For a large percentage of literary papers collected by university archives and manuscript repositories, copyright will not expire for several decades. As a result, it is likely that, in the future, many more researchers will face restrictions on use of this material. The archivist has little or no control over such situations, since most authors and their heirs are conscious of the importance of intellectual property rights and surrender them with great reluctance. Declining to acquire literary papers because the donor will not transfer copyright would likely mean a sharp reduction in the growth of research collections, and the possible destruction of these papers by fire, flood, mould, or other damage if they remain in private hands. Accepting papers without the transfer of copyright complicates their use in the short term, but it achieves the goal of preservation that will ensure the availability of significant cultural assets for future generations of researchers.

A donor may influence use by controlling copyright, but this applies only to documents created by the author. Most literary papers contain correspondence from third parties, such as family members, literary agents, editors, publishers, other authors, and readers. While individuals own the intellectual property that resides in the contents of such documents, they do not own or control the physical objects, and are usually unaware that their correspondence has been transferred to an archive. These papers can contain personal information of a sensitive nature that was communicated to the author on the assumption of confidentiality, and with no expectation that opinions or revelations would end up in the public domain. In other cases, third parties are represented as subjects in correspondence, and again, have no control over the disposition of personal information contained in documents that may harm or embarrass individuals or their families. The Code of Ethics developed by the Association of Canadian Archivists makes it clear that practitioners should "make every attempt possible to respect the privacy of individuals who created or are the subjects of records, especially those who had no voice in the disposition of the records."[6] Short of refusing to accept such papers, the archivist's only recourse is to impose access restrictions. Unfortunately, there are no clear guidelines for the archivist who is forced to abandon the possibility of being "neutral, objective, impartial," and to assume power over shaping cultural memory (Cook and Schwartz 1–2).

In an issue of *American Archivist*, Sara Hodson offers this summary: "Faced with the competing ethics of free and open access to research collections and the safeguarding of people's rights to privacy... how can curators and archivists devise appropriate policies for administering modern personal papers? Unfortunately, no good answers exist" (211). Perhaps some guidance can be taken from the literature and practices that have emerged from almost three decades of administering freedom of information and protection of privacy legislation in Canada. Considerable work has been done to identify the characteristics of personal information, assess the risks associated with access, and develop protocols to support scholarly research. These initiatives include research agreements based on provincial regulations that require applicants to identify the purpose and scope of their research, to agree to publish anonymous data stripped of personal identifiers, to keep research notes in a secure location, and not to share their notes with other researchers, libraries, or archives. Such agreements, developed within the context of managing government records, have been applied to private sector records acquired by academic archives to find a reasonable compromise between privacy and demands for scholarly access. As with most compromises, there are drawbacks for both parties. Researchers must be vigilant in maintaining the confidentiality of notes that contain personal identifiers in an age when computer theft and hacking into shared networks make electronic data particularly vulnerable. Archivists and their sponsoring organizations must bear the burden of enforcing these agreements. In the case of British Columbia, the Information and Privacy Commissioner ordered the provincial archives to develop criteria for storing and encrypting electronic data collected through research agreements, and to conduct random audits of researchers' computers to confirm compliance (Clément 1–3). Moreover, archivists are forced once more into the role of censor or gatekeeper, as they consider the intentions of researchers when approving applications for research agreements. Although such procedures improve the response of archivists to Hodson's search for policies that balance the competing ethics of access and privacy, they do not make for easy answers.

In the end, archivists must mediate between offering "supportive collegiality" to researchers and operating within the legal and ethical boundaries established by donors and the contents of literary papers (Overbeck 62–69). The acquisition of literary papers provides opportunities to make donors aware of standard research practices, the desirability of openness in promoting the pursuit and dissemination of knowledge, and the need for clear and reasonable restrictions that protect the privacy of authors and third parties, restrictions that can be managed easily and are reviewed and updated on a regular basis. Although such an approach to archival management may not meet the immediate and pressing needs of researchers who must satisfy the requirements of funding bodies and publishers, it provides some assurance that an extensive body of Canadian literary papers will be available to support the preservation, pursuit, and dissemination of knowledge well into the future.

Notes

1 For research assistance, we wish to thank Danielle Deveau.
2 See Panofsky (1992) and John Lennox and Ruth Panofsky (1997).
3 See Panofsky, ed., Adele Wiseman issue, *Room of One's Own* (1993).
4 See McCaig, 15.
5 See Hodson, 194–211.
6 Association of Canadian Archivists, *Code of Ethics*.

Works Cited

Association of Canadian Archivists."Code of Ethics." *Archivists.ca*. n.d. Web. Apr. 13, 2005. (http://archivists.ca/about/ethics.aspx).

Clément, Dominique. Memorandum Re. BC Archives Audit of UVic Office. *Canada's Human Rights History*. Sept. 27, 2007. Web. Apr. 13, 2005. (http://www.historyofrights.com/PDF/memo_access.pdf).

Cook, Terry, and Joan M. Schwartz. "Archives, Records, and Power: The Making of Modern Memory." *Archival Science* 2.1–2 (2002): 1–19. Print.

Craig, Barbara L. "What Are the Clients? Who Are the Products? The Future of Archival Public Services in Perspective." *Archivaria* 31 (Winter 1990–91): 135–41. Print.

Fulford, Robert. "Build a Literary Legacy for Yourself: Smart Aspiring Writers Have Their Archives Ready." *National Post* May 24, 2005: AL1. Print.

Geselbracht, Raymond H. "The Origins of Restrictions on Access to Personal Papers at the Library of Congress and the National Archives." *American Archivist* 49.2 (1986): 142–62. Print.

Hodson, Sara S. "In Secret Kept, In Silence Sealed: Privacy in the Papers of Authors and Celebrities." *American Archivist* 67.2 (2004): 194–211. Print.

Lennox, John, and Ruth Panofsky, eds. *Selected Letters of Margaret Laurence and Adele Wiseman*. Toronto: U of Toronto P, 1997. Print.

McCaig, JoAnn. *Reading in Alice Munro's Archives*. Waterloo, ON: Wilfrid Laurier UP, 2002. Print.

Overbeck, Lois More. "Researching Literary Manuscripts: A Scholar's Perspective." *American Archivist* 56.1 (1993): 62–69. Print.

Panofsky, Ruth. *Adele Wiseman: An Annotated Bibliography*. Toronto: ECW, 1992. Print.

———, ed. *Adele Wiseman*. Spec. issue of *Room of One's Own* 16.3 (1993). Print.

Personal Ethics: Being an Archivist of Writers
Catherine Hobbs

What does it mean to "do right" by someone's archives? This is the question I ask myself before all others when I work with the archives of Canadian writers. The question has two components: "What does it mean to 'do right' by this person while treating his/her archives?" and "What does it mean to 'do right' by this writer's literary oeuvre in dealing with these archives?"

Archival theory has done a terrible job of accommodating the particular needs of individual people's archives. By and large, archival procedures have been based on models for dealing with organizational records (from government or business), as if personal archives were just smaller and less organized versions of these. As I have argued elsewhere, this oversight is difficult to absorb into professional work.[1] Archival theory has also made little effort to accommodate adequately the particular exigencies of literary archives. This lack of theory is ironic, since literary archives have been subject to early and active acquisition by archival and special collection institutions in many countries.[2]

Literary archives have a particular resonance for archivists precisely because writers are "creative wordsters, and therefore many of the documents writers produce are invested with a creative vision in ways not duplicated by any other archival genre."³ Acts of documentation blend very closely (in space and time) with acts of literary creation. Words are the tools of both literature and textual records, which are the dominant form of documents in archives. Paper or digital forms, which mimic the printed page, are the foundation for both. Textual documentation is the birthing place for the new literary work in ways that even archives from the other arts cannot duplicate, because of the writer's creative relationship to language. For example, a musician who may create a work either on the page (by notation) or on an instrument, makes the page one of several possible sites to document an idea, and notation one of a number of means. In literary archives the medium, language, and idea cohere together: literature exists within language and text. There are ways in which the interpretive imagination directs us to think of the "author of intention" (Hobbs, "New Approaches" 114):⁴ that is, a kind of fictional intent/self-representation behind all documents. There are ways in which authors use, reuse, and reconceptualize not just the facts of their lives but also their documentation to make new literary projects. Finally, there are ways in which a narrative or multiple narratives are suggested by personal archives;⁵ the perception of narrative is heightened because we are dealing with authors, after all, with the weight of literary intentions and creative use of language behind them.

When working with personal archives, every question of contact, acquisition, treatment, and interpretation is ethically marked, insofar as the choices of the archivist reflect a perception of the life lived by a particular individual and the interactions with others around that individual. Working with literary archives also subjects archival procedures to ethical decision-making because documentation slips toward literary interpretations and archival practices might have very real implications for the later interpretation of that literature. For example, quite obviously intentional or unintentional reorganization of archives might affect literary biography as much as it can alter our sense of how that literature developed.

The positions of the archivist are as follows: *interlocutor* about the archives with the creator, when the archivist makes contact with and then visits the creator; *first stage interpreter*, when the archivist identifies and describes documents in finding aids; and in some sense, *preliminary biographer*, when the archivist distills the facts of a person's life and circumstances in order to interpret the documents.⁶ It is the archivist's precarious privilege to be a first-comer (although in some cases not "the" first-comer) and to carry out an interpretation upon which other interpretations will be constructed.⁷ The forensic aspect (we destroy some evidence as we encounter and interpret it) is, by and large, an unexamined peril of the profession.

However, recent archival theory has opened up more self-conscious ways for archivists to conceive of their work and proceed with it. There is also room to adapt our tools and approaches to meet personal archives on their own ground.

Personal Contact during Acquisition
It is by the grace of the individuals who create archives that we have archival collections in repositories at all. My own approach to planning acquisitions involves immersing myself as much as I can in the way that literature is being created now. This approach has as much to do with research in written sources as with listening for comments about the subtle connections between writers and the individuals surrounding them. Who knows whom and who aids whom? Who was previously married to whom? This information, in turn, provides an understanding of the subtleties of an individual's situation.

When first starting my career, it had not fully occurred to me that I would need to be familiar with both the official and unofficial stories of these individuals. Where would I find the information neither taught in schools nor published? But digging around is not done for a vicarious thrill of "knowing something about somebody." Like health care professionals, archivists are not there to share anyone's secrets, but to use information to find a solution that fits the documents and the personality of the donor/creator.[8] This attention to personal details is an honest professional attempt to make the archival process fit the (sometimes tacit social and ethical) demands surrounding the archival material. This attentiveness forms the bedrock of professionalism displayed by archivists about personal archives.

Acquisition is the point at which documents in private possession are transferred to a public repository. This new state of affairs is incongruous with the private nature of these papers. Archivists must adhere to two unwritten ethical imperatives when dealing with personal collections. The first of these is the need to be aware of what this transfer feels like to the individual concerned. When making acquisition site visits or corresponding with archival donors, the archivist must pay close attention to how a donor behaves and gauges his or her comfort level with the process. Our approach is to explain fully archival processes and acknowledge that, ultimately, creators have the prerogative to do what they like with their archival material before the property is legally transferred to an institution. This consideration of viewpoint is extended to discussions of what material, if any, to restrict within the incoming acquisition. Later, the archivist vets the correspondence in light of the donor's privacy and third-party issues. This approach to the creators of archives is neither simply "networking" nor establishing for the archival institution an ongoing relationship of trust, although it is often perceived as such. Centred on personal archives, this approach involves "doing right" by the archives vis-à-vis the creator and other people whose materials are included, and understanding the creator's lived situation as much as possible.

The second unwritten ethical imperative that permeates all aspects of archival activities is to do justice to the fact that the archives are linked to a life. Personal archives were physically and intellectually part of someone's life, a life that they, in turn, evince. A person struggled to live through real time with documents as part of this process, sometimes using documenting or writing as the modus vivendi (as is often the case with creative writers). Archives are material evidence of living in time and space, both by virtue of their physicality and their intellectual and physical interrelations. In the case of creative writers, there is also evidence of the links between physical acts and creative decisions and activities. For example, revisions of a literary work are manifested in the crossing out and insertion of words at a particular moment, and whole sections of a work might be shifted in sequence in a manuscript. Archivists are the ones who are on site soonest after archival and literary creation. This position brings with it an ethical burden which, if not overtly articulated in our professional literature, is made evident in archivists' day-to-day work of interpretation.

The relationship of the creator to documents and the links to acts of creation should be a focus of archivists doing this work; however, the fact remains that our professional literature on appraisal (that is the decisions about what to acquire) advocates the belief that the terrain to be documented on a macro level is a more important focus than these questions of relationship between a creator and his or her fonds. Archivists are advised to take on large strategies for acquisition in particular subject areas.[9] Of course, archivists need to create plans and, in doing so, consider the current research trends and look beyond to the important phenomena of the potential documentary universe. In creating this archival cosmic map about what to acquire in general, politics of acquisition come into play. There is a tension between documenting phenomena and encompassing famous creators. To a degree, archivists cannot avoid the perception that by pursuing certain acquisitions and not others they are creating a canon.[10] Other choices with greater implications about how to balance out the archival record determine the voices that are present in archives. These are large-scale questions to address, and no single approach is perfect.

The focus on the macro approach, however, allows archivists to evade ethical imperatives which arise from dealing with individual lives. Archivists use their tools in ways that lend a false sense of neutrality. We try to leave evaluative language out of our descriptions, for example. We also risk the pitfalls of organicism in thinking that fonds map easily over an individual's activities and provide a direct link to them as they once were.[11] Hinging our practices on the personal and creative life is essential, or else archivists are presenting these lives, and hence these archives, from the outside. Certainly within the current environment, the self-conscious archivist aware of postmodern archival procedure might make the appraisal methodology transparent and available to researchers,[12] and might seek to leave a trace of decisions through the use of arrangement notes,[13] for example, but there are other, subtler questions underlying our normative practices as well.

Arrangement, Description, and Interpretation
Of course, people's archives don't fit demurely into neat folders and tight boxes (either figuratively or literally), and anyone who tells you they do is choosing to be simple-minded. *A fonds d'archives* begins in rooms, on buses, on planes; travels in briefcases; finds temporary abodes in desks and cabinets. Each of these locations and shifts is evidence of an individual's choices and lived moments.

Original order (one of the most beloved and hackneyed terms in archives, and perhaps our most obscure principle) is key to this understanding.[14] In dealing with individuals, particularly writers, one can sense that the original working patterns they maintained in their life situations are significant and that they have shifted over time. Interpreting these patterns depends on when you encounter the writer, what has survived, and what they have done in terms of storage.

At the point of acquisition, archivists encounter archives in various states of rawness in terms of order. The newest document may yet be on the desk. Others may be grouped in piles, heaped in folders on the desk, or spread in a swath across surfaces, and still others may be neatly filed away in drawers or boxed in the attic.

Researchers who are familiar with finding aids will be accustomed to knowing very little about these original states of order and re-order. Yet what is the advantage of seeing this type of information? At the very least, it keeps vestiges of the process of work and the uses of the document by the creator. By not typically including such information in finding aids, archivists give the impression that the fonds, or at least the fonds conveyed through the description, is consistent in form. These descriptions imply orderliness. This "dressing up" of personal lives diminishes the human aspect of the material and borders on the unethical.

Titling and Editing

The *Rules for Archival Description (RAD)* currently in use in Canada were not particularly developed with personal archives in mind. Although it is possible to incorporate additional contextual information and notes on the writer's relationship to the archives, such as is gathered in a site visit for archival appraisal, this practice is not common. Additionally, there are norms embedded in *RAD* that obscure arrangements and formalize elements of description at the expense of the creator's personal choices. For example, one of the archivist's jobs is to determine the titles for files when processing archives and writing finding aids.[15] Titles for series are fairly obviously constructed from an interpretation of the creator's activities. However, file titles have a deceptive simplicity. They imply the creator made an active choice to group documents together and identify them collectively, thereby suggesting an intimacy to the thoughts and actions of that creator. Editing occurs on an almost unconscious level for the archivist determining the title for what were personal documents (either for a given title or one supplied by the archivist to accurately reflect the contents of that file). Impressions are built into this process, and it is likely that each archivist would construct the same title in a different way. It is important, in my mind, to make note of which file titles the archivist developed in the absence of a visible title on a file folder. This option is possible in *RAD* (as it was in previous descriptive practices), but not often followed. If these details are not made clear, the researcher is inclined to think these titles were created by the author of the archives.

Title creation has increased the potential for deception when dealing with literary writers' fonds. Some of the conventions of capitalization, punctuation, and italicization followed in literary works are at odds with the *Rules for Archival Description*. The *Rules* stipulate capitalizing only the first word in a title, as is the bibliographic convention, but this rule becomes particularly problematic when a fonds title contains the title or working title for a literary work within it.[16] A better approach to take would be to indicate as clearly as possible the creator's decisions and to use his or her own conventions within a finding aid. If, for example, the creator has a tendency to capitalize important words on the title tab of a file folder, this habit could be transferred into the finding aid. We cannot keep the original file folders (except in exceptional circumstances), but in this way, the minute decisions made about naming are conveyed to the fonds, as is some of the creator's working conception.[17] There are other personal details or complications that conflict with decision-making in different *RAD* fields, such as dates, for example. All of these cannot be discussed in the present article, but each is constructed through an archivist's active interpretation and conveys the same type of simple homogeneity, which is deceptive in the context of the creator's actual personal life.

Sometimes editorial decisions in finding aids are more overt. For the organizational fonds of the International Authors at Harbourfront Centre Toronto, Harbourfront had transferred, among other series, a group of files containing their correspondence with authors, but only of those who had passed away. The question arose in my mind, "Should I change the series title Dead Authors files (as they were called around the office) to simply Authors files?" This change would take into account the possible audiences for the finding aid and restrain the glibness of the series' title. At other times, the interpretive language comes from creators themselves. With the best of intentions, writers often edit finding aids—as they would publications—when the archivist sends the lengthy list and description of their archives, seeking confirmation of the facts. The crux of the problem is, if we archivists hide behind our historic self-effacement (our own authorial fallacy), we leave no trail at all of the thoughts or collaborations that went into the finding aids. Often, these omissions result from a lack of time. In a number of cases, I have indicated "the author notes that…" or "author's list describes…" to delineate clearly where the creator has made specific note of something and to incorporate his or her own language. Making these decisions more overt and informing the research community about them is both ethical and essential to provide an accurate composite picture of this process.

The Creative Archival Turn

As literary and cultural studies engage more with the genre of the archives, archivists are better able to embrace our ironic situation in critical commentary; and there exists another possibility for us to take a creative turn as an interpreter to enliven the fonds for researchers. As Maryanne Dever explains, there is a life narrative that suggests itself to readers of archives, particularly caused by reading the documents in sequence and in our interpretation of their omissions.[18] An archivist is always prey to these narrative interpretations and to imposing false linearity on life events; however, he or she experiences more than just this impulse toward threading a narrative. Perhaps more relevant to the archivist's situation when dealing with personal archives is the necessity of trying to tease out life events, decisions, and acts of documentation when confronted with the whole fonds all at once. There is a certain circularity or infinite *mise en abyme* based on knowing the details of someone's life and literature and reflecting them in the archives the way that an archivist does. The archivist encounters opacity and the vague period when particular motivations or projects take root.

She follows the gradual distillation of some of the creator's preoccupations into projects and the fading or continued latency of others. The finding aid acts to formalize these origins, or overlooks them.

I encountered an additional layer of literary circularity when writing about the Carol Shields fonds. As a writer, Shields was tremendously interested in the lives of others. She created copious archives filled with personal correspondence, while at the same time amassing the details of ordinary lives she might use in fiction. She also had experience doing literary research, and an ironic perspective of archives was abundantly evident in her fiction. Her character and experience made her a very generous archival donor who had a certain degree of self-consciousness about the act of donating her archives. But this generosity and self-consciousness was matched by an awareness about documents and fiction: she knew that not everything would make its way into fiction, documentation, or biography, and that life exceeded these boundaries by its sheer volume of detail and ephemerality. Her fiction crossed the fictional/fact divide, evident in her use of family photographs to illustrate characters in *The Stone Diaries* or her deliberate changes to details of Winnipeg as the backdrop to *The Republic of Love*.[19]

Encountering this blurring made me, as her archivist, reflect on the circularity of life/archives/fiction relationships. Shields's fiction itself overturned the idea of a one-to-one transfer of biographical information: she played with the elements of her life and the lives of others and churned them together to transform them into her fiction. As an archivist, I felt it was my role to interact creatively, or at least laterally, to demonstrate what I knew about her particular preoccupations as they threaded in and out of life to fiction and back again. I was (hopefully) also overturning the nineteenth-century idea of an archivist as a gatekeeper of truth in response to her playfulness. For example, I suggested that her mother's diary (details of which she adopted for *The Stone Diaries* and *Larry's Party*) could no longer be read in its own archival context because it was subsumed into the daughter's (Shields's) archival fonds as well as into her own fiction.[20] This diary surfaces both as a physical object described in *Larry's Party* and in the transfer of details from women's lives and descriptions of a trip to the U.K. found in Shields's fiction. What was the status of a document that made a cameo appearance in fiction? The diary accrued new contextual information in both the fictional and "literal" worlds. In some way, I hoped my act of theoretical writing was a complementary gesture to the self-conscious and ironic archives creator. I was calling attention to her subversion of the document's place in archives, overturning the ideas of provenance and original order,[21] and turning archival context into a myriad of reflections:

fact, intention, idea, and metaphor, blended in a non-privileged way. In fact, this process might be the closest and most responsible act toward literary archives—acting to let the signs float and interrelate without end or stopping to point at fact or fiction. In a sense, this unanchored reflection encompasses the work and life of creators like Shields in a meaningful way because using the details of life and thoughts about documenting to create fiction and archives, developed in a foment and not uni-directionally, was characteristic of her.

In the end, archival work is an approximation of an ideal, and the archival fonds a simulacrum of activities. The deceptive simplicity of this relationship is that it inheres in physical documentation (although, of course, the rise of digital storage is bringing us away from this physicality). We sense a concretization from the rootedness in the physical and an elusive and illusive connection to that which was once real.[22]

Currently, many archivists sense that archival work has continual and renewing value and that the moral imperative is to aim to do it correctly, however imperfect or fragmentary the results may be. Self-consciousness is a strong element of this approach. We need to be earnest about what we are trying to do, and realistic about it at the same time. Such an approach retains a self-critical edge and documents decision-making. Archivists are not afraid to interpret, but we are careful to show it is an interpretation. On the one hand, we aim to leave a visible trail; on the other hand, archivists can also throw up a myriad of interwoven referents about the archives in response to the circularity of our professional endeavours. These are two imperfect but perhaps complementary gestures to get at the content and meaning of personal archives of literary figures, and thereby to treat these figures appropriately ("do right by them") in ways not previously addressed.

Notes

1 See Hobbs's "Reenvisioning the Personal."
2 In Canada and Australia, the acquisition of literary archives by archival institutions or university special collections began in or before the 1970s. By the early 1990s, literary archival holdings had grown robust and experts defined well-articulated fields of acquisition in both countries. These developments stand in contrast to the longer traditions of Britain, France, and America (which are concomitant with their literature and literary study).
3 For a fuller discussion of the "writer of intention" see Hobbs's "New Approaches," 2, 109–19.
4 Hobbs, "New Approaches" 113.
5 For an exploration of this drive toward fictional narrative, see Dever's essays "Reading Other People's Mail" and "Marjorie Barnard Falls in Love."
6 As McCaig discusses in *Reading In: Alice Munro's Archives*, power dynamics are at play over the truth of archives, and archivists play a role in the interpretation

and availability of records which shapes the ability of researchers to interpret them (13–16).
7 Archives are not always acquired by archivists in rough form from the creator. Literary executors, family members, lovers, friends, and scholars can each influence the arrangement and keeping of archives by archives creators, and thereby alter what eventually comes to the archives as a fonds.
8 The *Code of Ethics* of the Association of Canadian Archivists states that "[a]rchivists make every attempt possible to respect the privacy of the individuals who created or are the subjects of records, especially those who had no voice in the disposition of the records."
9 The Documentation Strategy developed by Helen Samuels has been proposed as a useful avenue for private archives acquisition planning (see Pollard 149).
10 For a fuller discussion of canonization and literary archives, see Tector's "The Almost Accidental Archive."
11 According to the Canadian Council of Archives, the *Rules for Archival Description* describe the fonds as "[t]he whole of the documents, regardless of form or medium, automatically and organically created and/or accumulated and used by a particular individual, family, or corporate body in the course of that creator's activities or functions" (D-5). For a discussion of reconceptualizing the fonds and departing from notions of organicism, see MacNeil, 10.
12 Barbara Craig conducted a survey of the appraisal practices of Canadian archivists and found that despite the interest in these decisions by the public, "only twenty percent (19.7%) [of archivists surveyed] indicated that appraisal and decision information was provided as a matter of course through finding aids and other catalogue records" (24).
13 An arrangement note describes the intellectual arrangement of a fonds, and may include information about reorganization(s) by the creator, arrangement by the archivist, changes in the classification scheme, or reconstitution of original order (Association of Canadian Archivists, 1.66).
14 The concept of original order is meant to safeguard the arrangement of archives in the manner they were arranged by the creator. The concept hinges on the idea that documents retain additional or relational meaning in the context of the other documents in a fonds. This concept has a long history within archival theory and many theorists site the so-called Dutch Manual by Muller, Feith and Fruin (first published in 1989 and translated into English in 1940) as the work which positioned original order as a central concern for archivists.
15 For full definitions of the archival terms "fonds," "series," and "file," see the *Rules for Archival Description*.
16 The bibliographic convention referred to here is library cataloguing. This can be defined as "the convention of book cataloguing," or "the convention from library cataloguing."
17 In the context of digital archives, there are additional layers of complexity and more choices to be made about retaining personal approaches to structuring archives. Some of these have been investigated by projects like the PARADIGM (Personal ARchives Accessible in DIGital Media) Project, and the Salman Rushdie Digital Archives Project at Emory University. Technology provides more powerful tools for discerning original order, and creates new choices for archivists to make in conveying these orders.
18 See Dever, 120–23.

19 For a full discussion of this approach to Shields's archives, see Hobbs's "Voice and Re-Vision."
20 These findings were discussed in my (unpublished) conference paper, "Reading the Genre of the Archive through the fonds of Canadian Writers."
21 For complete definitions of the two foundational and related archival principles, *provenance* and *original order*, see the Society of American Archivists' *Glossary of Archival Terminology*.
22 As Dever, Newman, and Vickery suggest in their introduction to *The Intimate Archive*, "Perhaps it is also the materiality of these artefacts that helps create the highly seductive but illusory effect of being 'closer to what actually happened'" (32).

Works Cited

Association of Canadian Archivists. "Code of Ethics." *Archivists.ca*. ACA, n.d. Web. May 7, 2010. ⟨http://archivists.ca/content/code-ethics⟩.

Canadian Council of Archives. *Rules for Archival Description*. Rev. ed. *Canadian council archives.ca*. CCA, July 2008. Web. May 7, 2010. ⟨http://www.cdncouncil archives.ca/RAD/RADComplete_July2008.pdf⟩.

Craig, Barbara. "Doing Archival Appraisal in Canada. Results from a Postal Survey of Practitioners' Experiences, Practices, and Opinions." *Archivaria* 64 (Fall 2007): 1–45. Print.

Dever, Maryanne, Sally Newman, and Ann Vickery, eds. *The Intimate Archive*. Canberra: National Library of Australia, 2009. Print.

———. Introduction. Dever, Newman, and Vickery 1–39. Print.

Dever, Maryanne. "Marjorie Barnard Falls in Love." Dever, Newman, and Vickery 41–79. Print.

———. "Reading Other People's Mail." *Archives and Manuscripts* 24.1 (1996): 120–23. Print.

Hobbs, Catherine. "The Character of Personal Archives: Reflections on the Value of Records of Individuals." *Archivaria* 52 (Fall 2001): 126–35. Print.

———. "New Approaches to Canadian Literary Archives." *Journal of Canadian Studies* 40.2 (2006): 109–19. Print.

———. "Reading the Genre of the Archive through the Fonds of Canadian Wrtiers." Archive Fever/Archive Fervour Conference. Aberystwyth, Wales. July 2008. Conference paper.

———. "Reenvisioning the Personal: Reframing Traces of Individual Life." *Currents of Archival Thinking*. Ed. Terry Eastwood and Heather MacNeil. Santa Barbara: Libraries Unlimited, 2010. 213–41. Print.

———. "Voice and Re-vision: The Carol Shields Archival Fonds." *Carol Shields and the Extra-Ordinary*. Ed. Marta Dvorak and Manina Jones. Montréal: McGill-Queen's UP, 2007. 33–58. Print.

Loftus, Mary J. "The Author's Desktop." *Emory Magazine*. Emory U, Winter 2010. Web. May 7, 2010. ⟨http://www.emory.edu/EMORY_MAGAZINE/2010/winter/authors.html⟩.

MacNeil, Heather. "Archivalterity, Rethinking Original Order." *Archivaria* 66 (Spring 2008): 1–24. Print.

McCaig, JoAnn. *Reading In: Alice Munro's Archives*. Waterloo: Wilfrid Laurier UP, 2002. Print.

Muller S., J. A. Feith, and R. Fruin. *Manual for the Arrangement and Description of Archives*. Trans. A. Leavitt. New York: H. W. Wilson, 1940. Print.

Pollard, Riva A. "The Appraisal of Personal Papers: A Critical Literature Overview." *Archivaria* 52 (Fall 2001): 136–50. Print.

Society of American Archivists. "Glossary of Archival and Records Terminology." *Archivists.org*. SAA, 2005. Web. May 7, 2010. (http://www.archivists.org/glossary/index.asp).

Tector, Amy. "The Almost Accidental Archive and Its Impact on Literary Subjects and Canonicity." *Journal of Canadian Studies* 40.2 (2006): 96–108. Print.

University of Oxford and University of Manchester. "Personal Archives Accessible in Digital Media Project (PARADIGM)." *Paradigm.ac.uk*. U of Oxford, U of Manchester. n.d. Web. May 7, 2010. (http://www.paradigm.ac.uk/).

Invisibility Exhibit: The Limits of Library and Archives Canada's "Multicultural Mandate"
Karina Vernon

> Silence marks lack of neither language nor identity. Rather, it is a form of communication that those who rely on the hegemonic word of private authority cannot hear.
> –M. NourbeSe Philip

Currently, Library and Archives Canada finds itself in an awkward position with regard to its "multicultural mandate." Articulated in its 2003 working paper, "Architects of Change: How the National Library of Canada Is Responding to the New Cultural Landscape," this mandate declares that "[m]ulticulturalism lies at the very heart of Library and Archives Canada. It is integral and fundamental to the institution as it is to Canada itself." "Canadians," it insists, "must be able to find their own communities' heritage and culture within our collection, or to access it in others'. They must see themselves, their past, in what we hold" (LAC, "Architects"). But tellingly, in a report titled "Directions for Change" published a year later, Library and Archives Canada admitted that accomplishing this multicultural mandate will involve some shifts in collecting emphases to ensure Aboriginal and ethnocultural communities' documentary heritage, reflecting their experience within Canadian society, becomes better represented in our collection. At times, LAC may assist a community to document its heritage, at the same time assuring that it is collected, preserved and made accessible—whether locally or as part of the LAC collection. (LAC "Directions")

In other words, the collections at Library and Archives Canada do not currently reflect the "heritage and culture" of all Canadians, only those of the nation's historically dominant cultural groups. Its multicultural collections, it seems, are lacking.

Library and Archives Canada is well aware of the latter fact. In 2004, LAC created the Multicultural Initiatives Office, first to address the perceived lacuna in terms of what it calls its ethnocultural collections, and second to "act as a champion for multiculturalism and build networks to ensure that LAC represents and serves the geographic, linguistic and cultural diversity of all Canadians" (LAC, "Knowledge Institution"). The year that it was created, this Multicultural Initiatives Office initiated a series of community consultations with members of "ethnocultural communities" across the country to determine why, to put it bluntly, people of colour and ethnicized people do not use or contribute to public archives in Canada—at least, not to the extent that LAC would like. Between October 2004 and February 2006, the Multicultural Initiatives unit of Library and Archives Canada assembled email, telephone, and in-person focus groups with individuals from six racialized and ethnicized communities, as well as librarians and archivists who aim to serve these communities (LAC, *Community Consultations*). The Multicultural Initiatives Office met with members of the South Asian community in Surrey, British Columbia; the Chinese community in Vancouver, British Columbia; the Somali community in Ottawa, Ontario; the black Anglophone and Haitian communities in Montréal, Québec; and finally, the Italian community in Ottawa, Ontario. The rationale for selecting these particular communities and not others is outlined in the Methodology section of the *Community Consultations: Report of Activities and Outcomes*:

> Some broad approaches governed the identification of invitees for each of the six in-person community consultation sessions hosted by Multicultural Initiatives and regional public library partners between October 2004 and February 2006. It was deemed important to solicit input beyond Ottawa and to conduct focus groups in disparate regions of Canada where feasible (in this case, Vancouver, Ottawa, Montréal). A balance was sought between newcomer perspectives and input from well-established heritage communities.

The report added that

> A secondary goal was to make contact with those who have not typically had significant dealings with LAC to date in order to maximize the two-way learning value of these sessions; while the focus groups facilitated information-gathering, they also presented opportunity to make Library and Archives Canada, as a new knowledge institution, known to potential constituents who may not have had LAC on the radar to date.

According to its report, then, by assembling focus groups with members of Chinese, Somali, Haitian, Italian, and South Asian communities, LAC "strikes a balance between newcomer perspectives and input from well-established heritage communities," and garners input from communities that have not had "LAC on the radar" and which the institution now hopes to attract.

One wonders, however, if these are the only racialized and ethnicized communities in Canada that could have fulfilled LAC's two stated objectives; aren't there other communities in Canada currently underserved by the national archives? Might the particular communities they chose have been selected for additional but unstated reasons? In LAC's efforts to institutionalize difference in their collections, it might have chosen these communities because they are recognizably marked as "visible" and "cultural" within Canadian society. (The communities thus become metonymic for racialized communities in Canada in general.) By consulting with members of the Chinese, Somali, Haitian, and South Asian communities in particular, LAC is seen as representing and integrating "difference" into the institution. Yet it is important to note that the internal differences of these communities are downplayed. Though the LAC report "acknowledges the diversity within and between communities" (20), the language of the *Community Consultations* report nevertheless represents each one as discrete, internally homogenous formations ("*the* South Asian community," "*the* Somali community"). This language works to construct the community as a manageable difference that can be slotted neatly into a mosaic type of multicultural model. The methodology used by the focus group to approach community consultation itself constructs these communities as homogenous and univocal, for it presumes that individual members can "stand" and speak metonymically for the "group."

Such assumptions about how the "individual" might stand for the group affects an approach to understanding the role that women played in focus groups. Their role is difficult to assess, since the *Community Consultations* report that makes public the focus group findings is never explicit about whether or to what extent a desire for gender parity was part of the methodology for selecting participants. While it is hard to determine whether women played a significant role, the report does indicate that women's issues were raised repeatedly in the focus groups. For instance, during the meeting of the Somali community in Montréal, a focus group member raised the point that young women of their community "encounter difficulty in accessing library services for themselves and their families" since they are, in many cases, "responsible for rearing large families (at times single-handedly)." One focus group member at that meeting posed the question, "How might we bring services *to them*?" (*Community Consultations* 30). Similarly, members of the English-speaking community in Montréal spoke about the specific need to focus on youth and women: "the young ones coming up are the issue—kids need a sense of purpose," one participant said. Another underscored the need to recognize "women in the community" (*Community Consultations* 34).

Significantly, the Multicultural Initiatives Office did not meet with any Métis, Inuit, or First Nations people, despite identifying gaps in LAC's "Aboriginal holdings." Instead, after the reconstruction and consolidation of the National Library and National Archives in 2004 into a single "Knowledge Institute," LAC created two *separate* initiatives to handle "Multicultural services and collections," and "Aboriginal Services and collections." Each of these initiatives has its own coordinator and is funded separately (Storey). The separation of the Multicultural and the Aboriginal at LAC is a point I will return to at the end of this paper. The report that came out of Multicultural Office's community consultations found, in a nutshell, that "in general, Library and Archives Canada was not a recognized entity within any of the communities consulted.... Across the board, these professionals said that their clients had little or no understanding of LAC and its potential relevance to them" (*Community Consultations*). Why then, do racial and ethnic communities in Canada feel that the national public archives are "irrelevant" to them? Even in spite of LAC's explicit and, I believe, sincere—although belated—multicultural mandate, fuelled by its genuine desire to see minority communities represented in the archives? What is wrong with the Multicultural Archive, and what has occasioned the sense of disconnection between ethnicized and racialized communities and the LAC?

The published report to come out of LAC's Multicultural Initiatives Office in response to these focus groups offers only limited answers to these questions. The report finds, in general, that the problem is one of "awareness": the cultural groups consulted are not sufficiently aware of the collections and resources offered by LAC; the institution is failing to promote its collections and services through community outreach programs; and various minority groups are not adequately informed of the important role formal archives can play in helping to preserve and pass on their collective histories. As the *Community Consultations* report puts it, "For the most part, Library and Archives Canada was not a recognized entity within any of the communities consulted" (4). The assumption here on the part of LAC, of course, is that everybody in Canada *wants* representation in the Multicultural Archives, that all racial and ethnic groups and women desire their documentary histories to be included, and that their histories would be preserved in the archives' terms—if only they were more aware of the archives. The unarticulated principle underlying LAC's multicultural mandate is that archival silence is a sign of marginalization and exclusion—a silence that belies the nation's and the archives statelegislated multicultural policies. Because the national archive (like the nation itself) gains "multicultural" identity and legitimacy only insofar as it manages to institutionalize and represent difference, the racialized silences in the archive "must" be filled. Everyone "must see themselves," even if it is in records that the archives itself helps to create. As the *Community Consultations* document states, "LAC must endeavour to become ever more inclusive of cultural communities, from established heritage groups to newcomer communities who have lacked representation in Canadian institutions to date" (49). In order to fill this archival silence, LAC's mandate states, "At times, LAC may assist a community to document its heritage, at the same time assuring that it is collected, preserved and made accessible" ("Directions for Library and Archives Canada").

Yet in its summaries of the focus group discussions, a different and more complicated story regarding this racialized and ethnicized archival silence emerges from the community consultations, and LAC does not seem prepared to grapple with its meaning. In summarizing the feedback from the various focus group discussions, the Multicultural Initiatives report notes, for example, that although "[f]ormal archiving is not considered a common practice within Somali culture, many Somalis maintain personal archives" (*Community Consultations* 31). Similarly, with regard to the South Asian community, the report notes that, "while the value of archives appears to be understood by many within the South Asian community, at present, there is a lack of systematic effort (from within or beyond the community) when it comes to collecting formal archival materials" (22). Of the members of the Chinese Canadian communities consulted, "it was noted that some community members have been storing archival community information as they await the development of an organized effort to bring these materials together" (26). Racialized and ethnicized communities in Canada, it seems, are busily archiving their own ancestral and community histories. They are just not consigning their collections to the nation's official and public institutions of memory.

Lest the findings of this report seem in any way anomalous, I should note that the report both confirms and generalizes a phenomenon I have already discovered with regard to black communities on the Canadian Prairies. Although the holdings of public archives on the Prairies include some material pertaining to the historical black presence there, a great deal of this material was, in fact, created by the archives themselves.[1] For instance, the Provincial Archives of Alberta ran an oral history project between the 1960s and 1970s in an effort to document and preserve the histories and memories of Alberta's early pioneers. One of the contractors who worked for the archives, Reevan Dolgoy, went to the community of Breton (once called Keystone) in central Alberta, to record the memories of the community's black pioneers. The pioneers who participated in the project were Mrs. Charles King, who arrived in Alberta in 1911 with her husband when she was nineteen years old; Mark Hooks, who was born to pioneer parents in Breton in 1926 and who later took a homestead himself; and Ellis Hooks, who arrived in Alberta with his parents in 1911 when he was five years old.[2] Together, these pioneers recorded six and a half hours of orature. These recordings are a treasure trove of history and memory, but in many ways they are marked by the circumstances of their making: throughout, the pioneers seem reluctant to speak candidly about sensitive issues, particularly their experiences of racism because they are speaking to an archive employee, a community outsider.

Aside from such archive-created material, the majority of the Prairies' historical black, and especially pioneer, archival legacy still exists outside of public archives, in private, family collections. If, as the LAC report indicates, this tendency is also the case with other "ethnocultural groups" in Canada, then this phenomenon is one that those of us who do archival research, particularly on black or otherwise racialized communities, need to know about, since the materials we find in public archives are likely only the tip of the iceberg.

It is difficult to estimate just how much of the Prairies' black archive remains outside public institutions of memory. But, in speaking with a descendant of a black pioneer family in Edmonton, Junetta Jamerson, I gathered that there are at least half a dozen significant family collections that have not yet been donated to public archives. Her own family has held onto their important family papers, and Jamerson knows of three other families in the Edmonton area with comparable collections. Significantly, it is women like Jamerson, more than men, who act as custodians of the Prairies' black history. Because the black pioneers who settled on the Prairies came from a more oral culture than a textual one, and because, as Gay Wiltenz notes in her *Binding Cultures: Black Women Writers in African and the Diaspora*, in diasporic cultures, women are the unacknowledged "masters" of storytelling who skilfully preserve and pass on family lore and history (xxiv), it has often fallen to them to act as the historians and archivists of their Prairie culture. Indeed, one of the Prairies' most important collections of oral history, the two-volume work *The Window of Our Memories* was compiled by three of Jamerson's relations: her grandmother Velma Carter, her aunt Wanda Leffler Akili, and her sister, Leah Suzanne Carter. Other significant examples of black Prairie women's archival efforts include Willa Reese (Bowen) Dallard's memoir in booklet form, *Memories of My Father: The Late Willis Bowen of Amber Valley, Alberta* (1978); Cheryl Foggo's memoir of four generations of her family on the Prairies, *Pourin' Down Rain* (1990); Patricia Clements's oral interviews with railway porters for the Manitoba Museum (1993); and Addena Sumter Freitag's *Stay Black and Die* (2007), an autobiographical play about growing up in Winnipeg's black community during the 1950s and 1960s.

I asked Jamerson why she has decided to hold onto her family papers rather than donate them to the City of Edmonton Archives, the Alberta Provincial Archives, or Library and Archives Canada, where family materials could be catalogued, kept in a climate-controlled environment, and made accessible to the public. She responded that, to her mind, making the archive public was equivalent to "giving it over to white people" (phone conversation). Jamerson's comment addresses two of several significant problems with the prospect of donating black archival material to Canada's public archives. First, doing so invariably involves "giving it over," or deterritorializing important cultural documents. For a community whose collective identity in many ways coheres around the documents that testify to a unique and shared history, maintaining cultural property rights and access to those documents is paramount. Jamerson's comment also addresses the concern that staff complements at public archives in Canada remain, by and large, white. Her comment effectively addresses the question of whether non-black archivists who may not be familiar with black Canadian or black Prairie history could adequately respect the particular materials that families like the Jamersons have chosen to safeguard and preserve.

In many ways, the personal archives collected by black pioneer families on the Prairies test the limits of the notion of archival "value," for they preserve a great deal of what institutional archives call ephemera: written and printed matter not intended to be retained or preserved. In library and information science, the term describes the class of published single-sheet or single-page documents which are meant to be thrown away after one use, and it can include material such as greeting cards, menus, tickets, pamphlets, and postcards. One of the concerns many black families have is that, upon entering a public archive, their materials would be handled, catalogued, and scrutinized by professional archivists who do not appreciate the memorial, spiritual, sentimental, and cultural values clinging to objects that might at first appear odd and unimpressive: the menu of a black community social function; a railway porter's sixtieth-anniversary souvenir program; a son or daughter's high school essay on Amber Valley (historically an all-black community in north central Alberta); an undated photograph of a run-down house surrounded by tall prairie grass. But, as Ann Cvetkovich reminds us in *An Archive of Feelings: Trauma, Sexuality and Lesbian Public Cultures*, when dominant cultures fail to chronicle the lives of minorities, it is often the ephemeral documents of ordinary people that bear the burden of remembering.

There are, in addition to the issues Jamerson's comment addresses, several other important reasons why black and otherwise racialized communities in Canada are choosing to store and maintain records outside of public archives. The historical origins of the museum and the archive itself work against racialized communities wanting to "see themselves" and their documents represented in the archive. As S. I. Martin observes, the museum, with its late-Victorian origins, historically "stood as a testament to British expansion into and documentation of the world at large" (197). "Let us never forget," Martin writes, "the degrading and enormously popular and large-scale public displays of people of colour (Singalese, Tamils, 'Bedouin Arabs,' Matabeles, Swazis, Hottentots, Malays) in so-called 'native villages' where they could be observed going through the motions of snake-charming or performing a 'superstitious bush dance'" (197). According to Martin, it is "inevitable" that the present-day view among blacks in Britain is "that museums, galleries and archives are still places which tend to be *about* us rather than *for* us" (197–98).

What is more, there is a perception among many racialized or minoritized communities both in Canada and around the world that public archives aren't living houses of memory so much as they are houses of forgetting. South African archivist Verne Harris recognizes the relationship between archives and forgetting in "Seeing (In) Blindness: South Africa, Justice, and Passion for Archives." Quoting Derrida, Verne notes, "[t]he work of the archivist is not simply a work of memory. It's a work of mourning. And a work of mourning...is a work of memory but also the best way just to forget the other, to keep it safe...in a safe—but when you put something in a safe it's just in order to be able to forget it" (5). Indeed, in Library and Archives Canada's focus group discussions, when members of the anglophone black community in Montréal were asked why they didn't use the resources of LAC, they responded that archives are off-putting because, to them, they are "dead places" (*Community Consultations* 35).

All of these are significant reasons why racialized communities in Canada might choose to archive their own personal and community histories, and these are issues that, to some extent, have already been theorized by other scholars. For instance, Jamerson's comment about "giving over" archival documents "to white people" raises a host of issues related to the area of cultural property rights. What kind of access to documents becomes available to families once their materials are housed in an archive? What are the implications of deterritorializing ancestral materials from local communities? These are questions that have been explored extensively with regard to Aboriginal communities, both in Canada and around the globe.[3] In the space that I have remaining, I would like to turn my attention to another aspect of the problem, one with which LAC's belated Multicultural Initiatives Report is unable to come to terms—that it is the ideological limits of multiculturalism and the Multicultural Archives itself that keeps racialized communities' archives hidden.

Institutional archives, as we know, find their justification grounded in concepts of the state. As Terry Cook reminds us, "archives traditionally were founded by the state, to serve the state, as part of the state's hierarchical structure and organizational culture" (10). Thus, archival science found its early legitimization in statist theories and models, and from the study of the character and properties of older state records. While the maintenance of governmental records and administrative continuity are still recognized as important purposes for archives, the principle justification for the institution today rests on being able to offer citizens a sense of identity, locality, history, culture, and personal and collective memory. State archives now serve a more explicitly ideological function: they aim to reflect, in the achievement of a single archival body, the unity and cohesiveness of the state as a whole. As Derrida argues in *Archive Fever*, "[t]he archontic principle of the archive is also a principle of consignation, that is, of gathering together" (3). "*Consignation*," Derrida elaborates, "aims to coordinate a single corpus, in a system or a synchrony in which all the elements articulate the unity of an ideal"—and here, I would insert *ideological*—"configuration. In an archive, there should not be any absolute dissociation, any heterogeneity or *secret* which could separate (*secernere*), or partition, in an absolute manner" (3; emphasis in original).

This fundamental problem (or secret, if you will) lies at the heart of the Multicultural Archives. As an articulation of the ideological configuration of the state, the archives, like the nation, are deeply fissured. But in the Multicultural Archives this splintering must remain secret. The archives must be cohesive—like the nation, a "difference studded unity"; all its holdings, including those of Canada's "necessary others" (Mackey 13) must be filled to plenitude. And yet the National Archives of Canada is, in its very structure, already divided. At Library and Archives Canada, the Aboriginal is thought of and indeed kept separate from the Multicultural, both spatially in its collections and its budgetary organization, and theoretically in differing and separate mandates. The archives evoke in its structure the same fault lines inherent in the settler-state. Yet Aboriginal and other racialized communities are currently being asked not only to invest their materials in this archive (thereby participating in the construction of themselves as national subjects along the lines that the state envisions for them) but also to "see themselves" and their histories somehow metaphysically reflected in the institution.

But these communities do not see themselves in the institution. As the Multicultural Initiatives Office notes in their reported feedback from the black anglophone focus group in Montréal,

> Participants want to see Black materials cross-referenced within libraries so that they might be discovered in multiple locations by a variety of means (i.e., not merely because they are housed in a special "Black Studies" section). Black Studies sections in libraries were described in terms of the ultimate Catch-22; while this domain may be necessary at times to facilitate resource discovery, it reinforces "otherness," relegating the Black experience to a single place (and dimension) in a collection. (*Community Consultations* 36)

In what ways does the division of the multicultural from the Aboriginal archive prevent us from seeing the ways immigrant, diasporic, and Aboriginal histories in Canada are closely intertwined? For instance, how does the imagined separation of the multicultural from the Aboriginal perpetuate the sense that diasporic communities and their histories are not immediately connected to Aboriginal people in Canada? In what ways does the separation of the multicultural and the Aboriginal at the archival level reinforce the problematic understanding of diaspora as a wholly deterritorialized phenomenon, which in turn discourages us from grappling with the fact that diasporic communities are deeply territorialized in Canada and on Aboriginal lands?

Whereas the 1980s and especially the 1990s were marked by an insistence on presence—disenfranchised groups seeking to be seen, heard, and included in the institutional structures and contexts that inform and shape cultural production in Canada—in the past two decades, those groups have chosen to act outside structures such as state archives. They have decided to work locally at establishing their own archives and sites of memory, consciously undermining the unity of archives that the theory of the state seems no longer capable of providing. One of the implications of these new tactics of invisibility and absence from archives is that we will need to read the "gaps," "silences," and "void regions" in the archival records at the state level differently: not as signs of disenfranchisement, exclusion, or victimage, but as potential signs of empowered self-exemption from archives, a form of active resistance against the fantasy of the total Multicultural Archive.

Notes

I am indebted to Sachiko Murakami for the title of this essay. Her beautiful collection of poetry *The Invisibility Exhibit* (2008) materializes in language Vancouver's invisible archives.

1. I am not critiquing archivists' efforts to insert blackness into the nation's historical record through these projects; in fact, I regard it is a blessing that such records exist. But, as Carter argues, "[w]hen captured by an archivist, through an oral history project, for example, the stories, histories, and records may not have the function or meaning intended by the original record creator." For an analysis of archives-created records, see Carter, "Of Things Said and Unsaid."
2. Provincial Archives of Alberta Accession # 78.65/23; Provincial Archives of Alberta Accession # 78.65/21; There are three cassette tapes of Ellis Hooks's orature. Provincial Archives of Alberta Accession # 78.65/32; #78.65/28; and 78.65/28.
3. See, for instance, Laszlo's "Ethnographic Archival Records and Cultural Property"; Cooper's "Issues in Native American Archives"; Greene's "Protocols for Native American Archival Materials"; and Wareham's "'Our Own Identity, Our Own Taonga, Our Own Self Coming Back': Indigenous Voices in New Zealand Record-Keeping" (2001). For a discussion on the problematic territorialization of Indigenous oral archives, see Kurtz's "A Postcolonial Archive? On the Paradox of Practice in a Northwest Alaska Project."

Works Cited

Carter, Rodney G. S. "Of Things Said and Unsaid: Power, Archival Silences, and Power in Silence." *Archivaria* 61 (2006): 215–33. Print.

Carter, Velma, and Wanda Leffler Akili. *The Window of Our Memories*. St. Albert: Black Cultural Research Society of Alberta, 1981. Print.

Carter, Velma, and Leah Suzanne Carter. *The Window of Our Memories. Volume II: The New Generation*. St. Albert: Black Cultural Research Society of Alberta, 1990. Print.

Cook, Terry. "Science and Postmodernism: New Formulations for Old Concepts." *Archival Science* 1 (2000): 3–24. Print.

Cooper, Cary A. "Issues in Native American Archives." *Collection Management* 27.2 (2002): 43–54. Print.

Cvetkovich, Ann. *An Archive of Feelings: Trauma, Sexuality and Lesbian Public Cultures*. Durham: Duke UP, 2003. Print.

Derrida, Jacques. *Archive Fever: A Freudian Impression*. Trans. Eric Prenowitz. Chicago: U of Chicago P, 1995. Print.
Green, Mark A. "Protocols for Native American Archival Materials." *Archival Outlook* (2008): 3. Web. Feb. 17, 2012. (http://www2.archivists.org/sites/all/files/AO-MarApr2008.pdf).
Harris, Verne. "Seeing (In) Blindness: South Africa, Archives, and Passion for Justice." *Ghandi-Luthuli Documentation Centre*. 2001. Web. May 26, 2011. (http://scnc.ukzn.ac.za/doc/LibArchMus/Arch/ Harris_V_Freedom_of_Information_in_SA_Arhives_for_justice.pdf).
Jamerson, Junetta. Personal phone conversation with author. Edmonton, Feb. 16, 2006.
Kurtz, Matthew. "A Postcolonial Archive? On the Paradox of Practice in a Northwest Alaska Project." *Archivaria* 61 (Spring 2006): 63–90. Print.
Laszlo, Krisztina. "Ethnographic Archival Records and Cultural Property." *Archivaria* 61 (Spring 2006): n.p. Web. Feb. 17, 2012.
Library and Archives Canada. "Architects of Change: How the National Library of Canada Is Responding to the New Cultural Landscape." *IFLA.org*. Aug. 2003. Web. Feb. 18, 2012.
———. "Directions for Library and Archives Canada." *CollectionsCanada.gc.ca*. June 2004. Web. May 11, 2010. (http://collectionscanada.ca/obj/012012/f2/01-e.pdf).
———. "Library and Archives Canada: Canada's Newest Knowledge Institution." *Conference of Directors of National Libraries*. 2006. Web. Feb. 19, 2012. (http://www.cdnl.info/2006/canada2006.rtf).
———. *Community Consultations: Report on Activities and Outcomes*. Collections Canada.gc.ca. Aug. 2006. Web. May 11, 2010. (http://www.collectionscanada.gc.ca/multicultural/005007-240-e.html).
Mackey, Eva. *The House of Difference: Cultural Politics and National Identity in Canada*. Toronto: U of Toronto P, 2002. Print.
Martin, S. I. "Inheriting Diversity: Archiving the Past." *The Politics of Heritage: The Legacies of "Race."* Ed. Jo Littler and Roshi Naidoo. London: Routledge, 2005. 196–202. Print.
Murakami, Sachiko. *The Invisibility Exhibit*. Vancouver: Talonbooks, 2008. Print.
Storey, Brook, Multicultural Initiatives Office. "Research Question: LAC's Multicultural Initiative?" Message to author. May 11, 2010. Email.
Wareham, Evelyn. "'Our Own Identity, Our Own Taonga, Our Own Self Coming Back': Indigenous Voices in New Zealand Record-Keeping." *Archivaria* 52 (Fall 2001): n.p. Web. Feb. 17, 2012.
Wilentz, Gay. *Binding Cultures: Black Women Writers in Africa and the Diaspora*. Bloomington: Indiana UP, 1992.

III. Responsibilities

Rat in the Box:
Thoughts on Archiving My Stuff
Susan McMaster

"Mouse turds or rat turds? A few mouse turds are nothing, they can be brushed off…"

I look with amazement at my neighbour and friend, Anne Goddard, formerly the literary archivist at the (then) National Archives of Canada, and a person I'd always thought of as precise, meticulous, organized, and very, very clean. She would paw through mouse turds?

"A pity to throw all that out, a whole big box. Letters are irreplaceable, especially before computers."

"It really smelled! I think it was a rat. Anyway, it's gone. I sent it out with the garbage this week."

"Hmmm. Pity."

Archivists are interesting people, living in the dreamlands of a long-gone past, their life's work to preserve it for an unknowable future. At the same time, they are immensely realistic, because they get to read all our shameful letters and late-night journal confessions. Finicky to the point of obsession, it's archivists who turn pages as if they were handling leaves of gold through our childish first drafts and blowhard lists of life goals and failed intentions. They see where the money and the time *actually* went, and whether all that effort made a difference to anyone at all. They see in our rat-dirtied discards the mysterious beginnings of the stories, the dead ends and darkness, the unexpected sunshine or shivering retreat from the rain and cold of internal storms. Theirs is not the ground lens of literature, but the stench and mess of the garbage-sifter.

And yet, what idealists. Who else but Anne and Paul, and Serge and Catherine[1] would have encouraged me with such hopeful expectation to bundle my boxes together, ratty or not, for the good of unknown descendants in centuries to come? Who else is planning for fifty years, one hundred years after my death, planning for the scholars and lovers of words who might delve into my random accumulations and find comfort, surprise, mystery, romance?

In the last three years, I have been archiving my papers, letters, photographs, documents, and objects—anything and everything that relates to my work as a poet, performance poet, and literary editor. I've had to consider what exactly it means to archive a writing life, my writing life. Along the way, I've encountered three rats: the rat in the box, the rat in the skull, and the secret rat.

The Rat in the Box

The first question, of course, is "Why?" Why archive my papers at all? For me, the first and most compelling answer came with finding that real and very smelly rat who nested in and excreted all over a box holding two years of my life in the basement. Over three decades of publishing, I'd accumulated a mountain of stuff I hadn't been able to bring myself to throw out—strings of letters from writer friends; albums full of photos and clippings; artifacts and drafts and scores, submissions and scrapbooks from collaborations like *Branching Out* (the first national feminist magazine), *First Draft* (an intermedia group), *Geode Music & Poetry* (a.k.a. *SugarBeat*, a performance group), and *Convergence: Poems for Peace* (which took art-wrapped poems from writers and artists across Canada to every Parliamentarian in the millennial year); recordings, including *Wordmusic, Dangerous Times, SugarBeat, Geode, Until the Light Bends,* and *Wordmusic 2*; and anthologies including *Dangerous Graces: Women's Poetry on Stage, Bookware: Ottawa Valley Poets, Living Archives* (a chapbook series from the Feminist Caucus of the League of Canadian Poets), *Siolence: Women on Poets, Violence and Silence, Waging Peace: Poetry and Political Action,* and *Pith and Wry: Current Canadian Poetry*. Such projects involved many other creators and contributors besides me, so I just couldn't toss the records into the trash.

On top of that, there were all my own personal manuscripts, notes, objects, and correspondence for scores of periodical and anthology publications and books, starting with the wordmusic volumes *Pass this way again* and *North/South* (wordmusic is a scoring system for multiple spoken voices that we developed in *First Draft*), and encompassing the poetry collections *Dark Galaxies, The Hummingbird Murders, Learning to Ride, Uncommon Prayer: A Book of Dedications, Until the Light Bends, La Deriva del Pianeta* (Italian translations of my science poems), *The Gargoyle's Left Ear: Writing in Ottawa* (a memoir), and *Crossing Arcs: Alzheimer's, My Mother, and Me*, ending—for now—with *Paper Affair: Poems Selected and New*.[2] Sentiment, vanity, superstition, materialism—who knows what causes me to be a hoarder, while others blithely dump their past on the roadside at the beginning of each new journey? Or on me, I should mention, as they knew I'd take it in.

And all of this accumulation had been shoved into boxes and onto shelves in my crumbling, hundred-year-old basement, filling it finally to bursting. To bursting pipes, at least, to leaking walls, floods large and small, mildew and mould, summer dust and winter condensation, cat scat piles and mice trails and, finally, the stink that led me to that messy rat nest. So "why" was simple to answer. This stuff was no longer safe where it was. Time to toss it, or pass it on!

The Rat in the Skull
So I cruised the Internet and sent out letters to archives across the country that collect work from poets, listing what I had, and why it might be of interest. As I was just about to publish my selected poems, it seemed a perfect time to start a new, clutter-free future.

But not right away, apparently. Some places didn't reply, while others did, noting that they already had their list of donors full for years to come, or that they concentrated on regions or topics into which I didn't fit, or that my work was not of broad enough interest. Did that feel like rejection? You bet it did! My life's work wasn't worth a second glance or a second storage?

And here's where the disembodied "rat in the skull" began its gnawing.[3] What vagaries of vainglory would make me, a poet of sufficient achievement but certainly no superstar, think my bits of litter and castoff skins worth preserving? What could render my doings and writings so important that they should be handled with white cotton gloves? What self-delusions would be exposed to ridicule from without or within by the presumption of handing my garbage over to the trash organizers? And what kind of ego leads a writer to archive her own work before she dies?

Was this, one might wonder, a female skull rat chewing on my daring? Maybe, given that I was raised in the fifties and sixties, and am still capable of reverting to a "take your status from your man" mentality. The act of self-assertion involved in proposing my material for archiving required a certain confidence, known better to me as "showing off"—as in Alice Munro's famous title, *Who Do You Think You Are?* And yet, raised in Canada in the literary company of such renowned female models as Munro herself, Margaret Atwood, Dorothy Livesay, Bronwen Wallace, and P. K. Page, it's hard to fall back on that as an excuse. Skull rats seem to thrive among writers of all genders and stripes. We are very good at breeding them—and at constructing impossible mazes for them to navigate!

One person who tried to ensure I didn't feel humiliated was Catherine Hobbs, the Literary Archivist at the Library and Archives Canada, whose letter began, "Certainly, you are correct in thinking that those unpublished materials are archival." She sugared her "I'm afraid at this time..." by lumping me in with "interesting writers of note," and wound up with "I would encourage you to pursue this," listing possible university repositories such as York, McMaster, Toronto, and Calgary. "It is encouraging to me that so many writers these days are recognizing the value of archival work in preserving literary history," she added. It was one of the gentler rejection letters I've received, and as a poet, I have a fine scrapbook full of those (well, actually, it's archived now).

Rebuffed but reassured, I sent out a few more letters to the suggested places and received a few replies, but also remembered that my husband, when settling his parents' estate, had found a home for records and regalia from his father's machinists' association in the City of Ottawa Archives. And that my grandmother's scrapbooks from her stint as a housemother in a residential school had been warmly welcomed by the Anglican Church. If my work wasn't held in the national collection, why would I send it to a university I hadn't attended in a city where I hadn't lived? On the one hand, I wrote to Carleton, but received a lacklustre reply. On the other hand, I'd already been approached about my papers once by Steven Artelle, a Lampman scholar and founder of the new Literary Heritage Society of Ottawa, which was at that moment working with a new and enthusiastic city archivist, Paul Henry, to expand its literary collection and mount a program of shows and events to highlight it. A "Poets' Pathway" project was already under way. Perhaps this was the time to follow up.

On being consulted, Jim Struthers, a historian friend and husband of poet Betsy Struthers, told me the City of Ottawa Archives was good and getting better. Anne from across the street agreed and encouraged me to go ahead with the project; she especially liked the idea of the stuff staying in town. I emailed Paul—who broke the pattern by greeting my tentative offer with flattering enthusiasm. We started to meet to discuss what a donation would consist of, what terms I wanted, what he expected, how the donation would be valued for tax purposes, and so on.[4]

By this point, I was also meeting with Catherine to arrange a donation of papers from the Feminist Caucus of the League of Canadian Poets to Library and Archives Canada. When I asked her about my decision, she also felt the city archives were the best choice because my files would be in town and cross-referenced to the national holdings wherever they overlapped. It was a knotty question, in fact, since I had quite a lot of material from league projects, and we had to decide whether to split my papers between two places. In the end, after talking to Paul as well, we agreed to place all of my papers together in the City of Ottawa Archive, with indicators that cross-referenced the deposits.

For me, it's great to think that a researcher tracking a topic through my work can easily travel physically between the national archive and the city one. This proximity offers a unique advantage. Going back to an earlier point, it's also a great pleasure to have my papers in the town where I've worked all my life and continue to work, and where I can drop in to consult them or ramble down memory lane any time.

During the long process of preparing and handing over material to the City of Ottawa, the skulking skull rat has been repeatedly backed into dead ends, chased around blind curves, and finally driven out of the mind maze entirely. Aid in this pursuit has been offered in turn to me by Anne, with her passion for my ratty box of leavings; Paul, in our long "donation" discussions; Catherine, with her sympathy for the tender egos of writers; and lately, Serge Barbe, the community archivist now handling my fonds—who must all go to the same "how to reassure the wilting donor" conferences. In the face of my gnawing doubts and obsessive tail-chasing, Paul said, "Yes, of course there's ego involved. It is an act of self-assertion, pride, even vanity to think your leftovers might be of interest to the society at large." It is surprising how simply acknowledging that fact—shining a light on the beast within—diminishes its size. But, he went on, once those papers are offered, it's not the donor who decides their value. That is the archive's role, which is less concerned with matters of fame than with a contextual consideration of the potential donor's work and life in the much larger cultural maze of contemporary and historical society. They takes ya, buddy, or they donts.

Of course, if they don't, Catherine told me kindly one day over tea, it doesn't mean your work is unimportant. Rather, it might mean that the scope is not as large—you might be a city rat, for example, rather than a national and international one. Or, you might be a smaller rat, yes, but you are still part of the pack, still having bits of biting and nurturing and foraging to do, still able to find a path through a certain confusing corner of the maze for others to follow. It's a combination of all those industrious rodent snufflings, from minor to major, that writes the history of the group and helps explain who we are, now, here, today. And there are many different archives all actively working together across the country to gather the elements of that larger story, from the eminent national collection to the local holdings of the smallest museum.

"What if we had Lampman's financial records, for example, or Scott's?" Serge said to me one day as I delivered the last of forty-four boxes full of dust and processed wood pulp. "How interesting that would be. Imagine if we had access to the kind and amount of stuff you're giving us today, for someone like Madge Macbeth—what an insight that would give us into the life of women writers a hundred years ago."[5]

The Secret Rat
The details of the donation agreement Paul and I worked out and the final content of the fonds are too long to explore here, except to say that a determined archivist will patiently find a way to overcome every scruple and answer every anxiety. But it remains the donor's task to decide what to send for archiving, and what restrictions, if any, to put on it.

And here is the home of the third rat, the rat of secrets.

Because what is most interesting to archivists? Letters, especially intimate ones that irretrievably and privately involve other people. Letters that may contain confessions, angers, anxieties, dismays, revelations of love or lust that were never intended to see the light of (public) day. Secrets that, if I were to reveal them, would definitely label me as a rat.

Or maybe not. For myself, most of my old history is of little interest even to me, and I don't mind what goes out there. Perhaps others feel the same, but how am I to know? How big of a task would that be, to contact all my possibly touchy correspondents from the last five decades?

In my files there are letters, for example, from some of the big stars of Canadian poetry. Most are mundane, but in a few, the correspondent and I are working out ticklish issues concerning publication and remembered history, or discussing difficulties with certain irascible or odd peers. These discussions are definitely related to our writing life. But do I have the moral right to deposit such letters without consultation, even though technically I do have ownership of the physical items, if not the words themselves?

And that's the real third rat in the box. Not the actual little critter that crawled into our basement through—well, let's abandon that path right there. But the question of what betrayals I might be committing, what secrets I might let escape from my box in an old wood filing cabinet, what random musings and embarrassing gossip I might reveal for general perusal decades after they were dropped into my mailbox with none of us thinking that these shambles and messes, petty sins and judgments would be exposed to public glare. Stories that maybe shouldn't be told and aren't mine to tell anyway, although as one end of the communication line or one half of the experience, they are still partly my own. How to judge what to keep and destroy, what to protect with long-term seals and what to leave to the disinterest of the future (for how much do we really care now about the peccadilloes that loomed so large in our ancestors' shamed hearts)? Do letters from my best friend that refer only peripherally to my writing have a place in the archive? Old love letters? Children's letters? I can put a restriction on material I judge to be sensitive, so a scholar can read but not quote from it, but I can't prevent a paraphrase. I can seal it away totally for a hundred years, but what good is material that can't be accessed? Might as well throw it out after all, don't you think?

The Pack
And this is the implied query in my friends' eyes as I try to persuade them to archive their own records. "All that stuff!" I say. "Don't you want to get rid of it and yet keep it safe? A clean conscience and a clean basement!" Because I know that, while I still struggle with the details of how to handle the last really difficult documents, I am finally free of my own ratty worries. First, because the answer, as is so often, is not a simple yes or no, but is practical and situational. I'm reviewing my correspondence and papers as I package them for archiving, and where it seems courteous and possible, asking permission; so far, no one has asked me to seal their letters.

Second, beyond these details, and donning for a moment the archivist's gloves and glasses, I can see within my messy boxes and those of my friends not only individual ramblings and false starts, but a whole community of writers actively exchanging, arguing, communicating, disagreeing, collaborating, gossiping. I see tangible paper records of what the situation is for artists here in my town today and how it's been during my lifetime. I see how the well-intentioned initiatives of government and community and poetry-loving matrons/patrons work or don't work to support the actual making of literature. I see classes given and taken, poetry groups formed and torn apart, good ideas fulfilled and bad ones abandoned, and vice versa. I see artists of many disciplines working together to do great things—or not. I see libraries, bookstores, community centres, theatres, stores, festivals, and reading series offering facilities that make these things possible. I see letters about how families, and friends, and employers, and peers interrelate with the spouses, parents, siblings, staff, and friends who lead this multifaceted, often chaotic, writer's life.

I see the poet not as a single ego but as a working member of a cultural community. And, like any good worker, keeping records of her daily tasks, for the interest and use of others, now, and to come. Part of the pack.

Notes

1 Anne Goddard, former Literary Archivist, National Archives of Canada; Paul Henry, City Archivist, City of Ottawa Archives; Serge Barbe, Community Archivist, City of Ottawa Archives; and Catherine Hobbs, current Literary Archivist (English-language), Library and Archives Canada.
2 The donation remains open in that I will keep adding new material, such as manuscript drafts and letters, as they accumulate. For a detailed publications list, please see http://web.ncf.ca/smcmaster.
3 With apologies to Ron Hutchinson, I've made free use of his title *Rat in the Skull*.
4 My main concern was to retain reasonable trade publication rights for myself and my heirs. This concern was satisfactorily resolved, partly by slightly rewording the donation agreement, and partly through Paul's explanations of the responsibilities the curators of fonds assume. For example, they undertake not only to care for the physical objects but also to protect the integrity of the work and the reputation and rights of the author by controlling access to and use of the materials by scholars and the public, even if these have not been restricted by the donor herself.
5 Ottawa literary leader Madge Macbeth (1881–1965) wrote hundreds of articles, stories, and plays, as well as twenty novels. Her obituary in the *Ottawa Citizen* notes that her scathing commentary on political and social intrigue and her frank discussions of sexuality created controversy. A fervent nationalist, she was instrumental in founding both the national radio system that would become the CBC, and the Canadian Authors' Association (she was its first female, and only three-time national president). Her papers are held in the City of Ottawa Archives (MG059). Discussions about what belongs in the archive continue as I delve down into my third year of sorting and delivering. One such discussion led Serge and me to include records of my receipts and expenses as a writer, on the rationale noted here. At the moment, however, the fonds does not include strictly personal papers or memorabilia from or about my family or non-writing friends.

Works Cited

Hutchinson, Ron. *Rat in the Skull*. London: Methuen Drama, 1984. Print.
Munro, Alice. *Who Do You Think You Are?* Toronto: Macmillan, 1978. Print.

Letters to the Woman's Page Editor: Reading Francis Marion Beynon's "The Country Homemakers" and the Public Culture for Women
Katja Thieme

Research on women's suffrage constitutes an increasingly diverse academic field, producing studies not only on the history and politics of different national suffrage movements but also on suffrage theatre (e.g., Stowell), literature (Green; Petty), marketing (Finnegan; Morrisson), sexuality (Kent), and fashion (Behling). Although some attention has been paid to suffrage debates in non-European countries (including China, Japan, and South America),[1] by far the greatest degree of English-speaking scholarship continues to concentrate on British and American suffragists. This focus is the result of the fact that these were powerful countries and influential cultures, and is also a reflection of the diversity of archived material available for the study of the suffrage movements in them. Both movements left behind considerable records, including pamphlets, correspondence, minutes, yearbooks of regional and national suffrage organizations, and a rich record of print runs of various suffrage magazines.[2] By comparison, scholarship on Canadian suffrage has been less prolific, partly a result of the relative absence of documents. Canada did not have the same breadth and intensity of suffrage activities, nor did it have, therefore, the same level of newspaper reporting or courtroom documentation. Of the organizations that were formed and the campaign activities that were carried out, relatively few documents remain. Aside from a very small number of magazines,[3] the Canadian suffrage movement produced very few of its own printed documents. The most extensive record that remains can be found in the various woman's pages of local newspapers, a number of them edited by outspoken suffragists,[4] and in the suffrage commentary that was published in newspapers and magazines.

In spite of the paucity of archival materials or archives, we can find useful ways of approaching what we have preserved for the benefit of the cultural and historical record on women's political interventions. Indeed, the very lack of such documentation demands that we find new ways of reading to compensate for gaps in the record. Although the documents on Canadian suffrage might not support the same degree and diversity of study that is being produced about other national suffrage movements, researchers can nevertheless take a range of approaches that may illuminate and challenge what we already know about Canadian suffrage debates.[5] From a rhetorical perspective, for example, the women's suffrage movement gives us insight into the discursive formation of new subject positions and the rhetorical process of social and political change. One site where women shaped increasingly public and political subject positions for themselves was the woman's pages, especially those where readers played a large role by sending in letters and reports. My essay focuses on the woman's page in the *Grain Growers' Guide*, edited between 1912 and 1917 by Francis Marion Beynon. I approach this material with questions that have become prominent in rhetorical studies of women's writing. How were women called forth to speak, and what were their motivations to participate in public debate? How did woman's page editors shape the conditions under which they themselves and other women could articulate their concerns? Following from that, how did suffragist editors like Beynon create the situations in which they and other women could speak publicly and politically about issues such as women's suffrage?

Recent rhetorical scholarship provides particularly useful ways in approaching suffrage discussions in Canadian newspapers and magazines. Rhetorical research looks with great interest at texts that literary study might deem ephemeral or supplementary. These are the kinds of texts that are often the only record of activities by marginalized or historically forgotten persons and groups: personal and professional correspondence, petitions, minutes of meetings, reports of various associations, the technical documents produced in various trades and professions, ledgers, inventories, and scrapbooks. Rhetorical scholars look at these texts differently, and asks different questions than those conducting historical or sociological investigation. For instance, scholars of rhetoric are interested in the sense of need or motive that calls people to speak in certain situations, in the kinds of speech and textual forms—the genres—that are produced by recurring motives and situations, the way speakers address and constitute their audiences, and the kinds of action that different forms of speech perform. By examining the conditions and actions of different types of speech, rhetorical study has moved beyond the notion that "rhetorical" describes exceptional speech samples. Most of us no longer search for particularly successful or elegant specimens of persuasion, but instead consider all speech as rhetorical, and thus worthy of rhetorical analysis. As a result, a much wider variety of material has become the subject of rhetorical study. In feminist approaches to rhetoric, this shift away from "outstanding" speech samples has been particularly important.

In the 1980s and early 1990s, feminist scholars such as Karlyn Kohrs Campbell, Andrea Lunsford, and Cheryl Glenn turned their attention to women's rhetoric and attempted to foreground great women who had been lost from rhetorical history. Other studies followed, focusing on influential women speakers and analyzing how they managed to deliver speeches and garner public attention at times when women's public speaking was not encouraged and was often met with hostility. Such research has taught us about American women speakers such as Methodist minister and suffragist Anna Howard Shaw (Linkugel and Solomon) or moral reformer and abolitionist Angelina Grimké (Browne). In the Canadian context, feminist research that focuses on texts and speeches by single figures has expanded our knowledge of late-nineteenth- and early-twentieth-century writers such as Agnes Maule Machar (Fiamengo), Pauline Johnson (Strong-Boag and Gerson), Sara Jeannette Duncan (Dean; Fiamengo), Kit Coleman (Freeman; Fiamengo), and Nellie McClung (Devereux).

For the most part, research that investigates the texts of individual women is, as Robin Jensen calls it, "product-oriented": it focuses on the texts and opinions of prominent women and does not usually analyze the speech productions of a wide group of participants. There is also recent work, which is more "process-oriented" in that it analyzes collective rhetoric by women. Often, these are women who were not publicly celebrated or even publicly recognized at the time. How are we to analyze the texts of these women? What can we learn about a movement's genres and the actions these genres perform? Researchers interested in the collective rhetoric of groups of women focus, for instance, on American women's suffrage journals (Solomon), nineteenth-century temperance activists

(Mattingly), U.S. women's anti-slavery petitions (Zaeske), or writing- and speech-intensive education programs for women (Hollis). Jensen observes that these projects "broaden our sense of what rhetoric is" (101). They teach us how speech creates a diverse range of subject positions, and how these subject positions are enacted through genre.

Such a shift in rhetoric's attention is particularly fruitful when studying the discourse of marginal and disadvantaged groups. The often uneven record that we have of women's involvement in historical events and movements rarely allows us to tell seamless narratives, even in the case of the most prominent women. More typically, the historical material provides us with momentary glimpses of a flurry of activities, which are carried out by a score of women, most of whom remain largely unknowable. Rhetorical study of these movements is interested all manner of speech situations, any kind of text, and all debate participants. This kind of approach locates these texts and analyzes their development and the work they do.

My work is very much influenced by what Jensen calls "process-oriented" approaches to rhetoric, even if, on the surface, my topic here seems somewhat "product-oriented" in its focus on one central figure. While I concentrate on one editor, Francis Marion Beynon, I look at her work with an eye to collective processes. The process of increasing women's opportunity to speak required collective effort. At the same time, however, some women were better placed and in more powerful positions to affect this process. Woman's page editors were among these powerfully positioned women, and editors like Beynon were in a privileged position to foster a sense of collectivity among Anglo-Canadian women.[6]

Francis Marion Beynon was the editor of the woman's page in the *Grain Growers' Guide* from 1912 to 1917, calling her page "The Country Homemakers."[7] The journal as a whole ran from 1908 to 1928 and had its offices in Winnipeg. It was published by the Grain Growers' Grain Company—a co-operative of Prairie farmers—and by the grain growers' associations of Alberta, Manitoba, and Saskatchewan. I accessed the microfilm version available at the University of British Columbia library. The *Guide* had had several woman's page editors before Beynon, but she was the first to work full time. As Anne Hicks explains, along with editing "The Country Homemakers," Beynon edited and wrote "The Sunshine Guild" pages, secured space for the reports of the women's auxiliaries of the grain growers' associations, wrote a biweekly column called "Country Girl's Ideas," and managed the children's page. Her sister, Lillian Beynon Thomas, was woman's editor of the *Manitoba Free Press*. Beynon was also a co-founder of the Winnipeg branch of the Canadian Women's Press Club, and was involved in the Political Equality League of Manitoba. In January 1914, she acted in the famous mock parliament at the Walker Theatre in Winnipeg. The event was organized by the Winnipeg Political Equality League and featured the organization's key members in the positions of the provincial parliament at the time. Beynon and her sister, Lillian Thomas, acted as members of the opposition. Nellie McClung was the Premier, Kenneth Haig was the Attorney General, Isabel Graham the Speaker of the House, and Genevieve Lipsett-Skinner the Minister of Economy and Agriculture. In 1917, Beynon's time at the *Guide* came to an end because she disagreed with Editor George Chipman about Canada's involvement in the First World War. She was one of very few Canadian feminists who remained staunchly pacifist throughout the war (see Cook; Roberts). After she lost her position, she followed her sister Lillian to New York where, in 1919, she published her semi-autobiographical novel, *Aleta Dey*.

In her ground-breaking work on female journalists in Canada, Marjory Lang notes that woman's page editors owed their jobs not only to an increasing interest in women's commercial power because of their growing importance as targets for newspaper advertising but also to their own involvement in the burgeoning women's club movement. Thus, while these editors were often stand-alone and idiosyncratic figures within a male-dominated newspaper scene, they were also representatives of a collective force of women. They were not just representatives, Lang notes, they were also prime movers in and promoters of these clubs. Such involvement in one's journalistic subject matter was not unusual at the time; the idea of journalistic objectivity did not gain hold until after the women's club movement had lost much of its political momentum. Lang describes this situation as an early stage in the ascendance of female journalists toward what later became two separate areas of activity: the independent journalism of the disengaged observer and the professional work of the public relations officer. For Lang, this later change in the role of the woman's page editor is in tune with "the falling off of voluntarism and encroachment of professionalism in the arena served by women's clubs" (217). Beynon wrote at exactly the time when the relation between woman's page editors and the political ambitions of women's clubs was most potent. She used her position quite actively to produce a collective debate on the newspaper page and to create other occasions when women could meet and debate with one another.

By the 1910s, letters to the editor were a genre of public debate in which Canadian women could occasionally participate. Like those sent today, letters sent to the editor-in-chief were visually set apart from the editorial pieces to which they responded. They were usually published on a different page and under a separate rubric than editorials and main articles.

The *Grain Growers' Guide*, for instance, had a separate page for its letters called "The Mailbag." I need to describe the layout of the "Mailbag" page briefly in order to better contrast this section to Beynon's rhetorical efforts. During the years under consideration, letters published on the "Mailbag" page usually started with the address line "Editor, Guide," creating a rather different tone than the more personal "Dear Miss Beynon." "Mailbag" letters were usually signed with the letter writers' first name, or initials and last name, along with their hometown and province. It was not common for these letter writers to use pen names. Although letter writers offered their thoughts and names on this page, the editor did not (during Beynon's time, the editor was George Chipman). Only rarely did he respond to one of the letters; and if he did, it was done usually in order to swiftly "correct" what he saw as a writer's false or mistaken claims. On the letter page, the most discernible presence of the editor was a routinely included brief titled "Notice to Correspondents," which reminded them that they could "freely exchange views and derive from each other the benefits of experience and helpful suggestions," and that "every letter must be signed by the name of the writer, though not necessarily for publication."[8]

On Beynon's woman's page, letters were often placed in the middle of the page, directly following her editorial piece (which she signed with her full name) and before brief articles on cooking, baking, or sewing. Quite frequently, they were printed with an immediate, short response by the editor herself, signed "F. M. B." Most letter writers who contributed to the woman's page edited by Beynon used pen names. Some of these letter writers might have included their real names with their addresses, for instance, when they asked for the books and pamphlets that the *Grain Growers' Guide* was distributing among its readers; thus, their names would have been known to Beynon. It appears that Beynon kept careful record of the pen names since she occasionally modified someone's choice of name when she noticed that it had already been used by someone else. Several readers published repeatedly under their chosen names. On the surface, the widespread use of pen names among Beynon's readers made the discussion more anonymous—a few of the readers made critical note of that and then demonstratively signed their letters with full names. However, this anonymity also enabled discussion in relation to stories about hardship, poverty, and mistreatment (a point that is also taken up critically when a reader calls for more political and less personal writing). Clearly, letters to the woman's page functioned differently than those sent to the main editor of the same periodical: they were of a different nature, constituted a substantial portion of the page, and provided readers with a role in shaping the woman's page content.

The differences between letters to the main page editor and letters to the woman's page were related to how women like Beynon conceived of their role. Beynon saw herself as actively fostering a sense of community among her readers. When women indicated in their letters that they were new to reading the page or writing public letters, she often made a point of welcoming them to the "circle" or "family." Beynon's community-minded approach to her editorship was not unusual among woman's page editors. Lang highlights how these female editors differed from main page editors in their friendly and accommodating tone toward readers and letter writers. She notes that woman's page editorials often took the form of an "'over-the-fence' chat, projecting the illusion of private communication into a public venue," and that female editors provided a "surrogate friend" for the rural reader (Lang 10). In their writing on social and club activities, these editors were "active moulders of a culture of women," in effect creating a "newspaper within the newspaper" where "women were the newsmakers" (10). Those journalists who were considered club reporters were particularly instrumental in creating this culture of women, as they simultaneously played the roles of club member, club advocate, and club reporter. As I mentioned, Beynon wrote at a time when women's clubs were still surging in popularity and were becoming increasingly confident in their ability to address and change social conditions. The central space that was given to these letters by women was a crucial aspect of this Anglo-Canadian women's culture which extended across a diverse range of clubs and charities, and in many cases included suffrage organizations.

In 1908, the *Grain Growers' Guide* had declared that it supported women's suffrage in the editorial of its very first issue. Beynon, too, left no doubt that she was in favour of women's rights. However, her desire to promote women's right to vote was sometimes trumped by her hope to foster discussion among women, including those that involved their right to vote. This attitude was particularly evident in the first year of her editorship, when she was most eager to establish a sense of community among her readership. In July 1912, she declared that she was so impressed with Olive Schreiner's book *Woman and Labor* that she decided to summarize parts of it in consecutive columns. This summary begins with a piece entitled "The Woman's Movement." In the same issue, she also included a letter by "Albertan," who first described wildflowers in order to provide "a breath of country air" and then advocated for Beynon's page to concentrate on issues of motherhood and care of children.

> And about your page, I think it should deal in the subjects most near and dear to the woman heart. How to care for our babies and economize our work, to give us more time and strength for our loved ones.

> I am sorry to say, and yet I feel it true, that many of our women today are fighting against motherhood because it binds them at home, away from their good times, or because "John does not like babies."
>
> Can you not in your page to women show them what a great life work it is to train children to be true, honorable citizens? (9)

Along the same lines, Albertan also notes her opposition to women's suffrage: "As to votes for women, I think if she does her duty by her children she has no time for votes, but I do think she should be protected so that her husband could not sell their home and leave her homeless" (9). Despite her earlier declaration of admiration for Schreiner's book, Beynon did not directly respond to Albertan's opinion about suffrage. Instead, she lauds her description of flowers and invites her to write again: "Your letter did indeed bring a breath of country air and as you described them I could fairly smell the wild flowers as they appeared one after another. Do come again, and soon" ("Harking Back" 9). Like a polite conversationalist, she highlights the most innocuous part of Albertan's letter and sidesteps the more controversial points.

We might view this civil response as too timid, unwilling to risk opposition. But there are other ways of reading this exchange. We could note how differently resources are distributed in this situation: it is Beynon who has control over which letters will be chosen for print as well as whether or not, and how, she will respond to them. In full command of this power, she decided to print Albertan's letter, to respond in an encouraging way, and to invite more letters like it. Her response is meant to indicate her openness to a variety of voices, including those that disagree with her on certain issues. Beynon takes on the role of a facilitator. The actual debate is, in this and in many following cases, carried out among her readers. For instance, a few issues later, Beynon published a letter by "Progress," who spoke against Albertan's views on suffrage. First, Progress also praises Albertan's description of wildflowers, but then she notes,

> I don't quite agree with Albertan in her opinion on votes for women, however. I also am a farmer's wife and as we have seven children (the eldest only nine years of age) and I do all my own work, I am kept just as busy as a bee from early morning until late at night and I am happy in my work. But if we only had woman's suffrage I would find time to vote I can assure you.... I have always believed in woman's suffrage, but since we have taken The Guide and have read of the splendid improvements that are going on in the four states of America, where women have the franchise, I have believed in it more than ever. My husband believes in woman's suffrage too, I am glad to say. (12)

The discussion following Albertan's letter was not the only instance when Beynon noticeably restrained her passion for the suffrage cause. In July 1912, she solicited ideas about the formation of women's clubs associated with grain growers' associations. Previous letters had already given her a sense of how welcome and useful such clubs could be, but Beynon wanted to be sure that all opinions were aired. "Do you like the idea?" she asked, and added, "If not, write and tell me why and I'll print your letter as readily as those in favor of the project, which I own I rather like" ("Harking Back" 9). To clarify what such clubs could do, she suggested that they could cover subjects such as "the preparation and uses of foods, care of poultry, making and marketing of butter, care of children and sanitation" (9). She added that there was no reason why these gatherings could not also "consider municipal, Provincial and Dominion questions—homesteads for women, Direct Legislation, suffrage or any other matter of great moment" (9). Beynon leaves the field open for whatever individual women grain growers' associations decide they want to tackle—everything from domestic to political issues, from issues related to farm life to provincial and federal legislation. In response to this list, Eva Sulman critiques Beynon's recommendation of small, domestic matters such as food preparation, poultry care, and dairy production. Instead, her letter suggests,

> With regard to the proposed clubs it seems to me that it should be our aim to keep the big issues in the limelight, and when we can solve these, all smaller matters will automatically adjust themselves.... The most important subject to women at present is the franchise which we shall no doubt secure in time, and we should endeavour to educate ourselves in such a way that we shall know how to use it to the best advantage. (9)

Sulman follows up with detailed arguments about the value of women's work and women's knowledge of politics. In her response to this letter, Beynon indicates once again that personally she is very much in favour of Sulman's advocacy for women's rights. As the moderator of the discussion, however, she also expresses respect for those who think otherwise: "Yours is a delightful letter and I heartily approve of your ambition to take up the wider issues, but you and I must admit that there are many splendid women in the West who are not interested in or even in favor of these movements" (Sulman 9).

Because of these discussions among the readers, a pro-suffrage tenor begins to develop on the "Country Homemakers" page. Beynon's own support of women's suffrage helps this development along, but it is really the letter writers who make evident the community's interest in women's rights. Increasingly, those who question the call for women's suffrage could expect subsequent letters to challenge some of their claims. Pro-suffrage responses typically outnumbered suffrage-skeptical ones. After the first year of her editorship, Beynon, too, responded more directly and critically to the claims of some suffrage skeptics. However, she also continued to emphasize the points she agreed with, even when she wrote detailed rebuttals of their views. At the moments when she appeared to deny suffrage-skepticism a sufficient hearing, some of her readers usually came to the letter writer's defence. For instance, in the fall of 1913, an extended debate develops in response to a female reader named "Wolf Willow." When the first of Wolf Willow's letters arrives, Beynon explains that she will immediately respond to it because this letter is "fair-minded, courteous and free from personalities which the editor of this department does not regard as argument" ("Answers to an Anti-Suffragist" 10). She believes that Wolf Willow is "honestly opposed to suffrage for very laudable reasons," because she wants "children to be better cared for and a better race of men reared" (10). Beynon asserts that these are ideals that she also subscribes to, the difference being that she believes women who can vote are better able to take care of their children, because they can direct Parliaments toward more protective legislation. A vibrant debate ensues over the following two months. In that debate, other writers challenge not only Wolf Willow's letters but also Beynon's rebuttals. Even as the editor and many of her letter writers confidently assert their pro-suffrage stance, they also remind one another that the debate should continue to be open to varying viewpoints. As one pro-suffrage respondent put it, letters such as Wolf Willow's "do a great deal of good, I think, as they bring out arguments for the suffrage movement for women which we otherwise would not know" (Pansy 10).

Especially at the beginning of her editorship, Beynon repeatedly encourages women to send letters. For instance, in November 1912, she issues a "cordial invitation to write to us on any of the questions that come up for discussion in this page or any others that are of interest to women" ("'We Don't Believe'" 10). On another occasion, she declares very openly that, if anyone "care[s] to write to me on any matter of interest to women[,] I shall be glad to hear from you at any time and to give your letters publicity at the earliest possible opportunity" ("The New Year" 10). The discussions thus prompted her to address not only the formation of women's clubs but also issues such as a wife's access to the family's income, and how to organize tours for women speakers. After initially describing these topics in her column, Beynon often returns in subsequent issues to tell her readers that she would like to see more responses. She urges them to share the valuable thoughts and ideas that they do not necessarily share with one another in their letters. She notes, "if only the women could be brought to realize how much their letters interest our readers, we would be deluged with them" ("A Word" 23).

As a result of the central presence of the letters (in some issues there are as many as five of them, taking up almost the entire page) and Beynon's repeated and open invitations, the readers are thoroughly engaged in a conversation with one another. Often they respond to one another's letters instead of Beynon's editorial pieces. They take issue with the conclusions drawn or evaluations made by other letter writers. They convey sympathy with the suffering expressed by some of the writers—related to the amount of farm and household work, health issues and care of children, lack of money, and the attitudes of husbands. Many of these writers note that they like the "Country Homemakers" page so much because of the letters printed there. Indeed, a surprising number of letter writers confess that they are writing their very first letter to an editor. They usually credit the discussion in the letters with having motivated them to do something unusual: taking a pen and writing something that they know will likely be published. Many writers say they are not sure of the genre's conventions, and express concern about the length and style of their letters. In her responses to such concerns, Beynon reassures these women, tells them they have no reason to doubt their letter-writing ability, and asks to receive more of their views in subsequent missives.

What we can infer from the volume of letters is that the "Country Homemakers" page was creating a growing community of women. A good number of readers picked up their pens and voiced their thoughts publicly for the first time; this engagement renders the page increasingly diverse. However, it was still far from inclusive when it came to questions of race and ethnicity. The letter writers seem to form a primarily Anglo-Canadian group of women. Few women declare what their ethnic background is, but the ones who do are almost always from English-speaking backgrounds. Places of origin repeatedly mentioned are Scotland, the United States, Ireland, and England. At least two writers refer to themselves as "Salopian," meaning they are from Shropshire. There are also allusions to the migration transpiring within the country when, for example, one woman signs herself "Halifax," while another notes that she is now living in British Columbia. There is a chance that some writers who do not declare their ethnicity are from a First Nation, of Central or Eastern European descent, or of Asian background. But if they are, it is not a fact they are inclined to announce in their letters or through pen names. That tendency contrasts with the pride conveyed through phrases such as "lass from Scotland," or "English lady." There are only occasional and often indirect hints of family heritages that are other than Anglo-Canadian. For instance, one woman who grew up in Canada (she refers to her father as "one of the best men in the West") calls herself "Brun Kulla," whereas another signs her letter with "Wife of Norwegian."

The fluency of each letter also suggests that the writers were very familiar with written English. If there were any deviations from the grammatical norm in the original letters, they were corrected before going to print. In other words, either these women already wrote what would have been considered "proper" English at the time, or the editing that was done created the impression of an excellent command of English among all the letter writers. Even those who declare that they are responding for the first time to a newspaper and are not sure about their writing seem to produce well-written letters. The page must have conveyed to its readers that an excellent command of written English was a prerequisite for participating in the debate, effectively limiting potential letter writers to those who felt they possessed this skill. The women who felt confident enough to write likely had a formal education; many of them probably came from Anglo-Canadian rather than from other immigrant backgrounds. Even though the Prairies saw an influx of people from non-English-speaking backgrounds, the growing community of critically minded women that formed in the *Grain Growers' Guide*'s woman's page would have had a strongly Anglo-Canadian appearance.[9]

Within that Anglo-Canadian community, however, Beynon's management of the page seems to have been quite successful at inciting women to participate in the conversation. In fact, the page hails these women into public speech—for the first time, in many cases—and interpellates them as capable and valuable letter writers. Beynon's page provides the women in that group with a speech situation in which their experiences and opinions carry great value. "The Country Homemakers" does this so well because it is open to a large variety of topics—women's suffrage is one subject among and related to others, such as how a husband and wife can handle their finances in an equitable way, how children should learn about sexuality and reproduction, and how to manage the demands of farm life. It is not only Beynon's repeated invitations that help to usher these women into public speech; instead, and perhaps even more significantly, it is the presence of other women speaking. Her management of the page shows how highly she values this presence, perhaps even more than she supports women's suffrage in itself at times. Her desire to increase women's political participation and respect their contributions is sometimes greater than her desire to champion suffrage as the topic of discussion. In other words, as my reading of the records that survive around the *Grain Growers' Guide* shows, she encourages female political participation in the widest sense, and that includes thorough debate about the very conditions of this participation.

Notes

1 See, for instance, Edwards, *Gender, Politics, and Democracy: Women's Suffrage in China*; Matsukawa and Tachi, "Women's Suffrage and Gender Politics in Japan"; and Lavrin, "Suffrage in South America: Arguing a Difficult Cause."
2 A list of American suffrage journals includes the Boston *Una* (1853–55); *Sibyl* (1856–64), the journal of the National Dress Reform Association; Susan B. Anthony and Elizabeth Cady Stanton's *Revolution* (1868–70); Lucy Stone and Henry Blackwell's *Woman's Journal* (1870–1917), the chief periodical of the National Woman Suffrage Association (NWSA); the Oregon *New Northwest*, edited by Abigail Scott Duniway (1871–87); the *Ballot Box* (1876–81); the Denver *Queen Bee* (1879–96), edited by Caroline Nichols Churchill; the *Woman's Column* (1888–1904); the Nebraska *Woman's Tribune* (1883–1909); and the *New York Suffrage Newsletter* (1899–1913). Part of this list was taken from Tierney.

In Great Britain, there were suffrage magazines such as the *English Woman's Journal* (1858–64), established by Barbara Boudichon and edited by Bessie Rayner Parkes and Matilda Hayes, and its successor, the *Englishwoman's Review* (1866–1910); the *Victoria Magazine* edited by Emily Faithfull (1863–80); the *Women's Suffrage Journal* (1870–90); the *Personal Rights Journal* (1881–1903), linked to the Women's Franchise League and the Women's Emancipation Union; *Jus Suffragii*, later retitled *International Woman Suffrage News* (1906–29) of the International Woman Suffrage Alliance; the *Women's Franchise* (1907–11), edited by John E. Francis; *Suffragette*, renamed *Britannia* (1912–18), the official organ of the Women's Social and Political Union (WSPU), with Emmeline and Christabel Pankhurst among its editors; Emmeline and Frederick Pethick-Lawrence's *Votes for Women* (1907–18), until the split between the Pethick-Lawrences and the Pankhursts; the *Conservative and Unionist Women's Franchise Review* (1909–16); the *Common Cause* (1909–20), the journal of the National Union of Women's Suffrage Societies (NUWSS); *Englishwoman* (1909–21), with Lady Frances Balfour, Lady Strachey, Cicely Hamilton, and Mary Lowndes on the editorial committee; *Vote* (1909–33), a periodical related to the Women's Freedom League; Dora Marsden's *Freewoman* (1911–12), the counter-publication to the WSPU, and Harriet Shaw Weaver's *New Freewoman* (1913), later renamed the *Egoist* (1914–19); the *Church League for Women's Suffrage* (1912–17); the *Women's Dreadnought*, edited by Sylvia Pankhurst (1914–24, renamed *Worker's Dreadnought* in 1917); the *Catholic Suffragist* (1915–18); the *Coming Day* (1916–20), published by the Free Church League for Women's Suffrage; and the *Women's International League* (1916–52). For a more complete list, see Crawford.
3 The difference in print output between the British and American and the Canadian women's rights movements is startling. Throughout the several decades of the movement, British and American publications are quite numerous and diverse (see previous footnote). In contrast, Canada had less than a handful: *Freyja* (1898–1910), an Icelandic-language women's rights magazine (see Kinnear); *Woman's Century* (1913–21), the journal of the National Council of Women of Canada; and *The Champion*, the publication of the Political Equality League of Victoria (1912–14).

4 Woman's page editors who were also women's rights advocates included Sarah Anne Curzon, associate and woman's page editor of the *Canada Citizen* (1882–84); Kate Simpson Hayes writing for the Manitoba *Free Press* (1899–1906); her successor at the *Free Press*, Lillian Beynon Thomas (1906–17); E. Cora Hind, the commercial and agricultural columnist for the Manitoba *Free Press* (1901–30), who also contributed to its woman's page; Flora MacDonald Denison, women's columnist for the Toronto *Sunday World* (1909–13); Francis Marion Beynon, woman's page editor at the *Grain Growers' Guide* (1912–17); and Violet MacNaughton, editor of the "Our Welfare Page" at the *Saturday Press and Prairie Farm* (1916–17) and later woman's page editor for the *Western Producer* (1925–50).

5 For recent engagement with Canadian suffrage, see Dorland and Charland, *Law, Rhetoric, and Irony in the Formation of Canadian Civil Culture*; Thieme, "Uptake and Genre: The Canadian Reception of Suffrage Militancy"; Kulba and Lamont, "The Periodical Press and Western Woman's Suffrage Movements in Canada and the United States"; and Kinahan, "Transcendent Citizenship: Suffrage, the National Council of Women of Canada, and the Politics of Organized Womanhood."

6 In her count of the professions and activities of 156 female suffrage leaders, Carol Lee Bacchi calculates that 25 percent of them were journalists and authors (6). Journalists thus made up the largest portion of Canada's suffrage organizers, followed by educators (15 percent) and doctors (12 percent).

7 For more information on Beynon's family background and pre-*Guide* history, see Hicks, "Francis Beynon and *The Guide*."

8 This notice appeared well before Beynon started editing the women's page. See "Notice."

9 In her anthology, Norah Lewis surveyed letters written to the woman's pages of six agricultural periodicals published between 1900 and 1920 (four of the magazines were from Winnipeg, one of which was the *Grain Grower's Guide*, and one each was published in Montréal and Saskatoon). Lewis finds that none of the writers indicated they were First Nations or Métis, only a few of the letters were written by men, and there didn't appear to be any from writers who were not fully literate in English.

Works Cited

Albertan. "A Whiff of Country Air." Letter. *Grain Growers' Guide* July 17, 1912, 9. Print.

Bacchi, Carol Lee. *Liberation Deferred? The Ideas of the English-Canadian Suffragists, 1877–1918*. Toronto: U of Toronto P, 1983. Print.

Behling, Laura L. *The Masculine Woman in America, 1890–1935*. Urbana: U of Illinois P, 2001. Print.

Beynon, Francis Marion. "A Word of Encouragement." Editorial. *Grain Growers' Guide* Dec. 4, 1912, 23. Print.

———. *Aleta Dey: A Novel*. 1919. Peterborough, ON: Broadview P, 2000. Print.

———. "Answers to an Anti-Suffragist." Editorial. *Grain Growers' Guide* Oct. 1, 1913, 10. Print.

———. "Harking Back to those Women's Clubs." Editorial. *Grain Growers' Guide* July 24, 1912, 9. Print.

---. "The New Year Stretches but before Us." Editorial. *Grain Growers' Guide* Jan. 1, 1913, 10. Print.

---. "'We Don't Believe in Women.'" Editorial. *Grain Growers' Guide* Nov. 13, 1912: 10. Print.

---. "The Woman's Movement." Editorial. *Grain Growers' Guide* July 10, 1912, 9. Print.

Browne, Stephen H. *Angelina Grimké: Rhetoric, Identity, and the Radical Imagination.* East Lansing: Michigan State UP, 1999. Print.

Brun Kulla. "The Country Teacher's Standpoint." Letter. *Grain Growers' Guide* Dec. 11, 1912, 10. Print.

Campbell, Karlyn Kohrs. *Man Cannot Speak for Her.* 2 vols. New York: Greenwood, 1989. Print.

---, ed. *Women Public Speakers in the United States, 1800–1925.* Westport: Greenwood, 1993. Print.

---, ed. *Women Public Speakers in the United States, 1925–1993.* Westport: Greenwood, 1994. Print.

Cook, Ramsay. "Francis Marion Beynon and the Crisis of Christian Reformism." *The West and the Nation.* Ed. W. L. Morton, Carl Berger, and Ramsay Cook. Toronto: McClelland and Stewart, 1976. 187–208. Print.

Crawford, Elizabeth. *The Women's Suffrage Movement: A Reference Guide, 1866–1928.* London: Taylor & Francis, 1999. *MyiLibrary.com.* n.d. Web. June 23, 2009. (http://lib.myilibrary.com/Browse/open.asp?ID=5027&loc=459).

Dean, Misao. *A Different Point of View: Sara Jeannette Duncan.* Montreal: McGill-Queen's UP, 1991. Print.

Devereux, Cecily. *Growing a Race: Nellie L. McClung and the Fiction of Eugenic Feminism.* Montreal: McGill-Queen's UP, 2005. Print.

Dorland, Michael, and Maurice René Charland. *Law, Rhetoric, and Irony in the Formation of Canadian Civil Culture.* Toronto: U of Toronto P, 2002. Print.

Edwards, Louise P. *Gender, Politics, and Democracy: Women's Suffrage in China.* Stanford: Stanford UP, 2008. Print.

Fiamengo, Janice Anne. *The Woman's Page: Journalism and Rhetoric in Early Canada.* Toronto: U of Toronto P, 2008. Print.

Finnegan, Margaret Mary. *Selling Suffrage: Consumer Culture and Votes for Women.* New York: Columbia UP, 1999. Print.

Freeman, Barbara M. *Kit's Kingdom: The Journalism of Kathleen Blake Coleman.* Ottawa: Carleton UP, 1989. Print.

Glenn, Cheryl. *Rhetoric Retold: Regendering the Tradition from Antiquity through the Renaissance.* Carbondale: Southern Illinois UP, 1997. Print.

Green, Barbara. *Spectacular Confessions: Autobiography, Performative Activism, and the Sites of Suffrage.* New York: St. Martin's, 1997. Print.

Hicks, Anne. "Francis Beynon and *The Guide.*" *First Days, Fighting Days: Women in Manitoba History.* Ed. Mary Kinnear. Regina: Canadian Plains Research Center, U of Regina, 1987. 41–52. Print.

Hollis, Karyn L. *Liberating Voices: Writing at the Bryn Mawr Summer School for Women Workers*. Carbondale: Southern Illinois UP, 2004. Print.

Jensen, Robin E. "Women's Rhetoric in History: A Process-Oriented Turn and Continued Recovery." *Quarterly Journal of Speech* 94.1 (2008): 100–12. Print.

Kent, Susan Kingsley. *Sex and Suffrage in Britain, 1860–1914*. Princeton: Princeton UP, 1987. Print.

Kinahan, Anne-Marie. "Transcendent Citizenship: Suffrage, the National Council of Women of Canada, and the Politics of Organized Womanhood." *Journal of Canadian Studies* 42.3 (2008): 5–27. Print.

Kinnear, Mary. "The Icelandic Connection: *Freyja* and the Manitoba Woman Suffrage Movement." *Canadian Woman Studies: An Introductory Reader*. Ed. Nuzhat Amin et al. Toronto: Inanna, 1999. 79–85. Print.

Kulba, Tracy, and Victoria Lamont. "The Periodical Press and Western Woman's Suffrage Movements in Canada and the United States: A Comparative Study." *Women's Studies International Forum* 29.3 (2006): 265–78. Print.

Lang, Marjory. *Women Who Made the News: Female Journalists in Canada, 1880–1945*. Montréal: McGill-Queen's UP, 1999. Print.

Lavrin, Asunción. "Suffrage in South America: Arguing a Difficult Cause." *Suffrage and Beyond: International Feminist Perspectives*. Ed. Caroline Daley and Melanie Nolan. New York: New York UP, 1994. 184–209. Print.

Lewis, Norah L., ed. *Dear Editor and Friends: Letters from Rural Women of the North-West, 1900–1920*. Waterloo: Wilfrid Laurier UP, 1998. Print.

Linkugel, Wil A., and Martha Solomon. *Anna Howard Shaw: Suffrage Orator and Social Reformer*. Westport: Greenwood, 1991. Print.

Lunsford, Andrea A., ed. *Reclaiming Rhetorica: Women in the Rhetorical Tradition*. Pittsburgh: U of Pittsburgh P, 1995. Print.

Matsukawa, Yukiko, and Kaoru Tachi. "Women's Suffrage and Gender Politics in Japan." *Suffrage and Beyond: International Feminist Perspectives*. Ed. Caroline Daley and Melanie Nolan. New York: New York UP, 1994. 171–83. Print.

Mattingly, Carol. *Well-Tempered Women: Nineteenth-Century Temperance Rhetoric*. Carbondale: Southern Illinois UP, 1998. Print.

Morrisson, Mark S. *The Public Face of Modernism: Little Magazines, Audiences, and Reception, 1905–1920*. Madison: U of Wisconsin P, 2001. Print.

"Notice to Correspondents." *Grain Growers' Guide* Feb. 23, 1910, 13. Print.

Pansy. "Wants to Broaden Her Life." Letter. *Grain Growers' Guide* Nov. 12, 1913, 10. Print.

Petty, Leslie. *Romancing the Vote: Feminist Activism in American Fiction, 1870–1920*. Athens: U of Georgia P, 2006. Print.

Progress. "An Ardent Suffragist." Letter. *Grain Growers' Guide* Aug. 7, 1912, 12. Print.

Roberts, Barbara. "Women against War, 1914–1918: Francis Beynon and Laura Hughes." *Up and Doing: Canadian Women and Peace*. Ed. Janice Williamson and Deborah Gorham. Toronto: Women's P, 1989. 48–65. Print.

Solomon, Martha M., ed. *A Voice of Their Own: The Woman Suffrage Press, 1840–1910*. Tuscaloosa: U of Alabama P, 1991. Print.

Stowell, Sheila. *A Stage of Their Own: Feminist Playwrights of the Suffrage Era*. Manchester: Manchester UP, 1992. Print.

Strong-Boag, Veronica, and Carole Gerson. *Paddling Her Own Canoe: The Times and Texts of E. Pauline Johnson (Tekahionwake)*. Toronto: U of Toronto P, 2000. Print.

Sulman, Eva. "Too Much Chicken Raising and Butter Making." Letter. *Grain Growers' Guide* Aug. 14, 1912, 9. Print.

Thieme, Katja. "Uptake and Genre: The Canadian Reception of Suffrage Militancy." *Women's Studies International Forum* 29.3 (2006): 279–88. Print.

Tierney, Helen. *Women's Studies Encyclopedia*. Westport: Greenwood, 1999. Print.

Willow, Wolf. "To Be Attractive Is Woman's Main Duty." Letter. *Grain Growers' Guide* Oct. 1, 1913, 10. Print.

Zaeske, Susan. *Signatures of Citizenship: Petitioning, Antislavery, and Women's Political Identity*. Chapel Hill: U of North Carolina P, 2003. Print.

Archival Adventures with L. M. Montgomery; or, "As Long as the Leaves Hold Together"
Vanessa Brown and Benjamin Lefebvre

In her introduction to the collection of essays *Working in Women's Archives* (2001), Helen M. Buss considers how each contributor to the volume has been working at "the tentative beginnings of what we now see as the fortuitous coming together of feminist theory, the breaking of traditional limitations set by the idea of a literary 'canon' of great writers and the increased use of archives to rescue a female tradition in writing" (1). In the case of L. M. Montgomery (1874–1942), the trajectory of her critical reputation in many ways mimics the dominant pattern tracked by the contributors to this current volume: she has long been (and in many ways remains) marginalized by the expanded canon of Canadian literature as a result of her gender, popular appeal, and misrepresentation, generalization, and devaluation as a children's writer. That said, she remains a unique case study as a result of the fact that all her books—including her most popular, *Anne of Green Gables* (1908) and *Emily of New Moon* (1923), and their sequels—remain in print in the twenty-first century; in fact, most of them have never been out of print.[1]

In addition to her continued popularity, the academic field of L. M. Montgomery Studies was significantly stimulated by the simultaneous appearance in late 1985 of the first volume of *The Selected Journals of L. M. Montgomery*, published by Oxford University Press, and Kevin Sullivan's adaptation of *Anne of Green Gables* as a television miniseries. Although the Sullivan production and its sequels renewed Montgomery's popularity by introducing her and her characters to the mass medium of television, the publication of the journals by an established university press had an unprecedented effect on Montgomery's status within and beyond the academy. As Cecily Devereux notes in her review of the fourth volume, published in 1998,

> [t]hese journals, the handwritten originals of which are held at the McLaughlin Library, University of Guelph, are extraordinary documents, not only in terms of the information they provide about living, writing, and being a woman in English Canada in the first half of the twentieth century, but also because they have radically complicated our understanding of Montgomery. ("The Continuing Story" 180)

Although the continued availability of primary Montgomery texts makes her an anomaly in relation to the recovery of women's writing in Canada, what has not been adequately documented is the central role that the archive has played in the recuperation of Montgomery as a subject worthy of study. The detailed work of researchers who have combed the Montgomery archives for crucial new information about the author and her work, and the publication of a number of posthumous Montgomery texts since 1960—including diaries, letters, photographs, scrapbooks, periodical pieces, and rediscovered typescripts, in addition to the five-volume *Selected Journals*—has led to a series of reconsiderations about her primary work and its significance.[2] Moreover, the "rescue" that Buss mentions above has, at times, been literal: as Mollie Gillen explains in her account of tracking down the nephew of one of Montgomery's correspondents just as he had decided to burn forty years of her letters, "I was just in time" ("The Rescue of the Montgomery–MacMillan Letters" 484).[3]

In what follows, two researchers with vastly different professional backgrounds discuss their respective approaches to and discoveries in the L. M. Montgomery archives, each drawn, personally and professionally, to the puzzle about the end of Montgomery's life in 1942. Vanessa Brown is an antiquarian book cataloguer in London, Ontario, who was a prize winner in the Bibliographical Society of Canada's 2009 National Book Collecting Contest for her collection of rare editions and ephemera related to Montgomery. Benjamin Lefebvre, an academic with a background in Canadian literature and cultural studies, edited Montgomery's rediscovered final book, *The Blythes Are Quoted* (2009), which was reportedly delivered to Montgomery's publishers the very day of her death. Of concern to both are statements made by Montgomery that show the decisions she made about documents and artifacts she wanted to leave behind as the official records of her life. Independently and collaboratively, Brown and Lefebvre discovered that, although the Montgomery archives reveal missing pieces to the overall puzzle, they also point to the impossibility of conclusive answers.

VB: My first exposure to Montgomery was the 1985 miniseries by Kevin Sullivan. I then made quick work of reading all the Anne books and everything else Montgomery wrote. I could closely relate to her heroines then, because I was a bookish child who used big words and lived a lot in my head. As I became an adult, however, I started identifying more with Montgomery than with her characters. I began to grasp the darker elements in her fiction and journals. Whereas as a child I used to look up to Anne, as an adult I look up to Maud and admire her ambition—as she found it in the poem "The Fringed Gentian"—to

> reach that far-off goal
> Of true and honored fame
> And write upon its shining scroll
> A woman's humble name. (Montgomery, *The Alpine Path* 10)

BL: I started out with *Road to Avonlea* (1990–1996), which was first on television when I was a teenager, and then with Montgomery's novel *The Story Girl* (1911), which was one of the books used as a foundation for the television series. I've never been the "typical" Montgomery reader—I tend to prefer the realistic social community aspects to Montgomery's work over the romantic parts (which I don't find believable) or the effusive nature descriptions (which I tend to skip). Still, there is something about Montgomery that I have found highly addictive. After reading *Anne of Green Gables* and its sequels in high school, I read and reread all her novels and collections of short stories, continued with journals, letters, and literary criticism, then went to graduate school to learn new ways to study her work. In a way, I've been attracted to the Montgomery archives because they've given me the opportunity to *keep on reading*—to postpone indefinitely the end to Montgomery's work.

VB: For antiquarians, the archives offer a similar never-ending treasure hunt. Although both academics and antiquarians seek buried treasure, antiquarians focus on the materiality of the objects themselves (preferably a first edition with a dust jacket!), rather than solely on the information they convey. Acquiring Montgomery-related items is likewise addictive in this way; despite or perhaps because of her popularity, first editions and the like are scarce. Even more so are letters and other ephemeral objects related to her life. The rarest Montgomery artifacts in several archival collections across Canada make them a reference point both for the uniqueness of the information they contain and for the value of the objects themselves, which are of interest to antiquarians and scholars alike. The archives also secure the availability of these important cultural objects, where in a free market the interests of private collectors can conflict with the needs of those studying Montgomery. In my collection, I have a book that belonged to Montgomery, and I know it should be in an archive along with the rest of her personal library. However, part of me feels that no one deserves to own it like I do, that no one will appreciate it like I will. The problem is that most collectors think this way. If it weren't for archives, all of these great Montgomery-related artifacts would belong to private collectors and would never be part of the public conversation about her work. If her journals and letters had remained in private collections, the field of Montgomery Studies would be very different today.

BL: We owe so much to archival collections at the University of Guelph, the University of Prince Edward Island, McMaster University, Library and Archives Canada, and the Confederation Centre Art Gallery and Museum in Charlottetown, not only for acquiring and preserving these unique documents, but also for making them available to those interested in researching Montgomery's life and legacy. Still, we shouldn't underestimate the combination of timing, good luck, and persistence that led to the acquisition of these materials in the first place. Mary Rubio, who edited Montgomery's journals for publication in collaboration with Elizabeth Waterston, tells the story of her effort to persuade the University of Guelph in the early 1980s to purchase Montgomery's journals from her son, Stuart Macdonald. Dr. Macdonald had inherited not only the ten ledgers of handwritten entries covering the period 1889 to 1942 but also the responsibility of having their contents published after a sufficient amount of time had elapsed. Guelph was the logical place for these items, primarily because it was the academic home of Rubio, Waterston, and the journal *Canadian Children's Literature*, which had published a special issue on Montgomery in 1975; it was also a logical place for the deposition of her papers because of Montgomery's connection to the archive's existing Scottish Studies collection (since she was a Canadian woman of Scottish ancestry). It was this connection that convinced the then-chief librarian—who also had fond memories of reading *Anne of Green Gables* as a child—to advocate for their purchase (Rubio, "Why L. M. Montgomery's Journals Came to Guelph" 476–77). Countless additional items were donated to Guelph after Stuart Macdonald's death in 1982, and today, Guelph's L. M. Montgomery Collection is a must-see for anyone looking for archival documents related to Montgomery.

VB: In spite of such extensive archives, researchers are often frustrated in their archival work because they are restricted to working with photocopies or digital images, even if they want to see the original object. My experience as an appraiser in handling valuable documents has often helped me get around these barriers. Someone studying Montgomery from an academic viewpoint could also benefit from this access. As Elizabeth Rollins Epperly noted in "Revisiting Archives," a lecture she gave at a conference devoted to Montgomery held at the University of Guelph in 2008, "[m]ost of us who visit archives and work with original materials do get to find things that no one else may have noticed." This desire to examine original artifacts is counterbalanced by the absolute necessity of preserving them for future generations. Every time someone handles a piece of paper, its integrity is weakened, which is why Guelph's plans to digitize archival documents related to Montgomery is vital for preservation (Bruce, Johnston, and Salmon 128). Still, I have to agree with Epperly that "copies, no matter how useful for one level of study, cannot definitively solve puzzles or subtly suggest intimate feelings" ("Revisiting Archives").

BL: Montgomery was conscious enough of the value of these important documents that she left detailed instructions concerning their use after her death, not only in her will but also in the items themselves. Beginning in the winter of 1919, Montgomery began to transcribe her journals into uniform ledgers, each one five hundred pages. She claimed to "be careful to copy it exactly as it is written" (*Selected Journals* [Sept. 2, 1919] 2: 341), although scholars find it hard to believe that she did so without making any alterations based on her growing awareness of their cultural value. Once this was done in 1922, she made an explicit declaration about her intentions for them beyond her lifetime:

> But today I finished copying my journal into uniform volumes. It has been a long piece of work but an interesting one....
> This journal is a faithful record of one human being's life and so should have a certain literary value. My heirs might publish an *abridged volume* after my death, if I do not myself do it before....

> I *desire that these journals never be destroyed but kept as long as the leaves hold together.* I leave this to my descendants or my literary heirs as a sacred charge and invoke a Shakespearean curse on them if they disregard it. There is so much of myself in these volumes that I cannot bear the thought of their ever being destroyed. It would seem to me like a sort of murder.... (Montgomery, *Selected Journals* [Apr. 16, 1922] 3: 51; ellipses and emphasis in original)

Montgomery's caveat about the possibility of an "abridged volume" would return in the 1930s, when she began a typescript of selected entries for precisely this purpose ("Edited version of L. M. Montgomery journals"). Rubio and Waterston would then use the handwritten ledgers as the basis for the five published volumes of *Selected Journals*. What I find fascinating here is the sheer effort to which Montgomery goes: even while acknowledging that only selections of their contents could (or should) be published, she also intended the ten uniform ledgers to stand on their own as the "official" record of her life. The process of the recovery of Montgomery's work is thus begun by Montgomery herself, in anticipation of future reconsideration.

The eventual publication of these journals certainly opened up the field of Montgomery Studies, because they reveal a woman who, even under the guise of absolute frankness, is surprisingly cryptic and elusive about several aspects of her life, particularly in the later journals concerning some of the dynamics in her own family. In many ways, her gifts as a natural storyteller might have impeded her commitment to writing a "faithful" record of her life, since the journals contain her version of how she wished to be remembered. In a retrospective diary entry dated January 9, 1938, but pertaining to events from January 1937, she revealed that although she had not written in her journal in over a year, she had nevertheless kept a daily record of events:

> But such records were little else than shrieks of anguish. I knew they must not be preserved as they were. They were too dreadful—too bitter. I shall copy some of them in a condensed form here, so that this account of a most unhappy life will be complete. But there are many things I cannot write—for this journal will be read by others when I am dead and there are some things it would not be good for anyone but myself to know. It is bitter enough that I know them—and can never forget them—and cannot tell them—to anyone. (*Selected Journals* [Jan. 9, 1938] 5: 120)

Bearing this kind of entry in mind, it is perhaps less surprising that her journals end abruptly almost three years before her death, save for two final entries—the first in July 1941, the second in March 1942—that show

Montgomery's despair with life. "Oh God, forgive me," she wrote in an entry dated a month before her death. This was revealed to the public with the publication of the last volume of her journals in 2004. "Nobody dreams what my awful position is" (Montgomery, *Selected Journals* [Mar. 23, 1942] 5: 350). The carefully vague phrasing of the annotation for this entry by Rubio and Waterston—"The 'primary cause' of death on her death certificate was 'Coronary Thrombosis'" (Montgomery, *Selected Journals* 5: 399)—clearly indicates that there is much more to this story.

VB: The first clues concerning the mystery that is Montgomery's death were revealed only a few years later, during the centenary of the publication of *Anne of Green Gables*. On September 27, 2008, Kate Macdonald Butler (Montgomery's granddaughter through her son Stuart) published an article in *The Globe and Mail* entitled "The Heartbreaking Truth about Anne's Creator," revealing her family's secret, that Montgomery "took her own life at the age of 67 through a drug overdose." Butler added, "I wasn't told the details of what happened, and I never saw the note she left, but I do know that it asked for forgiveness" (F1). At a conference held at the University of Guelph less than a month later, Mary Rubio revealed that she had the suicide note in her possession, and presented an overhead copy to a room of very interested scholars and enthusiasts. This conference was where we both saw the document for the first time. Rubio addressed several interesting discrepancies at that presentation as well as in her biography, *Lucy Maud Montgomery: The Gift of Wings* (2008), published shortly after the publication of Butler's article. As Rubio notes, "there was a very specific page number—176—at the top of it. The note, which was dated April 22 (two days before her death), was not, as they believed, and as Stuart believed all his life, specifically a suicide note." In fact, in Rubio's view, the note was actually "the final page of Maud's journal, her 'life-book'" (*The Gift of Wings* 575). Rubio speculates that 176 pages of loose sheets of paper contained notes for journal entries that Montgomery had not yet transcribed into her tenth ledger, which she had begun in 1936. The absence of these pages would account for the abrupt end to her journal entries in 1939, although it does not account for the two brief entries made in July 1941 and March 1942. As Rubio notes, "The question is: *where did the other 175 pages go?*" (*The Gift of Wings* 576; emphasis in original). To me, Rubio's question meant only one thing: there was an important, undiscovered Montgomery document out there, which I had to be the one to find. To the antiquarian, Rubio's supposition pointed to the best achievement a treasure hunter could possibly hope for. Of course, this mystery is just another example of how the truth about Montgomery always seems to be hidden behind a curtain, like her character Emily Starr's "flash."

I worked on the appraisal of Montgomery's suicide note for the University of Guelph a year after these puzzle pieces first came to light. One of the important factors I had to take into account when determining a value for the document was whether or not it was an actual suicide note. Having to make such a decision forced me to examine every option. In her biography, Rubio notes that Montgomery used a piece of scrap paper—the back of a Frederick A. Stokes Company royalty statement from 1939, to be exact—to write the note that would be found on her bedside table after her death. "This was not a recent scrap of paper on which she had scribbled out a suicide note, but part of the advance jottings that she did before copying her entries into a journal ledger later on" (Rubio, *The Gift of Wings* 640n104). However, as Rubio points out, Montgomery "had only twenty free legal-sized pages left in Volume Ten"—hardly enough space to transcribe 176 handwritten pages—"but the handwritten letter-sized pages could have been greatly condensed.... I doubt she would have [started another volume] because ten was a round number to end off a life" (*The Gift of Wings* 641n105). Rubio later questions whether Montgomery or her eldest son Chester destroyed the missing 175 pages, and, if so, whether it was Chester's act, whether they were destroyed before or after Montgomery's death. This single piece of paper, a decisive document in a woman's literary life, raises more questions than it answers.

BL: Figuring out where *The Blythes Are Quoted* fit into the puzzle of Montgomery's death was equally challenging, especially since my work on the book began long before any of these clues were revealed. Despite the fact that only sixteen of Montgomery's twenty novels survive in the form of handwritten manuscripts (typescripts and proofs being stages in the production process that were not preserved by her publishers), the University of Guelph has in its Montgomery collection three different typescript versions of this final book. These include one typed draft with numerous handwritten corrections and two seemingly complete versions that were not typed on the same typewriter, and that contain numerous textual variations. No handwritten version survives, and none of the three typescripts is dated. The book's contents are also an anomaly: instead of writing a new Anne novel, Montgomery rewrote several of her most recent short stories (some of which had been published in periodicals as early as 1931, and some of which have never been found in published form) to include Anne and her family, and added vignettes of poems (most of which had already been published) and dialogue between the stories. It is impossible to ascertain when Montgomery actually worked on this book, just as figuring out which typescript is the final copy is also a matter of conjecture. The typed draft and one of the "final" typescripts came from the files of Dr. Stuart

Macdonald; his final typescript was used as the basis for an abridged version, *The Road to Yesterday*, which was published in 1974. The remaining typescript was part of a group of files that belonged to Chester Macdonald and were donated to Guelph by his son, David Macdonald. I was surprised to find that both typescripts appeared to be complete, since most scholars and reviewers who had commented on the final book had assumed that it remained unfinished when Montgomery died. After reading the two finished typescripts side by side and considering the variations between them, I eventually concluded that the version in the Stuart Macdonald files was the final one.

I was hired as a research assistant for the final volume of Montgomery's journals, so I had the opportunity to read the last journal entries long before the public did, but it was only when I started researching Montgomery's obituaries that I discovered another clue: namely, according to the *Globe and Mail*, that the typescript had been "placed in the hands of a publishing firm" the day of her death (qtd. in Lefebvre, Afterword 513). The use of the passive voice made it impossible to confirm that Montgomery herself had dropped it off, but the article seemed to imply that it had been delivered in person, rather than mailed. It was only several months later when I discovered the copies of the typescript that had been donated by David Macdonald were also in the McClelland & Stewart archives at McMaster University. This detail revealed that it was this version—which Stuart Macdonald had apparently not known about—that Montgomery had intended to be published (Lefebvre, "L. M. Montgomery and Her Publishers"). In this case, new findings in the archives radically altered the claims made by earlier scholars.

VB: Likewise, the holdings at the McLaughlin Library at the University of Guelph led to a new understanding of the context of Montgomery's "suicide note." I examined a range of additional documents in the archives to help in my appraisal, including the typescript of her journals, which she had made for her son Stuart. The typescript for the tenth volume, which contains entries from 1936 onward, ends mid-sentence after eleven pages. This fact struck me as odd: why did she stop so abruptly if she intended this typescript to serve as the basis for a posthumous publication? Intrigued, I proceeded backward to the typescript of the ninth volume, which ends at page 175. That was when it hit me: I had found the missing 175 pages that preceded the suicide note—page 176—that was found next to Montgomery's deathbed. Montgomery had started to include the contents of the tenth handwritten ledger in her typescript for future publication, but changed her mind and decided to end with the ninth ledger. Suddenly, the wording of the suicide note on page 176 made sense:

> This copy is unfinished and never will be. It is in a terrible state because I made it when I had begun to suffer my terrible breakdown of 1940. It must end here. If any publishers wish to publish extracts from it under the terms of my will they must stop here. The tenth volume can never be copied and must not be made public during my lifetime. Parts of it are too terrible and would hurt people. I have lost my mind by spells and I do not dare to think what I may do in those spells. May God forgive me and I hope everyone else will forgive me even if they cannot understand. My position is too awful to endure and nobody realizes it. What an end to a life in which I tried always to do my best in spite of many mistakes. ("'Suicide' note written by L. M. Montgomery")

Montgomery had begun typing this abridged version of her handwritten journals as early as 1937 (*Selected Journals* [July 7, 1937] 5: 185). This note confirms that the project was completed under excruciating circumstances sometime after 1940. She had fallen and hurt her right arm that year, and this typescript would have been a good fallback project for her, since she wrote journal entries and the drafts of her novels in longhand, and typing would have presumably been less painful. Depending on when she began *The Blythes Are Quoted*, her injury could explain why there are three typescripts for that book but no handwritten manuscript. The year 1940 was also difficult for her emotionally, as Rubio outlines in her biography: Montgomery endured her husband's ongoing mental illness, the dissolution of her eldest son's marriage, her own increased reliance on prescription drugs, the beginning of the Second World War, and her frustration with a literary community that had begun to marginalize her as a children's writer (*The Gift of Wings* 566). The typescript version of her journals shows several passes of revision in different pens and in pencil. She could very well have worked on it in revision until just before her death, even though the typing was completed long before—after all, Rubio and Waterston note that a handwritten interpolation dated 1942 was added to the typescript version of a journal entry dated 1921 (Montgomery, *Selected Journals* 2: 434). The "suicide note" was a final handwritten note to accompany the typescript. As a postscript to the typed version of the ninth ledger, the single sheet found at Montgomery's death would indicate that, rather than offering missing notes for further journal entries, it contains her final instructions to her son with respect to this important record of her life.

Additionally, Montgomery used considerable scrap paper in finalizing the presentation of her typescript for Stuart. She wrote her original instructions on the paper boxes in which the typescript was stored; she outlined that the journals and their publishing rights should be given to Chester, and then his daughter Luella on her twenty-first birthday. Then she scratched these out, possibly as a result of the falling out she had with Chester in 1940, when his marriage dissolved, and glued new ones to the front of the paper boxes on scrap paper, on which she gave full rights to Stuart and his heirs. Montgomery was so distressed by Chester's separation that she added provisions in her will that disinherited him if he were not living with his wife at the time of her death (Devereux, "'See My Journal for the Full Story'" 242). It is entirely in keeping with these measures that page 176 was written on scrap paper. The date on the note—April 22, 1942, two days before her death—is also significant; this day could have been when she made her final revisions to the typescript and the final preparations to *The Blythes Are Quoted*. One possible scenario is that Montgomery met with Stuart on April 23, 1942, to give him the typescript of the journals, and perhaps even asked him to drop off her manuscript at the publishers the next day. Unbeknownst to him, this would have been her final farewell. If so, then these two documents made up her final act as a writer and mother. The puzzle can only be put together using pieces preserved by the archives: the suicide note, the typescript, and the original box covers.

BL: Montgomery's ambivalence about which of her sons should inherit the journals had concerned her for several decades, from the time they were children. When I started research for this article, I was intrigued by the number of ellipses in the published version of the 1922 entry, quoted earlier, in which Montgomery outlined her wish that the ten ledgers be preserved and their contents published. Curious as to what had been cut by Rubio and Waterston in the process of preparing these journals for publication, I discovered that both the handwritten original and Montgomery's own typescript contained further sets of instructions that are entirely in keeping with the preoccupations revealed in the note found by her deathbed:

> But to-day I finished copying my journal into uniform volumes. It has been a long piece of work but an interesting one. Perhaps a hundred years from now my descendants may read over this diary and regard it as an interesting heirloom. By that time they can give it to the world if they like. Everyone would be dead whom its publication could hurt and I would like it to be published in full *without omission*, save for this very paragraph I have just written. Cut it out, descendants!
>
> This journal is a faithful record of one human being's life and so should have a certain literary value. My heirs might publish an *abridged volume* after my death, if I do not myself do it before. It might be a good financial proposition for them. They should not include anything that would hurt or annoy anyone living.
>
> *I desire that these journals never be destroyed but kept as long as the leaves hold together.* I leave this to my descendants or my literary heirs as a sacred charge and invoke a Shakespearean curse on them if they disregard it. There is so much of myself in these volumes that I cannot bear the thought of their ever being destroyed. It would seem to me like a sort of murder.

I do not yet know to which of my boys I shall finally bequeath this journal. Time must show which is the fitter to receive and guard it. Perhaps as yet unborn grandchildren and great-grandchildren will pore over these pages, with curious interest in a life lived so long before, in a world that will have so wholly passed away. Will some great-great-granddaughter of mine ever bend her pretty young head over this page? If so—I salute you, dear! Here and now, across the gulf of generations, I put out my hand and say to you,

"I lived a hundred years before you did; but my blood runs in your veins and I lived and loved and suffered and enjoyed and toiled and struggled just as you do. I found life good, in spite of everything. May you find it so. I found that courage and kindness are the two essential things. They are just as essential in your century as they were in mine. Here's to you, little great-great-granddaughter, not to be born for a hundred years! I hope you'll be merry and witty and brave and wise; and I hope you'll say to yourself, 'If Great-great-grandmother were alive to-day I think I'd like her in spite of her faults.'" (Unpublished journals [Apr. 16, 1922] 5: 266–67)[4]

In the unabridged entry, we see more of the ambivalences and contradictions that are implied in the published version: on the one hand, Montgomery adamantly wants the journals published, but on the other hand, she leaves it up to her descendants to decide whether or not to do so. Moreover, she contradicts herself about whether to have the journals published with or without omissions. She ultimately left them to Stuart Macdonald, who then entrusted them to Rubio and Waterston and left it to their editorial discretion to select and edit them.

VB: No matter how much we learn about Montgomery's death, a great deal will always be left to speculation. I believe that either she kept back the final handwritten instructions for the typescript, her suicide note, because it betrayed her intentions to kill herself, or perhaps she wrote it as a definitive suicide note, using the typescript as a frame for her approach. It was poetic timing to have her final and most subversive text, *The Blythes Are Quoted*, dropped off at the publishers as she lay dying in her bed.

The original suicide note, owing another debt to the archives, shows that she crossed out the word "would" ("I hope everyone else would forgive me") and replaced it with "will," outlining a moment of decisiveness to end her life. She was also concerned with leaving final instructions about the publication of her journals, confirming the open question posed in 1922 about which son would inherit them. According to Alix Strauss, whose book *Death Becomes Them* (2009) traces the suicides of public figures, "for some, there is planning—which brings momentary relief. It's the well-crafted, highly-organized strategy that allows a suicide to write the notes and divide up her belongings, that gives her time to say her proper farewells" (11). In my view, the note found at Montgomery's deathbed was partly a letter of formal instruction to her son and lawyers, and partly a final note of farewell. In a way, one part of her wanted to express what she planned to do, but another part wanted to preserve the secrecy of those plans. Such ambivalence between disclosure and subterfuge is not only the dominant pattern of her journals but also characteristic of suicide. According to Edwin Shneidman, a world authority on suicide, "the prototypical suicide state is one in which an individual cuts his throat and cries for help at the same time, and is genuine in both of these acts" (135). Further, the note would make sense only to Stuart Macdonald, who had been given the typescript of her journal and who she could have presumed to be among the first contacted when her body was found, because of his profession. As Strauss notes, "[i]n many cases the letters are a puzzle, decipherable only to the people they're intended for" (17). What gives this story a kind of happy ending is that Stuart Macdonald understood the message. When he made a facsimile of the typescript to edit for publication sometime in the 1970s, he did not copy the tenth volume of her journals, respecting his mother's instructions. Moreover, in a 1974 interview in the *Globe and Mail* about his plans to edit the journals himself, he is reported to have said that the published journals would end at 1933 "because mother says some unkind things about people who are still living" (Carson, "Million Words"). The typescript becomes an intimate message to her son, but also a final offering to her readers. We can read Montgomery as having set up her journals and *The Blythes Are Quoted* as her suicide notes, the lengthy farewell of a prolific writer. After all, as Strauss remarks, "[s]ome suicide notes are meant for a single pair of eyes; others reach out to the masses" (19).

BL: In Montgomery's case, the note found on her deathbed is both intimate and public, as are the journals and final typescript that she confided to her son. And although *The Blythes Are Quoted* isn't mentioned explicitly in the note, the fact that she had apparently arranged for it to be dropped off on the day of her death indicates that she saw it as publishable, unlike the final ledger of her journals. Ultimately, what this all shows is both the rewards and challenges of using archival documents in an attempt to solve a puzzle about a well-known author. Although such discoveries make this kind of sleuthing so rewarding, researchers can never predict what clues will be unearthed next to modify earlier claims.

VB: It would be superficial to say simply that the archives make these discoveries possible. Rather, there is an interconnected and ongoing relationship between archives, antiquarians, and scholars that creates a dynamic of discovery and learning that is akin to a breathing organism.

The strength of this community is what rescues the stories of Canadian women, preserving them *and* renewing them for the future—the force that holds all the leaves together.

Notes

1 The two exceptions to this generalization are *The Watchman and Other Poems* (1916) and *Courageous Women* (1934), a book of essays co-authored with Marian Keith and Mabel Burns McKinley, both of which went out of print soon after their publication. Even the unauthorized collection of short stories, *Further Chronicles of Avonlea* (1920), which Montgomery fought in court for eight years to be removed from circulation, remains in print today.
2 In addition to the *Selected Journals*, the posthumous texts attributed to Montgomery have included three volumes of letters (*The Green Gables Letters* in 1960, *My Dear Mr. M.* in 1980, and *After Green Gables* in 2006), diaries (including a joint diary kept by Montgomery and close friend Nora Lefurgey, published in *The Intimate Life of L. M. Montgomery* in 2005), short stories, essays, and poems culled from periodicals (*The Alpine Path* in 1974, *The Doctor's Sweetheart* in 1979, *The Poetry of Lucy Maud Montgomery* in 1987, and *Akin to Anne*, the first of eight collections edited by Rea Wilmshurst, in 1988), and a book-length work not published in Montgomery's lifetime (*The Blythes Are Quoted* in 2009, which had been published in significantly abridged form as *The Road to Yesterday* in 1974). Archival documents and artifacts, including photographs, have also been a major focus of recent academic studies (Epperly's *Through Lover's Lane* in 2007 and Gammel's *Looking for Anne* in 2008).
3 Gillen used Montgomery's letters to G. B. MacMillan as a major basis for her 1975 biography, *The Wheel of Things*. Although a fraction of the letter collection was published as *My Dear Mr. M.* in 1980, the originals are available to researchers at Library and Archives Canada, as are Montgomery's letters to Ephraim Weber.
4 This extract appears in near identical form in Montgomery, "Journals of L. M. Montgomery," 5:85.

Works Cited

Bruce, Lorne, Wayne Johnston, and Helen Salmon. "The L. M. Montgomery Collection at the University of Guelph." *Canadian Children's Literature/Littérature canadienne pour la jeunesse* 34.2 (2008): 124–29. Print.

Buss, Helen M. Introduction. *Working in Women's Archives: Researching Women's Private Literature and Archival Documents*. Ed. Helen M. Buss and Marlene Kadar. Waterloo: Wilfrid Laurier UP, 2001. 1–5. Print.

Carson, Jo. "Million Words in 10-Volume Diary Tell Lucy Maud Montgomery's Own Tale." Interview with Stuart Macdonald. *Globe and Mail* Oct. 3, 1974: W4. Print.

Devereux, Cecily. "The Continuing Story." Rev. of *The Selected Journals of L. M. Montgomery, Volume IV: 1929–1935*, ed. Mary Rubio and Elizabeth Waterston. *Canadian Literature* 177 (2003): 180–81. Print.

———. "'See My Journal for the Full Story': Fictions of Truth in *Anne of Green Gables* and L. M. Montgomery's Journals." *The Intimate Life of L. M. Montgomery.* Ed. Irene Gammel. Toronto: U of Toronto P, 2005. 241–57. Print.

Epperly, Elizabeth Rollins. *Imagining Anne: The Island Scrapbooks of L. M. Montgomery.* Toronto: Penguin Canada, 2008. Print.

———. "Revisiting Archives." From Canada to the World: The Cultural Influence of Lucy Maud Montgomery. U of Guelph. Oct. 25, 2008. Lecture.

———. *Through Lover's Lane: L. M. Montgomery's Photography and Visual Imagination.* Toronto: U of Toronto P, 2007. Print.

Gammel, Irene. *Looking for Anne: How Lucy Maud Montgomery Dreamed Up a Literary Classic.* Toronto: Key Porter, 2008. Print.

Gillen, Mollie. "The Rescue of the Montgomery–MacMillan Letters." McCabe 484–85.

———. *The Wheel of Things: A Biography of Lucy Maud Montgomery.* Don Mills: Fitzhenry & Whiteside, 1975. Print.

Lefebvre, Benjamin. Afterword. *The Blythes Are Quoted.* L. M. Montgomery. Ed. Benjamin Lefebvre. Toronto: Viking Canada, 2009. 511–20. Print.

———. "L. M. Montgomery and Her Publishers." *Historical Perspectives on Canadian Publishing.* McMaster University/Queen's University/University of Toronto Thomas Fisher Rare Books Library, 2009. Web.

McCabe, Kevin, comp. *The Lucy Maud Montgomery Album.* Toronto: Fitzhenry & Whiteside, 1999. Print.

Montgomery, L. M. *After Green Gables: L. M. Montgomery's Letters to Ephraim Weber, 1916–1941.* Ed. Hildi Froese Tiessen and Paul Gerard Tiessen. Toronto: U of Toronto P, 2006. Print.

———. *Akin to Anne: Tales of Other Orphans.* Ed. Rea Wilmshurst. Toronto: McClelland & Stewart, 1988. Print.

———. *The Alpine Path: The Story of My Career.* 1917. Toronto: Fitzhenry & Whiteside, n.d. Print.

———. *The Blythes Are Quoted.* Ed. Benjamin Lefebvre. Toronto: Viking Canada, 2009. Print.

———. "The Blythes Are Quoted." File 10-11, Box 31, Jack McClelland fonds, William Ready Division of Archives and Research Collections, McMaster University Library.

———. "The Blythes Are Quoted." Box 328, Series X, McClelland & Stewart fonds, Manuscript Bundles, William Ready Division of Archives and Research Collections, McMaster University Library.

———. "The Blythes Are Quoted—Original MS. with annotations by E. Stuart Macdonald." XZ1 MS A098001, L. M. Montgomery Collection, Archival and Special Collections, University of Guelph Library.

———. "The Blythes Are Quoted—Typescript." XZ1 MS A098002, L. M. Montgomery Collection, Archival and Special Collections, University of Guelph Library.

———. "Contracts, Picture of S. K. Woolner, MS. of 'The Blythes Are Quoted,' Journal and Literary Mss. of C. C. Macdonald, 1916–1945." XZ1 MS A100,

L. M. Montgomery Collection, Archival and Special Collections, University of Guelph Library.

———. *The Doctor's Sweetheart and Other Stories*. Ed. Catherine McLay. 1979. Toronto: Seal, 1993. Print.

———. "Edited version of L. M. Montgomery journals." XZ5 MS A021, L. M. Montgomery Collection, University of Guelph Archives.

———. *Further Chronicles of Avonlea*. 1920. Toronto: Seal, 1993. Print.

———. *The Green Gables Letters from L. M. Montgomery to Ephraim Weber, 1905–1909*. Ed. Wilfrid Eggleston. 1960. Ottawa: Borealis, 1981. Print.

———. "Journals of L. M. Montgomery; September 21, 1889 to March 23, 1942." XZ5 MS A001, L. M. Montgomery Collection, University of Guelph Archives. Print.

———. *My Dear Mr. M.: Letters to G. B. MacMillan from L. M. Montgomery*. Ed. Francis W. P. Bolger and Elizabeth R. Epperly. 1980. Toronto: Oxford UP, 1992. Print.

———. *The Poetry of Lucy Maud Montgomery*. Ed. John Ferns and Kevin McCabe. Toronto: Fitzhenry & Whiteside, 1987. Print.

———. *The Road to Yesterday*. 1974. Toronto: Seal, 1993. Print.

———. *The Selected Journals of L. M. Montgomery*. Ed. Mary Rubio and Elizabeth Waterston. 5 Vols. Toronto: Oxford UP, 1985–2004. Print.

———. *The Story Girl*. 1911. Toronto: Seal, 1987. Print.

———. "'Suicide' note written by L. M. Montgomery, April 22, 1942." XZ1 MS A098197, L. M. Montgomery Collection, University of Guelph Archives.

———. *The Watchman and Other Poems*. Toronto: McClelland, Goodchild, and Stewart, 1916. Print.

———. "Will, codicil and estate papers of L. M. Montgomery [1939]." XZ1 MS A098008, L. M. Montgomery Collection, University of Guelph Archives.

Montgomery, L. M., Marian Keith, and Mabel Burns McKinley. *Courageous Women*. Toronto: McClelland & Stewart, 1934. Print.

Montgomery, L. M., and Nora Lefurgey. "'. . . where has my yellow garter gone?' The Diary of L. M. Montgomery and Nora Lefurgey." *The Intimate Life of L. M. Montgomery*. Ed. Irene Gammel. Toronto: U of Toronto P, 2005. 19–87. Print.

Rubio, Mary Henley. *Lucy Maud Montgomery: The Gift of Wings*. Toronto: Doubleday Canada, 2008. Print.

———. "Why L. M. Montgomery's Journals Came to Guelph." McCabe 473–78.

———. Untitled lecture. From Canada to the World: The Cultural Influence of Lucy Maud Montgomery. U of Guelph. Oct. 25, 2008. Lecture.

Shneidman, Edwin. *Definition of Suicide*. New York: John Wiley and Sons, 1985. Print.

Strauss, Alix. *Death Becomes Them: Unearthing the Suicides of the Brilliant, the Famous and the Notorious*. New York: HarperCollins, 2009. Print.

Sullivan, Kevin, dir. *Anne of Green Gables*. Adapt. Kevin Sullivan and Joe Wiesenfeld. Sullivan Films, 1985. Television.

The Quality of the Carpet: A Consideration of Anecdotes in Researching Women's Lives
Linda M. Morra

I have an anecdote to share with you.

Some time ago, I gave a public lecture in Vancouver about modernist painter Emily Carr. Although Carr is renowned as a productive artist, having painted an impressive number of sketches and paintings, I had focused my research on her career as a public writer.[1] I was approached directly after the talk by an elderly man who told me that he had had some interactions with the family of Ira Dilworth, which he believed would be of great interest to me. Dilworth had inherited Carr's literary papers and became the executor of her estate because he served as her editor and had been one of her most faithful friends before she died in 1945.[2] Naturally, my interest was piqued, even though it was not a new occurrence to be approached thus. With moderate regularity, others bestow upon me anecdotes about Carr because of my expertise about her writing life. In such situations, I have been quite consistently willing to open myself up to the possibility that a story may be out there that will alter, shift, or contribute to the existing record on Carr. I quickly assented, therefore, to interviewing him, and made arrangements to have lunch with him and his wife in order to pursue the possible lead.

I arrived with my tape recorder and notebook and, after the lunch was concluded and his wife had retired for a nap, I settled back comfortably in an armchair, turned the recorder on, and proceeded to ask him about the memories that he thought would be of interest to me as a scholar of Carr and Dilworth.

"I had a date with his niece," he confided.

I mentioned the name of one of them, in bewilderment.[3]

"Yes," he confided, "that's her. I tried to go all the way with her on Dilworth's living-room carpet. Regrettably, I didn't get very far."

I waited. He regarded the floor pensively. I was certain there was more forthcoming, perhaps a story about Dilworth, or some other matter that would add to the record on Carr. After another moment or two of silence, I decided he needed some gentle prodding. "And is there anything else?"

"No," he shook his head sadly. "I never saw her again after that. I could tell you about Dilworth's carpet, though. It was a really nice carpet."

* * *

Initially, I had tossed this anecdote into my "research junk drawer," the place where we toss that hodgepodge of random items that cannot be easily categorized or that we regard as of little value; I declined from giving it further consideration for some time. But then questions began nagging, even clamouring for attention, until I could no longer ignore them. What did I make of the anecdote about the elderly gentleman whose attempts to seduce Ira Dilworth's niece failed—or read another way, the moment in which a woman refused to be coerced into a sexual liaison with him? Was this anecdote simply a detour from my research about Carr? How had I come to a decision that the gentleman's anecdote merited "junk-drawer status"? Why had I sidestepped including this one in my research, while using others, with little sense of hesitation? What criteria was I using that compelled me to include some, but not others? How did I know I was conducting my research in ways that were ethical? These last two questions have especially and consistently informed my research—and I continue to grapple with the processes of raising these questions and coming to answer them, however provisionally. This anecdote thus became important not only in and of itself but also for serving as a platform to consider and discuss two primary considerations in relation to my research on Canadian women's lives.

The first is related to the genre of archival materials—that is, those materials that we believe need to be safeguarded or are deemed "archive-worthy." These decisions have affected the preservation—or the lack thereof—of Canadian women's papers. As Catherine Hobbs notes in this collection, "[w]hen working with personal archives, every question of contact, acquisition, treatment, and interpretation is ethically marked, insofar as the choices of the archivist"—to which I might add, researcher—"reflect a perception of the life lived by a particular individual and the interactions with those others around that individual." Just as "professional archivists make decisions about those records that will be available to future generations as part of a collective cultural memory," I too as a researcher make decisions about which stories I will include in the narratives I write and share with others (Schultz viii). And just as professional archivists' criteria are formulated in relation to "an institution's specific mission" and to that which "might affect an institution's holding at a given moment" (such as "available space"), so I too consider my own research objectives and reflect upon a methodology that governs what I decide to keep, include, disclose, and dispose (Schultz viii). Like an archivist, I understand that much of what I am doing in the process does not "just take place in the library archives," but also extends well beyond it to "pursue supplementary information and additional perspectives about [my data] from existing people and places" (Kirsch and Rohan, Introduction 2).

The second consideration is related to the affective power of archival research, not necessarily of the material under scrutiny, but the researcher's relationship to it. I realized, moreover, that whether or not one considers using or preserving even the most spare of archival material—in, say, the form of an anecdote—the choice has implications for the positioning of writer, researcher, and archivist, and also for the relationships that are fostered (or not) between them. In *An Archive of Feelings*, Ann Cvetkovitch traces the importance of "ephemeral and unusual traces" left by lives that may not be subsumed by normative institutional practices and to which researchers must diligently heed (9). She notes that affective lives are necessary to challenge mainstream political ones and, more urgently, "affective experience can provide the basis for new cultures ... [i]t is organized as 'an archive of feelings,' an exploration of cultural texts as repositories of feelings and emotions, which are encoded not only in the content of the texts themselves but the in the practices that surround their production and reception" (9).[4]

On the subject of the first consideration—anecdotes, their identifying features, and putative insignificance—critic Jane Gallop has already spoken at great length, and she has addressed their designation as a genre. Indeed, in her book devoted to the subject, *Anecdotal Theory*, she defines that form as "a short account of some interesting or humorous incident," and as such, she argues that it has been positioned as diametrically opposed to high theory. She lists the binaries that are occasioned by such thinking: "humorous vs.

serious," "short vs. grand," "trivial vs. overarching," and "specific vs. general" (2). She might have added official vs. unofficial accounts, archived vs. un-archived, and print vs. oral story. By virtue of their "insignificant" status and compact nature, anecdotes are not necessarily substantial enough to be stored in archives as independent entities. In my experience, when jotted down in print, they are found in obscure folders, conveyed in passing in a letter, or shunted to the back of clipping files—if not completely omitted from archival institutions altogether. As such, they are often regarded as incidental, or as unofficial scrawl, a near cousin to graffiti.

Gallop therefore conceives of "anecdotal theory... to cut through these oppositions in order to produce theory with a better sense of humor, theorizing which honors the uncanny detail of lived experience" (2). To that end, she extends the arguments Joel Fineman made in "The History of the Anecdote" and those of Barbara Christian in "The Race for Theory." By considering their arguments jointly, Gallop locates the power of the anecdote in its disruption of "what is too fixed, too abstract, too eternal and ahistorical" (3). Fineman, who offers an example of "mid-eighties deconstructionist theorizing," and Christian, who offers an example of the championing of literature "against a theory which is to her mind grotesquely unliterary" (1), may have polarized theoretical approaches, yet they are read together by Gallop to showcase how the anecdote is both deconstructionist in impulse and highly literary and specific in nature. The anecdote emphasizes the immediacy of the moment and the real: it invites us to look "to the place where the literary is knotted to the real" (3). According to Gallop, its marginal status retains the power to cut through and undermine the abstractions of theory, and it does so by presenting itself in both literary and real terms. In other words, some anecdotes are sufficiently charged with an erotics that have the power to overturn or subvert totalizing narratives, to expand upon a record that may have been restrictive and limiting, and to create a "moment" or a sense of the real that theory would otherwise deny.[5]

The anecdote's specificity is thus integral to reacting against what comes to be regarded as mainstream or normative:

> The usual presupposition of theory is that we need to reach a general understanding, which then predisposes us toward the norm, toward a case or model that is prevalent, mainstream. To dismiss something as "merely anecdotal" is to dismiss it as a relatively rare and marginal case. Anecdotal theory would base its theorizing on exorbitant models. (7)[6]

Gallop elaborates on this facet of anecdotal theory by using Derrida's association of the exorbitant with "exteriority, with exits, departures, attempts to get out, and in particular with the attempt to get out of a rut" (8). In other words, she sees the anecdote as imbued with sufficient power that it can break out of restrictive structures, undermine monolithic or homogeneous approaches, or expand upon a formerly limited understanding. The repression of the anecdote is required for that limited understanding to retain its stability, coherence, and hegemony, and the anecdote's telling for its undoing. Gallop ultimately wishes to forge space and create a more receptive audience for anecdotes because she esteems their disruptive potential and their conveyance of the real.

On the one hand, in my consideration of the most ephemeral material, I had endeavoured to be a thorough researcher, following impulses and leads and considering even seemingly trivial details and anecdotes that might shed new light on Carr as a subject. As Gesa E. Kirsch and Liz Rohan note, researchers understand the importance of "attending to facets of the research process that might easily be marginalized and rarely mentioned because they seem merely intuitive, coincidental, or serendipitous.... Authors [may move] from a hunch, a chance encounter, or a newly discovered family artefact to scholarly research" (Introduction 4). They add that "genuine curiosity, a willingness to follow all possible leads, an openness to what one may encounter, and flexibility in revising research questions and the scope of a project to be key factors for conducing successful historical work" (Kirsh and Rohan 5). Not sufficiently substantive or weighty enough to be isolated on their own in larger archival institutions, anecdotes nonetheless may offer new leads or challenge the direction of a researcher. In my experience of archival work, I have found that anecdotes in oral—and sometimes print—form are more likely to illuminate a "moment" that in turn reveals character, a personality trait, or a dynamic that counters mainstream politics.

On the other hand, however, I had indeed quickly dismissed the gentleman and his disclosure after that encounter. Gallop thus correctly identifies one aspect of what I had observed about the anecdote shared by the elderly man with me—I had dismissed it, at first, because I regarded it as trivial, humorous, and specific. I also considered that, since the story had been relayed to me orally, I did not approach it perhaps as earnestly as I would a document, for example, in a government institution or archive; in the latter instance, I may regard the document as officially sanctioned and thus more legitimate (a bias I need to query), but certainly more easily reproduced. Researchers are able to cite these, integrate them into other published texts, and refer back to their origins as "viable sources." Yet, if literary forms communicated by word of mouth had once been perceived as an unstable form of knowledge transmission, such attitudes have surely changed. Indigenous forms of epistemology, and the complexity and intricacy of Indigenous traditions and histories, have been passed down orally; greater recognition for and viability of the oral form has increasingly rendered this attitude as untenable. Indeed, oral forms may carry as great or even greater weight than printed form.[7]

Yet even so, I valued a short and humorous account in the British Columbia Archives and Records Service (BCARS) which I discovered in a letter by Kate Mather and that suggested her relationship with and connection to Carr. Mather was reminding Carr of her "indomitable spirit," as evidenced by a situation in which a missionary collector approached Carr to ask for donations for the purposes of converting the Indigenous. To the missionary, Carr fierily quipped that she was "always glad [when she] heard one of them [had been] eaten by cannibals."[8] I did indeed find this anecdote humorous; yet, I used it in my research because it suggests both an aspect of Carr's personality and her political stance toward the colonization and religious conversion of the Indigenous.[9] However imperfect and politically incorrect her own attitudes were toward the Indigenous, her wit in that moment showcases her open defiance of such colonizing processes. Taken in isolation, her quip also gestures toward the stereotypical assumptions still held in that period about the nature and inclinations of the Indigenous—assumptions for which she evinced unmitigated scorn.

I had seen this anecdote as more significant because I regarded it as a "clue" to how the artist expressed her difference from prevalent cultural attitudes toward missionaries in the period. Lucilee M. Schultz, author of the preface to *Beyond the Archives*, implies that our research journeys are thus often marked by discoveries (possibly coming in the form of an anecdote) that then occasion twists and turns, detours and side trips—"all this as part of their research as a lived process" (vii). Methodologies might even irrevocably change in response to one's discoveries of material that is unusual, irregular, or unexpected. The reverse, however, is also true: our understanding of an anecdote may be altered when contextualized within a larger narrative. So, when I examine Carr's remark about the missionaries *in context* rather than in isolation, it takes on ironic overtones. She depended on the very missionaries she castigated to guide her through Indigenous territory and introduce her to the people she seemed to wish to champion.

I was ultimately more receptive to this anecdote's value because the recipient of Mather's letter was the very subject of my research—Carr herself. Its telling was thus much closer in proximity to the event and person described. Thus, it seemed to carry greater legitimacy for reasons other than intrinsic value and illumination of character, or for the implied assumptions about how women should have spoken and conducted themselves in that period. Indeed, it seemed to carry greater weight and authenticity than, say, the anecdote relayed to me by my gentleman interviewee, whose story was transmitted more than fifty years after the fact, and whose purpose was considerably less related to and vested in my research interests. Indeed, I might even have been satisfied with our brief exchange if I believed that the anecdote he relayed had greater potential to break out of restrictive structures, rather than inform them.

I then considered that my initial lack of interest in the gentleman's anecdote had less to do with its oral status and more to do with its "genre"—that is, since it might be characterized as mere gossip. Here again, Gallop is instructive: anecdotes are sometimes approached and dismissed as such. In this volume, however, T. L. Cowan notes that that "gossip-knowledge" may have "at least two kinds of reception," depending on their context. She quotes Lorraine Code's argument that gossip, as a "situated discourse... attuned to the location, the historical moment and the circumstances that generated it" (231), may be regarded as valuable to

> form[s] of knowing/knowledge, and, depending on the gossiper-audience relationship, it can serve different purposes: "In a climate of trust people gossip to think aloud about themselves and one and other, to work through extraordinary events, to know one and other better, and to establish community. In a climate of distrust, gossip is often malicious, playing with reputations, circulating truths better concealed, or half-truths elevated to the status of truth." (231)

In the case of the story shared between Mather and Carr, I remarked upon what Code would have identified as an atmosphere of trust, wherein two women felt safe to refer to a story of this kind.

That was when I realized that a central aspect of Gallop's consideration of how anecdotes function required re-examination. I had attended to the gentleman's desire to share his story with me because I believed that I too was operating in a climate of trust. His disclosure, however, affirmed my performance and authority as a Carr scholar, and created a dynamic that positioned me as someone who could serve as repository for his anecdote; however, his admission suggested that he was also playing with someone's reputation (as perhaps I now play with his) and that this desire was suspect in motivation. I allowed for this intimate encounter with the gentleman, who had subsequently little more to share with me than something I consider tantamount to boys' locker-room talk because, as a researcher specializing in women's writing, I do indeed accord some importance to the power of anecdotes and their role in establishing the intimacy required to render sometimes significant disclosures. The manner in which he shared it with me heightened the effect: he imparted it in his own home, when his wife was not present, and by doing so he tried to find a receptive, private, and sympathetic audience. The anecdote thus bore significance in another way that Gallop does not address: it not only conveyed a moment of "the real," as she suggests, but is significant in its potential affective power. Although he was not successful in establishing the kind of audience and connection he desired, I realized that he invoked a dynamic, sometimes effective, which women authors use to establish relationships with one another and with others in the publishing industry. Indeed, given my own research, I see some anecdotes as significant because they are invested with a kind of power related to the forging of intimacy. I came to some realizations about how intimacy is politically inflected in ways to suggest not only what is omitted from archives and why those omissions may exist but also how intimacy relates to strategies that late-nineteenth- and early-twentieth-century Canadian women writers used to access the public sphere in the face of being strategically denied a place therein. Carr certainly did so. It is also a means by which I sometimes respond to the research material at hand. In other words, anecdotes are organized in a hierarchy related to their value and use, but they may take hold by the affect they register.

In another research trip to the British Columbia Archives and Records Service, for example, I found a small piece of dried cedar pinned to one of Carr's well-loved editions of the poetry of Walt Whitman. Its relevance did not register in any significant way until I came across one of Dilworth's letters to Carr, dated Friday, April 16, 1943. Therein, he explained that he was returning "the sprig of cedars" that had been "on a long trip" with him to Toronto, specifically to the University Women's Club, where he had read from some of her work: "During 'Canoe' you could have heard a pin drop (even though the room was covered with luxurious deep carpet)." He had read these stories on her behalf because, at the age of seventy-two and fighting all manner of illness, she was scarcely able to make the trip herself. Apparently, Carr had given Dilworth this sprig of cedar as a token of her support and affection, and also as a reminder of her presence while he read her story. Dilworth honoured this gesture when he wore the cedar at the talk, and later returned it to her. In his letter to her, he expressed his appreciation: "had it not been for the warm spot over my heart where Small kept watch and for the sprig of your cedar, I think I might have got cold feet and run out on the good ladies." The fact that she kept the sprig of cedar and that it remains to this day in the British Columbia Archives and Records Service signified the importance of their relationship, the kind of trust and respect the two shared.

But why did she attach it to a volume of Whitman's poetry? Fred Housser, author of *The Group of Seven*, had bought her a copy of his Whitman's poems in 1930, which she took with her on a sketching trip in August of that year (Tippett 176; 178). Bess and Lawren Harris had also introduced her to his poetry, but when their sense of spirituality involved turning to Theosophy, Carr's friendship with them cooled. Yet her love for Whitman's poetry remained. At this juncture, Dilworth and his appreciation of Whitman filled a necessary void: the poetry became a beloved source of connection between the two and bears witness to their growing friendship. As I acknowledge when I speak about discovering the cedar clipping, it is touchingly relevant that Carr pinned it to that book, because the gesture evocatively captures Dilworth's importance to her. More importantly, the discovery of the cedar clipped to this volume becomes *my* anecdote, and its affective overtones suggest both why I was compelled by this research and why others often have a similar experience.

I understood better why the gentleman's anecdote was indeed significant, if not for reasons related to *my* agenda, certainly. His disclosure was not so trivial after all: it was a potent reminder of the prevalent male attitudes of the period that Carr had been struggling against. The telling of the anecdote registered his impulse to tell *his* story, to assert and insert himself in Carr's literary and historical record, to work against the story of a woman who tried to define her own life on her own terms. His failure to seduce Dilworth's niece might be thus read as his own personal failure, not just in sexual terms but also in terms of being represented in the historical record—unless he could find a proper witness with whom he might share his anecdote. I might read the anecdote as a man's struggle to define himself in the terms by which masculinity was set in the period: exertions of male sexuality over female sexuality. Or I might read it as his attempt to locate some sense of virility or longevity through the power of narrative.

I chose to read this moment, however, not as "exorbitant" in Gallop's (and Derrida's) sense of it—indeed, at this juncture, I regarded Gallop's sense of its purpose as strikingly incorrect. Anecdotes are not an indiscriminate group that collectively work in opposition to generalized theory. Indeed, I read that gentleman's anecdote as the urge of the patriarchal to impose itself, in however small a fashion, upon the narrative of a woman who struggled to wrest her own autonomy from the clutches of patriarchy—whose entire life might have been read in the 1950s as an "anecdote" outside of mainstream Canadian history. In its persistence, in its gaining of momentum, and in the expansive space it now occupies, Carr's story has not only eluded what scholars might have viewed as "anecdotal status" but has also gained mainstream status and, in turn, positioned the gentlemen's story as anecdotal. Gallop notes that the anecdote "as narrative...may also tend to elicit an urge to embed the incident in a larger story," as I am doing with the gentleman's anecdote by contextualizing it within patriarchal ideology (85). She adds that "such an urge would lead us away from contact with the singular moment into all-to-familiar directions—conventional narrative arcs, standard plots" (85). I might argue, however, that in distancing myself from that singular moment and refusing its place in Carr's narrative, I am also refusing the urge to contextualize the anecdote in a feminist narrative.[10] I have, of course, included his anecdote for the first time in my research here, but for different purposes: generally, to showcase how the research process works or how one's research agenda includes or excludes even the most seemingly trivial detail and, specifically, to shed light on how Carr was working against male attitudes that still lingered.

Whatever conclusions I draw, I must also examine my own position in relation to the elderly gentleman, for upon realizing that that anecdote was the only one he had to offer, and in my decision to turn off the tape recorder and beat a hasty retreat, I decided that this form of "excess" was one that I would not need; that it did not conform to the feminist narrative I wanted to convey and with which I was connected; that his anecdote's status and value rendered it of little relevance and, quite frankly, smarmy; and that I would not need (until now) to retell it to others or include it in future research publications. I had decided that the anecdote did not do much beyond addressing a man's need to recuperate his sense of importance to the larger sweep known as "Canadian cultural history," and to reminiscence about his own personal life.

In addition, I feel that I have, as Jacqueline Jones Royster notes, "an ethical responsibility" to those whom I study, and in this case, to her descendants and those of her loved ones, "who have a right to the respectful and dignified treatment of their ancestors" (qtd. in Kirsch and Rohan, "Being on Location" 25). The value of the anecdote must be conjoined with this sense of responsibility—with knowing the difference between "good" and "harmful" gossip. But then the question that I am obliged to raise is this: where do I focus my ethical responsibility, and how do I know what my ethical responsibility is when ethical questions themselves are contextually driven? How do I know whose and what interests to protect? Perhaps, in this instance, my ethical responsibility might have meant protecting his identity and the private sexual lives of others. I certainly did feel some sense of compassion for his need to have his story told as he approached his twilight years. However, I had a greater sense of protectiveness for the woman around whom his story circulated, so my sense of accountability ultimately moved in Carr's favour. In weighing ethical responsibilities and the story's value, I determined the anecdote about Dilworth's carpet did not merit further attention because it served no purpose in and shed no light on Carr's story—the only one that I happened to be invested in at that time. Nor did I wish to repeat a story that the gentleman would not share with his wife present—because, of course, he declined to share his anecdote until she had left the room. The manner in which she would be affected was a consideration in the process of exclusion as well.

This decision to exclude his anecdote also meant, as Kirsch and Rohan argue, that what is important to me is the largely unarticulated connection or intersection between my scholarly life and private interests about women's lives. Intellectual and affective matters intertwine. I must be aware not only of this intersection but also, as feminist archival research demands, of how knowledge is produced positionally. I must be aware of my ethical choices, which have a bearing upon what I decide should enter into the narratives I tell about Carr, or my other research subjects. So it is that I have habitually sidestepped recounting the narrative related to Dilworth's carpet, and instead shared the anecdotes about the missionary, the sprig of cedar, and the one I have yet to tell about Carr's stamp box. This story was communicated to me by a woman who mailed me a small silver stamp box after I gave another public lecture in Vancouver about Carr's life and correspondence. Before mailing me the box, the woman informed me how it came into her possession: her mother had purchased it from Carr herself in the 1920s, when she was in dire economic straits and selling her possessions in order to make ends meet. Only a couple of weeks later, much to my great surprise and delight, I found an envelope with the delicate silver box neatly wrapped inside, tucked in my mailbox at the University of British Columbia. The woman sent it to me because, as she said when we spoke, she felt that my research interests and commitments meant it rightfully belonged in my possession.

This anecdote I repeatedly share with my students not merely because it supports ideas in circulation about the material conditions in which Carr lived, although that certainly is a factor. Yet, if I adhered to postmodern notions about knowledge and understanding about the past, I would be obliged to conclude that the only Carr there is is that which represents my interpretation of the person called Carr. If I argued that the only relevance Carr bore was that which she represented for me (her endurance, her struggle, her commitment to her art career even in the face of economic crises), it would merely become a self-interested and esoteric project.[11] But what of that moment between me and the woman who gave me the stamp box? The anecdote, in this example, serves as evidence of the momentary connection between not only me and my subject matter but also me and another woman, both of whom agreed albeit briefly about the knowledge produced about Carr. The power of the anecdote, then, is not only in its capacity, as Gallop would suggest, to convey a "moment" but also its ability *to re-create* another such moment between two or more interested parties. In that re-creation, however, we may shift the emphasis and meaning for our own purposes. What my gentleman interviewee meant to convey in telling me his anecdote is quite distinct from what I mean to convey when I repeat it here. The context in which the anecdote is repeated matters.

So, in recounting all of these anecdotes here, I am demonstrating how I make decisions about the process by which I determine what is worthy of being kept, relayed, transmitted; what is worth bearing witness to and has historical significance and value; what is of greater value in the hierarchy of anecdotes; how I contribute to the production of meaning; and where my ethical commitments lie. I demonstrate the criteria I use to determine what material I choose to include or not to include, how I follow "clues" or "leads" that may enrich the record (as I believe it ought to be), and how and to what extent my connection to the material is necessary for the conversation. As Kirsch and Rohan argue, some of the

> most serious, committed, excellent historical research comes from choosing a subject to which we are personally drawn, whether through family artefacts, a chance encounter, alocal news story, or some other fascination that sets us on a trail of discovery, curiosity, and intrigue. That personal connection can make all the difference in our scholarly pursuit: it brings the subject to life and makes us more likely to pursue hunches, follow leads, and spend extra time combing through archival materials. (Introduction 8)

I should add that it makes me likely to listen to anecdotes or interview possible candidates who can add to the archival record. We are more inclined to do so than we would without the said "personal attachment" (Kirsch and Rohan, Introduction 8). Sometimes those anecdotes lead me to places I personally do not find of value—unless, as in the case of the first anecdote, I were conducting a foray into male heterosexual practices in mid-century Canada. My objective in relation to my research on Carr, and now others, including Sheila Watson, Jane Rule, M. NourbeSe Philip, and Pauline Johnson, however, is related to a feminist agenda. In the case of Carr, I was interested in recovering the writings of a woman whose initial status, literary and otherwise, was somewhat tenuous because of her gender. Having decided that the first anecdote I conveyed in this paper did not add to the conversation, aside from what I am broaching here, from showcasing the kind of narrative that Carr had assiduously circumvented, and from the "moment" I have been trying to create now, and having decided instead that it contributed to a larger patriarchal narrative which I have already heard far too often, I can toss it back into the junk drawer, where I believe—at least for now—it rightfully belongs.

Acknowledgements

I acknowledge Kaitlin Blanchard for suggesting that I read Jane Gallop's *Anecdotal Theory*. I am grateful to Jessica Schagerl, the conference participants at the Archives in Canada conference, and the readers of the manuscript for WLUP for their feedback. I acknowledge SSHRC, the FQRSC, and Bishop's University for support while I worked on this paper.

Notes

1. Carr's career unfolded between approximately 1937 and 1945, when her deteriorating health obliged her to turn to and rely almost entirely on a different medium for artistic expression. Carr began with a series of literary sketches that would constitute the core of *Klee Wyck*, but then produced so much in this nine-year period that she was able to complete the final drafts for seven books (although some of the writing had been done earlier).
2. See Tippett and Morra.
3. I am declining to offer the name of Dilworth's niece in the interests of her privacy.
4. So Stoler also notes in *Along the Archival Grain* that one may locate in the archive "uncensored turns of phrase, loud asides in the imperative tense, hesitant asides in sotto voce," and that these "make up a 'hierarchy of credibility,' scales of trust that measured what forms of witness, words and deeds, could be taken as reliably relevant" (23).
5. Gallop notes that, although "it is the feminist in me who claims recognition for the women who make me think, deconstruction seconds the gesture by insisting on the 'occasional,' on the event, the moment, as the site of productive thinking" (5).
6. She notes that "'Resisting Reasonableness' explicitly associates 'exorbitant' with the excessive, romantic, perverse, unreasonable, and queer. But the word carries with it a very specific allusion which remains unspoken in the essay. In the middle of Derrida's *Of Grammatology*, the book in which he sets out his program for deconstruction, is a methodological statement entitled 'The Exorbitant Question of Method.' The model for exorbitant theorizing is Derrida." (Gallop 5)
7. See, as examples, Archibald (2008), Ruffo (2001), and Battiste (2000, 1986).
8. Letter from Kate Mather to Emily Carr, July 14, 1942, BCARS.
9. Clearly, I had also taken into consideration the *temporal distance* from the event or character described, and the *reliability and authenticity* of the anecdote, which I measured according to who was doing the telling and his or her motives.
10. So Gallop adds that "[t]his contradiction between capturing the singular moment and a drive to insert the moment within a familiar plot may not be just a problem for this particular story but a tension intrinsic to the anecdote" (85).
11. In *What Are Achives?* Craven argues that in the archive—as in an anecdote—an individual may find meaning "because the document means something to him," but she adds that it also works to produce meaning about "that individual's cultural or community identity" (17). In other words, what is at stake is not merely a personal, but also a collective identity.

Works Cited

Archibald, J. *Indigenous Storywork: Educating the Heart, Mind, Body, and Spirit.* Vancouver: UBC P, 2008. Print.

Battiste, M. *Protecting Indigenous Knowledge and Heritage: A Global Challenge.* Saskatoon: Purich, 2000. Print.

Battiste, Marie. "Micmac Literacy and Cognitive Imperialism." *Indian Education in Canada: The Legacy.* Ed. J. Barman, Y. Hebert, and D. McCaskill. Vancouver: UBC P, 1986. 1: 2344. Print.

———, ed. *Reclaiming Indigenous Voice and Vision.* Vancouver: UBC P, 2000. Print.

Carr, Emily. *Klee Wyck.* Toronto: Oxford UP, 1941. Print.

Code, Lorraine. "Gossip." *Encyclopaedia of Feminist Theories.* Ed. Lorraine Code. New York: Routledge, 2000. 230–31. Print.

Cowan, T. L. "'I remember...I was wearing leather pants': Archiving the Repertorie of Feminist Cabaret in Canada." This volume.

Craven, Louise, ed. *What Are Archives? Cultural and Theoretical Perspectives: A Reader.* London: Ashgate, 2008. Print.

Cvetkovich, Ann. *An Archive of Feelings: Trauma, Sexuality, and Lesbian Public Cultures.* Durham: Duke UP, 2003. Print.

Gallop, Jane. *Anecdotal Theory.* Durham: Duke UP, 2002. Print.

Hobbs, Catherine. "Personal Ethics: Being an Archivist of Writers." This volume.

Kirsch, Gesa E. "Being on Location: Serendipity, Place, and Archival Research." Kirsch and Rohan 20–27. Print.

Kirsch, Gesa E., and Liz Rohan, eds. Introduction. *Beyond the Archives: Research as a Lived Process.* Carbondale: Southern Illinois UP, 2008. 1–12. Print.

Mather, Kate. Letter to Emily Carr, July 14, 1942. Box 4, File 23. MS 2763. Parnall Fonds, BCARS.

Morra, Linda. *Corresponding Influence: Selected Letters of Emily Carr and Ira Dilworth.* Toronto: U of Toronto P, 2006. Print.

Parnall Fonds, British Columbia Archives and Records Service (BCARS). Victoria, British Columbia.

Ruffo, Armand Garnet, ed. *(Ad)dressing Our Words: Aboriginal Perspectives on Aboriginal Literatures.* Penticton: Theytus, 2001. Print.

Schultz, Lucille. Foreword. *Beyond the Archives: Research as a Lived Process.* Carbondale: Southern Illinois UP, 2008. vii–x. Print.

Stoler, Ann Laura. *Along the Archival Grain: Epistemic Anxieties and Colonial Common Sense.* Princeton: Princeton UP, 2009. Print.

Tippett, Maria. *Emily Carr: A Biography.* Toronto: Stoddart, 1979. Print.

"I want my story told": The Sheila Watson Archive, the Reader, and the Search for Voice
Paul Tiessen

Where the Voice Is Coming From
During the late 1980s and into the 1990s, Sheila Watson (1909–98) helped her husband Wilfred (1911–98) process his material, which went into his archive. Then, without help from him, she turned to the task of establishing her own. She wanted hers to find a home separate from his or, for that matter, from that of her dear friend, Marshall McLuhan (1911–80). She seems to have felt it imperative that the primary voice embodied in her archive—although it contained much by way of the respective voices of Wilfred and Marshall, just as theirs contained much of hers—should, in various ways, remain distinct from the primary voices in theirs. She might have also appreciated that among the three archives, hers, constructed last, would contain something of a last word.[1]

At the same time, her own agency in determining the course of her archive notwithstanding, Watson was aware that an archive involves a complex series of subjectivities, beyond those manifested in its material: for example, the interventions when there is an institutional reordering and renaming of its parts. There is also the reader, or the researcher—

typically alone, and possibly unknown to the original creator—equipped with his or her own presuppositions and reading experiences, motives, and ambitions.

A researcher, listening (as it were) to the archive, finds soon enough that a writer's voice may seem strange and unexpected, as disembodied as it is embodied, and quite unlike that writer's published voice—for with the published voice, an ongoing history of readers produces coherent clusters of meaning around it. The archive voice may seem intimate and unguarded, yet surprisingly indeterminate and vague, especially in the utter absence of a history of readers for that archival material.[2] A Watson researcher might ponder in vain questions of tone or point of view in a few words or phrases scratched on a cigarette pack, or in images and shadows in a stack of photographs. A biographer—such as F. T. Flahiff, author of *always someone to kill the doves: a life of Sheila Watson*—contends with "facts" in an archive that invite unexpected interpretation. Flahiff happily had the opportunity to interrupt the archiving process and explore the Watson papers prior to their being processed according to institutional categories. A film/media history scholar interested, as in my case, in Watson's "theory" of media and communication attempts to give to Watson's little-known media interests the fullest possible expression, without losing sight of the historic moment in which she gave voice to them. Both a biographer interested in a hitherto little-known but dynamically lived life like Watson's and a film/media history scholar interested in obscured debates by Watson about media, technology, and communication will very likely challenge fixed ideas and create new knowledge on the basis of the archive. Complications surrounding such re-presentation stem from the complex relationships among original creator, the reader or researcher, and the voices in the archive.

Watson's former colleague Rudy Wiebe offers a paradigmatic reading of such complications. In his "Where Is the Voice Coming From?" (which he wrote in Edmonton in 1971 when he and Watson were teaching at the University of Alberta), Wiebe identifies the ethically charged negotiations between a researcher and the original creator of the archive. He identifies dilemmas posed by the temptation of appropriation. When Wiebe's researcher, in pursuit of "facts" about the historic Cree warrior Almighty Voice, is led finally to hearing "an incredible voice...a voice so high and clear, so unbelievably high and strong in its unending and wordless cry," he can know only that he has no means to comprehend that voice ("Where" 143). He cannot contain its transcendent meanings, so incommensurable with his own reductive scientific methods. He makes an interpretative judgment based on and acknowledging his limitations: "I say 'wordless cry' because that is the way it sounds to me." He does not, as he says, understand the Cree language himself, and his lack of knowledge is underlined by the unavailability (as he wryly puts it in the closing paragraph) of a "reliable interpreter who would make a reliable interpretation" (143). Wiebe's narrator, in effect, cautions researchers to proceed with humility and integrity when entering into conversation with a voice that speaks from outside or beyond the apparently finite evidence.

Wiebe repeats this warning in "Bear Spirit in a Strange Land." He discusses his discovery of the sacred bundle of the Cree Chief Big Bear, silenced and contained in a tiny, windowless archive in New York's American Museum of Natural History. Aware of "proper ceremonies" for opening the bundle, he confesses, "I am no proper person" (Wiebe, "Bear Spirit" 148). As a privileged "white man" he reminds us of issues of appropriation, self-disclosure, and conflict of interest, for he knows that he cannot find in himself the sacramental approach essential to his quest (148). Yet, in the same story, Wiebe alerts us also to the lure of what we might call the "archive fallacy" of a single-minded researcher working with the risk of preconceived expectations, who finds in an archive the very object that he or she has set out to see and touch. Wiebe catches a glimpse, on entering that tiny room, of a vast and little-known world: "it is as if out of the darkness an entire culture had exploded" ("Bear Spirit" 145–46). But the room is only a distraction for him. He remains steadfast in his quest for the bundle with a numbered tag that the archivist locates in a small drawer; indeed, his desire to touch the bundle remains his priority (146).[3]

Modernists and Mass Media
Much of my enthusiasm for archives has been governed by my interest in literary modernists' debates since the 1920s about the effects of non-literary media such as film, radio, television, and related technologies on literature, art, and culture. In the face of the long-standing tendency to see a writer's approach in terms largely of literary contexts, I test ways of finding a fair and balanced view of a modernist's media theorizing—often contained, for various reasons, in the vaults of archives rather than in published accounts—relative to his or her overall achievement. In fact, literary modernists active in Canada from the 1920s to the 1970s have offered many, if still only barely heard, variations of media theory that address categories proposed by their internationally famous contemporary, Marshall McLuhan.[4]

Watson, it happens, speaks firmly to the field of media and communication studies. She is, of course, known and admired for her critically acclaimed modernist novel, *The Double Hook*, as well as her career as a teacher of modernist literature at the University of Alberta during the

1960s and 1970s. Flahiff contextualizes these achievements, and more, in his elegant and evocative study of her life and work; however, perhaps because media theory would seem marginal to her concerns in light of her public persona, he does not draw attention to her grappling with it.

That McLuhan was Watson's dissertation supervisor and, indeed, her friend, makes questions we might ask about conversations between them concerning media, and about ways we might understand those conversations when they manifest themselves in the archive all the more interesting.[5] Wilfred and especially, of course, Marshall had plenty to say in the public realm about media, technology, and communication in relation to culture and society; their unpublished letters suggest that they were eager to draw Sheila into their discussions. She had to remind the two men that their respective approaches to media theory were not necessarily hers. She pointed out that she was not part of their decade-long dialogue concerning *From Cliché to Archetype*, the book that the two men discussed throughout the 1960s. In an undated letter (from a "Thursday," seemingly early in September 1964), she pointed out to McLuhan that it was with Wilfred, not her, who he was developing that book. "I am really on the periphery of the cliché-archetype dialogue," she insisted.

Investigating questions of media and communication, we know Watson did explore the cultural impact of the camera in a chapter of her 1965 dissertation, *Wyndham Lewis and Expressionism* (available only as unpublished text until 2003). She carried forward some of those analyses in her essay for the November 1967 issue of *arts/canada* and, to a lesser extent, in a 1978 text that she wrote for Athabasca University. To be sure, *The Double Hook*, as she herself once put it in conversation, might very well evoke the "cinematic camera" of the *nouveau roman* of an Alain Robbe-Grillet. In critical attention given to Watson, however, these technological preoccupations of hers have been relative side notes. For most readers, she belongs primarily in spaces developed by New Critical practices, with their attention to literary text as literary text, rather than as partner to other technological forms.[6] But from 1961 to 1964, while she was completing her dissertation and he was publishing *The Gutenberg Galaxy: The Making of Typographic Man* and *Understanding Media: The Extensions of Man*, Watson corresponded with McLuhan about her work in terms that included a preoccupation with mass media. She submitted her dissertation to him and her doctoral committee late in the very year that he, in May, published *Understanding Media*. His work included one chapter on the photograph; hers, one on the camera.

The Archive as Performance

The Sheila Watson Archive opened in 2007 in Toronto. In her introduction to the *Sheila Watson Fonds Finding Guide* published in June 2007, Anna St. Onge, the archivist assigned to the task at the time, gives a description of the provenance of the new archive—complete with books from both Sheila and Wilfred's libraries—housed at the Kelly Library at the University of St. Michael's College in Toronto:

> HISTORY OF THE SHEILA WATSON FONDS: Sheila Watson identified her friend Dr. Fred T. Flahiff as her literary executor and sent her archives to him between 1994 and 1998. Following her death in 1998, Flahiff donated the bulk of the Watsons' library to the John M. Kelly Library in 1998. The whole of the archival fonds was donated to the John M. Kelly Library Special Collection in 2006. (6)

During 2006 and 2007, St. Onge arranged and described the collection, and created the 141-page *Finding Guide*, along with a detailed thirty-six-page guide describing drafts of manuscripts.

Flahiff writes a fuller account and expands on the significance of his privileged position from 1994 onward in relation to the publication of his biography. When she was in her eighties, Watson became preoccupied with "a need to ensure that her own past would not be lost" (*always* 324). She would not respond to overtures from Library and Archives Canada made as early as 1992, nor to encouragement from Flahiff that she consider Ottawa—where lay the literary remains of McLuhan—as a home for her work. She was likewise determined that her papers not end up alongside her husband's in Edmonton where she, like him, had had a distinguished career at the university. "She felt no hostility towards the institution or the city, only reluctance to be archivally proximate to Wilfred" (*always* 325–26). After difficulties in her life with Wilfred, it seems that she sought peace apart from him in death.

During the last four years of her life, Watson sent twenty-five banker's boxes of books and seventy or eighty boxes of papers to the much younger Flahiff in Toronto. After her death (and also, as it happened, Wilfred's death only weeks later), she left behind many other materials, notably her and Wilfred's books: 7,280, in fact. They were hauled from Nanaimo (where the Watsons had moved from Edmonton in 1980) to Toronto by two young women who accompanied Flahiff to the West Coast and who drove the books back across Canada by truck (Flahiff *always* 325).

Watson hoped the materials would be kept together, perhaps in the hope that a coherent and complete archive—her private journals comprising its spiritual core—would increase the imminent prospect of a biography of her life. Implicit in its telling was her assumption that its readership would have one notable absentee: Wilfred. Flahiff is open about the dilemma for a biographer. Their "long, sometimes tortured and always tortuous, relationship" (*always* x) would be cause for a prospective biographer, especially one close to them both, to defer any attempt at a telling of her life. For it soon became clear to Flahiff that her papers held pent-up and hitherto unspoken words. When he actually uncovered her private journals, Flahiff phoned her and addressed what he saw as their incredible importance both as history and as art. She made her views clear during their conversation: "I told her [writes Flahiff] they must be published, but because her relationship with Wilfred so dominated these journals—literally, from first entry to last—their publication would not be possible until after his death. There was silence at the other end of the telephone line, and then: 'I want my story told'" (326; see also ix and 90). The implicit urgency in her words seems clear—it reflects her own understanding of a narrative about her life as one that she herself had suppressed and, in effect, deferred. Hers was, as she understood it, a counter-narrative, upsetting established presuppositions of her life being set in a happily functioning marriage and of simplistic readings of the (conventionally gendered) trajectories of her and Wilfred's fifty-eight-year relationship.[7]

Of course, in sending her bankers boxes directly to Flahiff, Watson was sending them to a potential biographer. It is true that when she had said to him, "'I want my story told,'" she did not say that he should be the one to tell it, "but only to ensure that it be performed" (*always* ix). But Flahiff saw that he was not only the first reader, he was one of the best of all possible readers of her archive and life. He reimagines her story for our own day not only as scholar and friend but also as a kind of fellow artist and, given his deep capacity for empathy and his history of overlapping associations, a sort of autobiographer as well as biographer. He knew Watson and her world well (see, for example, 185–87, 204–5); but at the same time he understood that, as a scholar, he was responsible both to the material and its creator and to himself and his future readers. He recognized, moreover, that once an archive is institutionalized, it remains in conversation with the future. That he called his work "a life" rather than a biography registers his belief that what he wrote was, in a sense, provisional (x). Responding with intellectual sensitivity and ethical insight to "where the voice was coming from" became a multifaceted element in the story that he was both researching and telling.

Watson knew about the contingencies of biographical representation, subjectivity, and power. All the more reason perhaps, in her gesture of sending Flahiff her unpublished remains, for her invoking something of the sacramental: "She said to me... 'I am sending you my life'" (*always* x, 244). But—and Flahiff must have sensed this—Watson surely had a playful twinkle in her eye, for she could have undertaken her personal journal, after all, with an imagined (future) audience at least partly in mind. Without reducing the place of the researcher/biographer implicit in the gesture of sending her work forward in one vast body was a satisfaction that it would lead to a biographic performance that she could join in a discourse of collaboration, as a partner co-engaged in the telling of her life. Significantly, Flahiff's most vivid gesture in acknowledging Watson's participation was to make her the explicit teller of her own story in the very heart of his biography: pages 91–174 are drawn directly from her journal.[8]

The expectation that a writer might position herself as participant in the circulation of her unpublished work was, in an interesting respect, anticipated by Sheila and Wilfred back in 1959. He (from Edmonton) wrote to her (in Toronto) that writers such as they should circulate their work only in unpublished form, thus speaking without the interference of any number of hands. Mindful of writers in the Soviet Union, he said in an unpublished letter, dated February 7, 1959, "I cd. [*sic*] envision a day when serious writers everywhere, like the desk-drawer Russians, such as Pasternak, will only circulate their writings in MS. It will be like a return to the Middle Ages. In print will appear all the State-supported and Business-subsidized TRASH. No serious critic will pay attention to this. We have, after all, our typewriters. We have paper. What more, really, do we want?" He was responding to her efforts to get *The Double Hook* published in a way that satisfied her ideas about production. Preoccupied with questions of book design, a possible dedication, a preface, blurbs—she had shared with him her concerns. He put forward perhaps too fervently the value of the unpublished text, for *The Double Hook* was on its way to becoming central in our Canadian consciousness as a published work. Further, his proposal for an underground circulation of manuscripts would do away not only with interventionist hands but also with a public community of readers, and so raises its own complicated questions of voice. Still, Wilfred was endorsing the importance of unpublished work, precisely the work that a biographer, or an academic curious about a literary modernist's media theorizing, finds invaluable.[9]

The Archive and the Telephone

Here I will give a bare outline of the current beginnings of my archive-based quest for the substance and flavour of Watson's media-theorizing stance, especially in relation to her associations with McLuhan. However, rather than investigating her media theory, I largely restrict myself to exploring further what I have learned about archives and archive voices, from not only my brief visits to the new Sheila Watson archive but also earlier visits to the McLuhan and Wilfred Watson archives.

My reading of Watson in relation to McLuhan reminds me that "archive" might be added to McLuhan's inventory of media, where medium becomes part of message and where medium becomes, also, environment. In relation to each other, the archive and the public record, as well as any given cluster of archives, are also counter-environments, fluidly and indefinitely affecting each other in hybridizing transformations. Implicitly evoking McLuhan, Aritha van Herk observes that a literary archive is a "tiny low-tech flame," but one that speaks beyond its cabinets and containers: "Most archives do not sit cosily in their acid-free boxes, glowing with a sepia nostalgia. They perform, declare, argue and shout; they speak a record of change and movement, discovery and revision" (156, 158–59). Much depends, of course, on the researcher.

Watson began PhD studies in Toronto in September 1956. She had just returned to Canada from a year in Paris. As Flahiff points out in his Preface to the published version of her dissertation, "she had already written her two novels, *Deep Hollow Creek* and *The Double Hook*, although neither had yet been published, and she had written all but one of her six short stories" (Flahiff, Preface n.p.). When she announced that she wanted to work on Wyndham Lewis, she was passed along to McLuhan "because Lewis," as she explained to a friend, "was Mr. McLuhan's territory." She saw Lewis as "particularly concerned with the literature of ideas...perhaps one should say the literature of salvation." Embedded in Lewis's literature of ideas was his analysis of the effects of the camera.[10]

Unlike her supervisor McLuhan, Watson, echoing Lewis, did not emphasize Gutenberg and the linearity of movable type as culprits in the unbalancing of the human sensorium. Rather, she concentrated on the camera and related instrumentation. These, she said, were central to the "visual revolution" of the nineteenth and twentieth centuries and lay at the heart of the effects of communication technology. She observed that Lewis was anxious about the future of the artist in the face of such contemporary "technological magic" (Watson, *Wyndham Lewis* xvii).[11] He was concerned about contemporary scientific pressures to isolate the eye as though it were a specialized instrument. In fact, he opposed "any specialization of a particular sense," whether tactual, visual, or aural (Watson, *Wyndham Lewis* 100). For Lewis, the artist's vision, based on the wholeness of the sensorium, opposed the scientist's.

Her dissertation chapter title, "The dead hand of the nineteenth-century robot: the camera eye," conveyed something of her own attitude.

At the same time, it recalls the title of McLuhan's chapter, "The Photograph: The brothel without walls," in *Understanding Media*. Her title is apocalyptic, sober, cryptic; his, playful, teasing, audacious.

* * *

In the Sheila Watson archive, there is a letter postmarked July 19, 1962, from McLuhan to Watson. In it, he told her he was working on the photograph chapter of *Understanding Media*. He explained, for example, as he was to write in *Understanding Media*, that he was interested in photographs as "visual reports without syntax" (see McLuhan, *Understanding Media* 258). The photograph "enables things to say themselves automatically," he said. Emphasizing the photograph-as-process rather than the camera-as-apparatus, he stressed that "the photograph is not a machine, but a chemical and light process" (264). With the photograph of the early nineteenth century came a break that echoed "the Gutenberg break between the Middle Ages and the Renaissance," he wrote in *Understanding Media*. "Photography was almost as decisive in making the break between mere mechanical industrialism and the graphic age of electronic man. The step from the age of Typographic Man to the age of Graphic Man was taken with the invention of photography" (259).

Driving home his categories of extension/amputation, McLuhan, drawing on Joyce, told Watson that Joyce saw the photo as a rival of the spoken and written word: "The technology of the photo is an extension of our own being and can be withdrawn from circulation like any other technology if we decide that it is virulent. But amputation of such *extensions* of our physical being calls for as much knowledge and skill as are prerequisite to any other physical amputation" (*Understanding Media* 262). McLuhan argued that the photograph, overcoming the tendency of the phonetic alphabet to sever the word from gestures and human postures, brought attention back to "physical and psychic posture" or "gestalts" alike (262–63). He suggested (in his letter to Watson, if not in *Understanding Media*) that, for writers like Gertrude Stein, the photograph as "gesture and gestalt" had become the substitute for the word. But he suggested to her that for Lewis writers such as Stein are "enemies of language," though Lewis, he suspected, offered no adequate analysis of "the process in question."[12]

Watson—as the archive demonstrates—responded the next day in a letter dated July 20, 1962. Drawing attention to McLuhan's statement that "Stein etc. were for Lewis enemies of language" and drawing on Konrad Fiedler's nineteenth-century art theory and Lewis's response to Fiedler, she said to him that the term "form-language" rather than "language" should be used in the discussion of Stein. In her view, Lewis was objecting to Stein's tendency to confuse the metaphors she used to describe her own experiment: "Lewis's objection to Gertrude Stein was that she suggested that she was using the form-language of plastic art when what she was using was the form-language of the camera or the machine or a chemical process as you say. The result [in Stein's work] was a...bastard form." Lewis respected the distinction between form-languages. She concluded,

> I am not arguing on Lewis's side. It seems to me that his problem was the problem of an artist who used two media—that he was primarily interested in gesture and gestalt—that is in a plastic medium—that he was interested in the architectural possibilities of the medium, not the representative possibilities—that his black & white drawings respect the possibilities of translation by photographic method—that is the limitation of translation.

Watson shifted attention from McLuhan's photograph-as-process to Lewis's camera-as-machine and implicitly interrogated McLuhan's claim that "the photograph is not a machine." She reacted to his analysis of the photograph as automatic statement sans syntax. The camera eye offered, at best, a "rough net" in relation to the world of human action, she argued. Going further, she took aim at the key term in his lexicon, "extension." She distinguished between extension and power: "a photograph is a limitation not an extension of the person—though it may extend the person's power, a recording is not the extension of a voice or an instrument but a limitation of it—the more abstract and limited, the more range or operation in time but the less intensity of being. At least this is Lewis's point." She pursued McLuhan's reference to "process," too, countering his discussion of photographic "process"—process, for her, representing mechanical reductionism.

After signing off, she followed in a kind of postscript with a reference to the work of William Ivins and his interest in the phenomenon of "man" having been "more drawn to the visual than to any other form because of its *directness*" (emphasis in original). Seeming to take aim at McLuhan's emphasis on the auditory and alluding to Henri Bergson and Ezra Pound, she added, "Despite Bergson, this is one of the most visual of all visual ages as Pound recognized when he said the 'image' was picture just coming over into speech."

* * *

Another burst of media-related correspondence occurred from late August to early October 1964, as we discover in the archival record. McLuhan again put his perspectives before Watson, this time concerning "environments."[13] In a September letter that was later published, he summarized for Buckminster Fuller the flexibility that the term gave him: "If one says that any new technology creates a new environment, that is better than saying the medium is the message. The content of the new environment is always the old one. The content is greatly transformed by the new technology" (McLuhan, *Letters* 308–9).

In a quick succession of four letters over five weeks, McLuhan tried to sweep Sheila's interest toward his (and Wilfred's) discovery of the interplay of environments. He spoke to her of the "Watson-McLuhan principle," that a new environment transforms an old environment into a new art form (unpublished letter, Sept. 28, 1964). Citing Lewis's 1931 *The Diabolical Principle and the Dithyrambic Spectator*, he argued that Lewis invited analysis in terms of this principle.[14]

During these five weeks, from what I gather from at least two extant but unpublished letters from her to him, Sheila sidestepped the use of environment as a descriptive or critical term. Then things got complicated in ways I had not anticipated. To my shock and, indeed, dismay, another medium, the telephone conversation, intersected with the "tiny low-tech flame" of the archive. Precisely on October 7, 1964, it seems from archival evidence, one party in the correspondence (but which one?) made a phone call to the other. Presumably, they were using the telephone to seek clarity on the drift of their epistolary conversation.

A phone call—an interruption in a print archive of letters, but an interruption probably laden with density of content for its two participants—can usurp for the researcher an epistolary momentum. With the phone call, the print archive itself takes on new meanings and seems to offer both more and, with the foregrounding of this gap, less than before. Of course, the startling but eloquent "silence" of a phone call, with no summary of its "contents," in the midst of intense debate via correspondence reminds us that an archive is, in any case, typically an environment of gaps.

But the phone call gap makes the researcher, with his or her intense desire to know, feel not only extraordinarily left out but also, paradoxically, drawn in; it allows the researcher to recognize that he or she is voyeuristically occupying a corner of a triangular relationship by eavesdropping on a conversation between two intellectual friends, and that this kind of eavesdropping afforded by the archive can be productive. During the phone call, the dialogue between archive and researcher temporarily ends, yes, but it also—as a counter-environment—invites productive speculation by the invigorated and stimulated, if humbled and excluded, researcher. It invites the researcher to engage all the more fully with papers and pages grounded by their tactility, their sound, their smell, their look. It might lead the researcher with renewed vigour to the boxes of archived files, now exhilaratingly freed—surrounded by the archive's maddening but liberating plethora of undated letters, for example, or boxes filled with inked jottings on those cigarette packages—from any kind of dogmatically fixed (if comforting) order and linearity. The presence of multiple environments in relation to one another can prove epiphanic, and surely they invite the archive researcher to shuffle the open-ended universe of papers and pages, and perhaps become all the more a (co-)producer of a new text.

As Wiebe has shown, the archive does not, in the first instance, belong to or take particular heed of the researcher or of his or her hopes and expectations. Letter writers are not obliged to include the researcher as audience. Letters themselves belong to a medium different not only from the telephone conversation but also from other artifacts collected in a literary archive: jottings, journals, notebooks, drafts, manuscripts, books. Each of these invites different relationships with archive readers. The phone call is a reminder of the subjectivities—the creator's, the reader's, the archivist's—that are invested in an archive.

I conclude by noting that Watson and McLuhan responded in subsequent days by letter to their telephone conversation, and so continued to lend the eavesdropping researcher the generosity of the archive.[15] McLuhan, referring the next day, October 8, to their phone call, wrote Watson about Lewis's understanding and shortcomings with regard to issues linking art and technology to extensions and environments. Watson responded to this "post telephone conversation letter" (as she called it) and also to a letter from the week before the phone call. She dated hers simply (and, at least for effect, traumatically?), "Any convenient date." (It must have been around October 10.) She claimed that she was not sure how to find her bearings with respect to terminology that did not belong to her but that belonged rather, as she put it delicately, to "the area of your [i.e., McLuhan's] insight." Yet, of course, she did find her bearings in that letter of "any convenient date." She suggested that Lewis's ideas concerning extensions and environments did not exactly match what McLuhan seemed to be suggesting. "Lewis sees man's extensions as abstractions," she wrote firmly. She saw herself and McLuhan as operating within different registers, drawing on different frames of thought, he from what she called, in a letter to him, "your point of view." In fact, she had distanced herself from McLuhan earlier (in the letter marked only "Thursday," but likely from early September 1964), seemingly in response to his questioning her about Lewis's exploration of "extensions" in the trilogy, *The Human Age*. She had therein assured McLuhan that she was giving his ideas much thought, but she was, at the same time, under enormous pressure to get her final copy of her dissertation off to him.

Things calmed down. McLuhan wrote a brief note to assure her that she need not, at such a late date, try to incorporate the "new environmental approach" into her thesis. Yes, he did think she might want to draw on it in the introduction to her dissertation that she was then working on, but only if she liked. However, he added that when she adapted her thesis as a book (as he dearly hoped she would, the sooner the better), she should then incorporate what he had earlier referred to as the "Watson-McLuhan principle."

Watson did manage to allude a couple times to "environment" in her introduction, but not in the body of the dissertation itself. She included, too, this statement (again with reference to Lewis's artists who, not unlike the common man, saw their power increasingly curtailed in the world of the camera and attendant technologies), drawing on McLuhan's language: "In *Blasting and Bombardiering* Lewis himself explained the futility of sallying forth on a duck-board walk in a world in which revolutionary technology had provided unequal and unexpected extensions and amputations of power" (Watson, *Wyndham Lewis* xviii; see also Gordon 382n41).[16] Those unexpected extensions and amputations of power were, for Watson's Lewis, deeply and darkly affected by human agency.

Watson was prepared to let Lewis's voice more or less float, without her explicitly added opinion, alongside the work of McLuhan (which she had always greatly admired). Yet, even in her apparently dispassionate and objective stance, it is not hard to imagine the sympathetic reading she was giving Lewis, and to Lewis's place, as foil to what during the 1960s seemed like the universally heard and totalizing media analyses offered by McLuhan. "I want my story told," she said to Flahiff more than thirty years after this 1964 exchange between herself and McLuhan. Through her presence in the archive, we can increasingly hear her as a contributor to media-effects debates among Canadian literary modernists.

Notes

1 F. T. Flahiff, Sheila Watson's biographer, gives a wise and witty account of her ensuring that her work would find an archival home (*always* 324–27). For Flahiff's own use of the papers that Watson sent him, see, for example, Flahiff *always*, x and 339. Wilfred's archival remains had been given a home in Edmonton during the 1990s at the University of Alberta; Marshall's had been established in Ottawa during the mid-1980s at what is now called Library and Archives Canada. For permission to quote from hitherto unpublished material by Sheila Watson and by Wilfred Watson, I wish to thank the estates of Sheila Watson and Wilfred Watson, respectively. For research and writing support, I am grateful to the Social Sciences and Humanities Research Council of Canada.

2 Exceptions might occur with exchanges of correspondence—though even then there can be many indeterminacies with respect to meaning.

3 In a 1980 conversation with Shirley Neuman and Robert Kroetsch concerning Wiebe's use of documents in his novel *The Temptations of Big Bear*, Wiebe identifies touch as central to the lure of the archive:

> I've had great experiences, great fun going to museums and holding in my hand the pieces of paper that people actually wrote on.... I was lucky in that when I was doing research on *Big Bear* at the National Archives, they still allowed you to get out the entire Louis Riel file, the literal stuff, so you can see the difference in ink, see that this is a totally different time of writing from that.... I don't know what that is, but I get a real charge out of holding an object in hand. (229–30)

In light of my preoccupation with the problem of subjectivity, representation, and power, it is interesting to note that, in the same conversation, Kroetsch, identifying Wiebe's self-reflexive method, says to Wiebe, "you are obsessed with finding a document and then obsessed with not believing it. One of the great things about *Big Bear* is the way you undo all the documents of the culture" (Neuman 233). Wiebe's reply to Kroetsch: "Yeah, but that doesn't mean that I don't discover a large meaning which has perhaps escaped the untutored eye of a lot of people" (Neuman 233).

4 I examine some of the Canadian literary figures who, along with their contemporary McLuhan, have explored cultural and communication issues involving modernism in relation to technology, mass media, and cinema, in the essays "Dorothy Livesay, the 'Housewife' and the radio"; "'Shall I say, it is necessary to restore the dialogue?'"; "Film, culture criticism, and institutional form"; "Literary Modernism and Cinema"; "A Canadian Film Critic [Gerald Noxon] in Malcolm Lowry's Cambridge"; and "From Literary Modernism to the Tantramar Marshes."

5 My present study of the archive emerges in part from my presentation "Phoning McLuhan, October 7, 1964: The Watson archives and the limits of communication" to the Canadian Communication Association meetings at the Canadian Congress of the Humanities and Social Sciences held in 2008 at the University of British Columbia, and, more generally, from my current SSHRC-supported research on McLuhanism, modernism, and mass media. I am grateful for comments about my study of the archive from many archivists, including most recently Anna St. Onge and George Brandak, and from communication and culture scholars Martin Dowding, Paul Heyer, Petra Hroch, and Matthew Tiessen. For her thoughts about Rudy Wiebe's approach to archives in his work, I am grateful to Hildi Froese Tiessen.

6 See Watson's "The Great War, Wyndham Lewis and the Underground Press" and "How to read *Ulysses*." The text of her thesis was published in its original form by MLR Editions Canada in 2003. The reader for a possible earlier publisher, Oliver & Boyd of Edinburgh, who recommended certain revisions to make it more readily accessible to a wide audience, wrote, "[T]he work is deep and imaginative, and the matter is necessary for anyone who wishes to understand more thoroughly than has before been possible the cross currents of literary and artistic and philosophical thought during the first half of this century'" (Flahiff, Preface n.p.).

7 That Watson should have insisted on her archive going to Toronto is an indicator that, with archives, the symbolic logic of a (re)turn to a homeland sometimes outweighs tendencies toward some other—sometimes lucrative—form of perhaps more diasporic dispersal. Toronto at one time would not have seemed likely: "'Only the most deliberate exercise of caritas would unite me with Toronto in any way,' she had written to her husband in the fall of 1956. But time was kind to Toronto and

to Sheila's view of it" (Flahiff, *always* 1). Indeed, some of Watson's ashes, upon cremation, went to Toronto—or at least the third not spread in the Caribou country of British Columbia or into the Fraser River. Flahiff and some friends buried the Toronto portion beneath the ailanthus—the "tree of heaven"—growing behind his home in the centre of the city. Her Toronto ashes find an echo in her literary remains being moved to St. Michael's, also a destination that Flahiff had proposed to her: "she was satisfied that she could live—and die—with that decision. It represented a kind of homecoming for her.... From her earliest experience, she appreciated that an institution could contain a home" (*always* 326).

8 See pages 86–90 of *always* for Flahiff's discussion of the origins and history of Sheila's journal.

9 Wilfred's own archive—especially his notebooks—recalls the Middle Ages–like status he envisioned for the unpublished manuscript. For a discussion of Wilfred's unpublished notebooks, see pages 106–8 of my essay, "'Shall I say, it is necessary to restore the dialogue?'" Pages 95–106 of that essay consist largely of a series of direct quotations from those notebooks. Actually, and luckily for readers, much of Wilfred's work would be published late in his life. But at the same time, in his unpublished notebooks his archive houses much of the evidence of his imagination and intellect, without the intervention of publishers and other practical interpolators.

If he had been too idealistic in his vision of the manuscript in his 1959 letter to Sheila, Wilfred nonetheless was foregrounding the idea of the archive as a central communication technology in terms that have become familiar today. Sheila would have agreed. As O'Driscoll and Bishop put it—in effect expanding on McLuhan's idea of "environment" (see below)—the archive provides an intentionally "intervening" and "deeply mediat[ing]"moment of illumination that can profoundly influence "every stage of cultural circulation" (4, 6). Even today, after postmodernism, the archive as "medium" retains something of its status as "message" in conferring authority related to its place of primacy and subversiveness in a cultural process. It remains a place of privilege, physically and culturally (O'Driscoll and Bishop 5).

Aritha van Herk sums up what an unpublished manuscript by an avant-garde artist (like Wilfred or Sheila) might achieve as an "activist archive": "The activist archive gestures toward resistance and distrust, displacement, settlement and survival. The activist archive refuses to endorse the official 'reality,' the broad stokes of a master narrative sweeping difficulty through a crack in the floor. The activist archive, like Hamlet, knows that murder will out" (159).

Boris Pasternak's manuscript for *Doctor Zhivago* had been smuggled out of Russia by the publishing house Feltrinelli for publication in Russian and Italian in Milan in 1957, with the English-language text published in 1958 in New York.

10 Watson may have read Lewis as early as the 1930s at UBC, or at Toronto during the 1940s, but she does not mention him in her surviving papers until she made a November 18, 1955, journal entry in Paris: "'On the 16th I went to Galignani's and came back with Wyndham Lewis' *Monstre Gai* and *Malign Fiesta* [the last two and then just-published parts of Lewis's trilogy, *The Human Age*].... Yesterday I read the first part of the Lewis. It is the best thing I've read for some time. There is no malice, no excitement, no castigation...'" (Flahiff, Preface n.p.; see also *always* 124–25).

11 In drawing on Lewis, Watson produced a darker view of media-and-society than the one projected by McLuhan in *Understanding Media*. McLuhan, citing Lewis, paints a robust picture of the artist as "the man of integral awareness," whether he

operates in science or in the humanities (96). Thus, to take one example, Watson's overall treatment of radio is grimmer than McLuhan's; she found in Lewis's treatment of radio, taken in terms of both medium and programming (starting with the BBC as early as the 1922–26 period), his concentration on a seemingly inevitable merging of unexamined links between "technological developments and political events" (Watson, *Wyndham Lewis* 216).

12 McLuhan's July 1962 comments to Watson concerning the photograph are, in many respects, an exact anticipation not only of his argument but also his wording in the photography chapter of 1964's *Understanding Media*. In that book, however, his writing is also much more expansive than it was in his letter concerning the photograph.

Watson reminded readers that for Lewis, the camera should be made subordinate to human intelligence (*Wyndham Lewis* 92). Through the application of its techniques in photography and cinema it has "helped to destroy man's feeling of organic unity and his sense of identity" (95). She drew on William Ivins's idea that the photograph had become "the subliminal norm for the appearance of everything" (99) in observing Lewis's alignment of the photograph with contemporary scientific techniques, which "tended to isolate the various senses—especially the visual" (100).

13 Also in September 1964, Watson submitted a draft of her dissertation to McLuhan, with a final draft following in December. To complicate things further, at the same time, from the end of August to mid-September, Marshall was corresponding with Sheila specifically about his writing something on *The Double Hook*. When McClelland & Stewart wanted to add it to their New Canadian Library series, they turned first to him for a preface. He agreed to write one, but only—as he wrote to Watson herself—if she would provide him with an outline of the "'basic themes and structure'" of the novel (Flahiff, *always* 237). In the end the task—or opportunity—went to someone other than McLuhan.

14 Marshall had already flooded Wilfred with a small torrent of applications of the term "environment." Indeed, in a February 1964 letter, Wilfred had perhaps suggested it to him, testing the idea that "extensions like the body, lever, wheel, car etc., can...be looked on as *intrusions of environment into*, as well as extensions of.... [T]his means an involvement of man in his machinery, as a reflex action consequent upon his extension by it?" (emphasis in original). Wilfred and Marshall ended up writing a chapter on "Environment" in *From Cliché to Archetype*. There they say that "counterenvironments created by the artist serve to raise...hidden environments [that is, the total culture in action] to the level of conscious appreciation" (*From Cliche to Archetype* 77). See Cavell 95–97 on McLuhan's address of environments, interface, and the development of critical awareness. See Gordon 307–13 on McLuhan's later elaboration of these environmental—and anti- or counter-environmental—categories in discussions of the hybrid effects of figure and ground dynamics.

15 McLuhan might have offered his own explanation of the surprise a researcher can feel when the archive seemed to have been snatched away, displaced by a telephone conversation. In his chapter in *Understanding Media*, "The Telephone: Sounding Brass or Tinkling Symbol?" he identifies the telephone as "an irresistible intruder in time or place.... In its nature the telephone is an intensely personal form that ignores all the claims of visual privacy prized by literate man.... The authority of knowledge [suited to the telephone rather than written text] is nonlineal,

nonvisual, and inclusive" (McLuhan 364–65). Yes, inclusive for the participants; exclusive, when it comes to the reader, the "invisible" eavesdropper of the archive who is never acknowledged by the two letter writers. For the archive reader (an eager variant of McLuhan's "literate man"), the manuscript and the telephone discourses in this case may be additive, yet they are incommensurate modes of communication.

16 Gordon, drawing on Watson's dissertation, fits Watson squarely into McLuhan's camp. In a series of nine endnotes that draw attention to McLuhan and Wyndham Lewis, Gordon leaves us with the impression that in her dissertation she straightforwardly endorsed McLuhan's program. Indeed, she engaged categories of thought that underlie McLuhan's approach to media but (as we have seen, based on the authority of the archive) she demurred when McLuhan invited her, in her dissertation, to join his program in terms more explicit than she was prepared to endorse. Instead, as in her discussion of the role of the camera, she established her own reading.

Works Cited

Cavell, Richard. *McLuhan in Space: A Cultural Geography*. Toronto: U of Toronto P, 2002. Print.

Flahiff, F. T. *always someone to kill the doves: a life of Sheila Watson*. Edmonton: NeWest P, 2005. Print.

———. Preface. *Wyndham Lewis and Expressionism*. Sheila Watson. Waterloo: MLR Editions Canada, 2003. 6 pp. Print.

Gordon, W. Terrence. *Marshall McLuhan: Escape into Understanding, A Biography*. Toronto: Stoddart, 1997. Print.

Marshall McLuhan Fond. MG 31 D156 R7593. National Archives of Canada.

McLuhan, Marshall. *Letters of Marshall McLuhan*. Comp. and ed. Matie Molinaro, Corinne McLuhan, and William Toye. Toronto: Oxford UP, 1987. Print.

———. *Understanding Media*. (1964) Corte Madera: Gingko P, 2003. Print.

———. Letter to Sheila Watson. Postmarked July 19, 1962. MS. Box 21, File 2006-01-352 (1). Sheila Watson Archive. St. Michael's College, Toronto.

———. Letter to Sheila Watson. Sept. 28, 1964. MS. Vol. 40 File 27. Marshal McLuhan Archive. National Archives of Canada, Ottawa.

———. Letter to Sheila Watson. October 1964. MS. Box 21, File 2006-01-312 (3). Sheila Watson Archive. St. Michael's College, Toronto.

McLuhan, Marshall, with Wilfred Watson. *From Cliché to Archetype*. New York: Viking, 1970. Print.

Neuman, Shirley. "Unearthing Language: An Interview with Rudy Wiebe and Robert Kroetsch." *A Voice in the Land: Essays By and About Rudy Wiebe*. Ed. W. J. Keith. Edmonton: NeWest P, 1981. 226–47. Print.

O'Driscoll, Michael, and Edward Bishop. "Archiving 'Archiving.'" *The Event of the Archive*. Spec. issue of *English Studies in Canada* 30.1 (2004): 1–16. Print.

St. Onge, Anna. *Sheila Watson Fonds Finding Guide*. Toronto: U of Toronto P, John M. Kelly Library, Special Collections. June 2007. Print.

Tiessen, Paul. "A Canadian Film Critic [Gerald Noxon] in Malcolm Lowry's Cambridge." *Flashback: People and Institutions in Canadian Film History.* Ed. Gene Walz. Montreal: Mediatexte Publications, 1986. 65–76. Print.

———. "Dorothy Livesay, the 'Housewife,' and the Radio in 1951: Modernist Embodiments of Audience." *The Canadian Modernists Meet.* Ed. Dean Irvine. Ottawa: U of Ottawa P, 2005. 205–28. Print.

———. "Film, Culture Criticism, and Institutional Form, 1936–1956: The Work of Vernon van Sickle," *Canadian Journal of Film Studies* 9.1 (2000): 80–100. Print.

———. "From Literary Modernism to the Tantramar Marshes: Anticipating McLuhan in British and Canadian Media Theory and Practice." *Canadian Journal of Communication* 18.4 (1993): 451–67. Print.

———. "Literary Modernism and Cinema: Two Approaches," *Joyce/Lowry: Critical Perspectives.* Ed. Patrick McCarthy and Paul Tiessen. Lexington: UP of Kentucky, 1997. 159–76. Print.

———. "Phoning McLuhan, October 7, 1964: The Watson archives and the limits of communication." The Canadian Communication Association meetings, the Canadian Congress of the Humanities and Social Sciences. University of British Columbia, 2008. Lecture.

———. "'Shall I say, it is necessary to restore the dialogue?' Reading Marshall McLuhan According to the Principles of Wilfred Watson." *At the Speed of Light There Is Only Illumination: A Reappraisal of Marshall McLuhan.* Ed. John Moss and Linda Morra. Ottawa: U of Ottawa P, 2004. 95–145. Print.

van Herk, Aritha. "Ardently Archiving." *Topia: Canadian Journal of Cultural Studies* 20 (2008): 155–66. Print.

Watson, Sheila. "The Great War, Wyndham Lewis and the Underground Press." *arts/canada* 24.11 (1967): 1–17. Print.

———. "How to Read *Ulysses.*" *Modern Consciousness: Habits and Hang-ups.* Athabasca: Athabasca UP, 1978. Print.

———. Letter to Marshall McLuhan. July 20, 1962. MS. Vol. 40, File 27. Marshall McLuhan Archive. National Archives of Canada, Ottawa.

———. Letter to Marshall McLuhan. "Thursday" [early Sept. 1964]. MS. Vol. 40, File 27. Marshall McLuhan Archive. National Archives of Canada, Ottawa.

———. Letter to Marshall McLuhan. "any convenient date" [c. Oct. 10, 1964]. MS. Vol. 40, File 27. Marshall McLuhan Archive. National Archives of Canada, Ottawa.

———. *Wyndham Lewis and Expressionism.* Waterloo: MLR Editions Canada, 2003. Print.

Watson, Wilfred. Letter to Sheila Watson. Feb. 7, 1959. MS. Acc. #95-131 Box 11, File 203. Wilfred Watson Archive, University of Alberta, Edmonton.

Wiebe, Rudy. "Bear Spirit in a Strange Land" ("All That's Left of Big Bear"). *A Voice in the Land: Essays By and About Rudy Wiebe.* Ed. W. J. Keith. Edmonton: NeWest P, 1981. 143–49. Print.

———. "Where Is the Voice Coming From?" *Where Is the Voice Coming From? Stories by Rudy Wiebe.* Toronto: McClelland and Stewart, 1974. 135–43. Print.

"You can do with all this rambling whatever you want": Scrutinizing Ethics in the Alzheimer's Archives
Kathleen Venema

Archiving Alzheimer's

> Broached the subject of her memory over lunch yesterday with Mom. She seems like a stranger when she asks, defensively, "Do you talk about this with [your sister]? [Your brother]?" Mostly, though, except for some confusion—she has to work hard to remember that the butter pat is a butter pat and what a butter pat is for—she seems like herself.
> –K. Venema, Journal entry Dec. 17, 04

My mother was diagnosed with Alzheimer's disease in late July 2005. Alzheimer's disease, as many families know well,[1] is a progressive, degenerative disease of the brain characterized by two distinct aberrations: in the first, brain cells shrink or disappear and are replaced by dense, irregularly shaped spots, or plaques; in the second, thread-like tangles appear in otherwise healthy brain cells and eventually choke off those cells' functioning.[2] As it destroys brain cells, Alzheimer's affects memory, language skills, cognitive activity, and behaviour, so that work life, family life, social life, community involvements, hobbies, and sports are all increasingly compromised.[3] Certain medications can halt Alzheimer's "progress" for up to two years in some people, but the disease eventually resumes producing the characteristic plaques and tangles that obstruct ever more of the brain's messaging capacity.[4] The Alzheimer's Association website describes the situation succinctly: "Alzheimer's disease has no survivors.... It slowly and painfully takes away a person's identity, ability to connect with others, think, eat, talk, walk and find his or her way home."[5] The website writers likely mean the Alzheimer's sufferer's literal home, but they might also include every other place, past and metaphorical, that the sufferer has ever understood as "home."

For a family member, a diagnosis of Alzheimer's marks the beginning of an excruciatingly protracted period of mourning as a beloved other disappears. It often also marks the beginning of sometimes frantic work to fight the disease: a diagnosis of Alzheimer's means, after all, that a life—or at least, the memory of a life—needs to be saved. Perhaps not surprisingly then, a diagnosis of Alzheimer's frequently prompts a turn, usually non-theoretical, to narrative as both a therapeutic structure and a means of shoring up self, identity, and relationship, and to various kinds of archives as potential sites of knowledge.[6] Ian Frazier, who has written about his own father's struggle with Alzheimer's, describes an impetus for the narrative process in his Foreword to Joyce Dyer's story of her mother. "An offhand trick of [Alzheimer's] disease," says Frazier, "is to leave this memory [of disintegration and helplessness and confusion] freshest in the minds of those who survive. Afterwards... [g]rief may make a historian of you, an archaeologist of the ordinary details that evoke the vanished person's life" (Foreword xi–xii).

From a theoretical perspective, meanwhile, Alzheimer's offers a gold mine of possibility, enabling a quintessential, extended, and unrepeatable engagement with historical indeterminacy, the constructed nature of subjectivity, and the extraordinarily biased nature of both partial and provisional truths. From a theoretical perspective, Alzheimer's offers a unique encounter with Jacques Derrida's resonant claim that "the archive takes place at the place of originary and structural breakdown of memory" (11). But I am deliberately literal when I invoke Derrida, and therefore I am almost certainly missing the point: Derrida could not possibly mean that "the archive" takes place in the brains of Alzheimer's sufferers.[7]

* * *

> What a cliché: my mother's driving me crazy. No: my mother behaves as if she might be going crazy herself. Breathtakingly disturbing to hear her ask on Tuesday evening, after I'd rehearsed with her several times my proposed

plan for Friday afternoon ("meet me at Carriere's at 3 and then we'll go for coffee at Theatro; if Dad can pick us up at 5, we can go see the house [renovations], and still be on time to meet Gareth for supper"), "Why have I got 'Carriere' written on this paper?" "Because that's where I get my hair cut and that's where we're meeting," I say. "Why have I got 'yellow' written down here?" Mom asks. "I think you wrote that down because I told you that Café Theatro is painted yellow," I tell her. "Dear God," I think, hanging up, "maybe she really does have Altzheimer's [sic]?" It was like watching someone negotiate around literal holes in their brain. (K. Venema, Journal entry Mar. 10, 2005)

At the end of June 1986, I was a young junior high school teacher with three years of teaching experience in a small mining community in northern Manitoba. I left Canada two months later for Ndejje, Uganda, where I'd accepted a volunteer position with an international development organization committed to southern Uganda's peaceful reconstruction after a devastating civil war. Over the next three years, I wrote almost three hundred letters from Ndejje to friends and family in Canada.[8] My mother was the most faithful of my sixty-odd correspondents, and I've saved or retrieved the two hundred letters that she and I exchanged[9] and organized them into a careful, if informal, archive.

Like the "stuff" that Carolyn Steedman describes as filling many archives, the stuff in this one hadn't been disturbed for a very long time; exactly as Steedman suggests, "the stuff just sat there," in part because, as she claims elsewhere, "[y]ou find nothing in the Archive but stories caught half way through: the middle of things; discontinuities" (68, 45). Sometimes, of course, you find nothing at all in archives, although then Steedman insists provocatively that you "will find nothing in a place...an absence is not *nothing*, but is rather the space left by what has gone...the emptiness indicates how once it was filled and animated" (11). Alzheimer's casts an ironic and catalyzing shadow over the presences and absences of archives generally, and over the fact that my mother and I exchanged two hundred letters twenty years ago specifically, because we were missing from one another's daily lives. The letters that travelled between Winnipeg and Ndejje provided the opportunity for my mother and me be present to one another in an ongoing way; they eased the bewilderment of vast geographic separation; and their handwritten, enveloped, and stamped materiality stood in for the intimacy we'd lost. The informal archive I've created of those letters commemorates both the wracking dislocations we negotiated and the range of connections we achieved.

More than twenty years later, Alzheimer's disease means that my mother's life and mine are defined these days by discontinuities, disconnections, and absences like the ones that the archive simultaneously performs and seeks to redress. It may be in the archive that my mother and I will find the story we need to bridge the distances in time, space, and intimacy that Alzheimer's is cleaving between us—or it may not. The documented and documentable facts of my mother's life are laughably few, following a familiar pattern of post–Second World War emigration by Europeans to Canada.[10] Despite her lifelong passion for languages and literatures, she was prompted only once to make a regular record of her life, and that was in 1986, when I left Canada to live in Uganda. "Dad suggested that I start keeping a diary," my mother wrote on August 18, 1986, in the first of what would be her almost weekly letters to me at Ndejje, "so I bought a smallish notebook and have scribbled in it a few things every day.... [N]ow I can give you a practically blow-by-blow account of our lives since [the day] you left." She notes on the next page that, although she's trying to finish the letter so that it can be mailed, there's something from the previous week that she still wants to relate. "[That] diary," she writes, "is going to be invaluable."[11]

Twenty years after the fact, the diary and the letters that the diary made possible turn out to be, in fact, invaluable: my mother's records of her quintessentially and unremarkably Canadian life will almost certainly never appear in any archive but mine, and it will be out of my archive that a story will emerge, of who my mother was and what her life meant and means. It doesn't matter yet that Derrida calls my often-feverish project an instance of the death drive (12). What matters for now is that revisiting the letters may help me recover for both my mother and me what Lois Parkinson Zamora calls "a usable past."[12] The project I devise—to create a story of my mother's life from *what* my mother remembers about her life and *how* my mother remembers her life—bears a passing resemblance to the work Ann Cvetkovich describes in *An Archive of Feeling*, particularly when she notes that her book "should be understood as working as much to *produce* an archive as to analyze one" (8; emphasis mine).

When Cvetkovich describes the lesbian public cultures that she researches, moreover, as "hard to archive because they are lived experiences," or calls the cultural traces that those public cultures leave "frequently inadequate to the task of documentation," and notes that "[t]heir lack of a conventional archive ... often makes them seem not to exist" (9), she might also be describing the peculiar project of archiving the life of an unremarked Canadian immigrant who is disappearing under a proliferation of Alzheimer's plaques and tangles. But, while Cvetkovich unequivocally celebrates the ways in which new queer documentaries create affective archives as part of an ongoing project of "testimonials, memorial spaces, and rituals that can acknowledge traumatic pasts" (14), I hesitate. The subject of my affective archive is, by any measure, what G. Thomas Couser calls a "vulnerable subject," subject, by virtue of her illness, to abuse and exploitation, and vulnerable to misrepresentation (*Vulnerable* x). How do I, both respectfully and truthfully, archive and narrate the life of a beloved other who sometimes breaks what Paul John Eakin calls the third unspoken rule of self-narration—who does not, that is, always display "normative models of personhood" (114)? What kind of peculiar ethical dust am I raising because it's the *Alzheimer's* archives I'm both exploring and creating?

The Project

> Because trauma can be unspeakable and unrepresentable and because it is marked by forgetting and dissociation, it often seems to leave behind no records at all. Trauma puts pressure on conventional forms of documentation, representation, and commemoration, giving rise to new genres of expressions, such as testimony, and new forms of monuments, rituals, and performances that can call into being collective witnesses and publics. It thus demands an unusual archive, whose materials, in pointing to trauma's ephemerality, are themselves frequently ephemeral. Trauma's archive incorporates personal memories, which can be recorded in oral and video testimonies, memoirs, letters, and journals.
> —Cvetkovich 7

For almost two years now, I've spent most Friday afternoons with my mother, at which time I tape our conversations as we discuss the news, work on puzzles and word games, read out loud from one or another of the books piled around my parents' home, worry over political issues and philosophical or theological questions, write letters to friends, and, as often as it's feasible, read aloud the letters we sent to one another more than twenty years ago. Ironically, I've probably spent more time with my mother and learned far more about her life in the last two years than I would have if she hadn't been diagnosed with Alzheimer's. I've learned much more, for instance, about how her life has been permanently (mis)shaped, first by being sexually abused at a very young age by one of her father's employees, and not long afterward, by experiencing the privations and anxieties of growing up in occupied Holland during the Second World War. By now I understand far better, too, the significance of the fact that my grandparents emigrated at a point in my mother's life when, if they had stayed in the Netherlands, she would have pursued the higher education about which she had dreamed. My mother returns repeatedly in our conversations to that timing as the central fact of her adult existence: arriving in Canada dramatically reduced the scope of her life, and put an irrefutable end to her dreams.

As I work with both the archive that exists and the archive of electronic recordings that my mother and I are creating, I use my previous research into the colonial and gendered rhetoric of early Canadian exploration journals, archived fur trade texts, and fur trade women's domestic writing, to sharpen my focus on auto/biography as both creative product and subject of analysis. I adhere to my university's ethics requirements, and I have a copy of my mother's signed permission carefully stored in my project records, but the ethical questions still proliferate. I am, after all, both an academic researcher/writer and a daughter.

At the very least, I am not the first to face the questions. Richard Freadman, for instance, who has written a book about his father and their fraught relationship (122), grapples generatively with issues of trust, trustworthiness, and the changing selves and subjects of life writing, when he asks what values and assumptions are at work in the notion that we owe loyalty to the dead (125). In an examination of life writing about children's disabilities, Arthur Frank argues compellingly for an understanding of illness as an inherently moral experience and proposes that "[t]he writer of an illness narrative is primarily a witness, whose testimony speaks not only for himself or herself but also for a larger community of those who suffer. Being a witness is moral work" (177). Alice Wexler, meanwhile, describes the complicated issues of privacy, confidentiality, and disclosure that attend the work she's done to document her family's experience with Huntington's disease (163–69), and she examines some of the ethical issues that are raised when a researcher has access to archived material that is old enough to carry no *legal* liability but inadvertently offers genetic information about a highly stigmatized hereditary illness that could do harm to the living (171–73).

Couser's admonition for people like me and projects like mine, meanwhile, is admirably clear, if broad: "The closer the relationship between writer and subject, and the greater the vulnerability or dependency of the subject," he cautions, "the higher the ethical stakes and the more urgent the need for ethical scrutiny" (*Vulnerable* xii). When Couser declares, understandably, that a project like mine requires the highest possible level of urgent ethical scrutiny, he also implicitly, and likely unintentionally, underscores the role of *judgment* in the auto/biographical dynamic. Leigh Gilmore's extremely useful and explicit exploration of this dynamic simultaneously clarifies and complicates the way I understand my project. Gilmore, like Cvetkovich, finds trauma at the centre of memoir and autobiography, but she understands this as a fundamental contradiction. Indeed, it is precisely this contradiction that prompts her to examine what she calls "limit-cases" of autobiography, because, she explains, by doing so she can develop a context for understanding the paradox that the autobiographer be both unique and representative. While trauma has become a pervasive subject in contemporary self-representation, it is nonetheless experienced as that which breaks the frame.... Indeed, autobiography's paradox is foregrounded so explicitly that the self-representation of trauma confronts itself as a theoretical impossibility. (7–8)

According to Gilmore, the "limit-cases" that she examines "confront how the limits of autobiography...might conspire to prevent some self-representational stories from being told at all if they were subjected to a literal truth test or evaluated by certain objective measures" (14). "The truthfulness of knowledge about the self and trauma as it arises in relation to self-representation," Gilmore explains,

> immediately confronts the issue of judgment. The association of autobiography with representativeness, confession, and testimony suggests some of why this should be so. *So does the history of identifying memory as a central and vulnerable location of identity, and trauma as a threat to the self due to how it injures memory.* The prevalence of judgment is threaded through the recurring emphases in my study's limit-cases—kinship, law, silence, identity, and love—and offers a way to connect them to each other as well as to the prohibitions on speech that structure trauma. In requiring testimony to take certain forms, judgment defines what cannot be said as much as what can, and, in establishing these forms as truthful, produces form as the grounds for experimentation. Criticism takes the form of judgment as it meets self-representational records and seeks to name them, attempts to answer whether they are telling the truth rather than how, and deems certain ventures out-of-bounds. (144–45; emphasis mine)

Gilmore's formulation helpfully foregrounds the layers of discovery work I've set myself: if my mother's memory is the central and vulnerable location of her identity, and trauma threatens that identity insofar as it injures memory, I am in search of an already traumatized identity that is increasingly dislocated from itself as the physiological processes of Alzheimer's do more and more damage to the memory where that identity is located.

Gilmore's project clearly opts in favour of stories that are told from beyond the boundaries, although none of her limit-cases tackle the uncanny representations a self suffering from dementia might offer. Some life writing theorists, intrigued to determine where, exactly, the limits of "out-of-bounds" might be, at least approach the subject. Sidonie Smith, for instance, includes "people suffering from Alzheimer's disease" in her list of the "everyday impediments to autobiographical storytelling" that create limits on "our narrative 'lives'" (227). Smith's particular focus, however, is on autistic subjects, and she examines self-narratives by two high-functioning autistics that challenge the notion that they "inhabit an elsewhere beyond the limit" because they can be known only through others' representations (235, 231). Alzheimer's sufferers remain on Smith's list of subjects at the limit, however, and they remain on Eakin's too when he wonders, in "Breaking Rules," whether the "failed narratives" of individuals suffering from Korsakov's syndrome or Alzheimer's disease reflect "failed identities" (113). Although Gilmore's limit-cases include no subjects compromised by illness, she usefully describes the limit-cases in terms of Michel Foucault's ethics of self-transformation, explaining that "[limit-cases] expose the insufficiency of viewing ethics and law primarily as a code of conduct. They examine the relations among people that exist in the presence of trauma and attempt to historicize the relations from which trauma has emerged in order to conceive of a self who can differ from the identity trauma imposes" (146). My project proposes to discover my mother's self as fraught by trauma but also different from trauma's impositions. I propose to do so, however, by recalling to her already-traumatized memory the writing we did when we were more dislocated from one another than we'd ever been before.

The Letters

> Everything here is marvellously "African," magical and otherworldly, and the closer we get to Uganda, the more thoroughly "African" it feels. It's magical and otherworldly but also surreal to be in a place you've imagined for months and years.[13] The truth is, however, if someone offered tomorrow to reduce my term to just one year, I'd take them up on it in a heartbeat. If I'd known how much I'd miss you, I never would have come.... Home will always be home with you.[14]

When I re-examine the letters my mother and I exchanged between 1986 and 1989, I marvel at the ways our "real" correspondence aligns with what Janet Gurkin Altman observes about literary instances of epistolary form. "What distinguishes epistolary narrative from...diar[ies]," says Altman, "is the desire for exchange.... [T]his is the epistolary pact—" she elaborates, "the call for response from a specific reader within the correspondent's world" (89). "Write soon," my mother says, to end her first letter. She repeats the admonition in a postscript: "write soon." Eight days later, when she begins her second letter, she notes, "we haven't yet heard from you..." Not surprisingly, my mother's letters to me don't mirror my intense homesickness, although they reflect their own peculiar experience of dislocation. About two-thirds of the way through her second letter, for instance, my mother reports that she's registered for another university course and adds, with a poignant and uncharacteristic grammatical slip,

> Since I was downtown, I picked up another ball of that purple wool in order to finish the sweater you were knitting for me. I didn't have much heart for knitting lately; I still have to get used to you being all the way in Africa and then I can't knit right away. That doesn't make much sense, perhaps. I know I'll get back into it in a little while.[15]

"Write soon," she says to end that letter too. When she writes again eleven days later, on the September 7, she begins on a jubilant note: "We received your letter on August 28."[16]

My mother means the letter that inaugurated our correspondence, one I wrote to my parents on August 16, 1986, en route from Amsterdam to Nairobi. I didn't receive her letter telling me it had arrived, however, until October 3, when I was already halfway through writing my tenth letter back to her.[17] When I survey our archive now, I see more clearly how epistolary discourse mimics the experience of Alzheimer's. My mother and I wrote constantly because we wanted exchange and we performed exchange, but the archive of our letters reveals it to have been an exchange of scrambled messages, messages confused in and by space and time, messages that gesture toward but never achieve direct or linear communication. But this is nothing new. Epistolary language, says Altman, is "marked by hiatuses of all sorts, time lags...blank spaces and lacunae"; it is, she says, "the language of absence." In epistolary discourse, Altman adds, however, "[m(])emory and expectation keep the addressee present to the imagination of the writer" (140). And there's the rub: if memory and expectation keep the addressee present to the imagination in epistolary discourse, what keeps the addressee present under the ontologically rupturing conditions of Alzheimer's disease?

"Mom," I say, "shall we read the letters we wrote while I was in Uganda and see what that helps us remember?" "Of course," she says, because she loves and trusts me, and enjoys my company and the attention I pay to her. "I'll have to tape us talking," I tell her, "or I'll never remember everything we say. Is that going to be okay?" My mother agrees to the project, signs the consent form in a fully lucid moment, and when we sit down together to record what we read and remember, she often surprises me. "These were letters that *I* wrote?" she has asked when I've reintroduced the project, or, slightly differently, "*I* wrote letters?" Sometimes she shifts and multiplies the emphases and asks, "*I* wrote *letters* to *you*?" My project, that is, instantly and repeatedly betrays its origins in desire. There is no capital A-Archive, no capital-M Memory, no isomorphic mapping of one onto the other. Whatever the archive will do, it will not heal my mother's memory, and it will not bring her back to me.

But the archive does do *something*, and the work of archiving the archive does *something*. Michael O'Driscoll and Edward Bishop call their archiving anecdotes "private histories about encounters with private histories," and they suggest that what they archive, as they "enter the record of these private events into the archive...is the moment of forgetting" (2). However paradoxical it might be, even these moments of forgetting *manufacture* memory (Brown and Davis-Brown 22) and memories. And because, as Ann Cvetkovich says, "[m]emories can cohere around objects in unpredictable ways...the task of the archivist of emotion is...an unusual one" (242). Once into an afternoon of reading and conversation, my mother and I proceed as we can.

Many Alzheimer's sufferers recede into the background in social interactions, often because they no longer fully trust themselves to know what the conversation is about or whether or not their contribution will be appropriate and meaningful (Kuhn 41–42; Bell and Troxel 5–18). Unless she is very tired, my mother typically becomes more, not less, engaged during the afternoons that we have to ourselves to talk. She maintains compelling vestiges of her passionate interest in politics, theology, literature, pacifism, and social justice; cites reading as *the* great pleasure of her life, and recounts her life in terms of books encountered; and greets me sometimes having memorized poems from her childhood in the Netherlands. She is having more and more difficulty reading on her own, however, and I learned quickly that I can't ask her to read the letters that I wrote to her: they are too idiosyncratic, too non-linear, too "voiced," to make sense to a memory that's disappearing. So I ask her to read the letters she wrote to me, and she looks up from them frequently, saying, "I remember that," or, "I would never have remembered that if we hadn't read these letters." There are disconcerting gaps, of course, although, as Steedman reminds us, "an absence is not *nothing*, but is rather the space left by what has gone" (11).

Almost exactly one year after I arrived at Ndejje, my mother began her forty-third letter to me by letting me know that another one of my friends had taken her out for lunch, a habit several of my friends were in. "It has been a profitable time for me in regard to lunches lately," my mother adds, describing another recent outing. "Before you left," she writes, "I could always count on you to take me out. Now it's catch as [catch] can. But," she adds reassuringly, "that is not the only reason I miss you."[18] A little more than six months after we began our memory project, I chose this letter very deliberately: I haven't yet stopped missing my mother, and I wanted to hear her remember how much she missed me. "Do you remember that, Mom," I ask, while we reread the letter, "how we'd sit and talk over lunch? Can you still picture the little places we'd go to in Osborne Village?" My mother tries to say "Osborne Village," a popular restaurant district in Winnipeg, but the consonants won't line up properly. "Can you picture yourself in Osborne Village?" I ask. No, she says, she can't. "Do you remember our lunches?" I ask, and she answers valiantly, "Vaguely."

What she remembers as we talk is that "the ladies, the ladies I worked for, didn't they live in Osborne Village?" For about five years, beginning in the early 1970s, long before I left for Uganda, my mother cleaned house for three elderly women, all of whom lived in the Osborne area. On this afternoon, my mother and I take several minutes to remember each one of "the ladies," and then I say, "Mom, in 1987, when you wrote me this letter, you hadn't worked for the ladies in over a decade. Do you have a clearer recollection of that than of the time that I was in Uganda?"

Her answer is startling for its insight. "In a way," she says hesitantly, in part because she isn't sure of her answer, in part because she doesn't want to hurt my feelings, "yes, because it has more to do with your body than your thought processes. When you were in Uganda, there wasn't a lot I could do except think of you. And a thought," she says, shaping the air with her hands, "you cannot conjure up, but a thing, you can think, 'this is what it looked like.' ... If you arrive to clean someone's house and then you drive back home... you can see that in your head: 'now I was *there* and now I'm going *there*,' but a thought isn't like that; thoughts fly away on you" (personal interview, Apr. 11, 2008). And then my mother tells me again what she's begun to tell me during this first winter of conversation. "You have no idea," she says, "what I've forgotten. You have no idea how much I've forgotten." In this moment of enunciation, my mother fashions a kind of metaphorical "bag" of memories that she unsettlingly both remembers and forgets. In the moment of insisting that the memories are gone, that is, the memories present themselves to view, but only vaguely, uncannily: they are here but not accessible; gone but not (entirely) forgotten; here and gone, in the space where *heimlich* and *unheimlich* meet (Freud 156–57). Or, rather, my mother's deeply unsettling memory loss collapses Freud's two definitions of *Heimlich*—"that which is familiar and congenial" and "that which is concealed and kept out of sight" (156)—and conceals, albeit not entirely and not all the time, the shared past with which she and I should be most familiar, and with which she and I should feel most at home.

Recently my mother has begun to tell me, repeatedly, that she does not feel at home in Canada. She used to feel at home in Canada. After her first acutely distressing years as a new immigrant, my mother embraced her Canadian-ness with determination and with special eloquence for the vast and delicate light, bright, teeming Prairies that Lorna Crozier describes in her memoir, *Small Beneath the Sky*. Since Canada Day 2008, however, my mother has been telling me more and more frequently that she no longer feels "Canadian."[19] When she tells me, on a very recent day trip through southeastern Manitoba, that "there is just too much room here in Canada to know where you belong" (Sept. 5, 2009), she offers an odd refraction of Gilmore's early observations about the relationship between autobiography and citizenship. "The interface of singular and shareable," says Gilmore, who is not describing the narratives of Alzheimer's sufferers, although she could be,

> goes to the issue of political representation, for the autobiographical self who is cut off from others, even as it stands for them, is a metaphor for the citizen. Once separated conceptually from a nation, a family, a place, and a branching set of contingencies, how does an individual recognize this disestablished self? (12)

My mother is quick to point out about her "disestablished self" that she also does not feel "Dutch." What she feels, she tells me, is Frisian, and where she wants to go back to is Gasterlân, the southern region of the small province in the Netherlands where she grew up.[20] When I press her to account for this desire, given the fact that her village is now a bustling, suburban town, and the bucolic fields and quiet forests that she remembers cycling past and through have changed irrevocably, she tells me, after considerable thought, "Do you know what I am? I am homesick for the past" (personal interview, July 24, 2009).

When Steedman connects a desire for the Archive and the past to "home," "memory," "identity," and Freud's "uncanny," she echoes, almost certainly inadvertently, Gilmore's recognition that an autobiographer is required, paradoxically, to be both unique and representative (8). "To want to go to the Archive may be a specialist and minority desire," says Steedman, "but it is emblematic of a modern way of being in the world.... In the everyday world of the early twenty-first century, we operate...by means of a politics of the imagination in which the past has become a place of succour and strength, a kind of home, for the ideas people possess of who they really want to be." Like Freud's uncanny, by which the familiar finally coincides with its opposite, Steedman suggests that this modern identity is at once "a claim for absolute sameness...perhaps [with] a historical identity, located in the historical past" and, at the same time, "a process of individuation, the modern making of a...unique personality" (75–77). Steedman's and Gilmore's paradoxes uncover the fundamental fissures in my project. I am using archives of the record my mother and I made more than twenty years ago to find the two of us a past where we can be at home together. What my mother is remembering instead is a past and a home to which only she can return, and only in her memory. My mother's memories, however, both exist and don't; by some criteria, that means my mother sometimes has, and sometimes does not have, an identity. Someone still very recognizable as my unique mother remembers, but sometimes what she remembers is that she has lost many of her memories; she remembers that the home of her past has changed, but it's her home *in* the past that she'd like to get back to now. And I wonder, is there an ethical measure that obliges me to help her get there?

Conclusion: Searching for an Ethical End

> I've thought again this week that it's more than a little bit self-indulgent for us ("we"?) rich North Americans to spend a few years here in the "developing" world. Why am I here exactly? Surely to god, it's not to help "the poor Ugandans": all the Ugandans I've met so far will fare as well or better after I'm gone and if I'm not here for them, I must be here for me, and this must be another selfish, self-indulgent move in the series.[21]

My project is hedged around on all sides by ethical questions. I would not have committed three years of my life to a postwar rehabilitation project in Uganda—and, by extension, have created the conditions out of which the letter archive has been assembled—if my parents had not raised my siblings and me to ask, about big and small decisions, some version of the question "What is it good to be?" (Eakin, Introduction 4). And I would not have committed three years of my life to that challenge had my parents not also taught us that it is good to be a person who measures his or her own "good life" in terms of the "good" it enables in other people's lives, especially other people who have not enjoyed the kind of "circumstantial luck" that we have (Nagel qtd. in Barbour 90). Barbara Heron's examination of whiteness, gender, development, and the helping imperative reminds me ruthlessly, however, that claims to "goodness" hardly constitute the end of an ethical answer in a post-colonial world. "The operation of colonial continuities," says Heron,

> can also be detected in constructions of gender, which position white middle-class women as simultaneously subjects and non-subjects who may enhance their hold on bourgeois subjectivity through the performance of "goodness." This exerts a special pressure on middle-class white women to stake a claim to the moral high ground. Because it is ostensibly about "helping" Others, development work particularly fulfills this imperative for female members of the dominant group in Canada and other Northern countries. (7)[22]

So I can neither evade the intractable ethical questions that surround my project nor answer them. Nor could I have predicted the ethical issues that the project would require me to face.

As my mother's condition deteriorates and she becomes increasingly less able to follow the non-linear logic of even her own letters, I become proportionally more generously poststructuralist in my estimation of what constitutes "text," what constitutes "archived" or "archivable" text, and what counts as an archive. I will read just about anything with my mother and tape the conversation that the reading material provokes. On December 5, 2008, I sit down at my parents' kitchen table and find a handout called "Alzheimer's Disease Bill of Rights,"[23] which my mother promptly reads aloud to me. When I ask her what she thinks of the list, she is quick to assure me that she feels she has everything on the list and is not complaining. "I'm just annoyed that I have this disease," she tells me vehemently. My mother often talks to me about the experience of having Alzheimer's, and about her fear that she'll live as long as her mother and maternal grandmother did, because she knows that by then she will be almost completely incapacitated. On this particular afternoon, my mother revisits both her awe at the possibility that she might, at some point in the future, not be interested in the world around her, and her preference to end her life before that should happen. "[S]ometimes I look out of the window here, for instance," she tells me, "[and] then I think, would I not know any more that that was a car coming or would I not know any more that that's snow? I find it actually pretty damn scary, but I don't know what else to do except [my mother makes a choking sound] 'Give me a sword, I'll fall on my sword!' But who has a sword in the first place and it's too cumbersome; I'd rather have something that's bloodless" (personal interview, Dec. 5, 2008).

This is neither the first nor the last time that my mother will speak about euthanasia, but, on this afternoon, she frames it as a clearly ethical issue. "[B]eing sick," she tells me, "is one thing, but this is as though your life is dwindling away.... I hope I don't have to live as long as my grandmother or even Beppe and certainly not in this condition."[24] "I have an idea," she adds after a pause; "maybe in that rights of Alzheimer's people: maybe they should also add one thing in: the right to die." We discuss this possibility for almost fifteen minutes as my mother assembles compelling reasons to support her position. "If people want to make a war," she reminds me passionately,

> then it doesn't matter how many people are getting killed...and maybe... people sign up for war, they die, the strong fall,...but there are also people that do not want to have that war, and they can say, "no, I'm not going to go to war," and I should have the right to say, this is...a dead end...

circumstance.... Maybe we have to expand what the rights are for Alzheimer people.... [I]t's not legal now, but when you think about it from my position, then it should be; it should be. (personal interview, Dec. 5, 2008)

Over the very long winter that follows, my mother returns to the possibility of ending her life every time we visit and every time we speak by telephone. I come to dread our conversations: because my mother is increasingly fixated on the possibility and increasingly serious about carrying out a plan; because I can fully understand how my mother arrived at this conclusion; and because I know that she no longer retains the cognitive skills to carry out the necessary operations. Someone would have to help her.

It may now start to matter that Derrida calls my project an instance of the death drive. Or it may not. My mother wants to end her life because she suffers from Alzheimer's, but because she suffers from Alzheimer's, she will, sooner or later, deteriorate past the point when she can conceptualize euthanasia. I don't, therefore, *have* to do anything; I could just wait. Luckily, in February, my mother begins asking for something I can help her with: she'd like me to organize a family meeting at which she can tell us all about her plans. When we finally gather in mid-March, she is exquisitely eloquent about her fears for the future and her need for our support. She surprises me, however, by saying nothing about wanting to end her life (personal interview, March 15, 2009). Even more surprisingly, my mother has only rarely and never urgently spoken about euthanasia since that meeting, perhaps confirming Herbert Hendin's assessment of patients who request assisted suicide. According to Hendin,

> [I]n their depression, their ambivalence about dying, and their need to test the affection of others, medically-ill patients who request assisted suicide are not different from patients who become suicidal for other reasons.... Most are looking for a response that indicates that their fears will be addressed, that their pain will be relieved, and that they will not be abandoned. (qtd. in Couser, "Life" 204; emphasis in original)

And spring comes even to the Prairies. My mother's spirits lift as good weather returns, and on May Day she concludes a lively account of her opposition to Canada's military presence in Afghanistan with a recollection of her father's passionate interest in politics; her father's sister, who lived in their village in Friesland, with whom her father shared his often radical political and theological ideas; and a half-remembered story I've never heard before, about that aunt's first fiancé and his untimely death.

"What I can tell you," my mother says, repeating the name of the sister who told her this story, and reviewing the story's fragments several times, "is just bits and pieces...now you have to take them and...make them into a quilt in your head." In the conversation that follows, she and I explore the implications of knowing just bits and fragments of a story, and my mother tells me how grateful she is that she is not a judge and does not have to decide what is true and what is not. "But you can do with all this rambling whatever you like," she assures me, "I don't think you'll lie" (personal interview, May 1, 2009).

When Cathy Caruth describes trauma as standing at the strange epistemological crossroads "between knowing and not knowing" (3), she offers unexpected parallels with the experience of Alzheimer's, the "limits" that autobiography and life writing theorists scrutinize, and Foucault's description of the archive.

> The analysis of the archive...involves a...region...at once close to us, and different from our present existence, it is the border of time that surrounds our presence...and...indicates it in its otherness.... [It] deploys its possibilities...on the basis of...discourses that have just ceased to be ours; its threshold of existence is established by the discontinuity that separates us from what we can no longer say. (130)

My mother is still, paradoxically, both unique and representative of Alzheimer's sufferers everywhere; she both knows her memories and doesn't; and the story she and I are still able to make out of our strange archive is, in her evocative words, both "the truth at the moment and the truth as it becomes something else" (personal interview, May 1, 2009).

Notes

1 Half a million Canadians have Alzheimer's disease or a related dementia; of those, 71,000 are under the age of 65. In just five years, fifty percent more Canadians and their families could be facing Alzheimer's disease or a related dementia (Alzheimer Society website, http://www.alzheimer.ca/english/disease/stats-intro.htm). The World Alzheimer Report, released September 21, 2009, can be accessed at http://www.alz.co.uk/research/worldreport/. It reports that the illness is already prevalent at epidemic levels and predicts alarming increases, worldwide, in the next twenty years.
2 From the Alzheimer Society Manitoba website, http://www.alzheimer.mb.ca/a-ad.html.
3 Alzheimer's Association website, http://www.alz.org/alzheimers_disease_what_is_alzheimers.asp.
4 Researchers are at least five years (more likely ten) from developing their best hopes, specifically, tools for early detection, in concert with a vaccine that will prevent the disease from progressing. See Alzheimer Society Manitoba website, http://www.alzheimer.mb.ca/f.html, especially Dr. Jack Diamond's summary of current biomedical and social/psychological research (July 2005).

5 Alzheimer's Association website, http://www.alz.org/alzheimers_disease_myths_about_alzheimers.asp.
6 G. Thomas Couser is relying on a bibliography of pathography published in 1993 when he lists, among a large range of illnesses that have prompted life narratives, "even, *improbably*, Alzheimer's disease" and references a single such narrative (*Recovering* 9; emphasis mine). In fact, a proliferation of accounts—some by Alzheimer's sufferers themselves, often with the help of spouses, and many by the daughters of mothers with Alzheimer's—offers evidence of the way the disease regularly prompts a turn to writing as both therapy and the recovery of personal and family history. The following list is by no means comprehensive, but includes accounts by people diagnosed with Alzheimer's: Davis 1989; DeBaggio 2002 and 2003; Simpson 1999; Taylor 2007; and accounts by the daughters of mothers with Alzheimer's: Cooney 2003; Dyer 1996; Fuchs 2005; Kessler 2007; Karafilly 2000; Menzies 2009. Ray Smith has written about his and his wife's unusual response to her diagnosis in *Amazing Grace: Enjoying Alzheimer's*; because of its subject's high profile, John Bayley's *Elegy for Iris,* about his wife, the late philosopher and novelist Iris Murdoch, may be the best-known instance of an Alzheimer's narrative.
7 Missing the point as I am, I take both consolation and delight from Carolyn Steedman, who describes herself as "cling[ing] to the coat-tails of one figure of Derrida, one image, *one literal meaning* of 'fever'" and taking pleasure in "willfully asserting of a text so intimately connected by its authorship to the practice of deconstruction, that there *is* something there... in the first place" (10; emphasis in original).
8 Just seven years later, email would enter the public sphere and permanently change the ways most people in the West and many people around the world understand distance, time, separation, and intimate communication; in 1986, however, electronic mail was an unimaginable future. ("Email history," http://www.livinginternet.com/e/ei.htm.)
9 My mother and I exchanged more than two hundred carefully numbered letters, but sixteen of my mother's letters didn't ever reach me. My mother received all the letters I sent to her.
10 In 1952, my sixteen-year-old mother emigrated to Canada from the Netherlands with her parents and eight of her nine siblings. She was obliged to spend her first year in the new country taking care of her suicidal mother, and until she married my father in 1958, she contributed money from various factory and entry-level clerical jobs to her large family's combined income. In 1959, she became a Canadian citizen and gave birth to her first child. In 1977 she passed the Canadian high school equivalency exam, and over the course of the next eleven years, earned an honours undergraduate degree in French literature and religious studies.
11 G. Venema, letter to author, Aug. 18, 1986.
12 Zamora understands the phrase to signal the often-ironic ambivalence of history in a "new" world. "'Usable,'" she explains,

> implies the active engagement of a user or users, through whose agency collective and personal histories are constituted. The term thus obviates the possibility of innocent history, but not the possibility of authentic history when it is actively imagined by its user(s). What is deemed usable is valuable; what is valuable is constituted according to specific cultural and personal needs and desires." (ix)

13 Heron's discussion of the way the "Third World" is presented to the northern imagination as exotic spectacle is relevant here; Heron, following Soja's arguments in "The Spatiality of Social Life," proposes that "such representations become concretized and consequently seem second nature, so that they are inscribed in our understandings of the place long before we get there" (57–58).
14 K. Venema, letter to parents, Aug. 21, 1986. Written on the road from Nairobi to Kampala, five days after landing in Nairobi.
15 G. Venema, letter to author, Aug. 26, 1986.
16 G. Venema, letter to author, Sept. 7, 1986.
17 Most of my correspondents and I numbered our letters to one another, and I now use the records in the letters themselves and in the journal I was keeping in Ndejje to track the arrival times and the often inexplicable feasts and famines that characterized our exchanges. Indeed, my journal's details of letters sent and letters received mimic the "counting and managing" that Philippe Lejeune identifies as one of the earliest prompts for diary-keeping (51).
18 G. Venema, letter to author, Aug. 18, 1987.
19 There is neither time nor space here to examine the resonant nexus of nationalism, nationhood, citizenship, archives and archiving, trauma, and auto/biography that work by Steedman, Anderson, Cvetkovich, Gilmore, and Berlant creates.
20 Friesland is one of the Netherlands' twelve provinces.
21 K. Venema, letter to W. Bruce, Nov. 14, 1986.
22 See also Keizer, *Help: The Original Human Dilemma*, which is broader, less theoretical, and (perhaps therefore) less damning than Heron's analysis.
23 My mother received this document from a support group that she attends at Alzheimer Society Manitoba. The list includes items such as the following: "to advocate for one's own rights and those of others"; "to have appropriate, informed, ongoing, medical care"; "to be treated like an adult"; "to be free of unnecessary psychotropic medications"; "to enjoy suitable activities and be challenged to the level of one's abilities"; "to have regular opportunities and access to events outside of the home"; "to have physical and emotional support that is respectful to the individual"; "to live in a safe, structured, and supportive environment"; "to be productive in work and play as long as possible"; "to be with persons who care about one's life story and background"; "to be cared for by individuals well trained and understanding of dementia care."
24 "Beppe" is Frisian for grandmother; my mother is referring here to her mother.

Works Cited

Altman, Janet Gurkin. *Epistolarity: Approaches to a Form*. Columbus: Ohio State UP, 1982. Print.

Alzheimer Association."What Is Alzheimers?" *Alzheimer Association.org*. n.d. Web. Aug. 10, 2009. (http://www.alz.org/alzheimers_disease_what_is_alzheimers.asp).

Alzheimer Society Manitoba. n.d. Web. Aug. 10, 2009. (http://www.alzheimerb.ca/a-ad.html).

———. "Research." n.d. Web. Aug. 10, 2009. (http://www.alzheimer.mb.ca/f.html).

Anderson, Benedict. *Imagined Communities: Reflections on the Origins and Spread of Nationalism*. London: Verso, 1983. Print.

Barbour, John D. "Judging and Not Judging Parents." Eakin 73–98.
Bayley, John. *Elegy for Iris.* New York: St. Martin's, 1999. Print.
Bell, Virginia, and David Troxel. *A Dignified Life: The Best Friends Approach to Alzheimer's Care.* Deerfield Beach: Health Professions P, 2002. Print.
———. *The Queen of America Goes to Washington City: Essays on Sex and Citizenship.* Durham: Duke UP, 2002. Print.
Brown, Richard Harvey, and Beth Davis-Brown. "The Making of Memory: The Politics of Archives, Libraries and Museums in the Construction of National Consciousness." *History of the Human Sciences* 11.4 (1998): 17–32. Print.
Caruth, Cathy. *Unclaimed Experience: Trauma, Narrative, and History.* Baltimore: Johns Hopkins UP, 1996. Print.
Cooney, Eleanor. *My Mother's Descent into Alzheimer's: Death in Slow Motion.* New York: HarperCollins, 2003. Print.
Couser, G. Thomas. *Recovering Bodies: Illness, Disability, and Life Writing.* Madison: U of Wisconsin P, 1997. Print.
———. *Vulnerable Bodies: Ethics and Life Writing.* Ithaca: Cornell UP, 2004. Print.
———. "When Life Writing Becomes Death Writing: Disability and the Ethics of Parental Euthanography." Eakin 195–215.
Crozier, Lorna. *Small Beneath the Sky: A Prairie Memoir.* Vancouver: GreyStone, 2009. Print.
Cvetkovich, Ann. *An Archive of Feelings: Trauma, Sexuality, and Lesbian Public Cultures.* Durham: Duke UP, 2003. Print.
Davis, Robert. *My Journey into Alzheimer's Disease.* Wheaton: Tyndale House, 1989. Print.
DeBaggio, Thomas. *Losing My Mind: An Intimate Look at Life with Alzheimer's.* New York: Free P, 2003. Print.
———. *When It Gets Dark: An Enlightened Reflection on Life with Alzheimer's.* New York: Free P, 2003. Print.
Derrida, Jacques. *Archive Fever: A Freudian Impression.* Trans. Eric Prenowitz. Chicago: U of Chicago P, 1995. Print.
Dyer, Joyce. *In a Tangled Wood: An Alzheimer's Journey.* Dallas: Southern Methodist UP, 1996. Print.
Eakin, John Paul. "Breaking Rules: The Consequences of Self-Narration."*Biography* 24.1 (2001):113–27. *Project Muse.* Web. Dec. 3, 2008.
———, ed. *The Ethics of Life Writing.* Ithaca: Cornell UP, 2004. Print.
———. Introduction: Mapping the Ethics of Life Writing. Eakin 1–16. Print.
"Email history." *Living Internet.com.* Nov. 10, 2007. Web. May 29, 2008. (http://www.livinginternet.com/e/ei.htm).
Foucault, Michel. *The Archaeology of Knowledge and the Discourse on Language.* Trans. S. M. Sheridan Smith. New York: Pantheon, 1972. Print.
Frank, Arthur W. "Moral Non-fiction: Life Writing and Children's Disability." Eakin 174–94.
Frazier, Ian. *Family.* New York: Farrar, Straus and Giroux, 1994. Print.

———. Foreword. Dyer xi–xiv. Print.
Freadman, Richard. "Decent and Indecent: Writing My Father's Life." Eakin 121–46. Print.
Freud, Sigmund. "The Uncanny." *Literary Theory: An Anthology.* Ed. Julie Rivkin and Michael Ryan. Malden: Blackwell, 1998. 154–67. Print.
Fuchs, Elinor. *Making an Exit: A Mother–Daughter Drama with Machine Tools, Alzheimer's, and Laughter.* New York: Metropolitan, 2005. Print.
Gilmore, Leigh. *The Limits of Autobiography: Trauma and Testimony.* Ithaca: Cornell UP, 2001. Print.
Heron, Barbara. *Desire for Development: Whiteness, Gender, and the Helping Imperative.* Waterloo: Wilfrid Laurier UP, 2007. Print.
Karafilly, Irena F. *The Stranger in the Plumed Hat: A Memoir.* Toronto: Viking, 2000. Print.
Keizer, Garret. *Help: The Original Human Dilemma.* New York: HarperCollins, 2004. Print.
Kessler, Lauren. *Dancing with Rose: Finding Life in the Land of Alzheimer's.* New York: Viking, 2007. Print.
Kuhn, Daniel. *Alzheimer's Early Stages: First Steps for Family, Friends and Caregivers.* 2nd ed. Alameda: Hunter House, 1999. Print.
Lejeune, Philippe. *On Diary.* Ed. Jeremy D. Popkin and Julie Rak. Trans. Katherine Durnin. Manoa: U of Hawai'i P, 2009. Print.
Menzies, Heather. *Enter Mourning: A Memoir on Death, Dementia, and Coming Home.* Toronto: Key Porter, 2009. Print.
O'Driscoll, Michael, and Edward Bishop. "Archiving 'Archiving.'" *The Event of the Archive.* Spec. issue of *English Studies in Canada* 30.1 (2004): 1–16. Print.
Simpson, Robert, and Anne Simpson. *Through the Wilderness of Alzheimer's: A Guide in Two Voices.* Minneapolis: Augsburg, 1999. Print.
Smith, Ray. *Amazing Grace: Enjoying Alzheimer's.* London: Metro, 2004. Print.
Smith, Sidonie. "Taking It to a Limit One More Time." *Getting a Life: Everyday Uses of Autobiography.* Ed. Sidonie Smith and Julia Watson. Minneapolis: U of Minnesota P, 1996. 226–46. Print.
Soja, Edward. "The Spatiality of Social Life: Towards a Transformative Retheorization." *Social Relations and Spatial Structures.* Ed. Derek Gregory and John Urry. London: Macmillan, 1985. 90–127. Print.
Steedman, Carolyn. *Dust: The Archive and Cultural History.* New Brunswick: Rutgers UP, 2001. Print.
Taylor, Richard. *Alzheimer's from the Inside Out.* Baltimore: Health Professions P, 2007. Print.
Venema, Grace. Letter to author. Aug. 18, Aug. 26, Sept. 7, 1986.
———. Letter to author. Aug. 18, 1987.
———. Interview with Kathleen Venema. Apr. 11, Dec 5, 2008.
———. Interview with Kathleen Venema. Mar. 15, May 1, July 24, Sept. 5, 2009.
Venema, Kathleen. Letter to G. and D. Venema. Aug. 21, 1986.

———. Letter to W. Bruce. Nov. 14, 1986.
———. Personal Journal. June 1, 2004 to Apr. 12, 2005. MS.
Wexler, Alice. "'Truth,' Life Writing, and DNA." Eakin 163–73.
"WorldAlzheimer Report." *Alz.co.uk*. Sept. 21, 2009. Web. Sept. 21, 2009. (http://www.alz.co.uk/research/worldreport/).
Zamora, Lois Parkinson. *The Usable Past: The Imagination of History in Recent Fiction of the Americas*. Cambridge: Cambridge UP, 1997. Print.

Locking Up Letters
Julia Creet

My approach to the discussion of the dynamic of discovery and response that marks the encounter with Canadian women's archives considers the violence inherent in the process of archivization itself. Holding an archive of my mother's papers that I know to be of historical value, with what issues must I grapple while I consider their deposition? Her letters, in particular, trace the path of an immigrant who wanted to leave her past behind, and yet she preserved a paper trail that led to a tragic and hidden history a continent and lifetime away. I hold in my hands (or more accurately, in boxes in my closet) the future of her memory, and know that every option for archival preservation will constitute some manner of betrayal. I take literally Derrida's observation in *Archive Fever* that personal documents in archives are held under "house arrest" (2). Once private ephemera of private lives, letters become public documents held under institutional restraints, the institutionalization of domesticity locking lives in boxes. A necessary trade-off, we might say, in order to allow researchers to mine these long-dead souls (sometimes not-so-long dead, and sometimes not dead at all) for their historical relevance and revelations. No longer just the traces of a life lived, archived papers become public documents and their writers become public figures by virtue of their textual traces rather than their worldly accomplishments. Why would or should this incarceration concern us in an era when the personal archive of even the most ordinary life has become a treasure? Because, as Richard J. Cox argues, there are no innocent archives (*No Innocent Deposits*).

When my mother, Magda Creet (formerly Magda Farkas, neé Magdalena György), died in 1984, she left several filing boxes of papers and photographs, including the drafts of two "novels" in English, a collection of poetry, and a body of work in black-and-white portraiture. About half of her documents were letters she had received, some packaged when she left England in 1957 and still taped closed, and some filed in accordion folders according to the correspondent, or group of correspondents. Although almost all of the letters were written in Hungarian, she labelled the packages and file folders in English: "Old boyfriends," "Old girlfriends," "Imre Farkas from Pécs," "Zsuzsi Fabini from Budapest," and so on. The organization of her letters suggests an archival "instinct" embodied in the preservation and orderliness of her ephemera, a vernacular expression of institutional archival practices (Cox, *Personal Archives* 3).[1] The Hungarian letters were her narrative continuity, even if she never read them again. The labels indicated that her life was now fully organized in English and perhaps, too, she thought about who might sort her papers in the future, in the sort of abstract way that we occasionally wonder about what will happen to our remnants. Her archived past was in Hungarian; her instinct about her archival future manifested in English.

I don't read Hungarian, or at least I didn't read it at all when I became feverish with the need to reconstruct my mother's life. In the wake of an expressive life in English and a secret life in Hungarian, the letters became one of the focal points of my research, but only after a series of research accidents made me reconsider their worth. The letters were not, of course, written by her, but by her correspondents, and so at the beginning I doubted they would tell me much. Nonetheless, the bulk, longevity, and arrangement of the collections alone told me a great deal about her other life. Why my mother kept these papers, given the depth of her secrecy about her history, can only be answered speculatively. My argument for the past decade, which I have spent decoding and reconstructing her fractured lifeline, has been that, as much as she did not want to live with her past, she nonetheless did not want the record of it destroyed. Cox observes similarly that "personal recordkeeping is linked to the human impulse for resisting oblivion" (*Personal Archives* 3), and my mother had faced oblivion once before.

The facts, once I found them (in a letter), were tragic and brutal. In June of 1944, my mother and her family, including her first daughter, Judit, age three, along with their entire community were deported from the Hungarian town of Székesfehérvár to Auschwitz. As she put it—in a sentence that I missed until the third time I read the manuscript of her first "novel"—"I had not imagined a catastrophe which would wipe them all out leaving me intact to witness it." By the late 1960s, twenty-five years after the events that had destroyed her world, my mother's impulses were deeply riven. She desperately wanted to recreate a world that had once been, but at the same time, in an effort to protect herself from the past and us from the possible future, she camouflaged the origins and fate of her family. Her "novels" recreated an unnamed time and place; the letters maintained her last living links with a time that once was.

My mother's story is typical of many Hungarian Jews, a highly assimilated population deeply betrayed by their country, who decided after the war that the wisest political and personal path was to forget that they had ever been Jewish in the first place. Silence, a common response to the Holocaust in postwar Hungary, was reinforced by communism's commitment to homogeneity and the viciousness of the Hungarian crime. "How did you find out you were Jewish?" is a clichéd question in Hungary, one exported with Hungarian emigrants to their families.[2] What's unusual about my mother's story is the wealth of documentary evidence she left behind. For a story about silence, this one is exceptionally loquacious. The paradox was remarkable: while she had done everything to keep her secrets, she wrote in precise detail about each other part of her life and kept in her personal archive the ephemera of a private world, protected by a language she knew we could not read.

Why she never threw her papers out, or instructed my father to do so (although he did try, only to be stopped by my sister), remains a bit of a mystery. She didn't want to admit she was dying, so perhaps she never thought it was time to say. Embedded in her ephemera is the record of a life half obliterated, half disavowed—although well-lived in revenge—the importance of the record heightened by her ambivalence about both remembering and forgetting. In the absence of any clear instructions from her and the presence of such deep conflict, her papers became a cabinet of curiosities, which I pored over with archival feverishness. "Nothing is more troubled and more troubling," Derrida says of the word "archive": "the trouble of secrets, of plots' of clandestineness, of half-private, half-public conjuration, always at the unstable limit between public and private, between family and an intimacy even more private than the family, between oneself and oneself" (90). I am indeed troubled by the intimacy of her archive, how it interceded between her and herself, her and me, and, finally me and myself; it provoked my longing for "a return to an authentic and singular origin" (Derrida 91).

Coming to the end of these years of living with and in her archive, or coming close to the end, I hope, I must now contemplate the value of what I painstakingly deciphered, and decide if the preservation of her papers is in the public's best interest or simply a further intrusion on her private life.[3] Her archive is bifurcated into a life pre- and postwar, as was her life, but I am faced with a dilemma caused by a basic tenant of archival theory, namely that the fonds should reflect a complete life, or as complete as possible. The fantasy of the life completely recorded recalls Danilo Kis's "Encyclopedia of the Dead (A Whole Life)," and its nightmarish volumes chained in a grotto, or an infinite binary stream, and I am under no illusions that such a thing is either possible or desirable. The responsibility of the decision to preserve the record of an ordinary/extraordinary life, however, has become mine, and with it comes a complex set of narratives, and theoretical, practical, spiritual, religious, and ethical concerns bound up, particularly, in one package of letters.

What exactly my mother had survived and her reasons for turning away from Judaism (she was a card-carrying member of the United Church of Canada) were still unclear until close to the end of my research. Over the years, I had tracked down many of her old Hungarian friends. From them, I heard several versions of what had happened to her, and I knew the official history well enough. I accepted in the end that I would never really know everything. After all, that is the condition of writing history. Then something surfaced from a suitcase opened in a Budapest attic by a person in search of photographs: my mother's side of a lifelong correspondence with her first husband, Imre Farkas. Among his last paper traces, along with his records of membership in the Communist Party and a leather wallet that held nothing but a forty-year-old picture of her, were four decades of letters from Magda to Imre, neatly arranged by date in a vinyl binder. When Tibor Szeszlér opened Imre's suitcase, whose contents he had never really carefully examined—and which he had considered throwing out—he found in his attic something he had no idea was there. Some things, I believe, call out to be found. Tibor and his wife, Maria Rusz, began to read. My mother's first letter (in Hungarian) was scrawled on a torn scrap of paper. When Imre got it, he dated it "Summer 1945."

> Imre!
>
> We learned at the last moment that Baba [Imre's sister "Dolly"] is leaving. I don't even have time to write. I don't know what will happen to us, I won't leave for home until I know how you feel. I beg you, try to write everything to me, completely honestly, write everything. Don't let it affect you that I am alone and that I might need you. After all we've been through, there is only one important thing: to create a somewhat happy life and this cannot

be built on lies. I only want one more thing, that you know that I only have beautiful memories of you and of the three years that we lived together. I am terribly thankful for it, and, if it happens that we never meet again, you must also try to forget [page torn]

[verso] the many bad things that I did to you and remember only the lovely things and happy memories.

By the second letter, Tibor and Maria realized that they had found not only a correspondence of historical significance but also one that was intimate and disturbing. They knew enough of my story to surmise that I could not possibly know what was in the correspondence. The uncanny emergence of these letters sent me back into the boxes of my mother's archives; I had never thought to look at Imre's letters carefully. "Imre Farkas from Pécs" was a man we knew from afar as "Uncle Imre," an uncle who sent her fashion magazines from Hungary. Even though they had divorced in 1947, Imre and my mother had kept in contact until her death in 1984. The letters grew less frequent over the years, and Imre seemed to be the more loyal correspondent, but nonetheless, there I found the other half of a testament to a relationship and a time. We had two sides of a rare correspondence. They had written a total of about three hundred letters between 1945 and 1984. The earliest letters were carried by hand between Székesfehérvár, Hungary, their hometown, to which Imre returned immediately after the war when he escaped a labour battalion, and Kaunitz, Germany, where my mother was now a "displaced person," having survived Auschwitz and a forced labour factory in Lippstadt, Germany. The letters are deeply private and yet self-consciously public, as they carry community news and were written knowing anyone might read them in transit.

Imre's response to my mother's first letter is not perhaps what one might expect of a man who has just heard that his wife and her sister, his dearest family, are still alive. After his initial, brief letter, it takes six weeks for this second reply to reach her.

Székesfehérvár August 19, 1945

My Magda,

I wrote to you a few weeks ago and I wrote what happiness, relief came with the news that you two are alive, healthy, and that you don't suffer for anything. I wrote that I am physically healthy but all the adversity of the past year destroyed me spiritually. Perhaps inconsiderately—but with all my sense of responsibility—I discussed our business also in this letter. I know that what I say now you will receive with rightful doubts: I was considering your interests mostly. Unfortunately, I'm not certain that you received that letter so that's why I repeat the gist of it.

I am not cradling myself in the illusion that all the suffering of the last year will have changed our relationship. Both of us were counting a bit on this, but, unfortunately, it appears that the situation, instead of improving, has gotten worse. Those threads that held our marriage together—are all broken. I'm not writing this to you for any other reason than you have a chance to go to the West and there you will have the possibility to have a calm and secure life with no risks. There, you wouldn't be exposed to uncertainty, or lack anything, and if the only reason you don't do this is that the threads of home pull you back, this shouldn't hold you back. From my end, I release you from all your responsibilities to me. In my present state I would be a worse husband than I was in the past, not to mention that I am completely cleaned out financially. I have no home, furniture or clothes.... The world has altogether changed around us. It didn't turn out the way any of us hoped. I can live with this just fine, but I don't know how you would put up with it.... Faces that were not long ago cruelly evil now grin with overwhelming friendship.... For myself, I do not want to re-establish our marriage—it is in both of our interests—which certainly does not mean that you cannot rely on me to the utmost extent, as much as I am able. If you are mad at me for this letter, maybe it makes you feel better that from the time you were deported up until now, every minute was miserable because I knew you were suffering and I couldn't help you. During this time, I didn't allow myself the smallest joy, that sacrificing all pleasure would perhaps make your life better.... My Magda, no matter what happens to us, however distant we are from each other, I will always think of the you that was kind to me. Imre.

Mrs. Gams, who is here, said that she got a note from your father in the camp at Auschwitz in which he inquired about you. It happened a few days after you left.

For a first letter, Imre's seems mean and cold. Don't come home. Our marriage is over. There is nothing left for you here. The relationship was an uncertain marriage. She was perhaps cruel, and Imre stiff and somewhat controlling. She responds, as one might imagine, in fury. Feeling betrayed by her closest friends, some of whom had already returned to Székesfehérvár with stories from the camps, and by Imre, she recounts a history that must now have seemed a world away to her. No part of my mother's survival has come without feelings of guilt; Imre's letter has intensified these feelings unbearably. She begins her story shortly after the time she and Imre last saw each other, the day after she walked, holding their daughter's hand, through town to the brickworks behind the train station.

I won't reproduce that letter here, for it still seems too raw. What Maria translated for me the day I went to visit them made me desperate to run away from a history that I had spent years trying to find. And yet it became my Rosetta stone; all has been reinterpreted in light of it. This is exactly what my mother didn't want, for she had done everything to avoid being defined by the horrors of the past. Imre received her angry account of what had happened to her, to Judit, and to her family and, deeply sorry for having hurt her, he writes an apologetic opus in response. His typed, 10,000-word letter tells his side of the story from the last time they saw each other, in early June of 1944 until October 1945, an epic in which he is both the hero and fool. He tells of the guilt of surviving in relative safety—a story that suggests competing traumas. It is a remarkable testament to the banality of survival, to mimic a phrase.

Between 2003 and 2006, I had the first two years of their correspondence transcribed and translated, a laborious and expensive process. Subsequent letters document my mother's exuberant partying with the American and British soldiers who liberated her (parties that also occupied the bulk of her postwar diaries); Imre's opportunities for revenge in his new role as the postwar police commandant for Székesfehérvár; the dissolution of their marriage; and her difficult decision about how to get out of Germany and where to go next. In 1946, Magda writes to Imre asking that he remove her from the list of the Jewish community. He writes back that no list of the living exists, only a long list of the people who have perished. Her letters chart the beginning of her survival strategy: she sheds her previous identity, and a few years later, with my father's encouragement, she tries to forget who and what she lost. Yet she continues her correspondence with Imre and her remaining Hungarian friends, and it becomes the place in which she is able to maintain a relationship with the past using a language she is sure none of her second family will ever be able to read.

It is rare to have both sides of a correspondence like this, the early letters in particular, which describe at length the postwar conditions in Hungary and Germany and the fate of survivors who have returned or are moving on. Tibor Szeszlér, the man who discovered my mother's letters, is a lawyer centrally involved with documenting anti-Semitism in post-1989 Hungary. He graciously relinquished any claim to the correspondence, but asked me to consider depositing it in the archives of the Budapest Holocaust Memorial Centre. And here the complicated questions began.

The historical value of this correspondence relies very much on making both sides accessible to researchers. As a description of relationships to people, places, and time deeply torn, and the strange immediacy of a return to normalcy, these letters constitute a history of Second World War Hungary and its brutalities, and so surely they belong there. But, even though I have written extensively about the story that emerges from these letters, what would it mean to return my mother's letters to Hungary and to an explicitly Jewish archive? Surely the correspondence as a whole would be most useful to Hungarian researchers involved in their own battles about remembrance and the reconstruction of a Jewish past, but would this not symbolically enact the very worst of my mother's fears and literalize Derrida's metaphor? Does the evidential value of the letters outweigh her obvious wish to leave the past behind? What if I were to deposit their correspondence in a Canadian archive? The usefulness of the correspondence to Canadian researchers would surely be limited by the language in which it is written. What if I were deposit the letters with the translations (including all the inaccuracies)? These kinds of immigrant letters are precisely those that build a picture of the nation in formation (as a place where people can leave the past behind). These questions bring an interesting element to theorizing the materiality of our "encounters." As Millar writes, "[o]ur level of 'trust' for the record is inextricably linked to the contextual information available: factual *and* emotional. We must ask why the record was created, and why it was kept" (117). And why and in what context it was archived:

> [R]egardless of what theory an archives or archivist adopts to ground their methods, especially those for appraisal, the act of selection gives archivists an important role as a creator or author of their archives. Decisions of choice need to be explicit. Once these have been declared, they become part of the larger memorial process, as the archivist's florilegia, in this case not on individual documents, but more profoundly, on the large archival "text" we shape in appraisal. These texts, like any other, are then available for critical assessment by others. (Craig 288–89)

Three archival forces are at work here: my mother's need to create a record of her experience elicited by various contexts, provoked and otherwise; my "instinctive sense," as Cox puts it, to "care for personal and family archives" (*Personal Archives* 3); and the competing desires of archivists, whose solicitation, selection, and guardianship of personal records is critical to collective memory. Although driven by interests profound and genuine, the decisions of archivists are also part of the context of the archival record.[4]

So, let's consider the value of my mother's archive central to the questions of how or why to institutionalize it: its historical value (a bit of which I have already described); its economic value (two different things, but not unrelated); its political value in tracing her geographic exiles and migrations (Hungary to Poland to Germany to England to Canada); its personal value in tracing a worthwhile life (any life is potentially interesting); and its potential value in its usefulness and accessibility to the future, not necessarily in that order. To understand the complexity of some of these dimensions, I had conversations about the materials with archivists in three university libraries: Dr. Carl Spadoni, Director of the William Ready Archives at McMaster, Suzanne Dubeau, the Assistant Head of the

Clara Thomas Archives at York, and Paul Banfield, University Archivist at Queen's.[5] Each of the archivists expressed a strong interest in my mother's papers, each for a different reason in a different context.

The William Ready Archives has, as one of its foci, a collection organized around the theme of peace and war, particularly with respect to the role of British pacifists in the First and Second World Wars, including the diaries of Vera Brittain. In 2008, with the donation of the Michel Brisebois collections, the archive acquired "nearly 2,000 items originating from prisoners held in German concentration camps, internment and transit camps, Gestapo prisons, and POW camps, during and just prior to World War II" ("Concentration Camps"). So here, my mother's letters would be in good company; she would have been delighted to have ended up with Vera Brittain, whose writing she admired enormously. "The best archives are the ones that hit you right here," said Dr. Spadoni, placing his hand on his heart, having just read to us from Vera Brittain's diary the moment when she finds out that her fiancée has been killed in combat (personal interview). The value of the historical record is not, in his estimation, in the grocery lists—something we might arguably find enormously interesting in women's archives—but the extraordinary moments of ordinary lives. As historian Deborah Montgomerie observes in her book, *Love in the time of War*, "[l]etters written and received in times of great stress...become poignant artefacts. Wartime letters carry with them a burden of sorrow and senseless loss as well as treasured remembrance" (qtd. in Cox, *Personal Archives* 44). The evidential uses of documents (the usual criteria for archive depositions) cannot, in the case of letters and manuscripts, be severed from the emotional value of a document, although affect and memory are not things that can be archived in any traditional sense. As Millar argues, "the record ultimately serves many purposes and facilitates many responses, some evidential and some psychological. We must understand the symbolic context surrounding the creation and preservation of the record, but we must acknowledge the gap between the record, the event, and the emotion" (116).

So is the letter that describes the devastating events on the platform at Auschwitz the single most important piece of my mother's ephemera? It was, indeed, enormously important to me when I found it, and it justified years of frustrating and sometimes fruitless research, the payoff of a detective story that drives so many of our hours with papers. In my case, much of that time was spent in Hungarian archive holdings that I could treat only as an exercise in "diplomatics" of reading by form and function, which would be the way most English readers interact with her letters. When I held her Rosetta stone letter for the first time, I had no idea what it said.

The date, the length, the density of the writing in pencil, words written all the way to the margin, two-sided—her attempt to make the best use of scarce paper—all told me something, but the content was only slowly decipherable.

Dr. Spadoni agreed after our first conversation that the letters would be better housed in Hungary because of the questions of linguistic access. One must keep in mind that archives are much more about the future than they are about the past, in the sense that archivists must anticipate the interests of future researchers, and thus the question of the accessibility of the materials is paramount. Recently, however, Dr. Spadoni wrote to me to tell me that one of his archivists does indeed read Hungarian, and that the McMaster archives was enlarging its collections of their Second World War documents, so perhaps we might continue our conversation. But at McMaster, her letters and everything else in her leftover boxes would be framed by the history and aftermath of the Second World War, a piece of her life, arguably, no more than five years long. Was the war the most important part of her life? Yes and no.

Should perhaps her letters to Imre be joined with his to her? Certainly, the value of their testimony is indisputable. To return her letters to Hungary, however, would be to return her in some phantasmal fashion, or at least the knowledge of her, to a place that severed her. Could her soul rest with her letters as Jewish testimony in the Hungarian Holocaust Archives? She'd torment me for the rest of my days. Strangely, by the letter of the law (lest we forget the archives are the letters of the law), her letters do not actually belong me to me to deposit where I would. The physical letters are always the property of the receiver, while copyright remains with the estate of the writer. So her letters are properly Imre's property and thus belong to the Szeszlér's, and Imre's letters are mine. The Szeszlér's wish is to donate all the letters to a Hungarian archive, although they have, very graciously so far, left the decision to me. Clearly, some arrangement must be made to house these letters together, if not physically—which would be, after all, an artificial arrangement, uniting a correspondence that was written and received countries and, later, continents apart, some of the originals ending up back from where they were sent—then perhaps virtually, reuniting the correspondence of a couple who only ever saw each other again for three days after they were forcibly separated in June of 1944. But (and you may have noticed by now that this paper moves from one "but" to another) virtual historical archives that are accessible to all bring with them, as Daniel Cohen and Roy Rosenzweig write in *Digital History*, some "unsettling implications," not the least of which is who will own the digital information in the end (9). So no digital reunion, not yet, not while outdated notions of privacy, archival access, and ownership still have some currency. Beyond the problems of digital history, the letters are only one part of my mother's life, and certainly not the part that she would have wanted to be public.

Does my Rosetta stone letter have significance as a single item, as part of a correspondence, or does its importance accrue in the context of a fonds? According to Suzanne Dubeau, a fonds is the "person in documentary form," an "organic accumulation of documents, the by-products of ordinary life and business" (personal interview). Or, as Catherine Hobbs puts it, "the fonds of an individual is where personality and the events of a life interact in documentary form," or more haphazardly, "the flotsam of the individual life" (127, 131). Is it the extraordinary or the ordinary, the most traumatic slice of life or the reconstitution of one that constitutes the value of fonds? Both together, it seems obvious. The larger part of my mother's life was spent in Kingston, Ontario, the town I grew up in. She had four children and wanted very much to have the life of a writer, succeeding in this to a measured extent. Her greater talent lay in her photographic eye. She began to photograph the "old stones" of Kingston, its artists and writers, and those who had acquired interesting faces just by living; from there, she built a portrait studio in which she did studies in black and white. Her archive also contains about a thousand negatives of three hundred subjects, and albums full of portraits, some stunning, some awkward, some penetrating; twenty years of work which the mice at the farmhouse, where all of this material is currently stored, have found quite appetizing. She said that photography had allowed her to see the beauty in people, while in writing she saw only the grotesque. And then the other ephemera: clippings, manuscripts, rejection letters (about forty for her two manuscripts), poems, daybooks, lists, love notes (from Lippstadt), and diaries. Is her life in Kingston any less substantial than her previous lives? Should her later material traces be separated from what came earlier? An ethical archive would argue no, that the organic whole is the best record of a life, a screed that binds most university archives to non-competition. And traces of her migrations should be, logically, included in her accumulation (minus, in strict terms, the letters she wrote). So then the question becomes, what archives would be the appropriate place for everything? Her Kingston life and her Hungarian past, which would otherwise remain compartmentalized? Queen's might seem like a logical answer—Paul Banfield, the archivist who took over from my father, is very interested in the photographs and would happily take everything, even if temporarily, just for preservation. A few of my father's papers are there, his research for a book on Sir Sandford Fleming. So Magda and Mario could be reunited. After all, they were married for thirty years, and her life in Kingston was intimately his—a very good reason not to put her papers there. A significant bundle of letters are from my father, letters he would have hated being part of the public record, especially at Queen's, where they had rejected him on the eve of his doctoral defence. And housing her with one husband or the other seems pre-feminist. No, not Queen's, but yes, perhaps, in the end.

York perhaps? York's special collections are concentrating their holdings in Canadiana and Canadian literary papers, most notably Margaret Laurence's (though McMaster does indeed hold some of the author's paper letters), brought by Professor Clara Thomas, after whom the collections were renamed. Here my mother's organic ephemera could be gathered under the sign of a Canadian writer, including every bit of the path that brought her. However, Suzanne Dubeau's initial contact with me was not about my mother's papers at all, but about mine. Would I think of depositing my papers there, she asked, after seeing an article about my documentary based on my mother's remarkable combination of silence and textuality. Why me? Adolescent love letters. Why me? Undergraduate essays, high school sports badges, records of administrative frustration and tedium. Why me? Filing cabinets and boxes of research materials. What would I throw out first? Might I not like to keep her papers close to mine? So much of my archives is about her. And Imre's letters? They would stay in Hungary, where I have returned them, accompanied by directions to her papers and mine, with copies of her letters to him. And in my papers one would find copies of his letters, with transcriptions and translations provided, an anathema to the idea of singularity and originality, but in this case, the trail of research and origin tied back together. At York, then, I would be the anchor and her papers would be, in some sense, a by-product of mine, with their value accruing to me. But I like the way that Dubeau, who has a passionate interest in the archives of Canadian women writers, talks about standing in the vault and listening to the conversations between artists. She could stand and listen to my mother and I fight for eternity.

People don't always want to donate to archives, said Dubeau, they have to be convinced, an observation echoed by other archivists in conversation and in print. Papers usually come to an archive at the end of a career or life, at time of emotional instability already. Donors fear they will lose their memories in what has been externalized, that the deposition of papers will bring on memory loss itself. "An archivist dealing with personal fonds is often confronted with the power of the individual" (Hobbs 132) and/ or her family members. "Many individual donors have a deep emotional investment in their records and for them the donation is usually a highly personal and emotional transaction over which some are inclined to feel a certain level of *post partum* anxiety.... In a way, it is exporting their own life" (132–33; emphasis in original). I would be butter in Hobbs's hands. What convinces people like me to deposit papers? Worth. Historical value—who doesn't want to part of the historical record, preserved indefinitely in humidity- and temperature-controlled vaults?—and tax receipts. Her "flotsam" may be one of the last generations of paper archives, letters in particular, historical artifacts in more than one sense, along with our ability to read them (Cox, *Personal Archives* 41). So what is her historical value? What monetary value would her papers generate? Mine? How would an expert assess their fair market value? How big would my tax receipt be if I donated them?

As I spin this narrative of where to deposit her papers, impugning the desires of the dead seems to bear some ethical weight in the debate. What would she have wanted? It is an impossible question to answer, since she never made any explicit arrangements. She had irreconcilable impulses, torn as she was between erasing and preserving her history, an ambivalence that left the decision in our hands. However, much more evident than her wishes, or even mine, are the desires of the archivists who would very much like to see her papers become, in some sense, theirs. The proprietary nature of archives has never been quite so clear to me as it is now, for the process of acquiring private records involves a change of ownership. In contrast to government records, which are kept or transferred, "private fonds are 'acquired' or 'collected'...private archives are private property until a public institution acquires them" (Fisher 49). Would I be willing to give up ownership? I am, in some sense, possessed by her papers rather than possessing them (Cox, *No Innocent Deposits* 5). They are the last relics of her and, indeed, are tinged with an almost mystical quality. They are the last intimate traces of my mother's body and, more disturbingly, a tortured soul I never knew. Would giving them away (or selling them, in a sense) end this interminable melancholia? Most of the content I will publish in one way or another, but my relationship to the objects is nowhere near resolved, I have realized. When I think about it this way, I cannot bear the thought of parting with the boxes in my closet, for the incorporation of their contents has reconfigured my psychic, historical, and political topography (Butler; Eng and Kazanjian). I think I'll wait until I die and risk the damage that might come to this fragile matter. I promise to make a note in my will.

Having begun the process of thinking about these things, I will look very differently at archived papers from now on. The kinds of questions I will ask about them have changed. Before I begin reading in an archive again, I will want to know everything I can about their deposition: Who deposited them? Why? Why there? Who was the archivist who arranged for the deposition? Why did they want the papers? What I have realized is that the conditions of deposition inevitably frames what and how we read the human record, that how and where we lock up a life indefinitely will define how that life is read in the future and the past.

Notes

1. Richard J. Cox's *Personal Archives and a New Archival Calling* (2008) and *No Innocent Deposits* (2004) have been central to the rethinking of this paper, on which he offered valuable comments. A different version of this essay, with some overlap, appears under the title "The Archive as Temporary Abode" in Creet and Kitzmann.
2. See Erös, Kovács, and Lévai.
3. The products of my pursuit of this story have been various: a documentary video, *MUM* (2008), many academic articles, non-fiction essays on witnessing, testimony, archives and identity, and a collaborative autobiography which is currently in the final stages of editing.
4. The appraisal and selection of personal records or "manuscripts" is a subject that archivists and literary critics have been debating for some time, although quite separately, for the most part. For a good overview of the debates about the selection criteria for personal papers, see Pollard's "The Appraisal of Personal Papers." The collection of essays from the Sawyer Seminar, *Archives, Documentation and Institutions of Social Memory* offers one of the richest collections of essays by key thinkers about the contexts of archives themselves. Cox's *No Innocent Deposits* is centrally concerned with the issues of contemporary appraisal. Fisher has worked out the broad outlines of a theory of private archives in "In Search of a Theory of Private Archives." In contrast, see Gerson's lament in "Locating Female Subjects in the Archives" that "literary critics tend to regard the archive as a neutral zone, untouched by the questions of selection, evaluation and subjectivity that they apply to their own more self-conscious interpretive activities" (7). For my purposes, Hobbs's evocative essay, "The Character of Personal Archives," which was one of four essays on the topic in *Archivaria* 52 (including Pollard's), comes closest to addressing the psychology of personal fonds and their deposition.
5. I wish to thank Dr. Carl Spadoni, Suzanne Dubeau, Paul Banfield, and Myron Momryk, former director of the Multicultural Archives Program at Library and Archives Canada, for their willingness to tutor me in the basics of archival science and to discuss the particularities of my mother's papers.

Works Cited

Banfield, Paul. Personal Interview. July 15, 2008.

Blouin, Francis X., and William G. Rosenberg. *Archives, Documentation, and Institutions of Social Memory: Essays from the Sawyer Seminar*. Ann Arbor: U of Michigan P, 2006. Print.

Butler, Judith. *The Psychic Life of Power: Theories in Subjection*. Stanford: Stanford UP, 1997. Print.

Cohen, Daniel, and Roy Rosenzweig. *Digital History: A Guide to Gathering, Preserving, and Presenting the Past on the Web*. Philadelphia: U of Pennsylvania P, 2006. Print.

Cox, Richard J. *No Innocent Deposits: Forming Archives by Rethinking Appraisal*. Lanham: Scarecrow, 2004. Print.

———. *Personal Archives and a New Archival Calling*. Duluth: Litwin, 2008. Print.

Craig, B. L. "Selected Themes in the Literature on Memory and their Pertinence to Archives." *American Archivist* 65.2 (2002): 276–89. Print.

Creet, Julia, and Andreas Kitzmann, eds. *Memory and Migration: Multidisciplinary Approaches to Memory Studies*. Toronto: U of Toronto P 2010. Print.

Derrida, Jacques. *Archive Fever: A Freudian Impression*. Trans. Eric Prenowitz. Chicago: U of Chicago P, 1996. Print.

Dubeau, Suzanne. Personal Interview. May 13, 2008.

Eng, David L., and David Kazanjian. *Loss: The Politics of Mourning*. Berkeley: U of California P, 2003. Print.

Erös, Jerenc, András Kovács, and Katalin Lévai. "Comment j'en suis arrivé à apprendre que j'étais juif." *Actes de la recherche en sciences sociales* 56 (1985): 63–68. Print.

Fisher, Robert. "In Search of a Theory of Private Archives: The Foundational Writings of Jenkinson and Schellenberg Revisited." *Archivaria* 67 (2009): 1–23. Web. Feb. 9, 2010.

Gerson, Carole. "Locating Female Subjects in the Archives." *Working in Women's Archives: Researching Women's Private Literature and Archival Documents*. Ed. Helen M. Buss and Marlene Kadar. Waterloo: Wilfrid Laurier UP, 2001. 7–22. Print.

Hobbs, Catherine. "The Character of Personal Archives: Reflections on the Value of Records of Individuals." *Archivaria* 52 (2001): 126–35. Print.

Millar, Laura. "Touchstones: Considering the Relationship between Memory and Archives." *Archivaria* 61 (2006): 105–26. Print.

Momryk, Myron. Personal Interview. July 9, 2008.

Pollard, Riva. A. "The Appraisal of Personal Papers: A Critical Literature Review." *Archivaria* 52 (2001): 136–50. Print.

Spadoni, Carl. Personal Interview. Apr. 3, 2008.

World War, 1939–1945, German Concentration Camps and Prisons collection. *William Ready Archives*. McMaster University Libraries, Hamilton, Canada, n.d. Web. Feb. 8, 2010. (http://library.mcmaster.ca/archives/findaids/fonds/w/ww2german.htm).

Afterword
Janice Fiamengo

I have often regretted that my graduate work in English, while thorough in many respects, did not involve training in the theory and methods of archival research. Passionate about the interpretation of stories, I did not, as a doctoral student, imagine that I would one day sit helplessly in front of a large box of all-but-illegible letters in the Flora MacDonald Denison collection at the Thomas Fisher Rare Book Library. Nor did I expect to confront numerous boxes crammed with scribblers, arranged in no chronological order and each filled with handwritten recipes, prayers, literary quotations, observations, bits of stories and fragments of speeches, in the Nellie McClung collection at the British Columbia Provincial Archives. At such moments, I felt as if I had been given a treasure trove whose worth I could not measure, let alone begin to count, order, record, and analyze. Usually I had only a few weeks, at most, to extract something useful from the papers in order to justify the institutional money I had used for the visit. Although I had read in Acknowledgements pages the sincere and even effusive thanks offered by researchers to archivists and librarians who gave "invaluable assistance," I was fearful of archivists and determined to interact with them as little as possible, sure that they had already found me out for the fraud I was.

A bad moment came early on in my perusal of the McClung papers as I was recording with my pencil, which wore down with dismaying frequency, McClung's thoughts about the First World War. I was aware that good work had already been published on McClung's response to the war, and I was unsure how fully I should pursue this strand of investigation, particularly because my immediate interest was her feminist writing. Yet, given that the war had confirmed McClung's suspicions about the masculine bias of politics, I moved doggedly to the next scribbler, my hand already aching. After a few pages of laborious note-taking, I realized that McClung was now writing about the Second World War, not the First as in the previous scribbler. Overwhelmed by the unruliness of the collection, I got up for a washroom break. It would take weeks, I fretted, simply to organize it all, let alone to read and digest everything. In this thought, I was not alone. Carole Gerson has remarked on the unlikelihood that the papers of any male figure of McClung's stature would remain in such a haphazard state for so long (12). My problem, however, was even larger than the disarray of the materials. It pertained to matters of interpretation, citation, emphasis: what to do if I could decipher only parts of a letter, where to concentrate my energies, what to pass over. The practical problems were vast.

Moreover, I was disappointed to find myself so ill at ease in archives generally. Whether due to the stale air, the sharp looks (real or imagined) of the archivists, or the dismaying complexities and magnitude of my task, the experience of sitting with a collection for even a few hours usually left me cramped, dopey, and longing for a sugary snack. There are books to be written, I suspect, about the conventions of reading rooms and how they do or do not facilitate productive research. Despite my awareness of limited time, I often left the archives before closing time, feeling drained of energy and unable to muster the necessary focus. Where was the rush of discovery that I had imagined, or at least the sustained, alert attention of the dedicated literary detective? What was I really looking for, and how would I know if I found it?

In the end, I made what I could of the papers, and some of my discoveries enriched my work, particularly in the voluminous scrapbooks McClung kept in which an abundance of unidentified newspaper clippings chronicled contemporary responses to her books and speeches. It was not all bad news: the experience of touching materials "my" writers had touched, such as a "Votes For Women" pin that Denison had almost certainly worn, or a yellowed flyer advertising a talk by McClung, would stay with me for years and give me a heady sense of the living presences behind the writers' words that complemented my already strong interest in their published writings. Still, I never felt I had made the best use of the papers, and I never lost the sense of blundering through precious resources. And I still shudder when I remember inadvertently tearing some of the newspaper clippings in McClung's scrapbooks.

Such practical and emotional aspects of archival research are glimpsed in the pages of *Basements and Attics, Closets and Cyberspace*, and although they are not the volume's primary focus, they enliven a collection that offers invaluable opportunities to think about the approaches, ethical questions, and guiding assumptions of women's archives. The discussions here are both personal and professional, and they range widely: from the initial questions surrounding a decision to create a personal archive to the researcher's challenges in tracking down information. Such pivotal matters, such as how we know what counts as a significant finding, how we make sense of what is missing, and how we know what we can safely ignore, if there *is* anything we can safely ignore, are the source of provocative reflection throughout. Even the very idea of the archive, and what counts as a historical document, are searchingly reconsidered in essays by T. L. Cowan, Cecily Devereux, Karis Shearer and Jessica Schagerl, and Kathleen Venema, to name only a few. These essays ask us to think anew about how memory is shaped and preserved, and about the potentially transformative roles of scholars, activists, and creative individuals.

Other essays in the collection explore the challenges and disciplinary biases of more traditional types of archival scholarship. To take one example, Susan Butlin's discussion of her research into the life and works of Florence Carlyle, a painter who supported herself with commissioned pictures for an American calendar company, is candid in confronting the bias against commercial art that threatened to derail the study: had Butlin not faced and overcome this bias, she reflects, her account of Carlyle's painting life would have been skewed. The essay not only testifies to the painstaking work involved in such a research project but also to the scholar's struggle to find a just vision of her subject. Sometimes that vision is blocked or enhanced, and certainly it is always influenced, by the ever-changing emphases and priorities of scholarly disciplines. The increasing interest in women's popular art must have facilitated Butlin's reorientation of the project, and I wondered if whether, in the absence of such scholarship, Butlin might have been even more strongly tempted, as I'm sure I would have been, to minimize or skirt altogether the evidence that she initially "looked at...out of the corner of [her] eye"?

Butlin's essay raises the fascinating question, addressed directly or indirectly in so many of these essays, of how contemporary valuations of worth inevitably affect the narratives we make of archival materials. No matter how careful our work, it is impossible to escape the influence of our institutional and community frames of reference, nor would we want to "escape" them, of course, since doing so would prevent our joining the conversations of our era. I was always aware in my work with McClung's papers that I was reading her materials through the lens of recent discussions, particularly the debates about race that had dominated feminist scholarship for a decade or more. In the 1930s and 1940s, as the aggressions of imperial Japan filled newspaper headlines, McClung made a number of sympathetic references to Asian communities on the Canadian West Coast in newspaper articles. I paid close attention to what, and how much, she wrote about the internment of Japanese Canadian citizens in 1942. She was one of the few to deplore their treatment, although not as vehemently or consistently as modern-day scholars might wish; I was disappointed not to find more references to the subject.

I have since questioned how much my need to join the charged conversation about McClung's racial attitudes—perhaps explicitly to defend McClung from some of her more unsympathetic detractors, or at least to complicate the picture they had presented—influenced what I noticed in the archive and how I interpreted it; and, perhaps more seriously, I question how the significance of race crowded out other impressions I might have formed, other details I might have noticed. Was it distorting or simply appropriate, even while distorting, that a specifically modern ideological perspective had become the measure of McClung's significance as a social activist? It was naive, of course, for me to imagine a pure consciousness through which to perceive her, free from ideology. Our implication in contemporary ways of seeing means that archives are inexhaustible, potentially revealing new meanings to every scholar, and almost certainly every generation of scholars, who searches in them. This understanding may free us from the impossible imperative of comprehensiveness, but it is unsettling to think that our work is so historically contingent.

Vanessa Brown and Benjamin Lefebvre address a related issue in their essay about the interpretative puzzle of the so-called suicide note found at L. M. Montgomery's deathbed. The note caused a justifiable explosion of interest among Montgomery scholars and fans when it was revealed in 2008, and led to some seemingly definitive pronouncements about the last days of her life. On further examination, however, the meaning of the note is far from self-evident, reminding us once again and in a most arresting manner that the private self we hope to encounter in the archive remains elusive, the truth of that self a matter always, even with concrete evidence, of conjecture and judgment. On a related issue, Linda Morra uses the engaging example of a man who sought to claim a connection to Ira Dilworth, Emily Carr's friend and correspondent, to explore the question of how researchers decide, often intuitively or by chance, to follow certain leads rather than others, and how we attribute meaning to memories and stories.

Morra's reflections on the usefulness of anecdotal evidence, and on the care required to interpret it, bring us back to scholars' need to consider assumptions about value. This is a problem in all humanities scholarship where choice of evidence and interpretation of texts are involved. It seems particularly relevant to feminist work on women's lives, given the feminist acknowledgement of a political agenda to recognize the primacy of gender in culture and to make women central to our accounts. To what extent does the emphasis on gender—on women's presumed differences from men, on the oppressions women have faced—determine our conclusions? What happens to scholarly objectivity in such research? If we decide that objectivity is impossible anyway, although it might still be worked toward, is it enough to acknowledge biases honestly? Or is it in the nature of a bias to be unconscious and unacknowledgeable?

The feminist commitment to redress bias may remind us of ongoing challenges. In my work with McClung more recently, I have found myself both compelled and restrained by my chagrined sense that her Christian faith has been often slighted or denounced by feminist scholars for whom Christianity is, uniquely among faiths, it seems, synonymous with exploitation and bigotry; in countering such bias, I recognize my inclination to present a McClung whose faith is inextricable from her achievements. This issue of conscious or unconscious advocacy is even more charged when a scholar feels herself working with sensitive cultural materials on behalf of vulnerable communities, as is the case with many of the essays here, and the writers approach their subjects with different convictions about their scholarly and personal allegiances.

More general ethical questions are raised by many in the collection, and remain haunting and urgent. In discussing her struggle over where and whether to deposit her mother's letters, Julia Creet addresses the wider question of what we owe to the dead. Ruth Panofsky and Michael Moir present a gripping account—more gripping perhaps for the absence of exclamation marks—of the problems created by Adele Wiseman's daughter's decision to require, and withhold, special permission from scholars wishing to quote from the author's papers. The issue of privacy is fraught and fascinating, as it emerges also in Andrea Beverly's account of her research into the Telling It conference, research that revealed the name of a participant who asked that her remarks and identity be removed from the book that emerged from the conference. Beverly's own decision not to reveal the woman's identity points again, in a different manner, to the potential conflict between privacy and access, as do the many questions asked here by creative writers about whether personal letters should be placed in open collections. How far should privacy requests be honoured? Does feminist scholarship distinguish itself by a special sensitivity to matters of privacy, even when requests may seem unreasonable? Where do the personal and the scholarly intersect, and how far should we probe in investigating subjects who are still alive, or only recently dead? The precise nature of the questions changes with each particular archive.

And always there remain the practical difficulties of the archives, which many of us know so well. Because archival work is often arduous and time-consuming, because it is risky for graduate students and young scholars in a profession that insists on timely completion of degrees and high productivity, it is important for scholars to discuss its complex processes, not only to share insights and strategies but also to encourage and equip one another. The papers collected here have begun to address the myriad difficulties, decisions, dead ends, disappointments, unresolved questions, interpretative quandaries, and provisional resolutions that researchers and writers confront. They also speak vividly of the joys of archival research, its great potential and satisfactions. As we become more self-critical about the institutional biases of archives and our own scholarly and personal prejudices, our opportunities to examine and theorize the practice of archival research will continue to develop. Such discussions are well worth pursuing.

Works Cited

Gerson, Carole. "Locating Female Subjects in the Archives." *Working in Women's Archives: Researching Women's Private Literature and Archival Documents*. Ed. Helen M. Buss and Marlene Kadar. Waterloo: Wilfrid Laurier UP, 2001. 7–22. Print.

Contributors

Catherine Bates is a lecturer at Keele University, UK. Her research and published work focuses on ethical reading practices and the micro-politics of mourning, messy archives and life writing, and the ways in which waste becomes imbricated within communication and everyday living. She is working on two monographs: *Alibis, Decoys and Backdoors: Robert Kroetsch's Resistant Life-Writings* and *Regarding Discard: Refigurations of Rubbish in Contemporary Literature*.

Andrea Beverley is originally from New Brunswick and lives in Montreal, where she is currently completing her doctoral dissertation in the Études anglaises department at the Université de Montréal. Her work focuses on contemporary Canadian women's writing and anti-essentialist feminism. Andrea is also a mother, a community volunteer, a teacher, and a member of the TransCanada/TransQuébec PhD Student Workgroup.

Vanessa Brown received her BA (Hons.) in English from the University of Western Ontario and works as an antiquarian book cataloguer at Attic Books in London, Ontario. A prizewinner in the 2009 Bibliographical

Society of Canada's National Book Collecting Contest, she collects rare editions related to L. M. Montgomery and her work.

Susan Butlin is the author of *The Practice of Her Profession: Florence Carlyle, Canadian Painter in the Age of Impressionism* (McGill-Queen's UP, 2009). Prior to receiving her PhD in Canadian Studies (2008), she worked as a curator. Her current research and writing projects continue in the areas of women artists and Canadian cultural history.

Sally Clark was born in Vancouver and is a critically acclaimed playwright who dazzles audiences with her penchant for dark humour, ironic wit, and sharp character portrayals. She has been playwright-in-residence at Theatre Passe Muraille, the Shaw Festival, Buddies in Bad Times Theatre, and Nightwood Theatre. She is also a painter, director, and filmmaker. When she was a resident artist at the Canadian Film Centre, she wrote and directed her award-winning short film *Ten Ways to Abuse an Old Woman*. Her papers are held in the Archives and Special Collections at the University of Guelph.

T. L. Cowan is Assistant Professor of Women's and Gender Studies and English at the University of Saskatchewan.

Julia Creet is an Associate Professor in the Department of English at York University. She has produced a documentary, *MUM*, about the memoirs of a Holocaust survivor who tried to forget, and she is completing a book of literary non-fiction based on the same story. She has published numerous essays on identity, memory, and testimony in various academic and literary journals, including *The Journal of Aesthetics and Culture, differences, Applied Semiotics, Paradoxa, English Studies in Canada, Resources for Feminist Research, Toronto Life, West Coast Line,* and *Exile*. Several of her essays have been translated into Hungarian and Polish, and others have been published in edited collections in Sweden and the Netherlands.

Cecily Devereux teaches in the Department of English and Film Studies at the University of Alberta. Focusing on women's writing and representations of women in nineteenth- and early-twentieth-century English Canada, she has published work on the politics of race, gender, maternalism, and empire in the Canadian context, and she is currently completing a book-length study of women's writing in English Canada, 1769–1914.

Janice Fiamengo is a professor of English at the University of Ottawa, specializing in Canadian literature. She is the author of *The Woman's Page:*

Journalism and Rhetoric in Early Canada (2008) as well as numerous articles on women's writing in Canada.

Catherine Hobbs is the Literary Archivist (English-language) at Library and Archives Canada. She is Chair of the Special Interest Section on Personal Archives in the Association of Canadian Archivists. In 2011, she was elected to the steering committee of the Section on Literary and Art Archives in the International Council of Archives. She has taught seminars and published articles on literary archives as well as personal archives and is an Adjunct Professor for the Public Texts Programme at Trent University.

Penn Kemp, an award-winning poet/performer, has published twenty-five books of poetry and drama, ten CDs, six videopoems, and a DVD. Some of her work can be found at http://www.myspace.com/pennkemp, and http://www.mytown.ca/pennkemp/. Penn presents her Sound Operas on http://www.chrwradio.com/talk/gatheringvoices. She was the University of Western Ontario's writer-in-residence for 2009–10. The League of Poets has proclaimed Penn a foremother of Canadian poetry. See also http://www.mytown.ca/pennletters.

Benjamin Lefebvre is a Leverhulme Visiting Fellow at the University of Worcester and the Director of the L. M. Montgomery Research Group. He edited Montgomery's rediscovered final book *The Blythes Are Quoted* (2009) and co-edited *Anne's World: A New Century of Anne of Green Gables* (2010).

Hannah McGregor is a doctoral candidate at the University of Guelph's School of English and Theatre Studies, where she is also a doctoral fellow at the TransCanada Institute. Her doctoral research engages with postcolonial theory and the ethics of reading and representation in the context of contemporary Canadian literature.

Susan McMaster is the President of the League of Canadian Poets and author or editor of some two dozen books, magazines, and anthologies. She has also made recordings with First Draft, SugarBeat, and Geode Music & Poetry. She was the founding editor of Canada's first feminist magazine, *Branching Out*, and has organized such projects as *Dangerous Graces: Women's Poetry on Stage* (Great Canadian Theatre Company) and *Convergence: Poems for Peace*, which brought poetry and art from across Canada to MPs and senators for the millennium.

Daphne Marlatt is a Vancouver poet and novelist whose work spans four decades. Her long poem in prose fragments, *The Given*, received the 2009 Dorothy Livesay Poetry Award. In 2009, she collaborated with filmmaker Aerlyn Weissman and wrote her first film script, a short drama called *The Portside*, which premiered that year at Vancouver's Gay Film Festival. On the coast and in Ontario, she has performed her poetry with the Minden Duo. Talonbooks recently released her award-winning contemporary Noh play *The Gull*, in a bilingual edition with a selection of photographs from the 2006 Pangaea Arts binational, bicultural production in Richmond, BC.

Michael Moir began his career as an archivist in 1982. He served as Director of Corporate Records Systems and City Archivist for the City of Toronto from 1998 to 2004, when he was appointed University Archivist and Head of the Clara Thomas Archives and Special Collections of York University Libraries.

Linda M. Morra is an Associate Professor in the Department of English at Bishop's University. Her publications include an edition of Emily Carr's letters, *Corresponding Influence: Selected Letters of Emily Carr and Ira Dilworth* (2006) and Jane Rule's autobiography, *Taking My Life* (2011), which was shortlisted for the LAMDA prize in 2012. She is currently writing a book-length study that examines five Canadian women as case studies in relation to archives and agency.

Ruth Panofsky is a Professor of English at Ryerson University, where she specializes in Canadian Literature and Culture. Her publications on Adele Wiseman include *The Force of Vocation: The Literary Career of Adele Wiseman*; *Adele Wiseman: Essays on Her Works* (editor); *Selected Letters of Margaret Laurence and Adele Wiseman* (co-editor); and *Adele Wiseman: An Annotated Bibliography*.

Jessica Schagerl holds a PhD from The University of Western Ontario, where she works in the field of institutional advancement.

Karis Shearer is an Assistant Professor in the Faculty of Creative and Critical Studies at the University of British Columbia (Okanagan), where she teaches Canadian literature and drama. Her ongoing research, which was supported by a 2010–2011 Canada–U.S. Fulbright Visiting Research Chair, is on Canadian poets' pedagogy. She has published articles on a number of Canadian writers, including Tomson Highway, Jane Urquhart, and George Bowering.

Katja Thieme studies Canadian writing from the late-nineteenth and early-twentieth centuries, particularly public debates about women's suffrage. She teaches academic writing, language theory, and Canadian Studies for the Arts Studies in Research and Writing course at the University of British Columbia.

Paul Tiessen teaches English and Film Studies at Wilfrid Laurier University. His recent work includes *After Green Gables: L. M. Montgomery's Letters to Ephraim Weber, 1916–1941*, co-edited with Hildi Froese Tiessen (UTP, 2006), and the art-historical text for *Woldemar Neufeld's Canada: A Mennonite Artist in the Canadian Landscape, 1925–1995*, edited by Laurence Neufeld and Monika McKillen (WLUP, 2010). He is writing a book on McLuhan and Modernism, with emphasis on work by Sheila Watson and Wilfred Watson, and co-editing works by Malcolm Lowry.

Kathleen Venema is an Associate Professor in the Department of English at the University of Winnipeg and has several publications on letters and archives, including "'a trading shop so crooked a man could jump through the cracks': Counting the Cost of Fred Stenson's *Trade* in the Hudson's Bay Company Archive," which appears in *National Plots* (WLUP, 2010).

Karina Vernon is an Assistant Professor of English at the University of Toronto Scarborough. She is a co-founder of Commodore Books, the first black literary press in Western Canada, and a member of the Hogan's Alley Memorial Project, a grassroots cultural organization engaged in local archival work toward the publication of an oral history of black Vancouver.

Index

A

Alzheimer's disease, 5, 14, 18, 209, 281–301; ethics of Alzheimer's archive, 286–88; memories and, 282, 285, 290–93, 296

anecdote, 8, 9, 17, 27, 52, 66–85, 105, 144, 249–62, 290; *Anecdotal Theory*, 252, 261; oral vs. written, 155–68, 198–99, 252–55; value of, 66–85, 249–62

antiquarians: relationship to archivists, 235–36, 245

archival collections: Adele Wiseman fonds, 16, 169–80; Alberta Provincial Archives, 199; British Columbia Archives and Record Service (BCARS), 254–56, 262; British Columbia Provincial Archives, 171–75, 177, 311, 319, 327; Canadian National Exhibition archives, 145; City of Edmonton Archives, 199; City of Ottawa, 210–11, 214; Clara Thomas Archives, 171–77, 311, 327; Daphne Marlatt Fonds, 161–68; Flora MacDonald Denison collection, 319; John M. Kelly Library Special Collections, 267, 279; Library and Archives Canada (LAC), 11, 17, 27, 31, 33–34, 157, 161, 165–68, 172, 193–204, 210–11, 236, 256, 267, 275, 316; Library of Congress, 31, 34, 45, 180; Literary Heritage Society of Ottawa, 210; Macmillan Company of Canada fonds, 171; McMaster Archives, 127, 171, 172, 210, 236, 241, 247, 310,

312, 314, 317; Museum London archive, 145, 146, 153; Penn Kemp fonds, 125–30; Provincial Archives of Alberta, 198, 203; Sally Clark fonds, 133–39; Sheila Watson fonds, 8, 11, 263–80; Susan McMaster fonds, 17, 50, 207–14; Thomas Fisher Rare Book Library, 247, 319; University of Guelph Archives and Special Collections, 134, 234, 236–41, 246–48, 326; Vancouver City Archives, 25; York University archives, 169–76, 327

archive: acquisition and, 2, 10–11, 33–34, 48, 179–85, 189, 190, 236, 251; Afghanistan and, 16, 107–24; alternative, 2, 4, 7, 11, 15, 16, 24, 26, 29–46, 47–63, 89; *arkhë*, 5, 23, 95; art history canon and, 14, 141–54; Black Prairie, 12, 17, 193–204; Christianity and, 323; creation of, 1, 2, 6, 9, 11, 49, 52, 79, 80, 101, 115, 127–30, 155–68, 170, 178, 182–91, 198, 203, 208, 264, 267–68, 285–87, 303–17, 321; cross-border, 13; as cultural commentary, 51; cultural memory and, 10, 35–44, 74–82, 91, 178, 251; definitions of, 1–15, 43, 52–54, 91–92, 99, 109, 115, 190, 260–61, 290, 297, 316, 322; deposition and, 2–5, 8, 11–17, 171, 236, 303–16; diaspora and, 110–21, 199–202; digitization of, 6, 15, 16, 18, 29–44, 47–62, 128–30, 182, 189, 190, 237, 312–13; as documentary, 107–24, 326; ephemera and, 5, 8, 16, 30–36, 74, 80–82, 132, 143, 188, 199–201, 234, 236, 251, 285, 303–15; ethics and, 5–17, 54, 57–61, 89, 91, 103, 107–22, 150, 155–65, 178–79, 181–91, 250–51, 258–60, 264, 281–96, 303–16, 321, 323; ethnic groups and, 26, 71, 157, 194–97, 225; Indigenous and, 3, 4, 29–44, 72, 203, 254; literary executor and, 13, 170–72, 190, 267; literature and, 1–2, 15, 93, 162, 176, 178, 182–84, 187, 233–46, 265; material history and, 127; media and, 5, 8, 30, 35, 40, 45, 58, 60, 68, 83, 87, 108–14, 121, 128, 129, 151, 190, 264–79; memory and, 7, 10, 14–18, 24–27, 35–36, 40, 44, 53, 67, 69, 74–82, 84, 89, 91, 105, 142, 198–203, 250, 251, 281–96, 303, 310–14, 316, 321, 323; multiculturalism and, 17, 25, 193–203; national identity and, 112; oral history and, 24–26, 198–99, 203; policies and, 144, 178–79, 155–66, 169–204; race, racial attitudes, and, 30, 41–44, 155–57, 194–202, 225, 322; repertoire-knowledges and, 65–85; restrictions and, 3, 9–13, 16, 57, 60, 161, 169–79, 212; rhetorical strategies and, 58, 216–28; theories of, 1–15, 43, 52–54, 91–92, 99, 109, 115, 150, 190, 201, 260–61, 290, 297, 316, 322; value of, 14, 24, 30, 32, 37, 41, 43, 48, 52, 56–59, 138, 163, 189, 197, 199, 200, 210, 211, 236–40, 243, 250, 256, 258, 286, 303–16, 323; writers and, 11, 12, 23–28, 125–32, 133–40, 155–68, 169–79, 181–89, 207–14, 264

archivist, and antiquarian, 235–45; privacy and, 14, 15, 27, 129, 135, 157, 160–69, 175, 177–80, 183, 190, 286, 313, 323–34; relationship with donor and, 180–92
Artelle, Steven, 210
Association of Canadian Archivists: *Code of Ethics*, 179, 163, 166, 178, 179, 190, 191
Audition, 108, 109, 111, 116, 117, 118, 119, 122. *See also* Pazira, Nelofer

B
Ball, Nelson, 127
Barbe, Serge, 208, 211, 212, 214
Baudrillard, Jean, 32, 44, 125, 130
Berlant, Lauren, 60, 62, 298
Beynon, Francis Marion, 15, 17, 208, 210, 212, 214, 215, 216, 218–30
blog, 6, 8, 69, 73, 75, 76, 77, 79; as archive 6, 8, 47–63; women and, 6, 48, 49. *See also* cyberspace
Breedlove, Lynn, 65, 66, 70, 78, 82, 84
Buss, Helen, 2, 19, 107, 117, 122, 123, 153, 167, 233, 246, 317, 324, 332

C
cabaret, feminist, 15, 16, 52, 65, 66, 68–76, 79–85, 262; Choice Words, 65, 66–70, 73, 75–76, 79–85
Canadian Authors Association, 214
Carlyle, Florence, 10, 14, 15, 16, 141–54; calendar paintings, 145, 148–51, 321; *Summer*, 147–48
Carr, Emily, 15, 149, 150, 153, 154, 249, 250, 253–62, 322, 328
Caruth, Cathy, 296, 299
CBC, 106, 111, 112, 115, 123, 214
Code, Lorraine, 7, 82, 84, 255, 262
Cox, Richard, 5, 6, 10, 19, 27, 49, 52, 57, 61, 62, 125, 130, 163, 166, 304, 310, 311, 315, 316, 317
Coyote, Ivan E., 65, 77, 78, 79, 82, 84
Cvetkovitch, Ann, 77, 82, 84, 109, 115, 123, 200, 203, 251, 262, 284, 285, 286, 290, 298, 299
cyberspace, 1, 2, 3, 4, 5, 321, 334; Internet and, 15, 31, 53, 58, 129, 209, 299. *See also* digital

D
de Certeau, Michel, 89, 90, 91, 98, 104, 105, 106, 121
Denison, Flora MacDonald, 228, 319–21
Derrida, Jacques, 4, 5, 7, 19, 49, 53, 80, 90, 92, 98, 105, 106, 123, 200, 201, 252, 257, 261, 282, 284, 295, 297, 299, 303, 305, 310, 317
Dever, Maryanne, et al., 7, 9, 10, 12, 19, 50, 62, 157, 187, 189, 190, 191
digital, 6, 15, 16, 18, 29–44, 47–62, 128–30, 182, 189, 190, 237, 312–13
documentary, 107–24; auto-Orientalizing and, 116, 121
donors, 98, 174–79, 183, 209, 314; control of archive and, 174–79

E
eBay, 8, 15, 29, 31–41, 43, 44, 45, 122n4
Engel, Marian, 8, 16, 87, 89, 92–96, 98, 99, 100, 103, 106, 162, 168, 332
ethics, 5–17, 54, 57–61, 89, 91, 103, 107–22, 150, 155–65, 178–79, 181–91, 250–51, 258–60, 264, 281–96, 303–16, 321, 323

F
female journalists, 16, 219
Feminist Archive North, 87, 88

Flahiff, F.T., 11, 264, 266–70, 275, 276n6, 277n7, 278n13, 279
Foucault, Michel, 92, 123, 288, 296, 299
Francis, Daniel, 30, 37–38

G
Gallop, Jane, 80, 81, 84, 251, 252, 253, 255, 256, 257, 258, 260, 262
Gerson, Carole, 2, 217, 231, 316, 317, 320, 324
Gilmore, Leigh, 286, 287, 288, 292, 298, 300
Goddard, Anne, 207, 214
gossip, 7–8, 27, 73, 82n4, 90, 213, 255, 258. *See also* anecdote
Grain Growers' Guide, 17, 216, 218, 220, 221, 226
Green, Rayna, 30, 36, 38, 40, 42, 44, 203
Group of Seven, 149, 150, 153, 154, 158, 257

H
Henry, Paul, 210, 214
Highway, Tomson, 39, 44
Hobbs, Catherine, 10, 16, 19, 50, 182, 191, 210, 214n1, 250, 262, 313, 317
Hutcheon, Linda, 142, 154

I
Indian maiden, 15, 29, 30, 31, 32, 35, 36–44, 45

K
Kadar, Marlene, ii, 2, 19, 107, 122, 123, 153, 154, 163, 164, 167, 168, 246, 317, 324, 332, 333
Kamboureli, Smaro, 121, 122, 123

Kandahar, 108–14, 117, 120, 123
King, Thomas, 38, 44
Kirsch, Gesa E., and Liz Rohan, 10, 19, 44, 45, 84, 251, 253, 258, 259, 260, 262

L
Laurence, Margaret, 169, 170, 171, 172, 176, 314
Lemon Hound, 15, 48–62
letters, 1, 4, 12, 14, 18, 27, 50, 52, 135, 142, 145–46, 158, 160–62, 169–77, 207–10, 212–14, 215–28, 234–36, 245, 252, 254, 256, 266, 269, 271–74, 278, 283–85, 288–94, 297–98, 303–18, 319, 320, 323, 324
Lewis, Wyndham, 266, 270–75
Library of Congress, 31, 34
Literary Heritage Society of Ottawa, 210

M
Macbeth, Madge, 151, 153n13, 212, 214
manuscripts, 54, 88, 89, 98, 135, 160, 162, 175, 176, 209, 240, 267, 269, 274, 311, 313, 316n4
Marlatt, Daphne, 13, 15, 23, 53, 155–59, 161, 162, 165, 166, 327
McClung, Nellie, 217, 219, 319–23
McLuhan, Marshall, 11, 263, 265–67, 269–79
Mojica, Monique, 39
Montgomery, L. M., 7, 15, 17, 141, 233–46, 322; *Anne of Green Gables*, 233, 234, 235, 237, 239, 246, 247, 248, 327, 328
Multicultural Initiatives Office, 194, 196, 202, 204
Munro, Alice, 8, 16, 89, 90, 96–99, 101, 104, 175, 177, 210

N
Naficy, Hamid, 111, 119
National Gallery of Canada (NGC), 143, 144

O
O'Driscoll, Michael, 109; Edward Bishop and, 4, 277, 290
oral history, 24–26, 198–99, 203n2

P
Pazira, Nelofer, 10, 16, 108–22
photographs, 3, 25–27, 29, 42, 80, 90, 92, 98, 102, 143, 145, 147, 148, 188, 200, 208, 234, 246n2, 264, 266, 271–72, 278n12, 304, 306, 313

Q
Queyras, Sina, 47, 48–52, 54–61, 63

R
Razack, Sherene, 114, 115
Return to Kandahar, 108–14, 116, 117, 119, 120
Rubio, Mary, 2, 141, 236–40, 242–44
Rules for Archival Description (RAD), 186, 190

S
Schultz, Lucilee M., 11, 251, 254
Sharer, Wendy, 35
Shields, Carol, 188, 189, 191

Society of American Archivists, 175, 191
Steedman, Carolyn, 5, 7, 8, 283, 290, 292, 297, 298
Stoler, Ann Laura, 5, 7, 61, 91, 99, 108, 109, 112, 114, 115, 261
Strong-Boag, Veronica, 151, 217

T
Telling It (conference), 9, 155, 156, 157, 159, 160, 163, 164, 165
Telling It (collective), 16, 155, 156, 157, 158, 159, 160, 161, 163
Thobani, Sunera, 109, 110, 112, 116, 117, 119–22
Thomas, Clara, 176, 314

U
University Women's Club, 256

V
Valaskakis, Gail Guthrie, 30, 35, 38, 40, 42
van Herk, Aritha, 103, 104, 270, 277

W
Watson, Sheila, 6, 8, 11, 15, 17, 260, 263–79
Watson, Wilfred, 6, 11, 270, 275
Wiebe, Rudy, 264, 265, 274, 276
Williams, Raymond, 150
Wiseman, Adele, 16, 169–77, 179, 323
Women's Art Club, 147

Books in the Life Writing Series
Published by Wilfrid Laurier University Press

Haven't Any News: Ruby's Letters from the Fifties edited by Edna Staebler with an Afterword by Marlene Kadar • 1995 / x + 165 pp. / ISBN 0-88920-248-6

"I Want to Join Your Club": Letters from Rural Children, 1900–1920 edited by Norah L. Lewis with a Preface by Neil Sutherland • 1996 / xii + 250 pp. (30 b&w photos) / ISBN 0-88920-260-5

And Peace Never Came by Elisabeth M. Raab with Historical Notes by Marlene Kadar • 1996 / x + 196 pp. (12 b&w photos, map) / ISBN 0-88920-281-8

Dear Editor and Friends: Letters from Rural Women of the North-West, 1900–1920 edited by Norah L. Lewis • 1998 / xvi + 166 pp. (20 b&w photos) / ISBN 0-88920-287-7

The Surprise of My Life: An Autobiography by Claire Drainie Taylor with a Foreword by Marlene Kadar • 1998 / xii + 268 pp. (8 colour photos and 92 b&w photos) / ISBN 0-88920-302-4

Memoirs from Away: A New Found Land Girlhood by Helen M. Buss / Margaret Clarke • 1998 / xvi + 153 pp. / ISBN 0-88920-350-4

The Life and Letters of Annie Leake Tuttle: Working for the Best by Marilyn Färdig Whiteley • 1999 / xviii + 150 pp. / ISBN 0-88920-330-x

Marian Engel's Notebooks: "Ah, mon cahier, écoute" edited by Christl Verduyn • 1999 / viii + 576 pp. / ISBN 0-88920-333-4 cloth / ISBN 0-88920-349-0 paper

Be Good Sweet Maid: The Trials of Dorothy Joudrie by Audrey Andrews • 1999 / vi + 276 pp. / ISBN 0-88920-334-2

Working in Women's Archives: Researching Women's Private Literature and Archival Documents edited by Helen M. Buss and Marlene Kadar • 2001 / vi + 120 pp. / ISBN 0-88920-341-5

Repossessing the World: Reading Memoirs by Contemporary Women by Helen M. Buss • 2002 / xxvi + 206 pp. / ISBN 0-88920-408-x cloth / ISBN 0-88920-410-1 paper

Chasing the Comet: A Scottish-Canadian Life by Patricia Koretchuk • 2002 / xx + 244 pp. / ISBN 0-88920-407-1

The Queen of Peace Room by Magie Dominic • 2002 / xii + 115 pp. / ISBN 0-88920-417-9

China Diary: The Life of Mary Austin Endicott by Shirley Jane Endicott • 2002 / xvi + 251 pp. / ISBN 0-88920-412-8

The Curtain: Witness and Memory in Wartime Holland by Henry G. Schogt • 2003 / xii + 132 pp. / ISBN 0-88920-396-2

Teaching Places by Audrey J. Whitson • 2003 / xiii + 178 pp. / ISBN 0-88920-425-x

Through the Hitler Line by Laurence F. Wilmot, M.C. • 2003 / xvi + 152 pp. / ISBN 0-88920-448-9

Where I Come From by Vijay Agnew • 2003 / xiv + 298 pp. / ISBN 0-88920-414-4

The Water Lily Pond by Han Z. Li • 2004 / x + 254 pp. / ISBN 0-88920-431-4

The Life Writings of Mary Baker McQuesten: Victorian Matriarch edited by Mary J. Anderson • 2004 / xxii + 338 pp. / ISBN 0-88920-437-3

Seven Eggs Today: The Diaries of Mary Armstrong, 1859 and 1869 edited by Jackson W. Armstrong • 2004 / xvi + 228 pp. / ISBN 0-88920-440-3

Love and War in London: A Woman's Diary 1939–1942 by Olivia Cockett; edited by Robert W. Malcolmson • 2005 / xvi + 208 pp. / ISBN 0-88920-458-6

Incorrigible by Velma Demerson • 2004 / vi + 178 pp. / ISBN 0-88920-444-6

Auto/biography in Canada: Critical Directions edited by Julie Rak • 2005 / viii + 264 pp. / ISBN 0-88920-478-0

Tracing the Autobiographical edited by Marlene Kadar, Linda Warley, Jeanne Perreault, and Susanna Egan • 2005 / viii + 280 pp. / ISBN 0-88920-476-4

Must Write: Edna Staebler's Diaries edited by Christl Verduyn • 2005 / viii + 304 pp. / ISBN 0-88920-481-0

Pursuing Giraffe: A 1950s Adventure by Anne Innis Dagg • 2006 / xvi + 284 pp. (photos, 2 maps) / 978-0-88920-463-8

Food That Really Schmecks by Edna Staebler • 2007 / xxiv + 334 pp. / ISBN 978-0-88920-521-5

163256: A Memoir of Resistance by Michael Englishman • 2007 / xvi + 112 pp. (14 b&w photos) / ISBN 978-1-55458-009-5

The Wartime Letters of Leslie and Cecil Frost, 1915–1919 edited by R.B. Fleming • 2007 / xxxvi + 384 pp. (49 b&w photos, 5 maps) / ISBN 978-1-55458-000-2

Johanna Krause Twice Persecuted: Surviving in Nazi Germany and Communist East Germany by Carolyn Gammon and Christiane Hemker • 2007 / x + 170 pp. (58 b&w photos, 2 maps) / ISBN 978-1-55458-006-4

Watermelon Syrup: A Novel by Annie Jacobsen with Jane Finlay-Young and Di Brandt • 2007 / x + 268 pp. / ISBN 978-1-55458-005-7

Broad Is the Way: Stories from Mayerthorpe by Margaret Norquay • 2008 / x + 106 pp. (6 b&w photos) / ISBN 978-1-55458-020-0

Becoming My Mother's Daughter: A Story of Survival and Renewal by Erika Gottlieb • 2008 / x + 178 pp. (36 b&w illus., 17 colour) / ISBN 978-1-55458-030-9

Leaving Fundamentalism: Personal Stories edited by G. Elijah Dann • 2008 / xii + 234 pp. / ISBN 978-1-55458-026-2

Bearing Witness: Living with Ovarian Cancer edited by Kathryn Carter and Lauri Elit • 2009 / viii + 94 pp. / ISBN 978-1-55458-055-2

Dead Woman Pickney: A Memoir of Childhood in Jamaica by Yvonne Shorter Brown • 2010 / viii + 202 pp. / ISBN 978-1-55458-189-4

I Have a Story to Tell You by Seemah C. Berson • 2010 / xx + 288 pp. (24 b&w photos) / ISBN 978-1-55458-219-8

We All Giggled: A Bourgeois Family Memoir by Thomas O. Hueglin • 2010 / xiv + 232 pp. (20 b&w photos) / ISBN 978-1-55458-262-4

Just a Larger Family: Letters of Marie Williamson from the Canadian Home Front, 1940–1944 edited by Mary F. Williamson and Tom Sharp • 2011 / xxiv + 378 pp. (16 b&w photos) / ISBN 978-1-55458-323-2

Burdens of Proof: Faith, Doubt, and Identity in Autobiography by Susanna Egan • 2011 / x + 200 pp. / ISBN 978-1-55458-333-1

Accident of Fate: A Personal Account 1938–1945 by Imre Rochlitz with Joseph Rochlitz • 2011 / xiv + 226 pp. (50 b&w photos, 5 maps) / ISBN 978-1-55458-267-9

The Green Sofa by Natascha Würzbach, translated by Raleigh Whitinger • 2012 / xiv + 240 pp. (5 b&w photos) / ISBN 978-1-55458-334-8

Unheard Of: Memoirs of a Canadian Composer by John Beckwith • 2012 / x + 393 pp. (74 illus., 8 musical examples) / ISBN 978-1-55458-358-4

Borrowed Tongues: Life Writing, Migration, and Translation by Eva C. Karpinski • 2012 / viii + 274 pp. / ISBN 978-1-55458-357-7

Basements and Attics, Closets and Cyberspace: Explorations in Canadian Women's Archives edited by Linda M. Morra and Jessica Schagerl • 2012 / x + 338 pp. / ISBN 978-1-55458-632-5

Not the Whole Story: Challenging the Single Mother Narrative edited by Lea Caragata and Judit Alcalde • forthcoming 2012 / 176 pp. / ISBN 978-1-55458-624-0

www.ingramcontent.com/pod-product-compliance
Lightning Source LLC
Chambersburg PA
CBHW071803080526
44589CB00012B/667